DISASTER
POLICY
AND POLITICS

DISASTER
POLICY
AND POLITICS

Emergency Management and Homeland Security

RICHARD SYLVES

UNIVERSITY OF DELAWARE

Los Angeles | London | New Delhi
Singapore | Washington DC

CQ Press
2300 N Street, NW, Suite 800
Washington, DC 20037

Phone: 202-729-1900; toll-free, 1-866-4CQ-PRESS (1-866-427-7737)

Web: www.cqpress.com

Photo credits: pp. 2, 26, 46, 76, 108, 132, 194, and 210 AP Images; p. 170 photo by David Rydevik

Cover design: Matthew Simmons/Myself Included Design
Cover photo: Corbis
Composition: Judy Myers

∞ The paper used in this publication exceeds the requirements of the American National Standard for Information Sciences—Permanence of Paper for Printed Library Materials, ANSI Z39.48-1992.

Printed and bound in the United States of America

12   2   3   4   5

Library of Congress Cataloging-in-Publication Data

Sylves, Richard Terry.
  Disaster policy and politics : emergency management and homeland security / Richard Sylves.
      p. cm.
  Includes bibliographical references and index.
  ISBN 978-0-87289-460-0 (pbk. : alk. paper)
  1. Emergency management—United States. 2. Intergovernmental cooperation—United States.
I. Title.

  HV551.3.S95 2008
  363.34'5610973—dc22

                                                                2008005706

TO MY PARENTS,

ROBERT AND JOANNE

Richard Sylves is professor of political science at the University of Delaware, where he has taught for many years. He specializes in public policy and administration and teaches courses in disaster policy, environmental policy, energy policy, public budgeting, and public policy. He has taught the dual-listed graduate and undergraduate course Politics and Disaster every year since 1988; this text grew from that experience. Sylves has held two post-doctorates, one as an associate producer for WHYY TV-12 Public Television News, which serves the Wilmington, Del./Philadelphia, Penn. area. He has served on a National Academy of Sciences National Research Council panel, received research funding from the Public Entity Risk Institute, and performed funded and unfunded research for FEMA both before and after that agency's transfer into the U.S. Department of Homeland Security. From 2002 to 2005, he served as an appointed member of the National Academy of Sciences Disasters Roundtable, where he participated in or helped organize workshops on various disaster-relevant topics, including 9/11, floods, earthquakes, and disaster prevention. His books include *The Nuclear Oracles, Disaster Management in the United States and Canada* (with William L. Waugh Jr.), and *Cities and Disaster: North American Studies in Emergency Management* (also with William L. Waugh Jr.), in addition to a great many articles and chapters. His BA and MA are from State University of New York, and his PhD is from University of Illinois at Urbana-Champaign.

Tables, Figures, and Boxes   xiv

Preface   xvi

CHAPTER 1   DISASTER MANAGEMENT IN THE UNITED STATES   2

CHAPTER 2   DISASTER MANAGEMENT AND THEORIES OF PUBLIC MANAGEMENT   26

CHAPTER 3   HISTORICAL TRENDS IN DISASTER MANAGEMENT   46

CHAPTER 4   UNDERSTANDING DISASTER POLICY THROUGH PRESIDENTIAL DISASTER DECLARATIONS   76

CHAPTER 5   THE ROLE OF SCIENTISTS AND ENGINEERS   108

CHAPTER 6   INTERGOVERNMENTAL RELATIONS IN DISASTER POLICY   132

CHAPTER 7   CIVIL-MILITARY RELATIONS AND NATIONAL SECURITY   170

CHAPTER 8   GLOBALIZATION OF DISASTERS   194

CHAPTER 9   CONCLUSIONS AND THE FUTURE   210

Notes   233

Bibliography   256

Glossary   264

Index   274

Tables, Figures, and Boxes xiv

Preface xvi

CHAPTER 1

DISASTER MANAGEMENT IN THE UNITED STATES 2

   EMERGENCY MANAGEMENT AS A PROFESSION 5

      Advancing Emergency Management as a Profession 6

   DISASTERS AS A FIELD OF SCIENTIFIC RESEARCH 7

   PRESIDENTIAL DISASTER DECLARATIONS 9

   FUNDAMENTAL CHALLENGES OF EMERGENCY MANAGEMENT 9

      Issue Salience 10

      Fragmented Government Responsibility 12

      Communities of Stakeholders 13

      Who Has Jurisdiction over Emergency Management? 14

      Local Governments and Decentralization Issues 15

      Political Aspects of Disaster 18

      The Problem of Disaster Insurance 18

      Technical Expertise 20

   PHASES OF EMERGENCY MANAGEMENT 21

      Mitigation 21

      Preparedness 23

      Response 23

      Recovery 24

   CONCLUSION AND SUMMARY 24

   KEY TERMS AND CONCEPTS 25

CHAPTER 2

DISASTER MANAGEMENT AND THEORIES OF PUBLIC MANAGEMENT 26

   NORMATIVE POLITICAL THEORIES: MANAGERS IN THE JEFFERSONIAN AND HAMILTONIAN STYLES 28

ORGANIZATION STUDIES 31

    Organization Culture of Bureaucratic Politics 34

    Best-Practices Approaches 34

    Analytical Approaches vs. Social Constructivist Theories 37

    Principal-Agent Theory 38

    Partisan Mutual Adjustment 39

    Intergovernmental Relations Theory 39

    Disaster Victims and Clients as Customers 41

KNOWLEDGE CODIFICATION AND KNOWLEDGE DIFFUSION ISSUES 43

CONCLUSION AND SUMMARY 45

KEY TERMS AND CONCEPTS 45

CHAPTER 3

HISTORICAL TRENDS IN DISASTER MANAGEMENT 46

THE COLD WAR AND THE RISE OF CIVIL DEFENSE 48

    The Civil Defense Act of 1950 48

    The Federal Disaster Relief Act of 1950 49

    Dual-Use Preparedness Programs 49

NATIONWIDE EMERGENCY MANAGEMENT 51

    Flood Insurance Policy History 54

    The Disaster Relief Act of 1974 54

THE BIRTH OF FEMA 56

DISASTER DECLARATION ISSUES 57

CIVIL DEFENSE AGAIN, AND CHANGES IN FEMA 59

    FEMA as an Instrument of Presidential Power 62

    Stakeholders in Disaster Policy 63

    From State and Local to Federal Emergency Management 64

    From Civil Defense to Homeland Security 64

ALL-HAZARDS MANAGEMENT 65

    The Rise of Terrorism 67

    Disaster Mitigation Becomes Law and Policy 68

TERRORISM REMAKES DISASTER MANAGEMENT 70

HOMELAND SECURITY PRESIDENTIAL DIRECTIVE 70

CONCLUSION AND SUMMARY 74

KEY TERMS AND CONCEPTS 75

CHAPTER 4

UNDERSTANDING DISASTER POLICY THROUGH
PRESIDENTIAL DISASTER DECLARATIONS 76

THE PRESIDENT'S CONSTITUTIONAL EMERGENCY
POWERS 77

FEDERAL DISASTER RELIEF LEGISLATION AND DECLARATION
AUTHORITY 78

Post-9/11 Disaster Declaration Authority 79

Catastrophes Enter the Mix, National Special Security
Events, and More 82

The Significance of the Changes 82

PRESIDENTIAL DISCRETIONARY POWER 83

FACILITATING THE PRESIDENT'S WORK 86

The White House Staff 86

The Secretary, Department of Homeland Security 87

The FEMA Director 87

The Role of Congress 91

The Role of Governors 95

FEMA'S ROLE IN THE DECLARATION PROCESS 98

PRESIDENTS AND DISTRIBUTIVE POLITICS 100

CONCLUSION AND SUMMARY 103

KEY TERMS AND CONCEPTS 107

CHAPTER 5

THE ROLE OF SCIENTISTS AND ENGINEERS 108

RESEARCHING HAZARDS AND DISASTERS 110

SOCIAL SCIENCES AND EMERGENCY MANAGEMENT 111

THE SCIENCE INFORMING THE POLICY AND POLITICS
OF DISASTERS 113

Mitigation 114

Preparedness 115

Response 117

The Medical Sciences and Disaster Response 118

Recovery 120

CASE STUDIES OF SCIENCE AND ENGINEERING APPLIED
TO DISASTER 121

The Policy and Politics of Earthquake Research and
Engineering 122

The Policy and Politics of Tornado Research 125

ENGINEERING AND PUBLIC INFRASTRUCTURE POLICY 128
CONCLUSION AND SUMMARY 130
KEY TERMS AND CONCEPTS 131

CHAPTER 6

INTERGOVERNMENTAL RELATIONS IN DISASTER
POLICY 132

INTERGOVERNMENTAL PROGRAM MANAGEMENT 134
Federal-State Agreements 136
The Impact of 9/11 on Federal-State Relations 139
Memorandums of Understanding 145
Mutual Aid Agreements 145
State-to-State Relations and Interstate Assistance
Compacts 145
Predisaster Preparedness and Response Agreements 146

THE NATIONAL RESPONSE PLAN, THE NATIONAL RESPONSE
FRAMEWORK, AND THE NATIONAL INCIDENT MANAGEMENT
SYSTEM 146
Implementation of the NRP, the NRF, and the NIMS 150

INTERGOVERNMENTAL DISASTER MANAGEMENT
CHALLENGES 156
Nonprofit Organizations and Volunteers 158
Volunteer Organizations in the Field 161

GOVERNMENT CONTRACTORS AND DISASTER
MANAGEMENT 163
Observations on Government Contractors and
Contracting 166
Positive and Negative Aspects of Subcontracting 166

CONCLUSION AND SUMMARY 168
KEY TERMS AND CONCEPTS 169

CHAPTER 7

CIVIL-MILITARY RELATIONS AND NATIONAL
SECURITY 170

PRESIDENTS, THE U.S. MILITARY, AND POSSE
COMITATUS 172

MILITARIZATION OF DISASTER POLICY 174
Disaster Response and Recovery Efforts 176
Military and State-level Disaster Management 177
The Rise of the North American Command 178

HOMELAND SECURITY TERRORISM PROGRAMS 180

The Homeland Security Advisory System 181

The Urban Area Security Initiative 183

The Law Enforcement Terrorism Prevention Program 186

The Emergency Management Performance Grant Program 186

The Assistance to Firefighters Grant Program 188

The Metropolitan Medical Response System 188

HOMELAND SECURITY GRANTS AND THEIR EFFECTS AT THE LOCAL LEVEL 188

CONCLUSION AND SUMMARY 191

KEY TERMS AND CONCEPTS 193

CHAPTER 8

GLOBALIZATION OF DISASTERS 194

THE U.S. RESPONSE SYSTEM 197

The U.S. Agency for International Development 197

The Office of U.S. Foreign Disaster Assistance 198

U.S. Ambassadors Declare Disasters 198

The Role of the Department of Defense and the U.S. Military 199

EMERGENCY MANAGEMENT IN OTHER NATIONS 200

THE UNITED NATIONS AND INTERNATIONAL DISASTER RELIEF 201

The UN Office for the Coordination of Humanitarian Affairs 201

The United Nations High Commissioner for Refugees 202

The United Nations Children's Fund 203

The United Nations Development Program 203

The World Food Program 204

The World Health Organization 204

U.S. DOMESTIC DISASTER RELIEF VERSUS THE U.S. INTERNATIONAL RELIEF SYSTEM 205

CONCLUSION AND SUMMARY 206

KEY TERMS AND CONCEPTS 209

CHAPTER 9

CONCLUSIONS AND THE FUTURE 210

DISASTER MANAGERS AND THEORIES OF POLICY IMPLEMENTATION 213

HISTORICAL TRENDS IN DISASTER MANAGEMENT 216

DISASTER POLICY AND PRESIDENTIAL POWERS 218

THE ROLE OF SCIENCE AND ENGINEERING 220

INTERGOVERNMENTAL RELATIONS IN DISASTER POLICY 220

CIVIL-MILITARY RELATIONS AND NATIONAL SECURITY 222

GLOBALIZATION OF DISASTERS 224

SPECIAL ISSUES 225

Natural and Human-Caused Disasters versus Terror-Caused Disasters 226

Do Americans Expect Too Much? 226

Winners and Losers in Disaster Policy 227

THE BIG QUESTIONS 230

Volunteers in Disasters 230

Gap Questions 230

FEMA and DHS, In or Out? 231

KEY TERMS AND CONCEPTS 232

Notes 233

Bibliography 256

Glossary 264

Index 274

TABLES

1-1 Needs of Stakeholders and Participants in Disaster Recovery   14

3-1 Federal Emergency Management Organizations   53

4-1 Presidential Approvals and Turndowns of Governor Requests for Disaster Declarations   100

6-1 States, Territories, and the District of Columbia, by Respective FEMA Standard Federal Region   137

6-2 Emergency Support Function Teams and ESF Coordinators   147

6-3 NVOAD Membership List as of May 4, 2007   160

FIGURES

3-1 Department of Homeland Security   71

6-1 Organization of the Framework   149

6-2 National Response Network   149

6-3 Incident Command Structure   151

6-4 Joint Field Office   154

6-5 Federal Incident Management Planning Structure   155

BOXES

Multiagency and Multijurisdiction Coordination   16

The Matter of Disaster Insurance   19

Polity, Power, and Responsibility   22

To Be or Not to Be a Profession   33

The Cuban Missile Crisis   35

America's Mayor and City Management   36

Turf Wars and Shifting Focus   42

Too Many Cooks?   52

"Civilianizing" FEMA?   58

Whither FEMA?   74

The Stafford Act   80

Anomalous Problems Invite New Declaration Precedents   85

The Presidential Disaster Declaration Process in Brief   88

The Role of News and Public Relations   92

Vague Criteria and Political Subjectivity   96

Overwhelmed or Over Budget?   102

Functional Federalism versus Pork-Barreling   104

Presidential Action and Project BioShield   119

The Great Midwest Flood of 1993   122

When Technology May Fail Us: The Case of Y2K   127

First Response and Management by Locals   134

Revisiting Who Gets What under a Presidential Declaration   138

Memo of the Month, RE: FEMA   141

The Bridge to Gretna Incident as a Failure of Intergovernmental Disaster Management?   142

Key Concepts of the National Incident Management System   152

A Short Revisit to Presidential Declarations   157

The Politics and Preferences of Volunteer Organizations   162

Find the Fault?   167

The Northern Command and Disaster Management   180

The Shifting Focus of Emergency Management   182

The Infamous Five-color Threat-level System of the Department of Homeland Security   184

Disasters and emergencies challenge people and their governments. Burned into the American psyche is how government officials performed after the 9/11 terror attacks of 2001 and after Hurricane Katrina in 2005. This book is written for those interested in a relatively new domain of public policy and governance: disaster policy and politics.

Disasters affect people and society in a great many ways. As disaster sociologist Dennis Mileti insists, disasters stem from more than simply "unexpected events." Disasters result from somewhat predictable interactions of the physical environment (earthquakes, hurricanes, floods, drought, tornadoes, and so on), the social and demographic characteristics of the localities that experience them (population, population density, education levels of inhabitants, economic level of development, social systems in place, and the like), and the durability and resilience of the constructed or built environment (such as buildings, bridges, roads, housing, and utility infrastructure).[1] Yet, disasters also challenge the operation, resilience, competence, and responsiveness of government as a political system.

In the United States, disaster, whether from natural forces or human cause, has long had its own public policy and politics. This is because disasters have long had political implications. The reverse is also true. First, humans are capable of producing disasters. Terrorism, failures of technology, and tolerated vulnerability to natural forces mean that disaster may be the result of human behavior. Second, owing to the national security relevance of disaster, stemming from public and official fears about the threat of nuclear attack in the past and the threat of terrorism in recent years, political actors shape people's conceptions of what a disaster is. That is, government officials and policymakers are in many respects coming to define, sometimes in concert with the news media, what disasters are and what constitutes a disaster or a disaster threat. Thus, in some ways disasters and emergencies are politically and socially "constructed" in the minds of the polity by those capable of influencing public opinion and public perceptions.

Disaster policy overlaps and encompasses portions of other policy domains. One of the reasons disaster policy and politics seem to defy easy explanation is that, although seemingly episodic and rare, disasters and emergencies affect almost every other domain of public policy (defense, health, social welfare, housing and urban development, labor, agriculture, commerce, education, environmental protection, transportation, energy, criminal justice, and others). Policy study, so often applied in other policy domains, furnishes a useful tool one may use to make sense of the politics surrounding past disasters. It helps one to anticipate and predict government's response and reactions in the aftermath of disasters.

Because emergency management fundamentally involves coordinated activity, and because much of this coordination work involves oversight and operational management of officials working at different levels of government and in different public and private settings, intergovernmental relations theory and analysis are most appropriate in disaster study. In addition, the framework of intergovernmental relations helps one appreciate that the definition of disaster is dynamic and is particularly influenced by political actors and forces.

MAJOR THEMES OF *DISASTER POLICY AND POLITICS*

The approach to disaster study taken in this book is through the study of public policy analysis, organizational management, and leadership. The book is thematic, intended to guide students through a wealth of material by employing a simple analytic framework and set of themes to help students in organizing the details and connecting them to larger concepts. Taken together, the framework and its concepts provide students with a way to understand disaster policy and politics.

The analytic framework focuses on the challenges presented in achieving effective intergovernmental relations across levels of government and through all-hazards emergency management. All-hazards emergency management saves us from a serial chapter-by-chapter study of earthquakes, hurricanes, floods, terrorism, and so on. Within the framework are four themes, which emerge in different ways and to different degrees in each chapter of the book.

The first theme concerns emergency management in the United States. Most people associate disaster policy with the emergency responder occupational groups they have come to know and trust: firefighters, law enforcement, and emergency medical personnel. Public emergency management continues to rely on the support and contributions of these essential occupational specialties, but emergency management both includes and extends well beyond these occupational specialists. Emergency management appears to be the "application" side of disaster policy. Although this is true, emergency managers also help in problem identification and policy formulation.

A second theme proposes that disaster policy and politics constitute a worthy field of academic study. Disaster research has long been part of many academic disciplines. This book draws from political science, public administration, sociology, and economics theory to demonstrate how disaster research has become a force in shaping disaster policy and how disaster researchers have become part of the politics of disaster in the United States. Disaster researchers continue to make both major and minor contributions to our understanding of disasters as political, social, and economic phenomena. They, as well as other scientists and engineers, have also advanced knowledge and understanding of natural and human-caused disaster forces. They have helped prevent or mitigate the effects of forces capable of producing disasters and they have used science and technology to forecast, monitor, track, and measure natural forces so that people around the world have been given advanced warning of disaster threats. Emergency management has evolved into a profession, and those seeking to learn the profession are pressed to master it through interdisciplinary and multidisciplinary education.

The third theme involves management again, but at the level of the elected executive. Presidents, governors, mayors, county executives, and city managers are major players in times of disaster and emergency. Past and present modes of intergovernmental relations in disaster management are examined and assessed from their vantage point. Presidents and the presidency itself occupy a central position in U.S. disaster policy and politics. How presidents lead, manage federal officials, cope with the news media, address federal-state relations, act on governors' requests for disaster and emergency assistance, define policy agendas, and choose political appointees for responsible posts all contribute to the ability to address the demands imposed by disasters and catastrophes. In many respects political, policy, and managerial decisions made by presidents and their administrations before a disaster significantly affect the ability of federal, state, and local government to mitigate, prepare for, and respond to disasters and emergencies. An overview of the tools of federal, state, and local interchange in disaster management is presented, as are several theories that provide a suggested course for analyzing the president-governor relationships that underlie presidential decisions to declare disasters.

The fourth theme of the book involves civil-military relations and homeland security. In the United States, the military is an instrument of federal and state government and has long played a role in disaster management, usually in the emergency preparedness and response phases. Since 1950, when modern-era American emergency management arguably got its start, disaster policy and politics have overlapped, been periodically dominated by, and paralleled U.S. foreign policy and national defense policy. The cold war era (approximately 1946–1990) of U.S.–Soviet conflict was a time when American federal, state, and local emergency managers had to work on matters of civil defense against nuclear attack. Civil defense of the cold war era sometimes complemented, but often confounded, emergency management aimed at natural disasters and nonwar human-caused calamities. During the 1970s and 1980s, as emergency managers (at all levels) matured in their ability to address natural disasters and as the need for civil defense against nuclear attack diminished, military dominance of disaster management waned. However, the rise of terrorism internationally, particularly the possibility that terrorists would strike inside the United States and that they might use massively destructive weapons, set the stage for the era of homeland security. The terrorist attacks of September 11, 2001, made at least part of the envisioned nightmare a reality. Today, once again, U.S. disaster policy and politics, as well as American emergency management, cannot be fully understood apart from their relationship with national security and defense policy.

ORGANIZATION OF THE BOOK

Chapter 1 explains what constitutes U.S. disaster policy and management. It furnishes a set of useful definitions, many employed in subsequent chapters. The chapter introduces and explains many aspects of emergency management, most particularly the phases of the field: disaster mitigation, disaster preparedness, disaster response, and disaster recovery. Also examined is disaster study as a field of scientific research. Themes, or threads, that appear in other chapters of the book, among them the political salience of disaster to the general public and its elected representatives, are introduced in Chapter 1, which also demonstrates that disasters and emergencies often create difficult problems for governments and their leaders.

A collection of theory tools that can be used to study disaster policy, politics, and management can be found in Chapter 2. Two normative theories, one Jeffersonian and the other Hamiltonian, are proposed as ways to understand and examine the work of disaster management. These two theories of disaster policy and management posit that there is a continual tension between the need to promote political responsiveness and representative democracy and the need to work dispassionately, professionally, scientifically, technocratically, and with minimal political bias. Chapter 2 also examines matters of bureaucratic politics and organizational culture as they relate to disaster policy, politics, and management. The chapter asks readers to ponder how emergency management will proceed as an academic and professional field. In addition, the chapter explores principal-agent theory, partisan mutual adjustment, the new public administration, and diffusion of knowledge subjects, all within the realm of disaster policy, politics, and management.

Chapter 3 examines the history of disaster policy and politics from the administration of Harry S. Truman to that of George W. Bush. The major defining federal laws of U.S. disaster policy are explained and summarized. The forms of disaster relief made available to state and local governments, as well as to victims of disaster, from 1950 to the present are described. Chapter 3 includes information about the establishment of the U.S. Federal Emergency Management Agency and its operations since 1979. The chapter carefully reviews how presidents from Truman on have shaped, used, and conducted disaster policy and management on a national level. Included as well are post-9/11 homeland security era matters important to understanding emergency management as it is being conducted in the twenty-first century.

Presidential disaster declarations are the main topic of Chapter 4. American presidents since 1950 have been able to issue declarations of major disaster. Governors are the only officials authorized to formally ask the president to issue their respective states and disaster-affected counties declarations of major disaster. Since 1974, presidents have also been able to issue declarations of emergency to requesting governors. Emergency declarations are predicated on the assumption that the declarations serve immediate life-saving needs; they may be issued immediately when a disaster occurs or when a disaster is imminent.

Examining the record of presidential declarations of major disaster is a useful way to learn about disaster management in the United States, an insightful way to investigate the geographical and historical record of U.S. disaster experience, and an illuminating way to grasp some of the politics of disaster. Thomas A. Birkland is correct in his assertion that disaster policy in the United States is driven by event-related policy change.[2] Disaster declarations are a good compendium of disaster events. The record of disaster declarations also reveals in some respects how presidents have coped with disasters and emergencies during their terms in office. Disaster law and policy are aimed at furnishing the nation, its subnational governments, and its people a "shock absorber" for catastrophes and calamities of many types. As averred in Chapter 4, one can understand much about disaster policy by studying the record and process of disaster declaration issuance.

Chapter 5 delves into the realm of the disaster researcher. People working in the physical, social, and biological sciences have long been engaged in various forms of disaster study. Disaster sociologists have pioneered and enriched the study of disaster in ingenious ways. Also, disaster researchers have become political interest groups in need of engaging in "big science" with the backing of government research funds.

In Chapter 6 the focus is the U.S. system of intergovernmental relations. For years emergency management has been perceived as chiefly a local government responsibility, and in many respects it remains fundamentally that. Nevertheless, state governments have come to assume more jurisdiction over management of emergencies and disasters, often in partnership with their respective local governments. Governors are major players in disaster policy and management. Likewise, and more especially so, the federal government has assumed more and more jurisdiction over major realms of disaster management. The National Response Plan and its 2008 successor, the National Response Framework, as well as the National Incident Management System, make up an administrative superstructure through which disaster policy is shaped and emergency management is collectively carried out. No less important in disaster management are the nongovernmental organizations: nonprofit organizations active in disasters and private corporations, particularly those responsible for managing vital public lifeline resources and infrastructure and those performing disaster-related work under government contracts.

Chapter 7 concerns civil-military relations and national security, topics touched on in earlier chapters. Here the issue of militarization of disaster policy takes center stage. The role of the National Guard in disasters and emergencies and the role of the military before, during, and after both the 9/11 terrorism disaster and Hurricane Katrina (2005) are explored. Included in the chapter is an overview of how anti- or counterterrorism federal programs under Homeland Security have affected the nation's system of disaster management. Civil defense, as a national security concern and as an instrument of national military defense, has long had a place in the history of U.S. disaster policy. The Continuity of Government program set forth in the 1950s has always been maintained and continues to this day.[3] When President George W. Bush was whisked away from Florida immediately after the 9/11 terrorist attacks, a national security operation, under Continuity of Government, was keeping the president out of harm's way until it could be determined whether or not more attacks were imminent and whether the president might be a target of one of those attacks.

Chapter 8 proceeds on three levels. Disasters have occurred in every nation of the world. On one level, the United States maintains a policy and capacity to help other nations that experience disasters and emergencies. Disaster policy is actually part of American foreign policy. The United States, as a major contributor to the United Nations, has helped various UN offices and programs address disasters and emergencies in other nations, particularly in developing nations, which may lack the capacity to engage in emergency management before, during, or after disasters. Both the United States and the UN engage in disaster relief work for various humanitarian reasons as well. The UN itself comprises the second level of analysis in Chapter 8. This chapter provides a brief overview of the UN and its array of disaster management programs. On a third level, Chapter 8 compares and contrasts U.S. domestic and international disaster management with UN disaster management. Some features of American emergency management have been emulated by other nations, but it is also true that American emergency management, owing to U.S. military and nonprofit organizational work elsewhere, has helped inform and improve emergency management for Americans at home.

Chapter 9 provides a conclusion and summary of major findings in the book. It also puts forward a set of observations about the likely future of disaster policy and politics. Included in this final chapter are a series of major questions, many of which have yet to be properly addressed by the public and elected representatives. The chapter is also a poorly concealed quest to draw readers to the field of disaster research and studies.

SPECIAL FEATURES

This book provides readers with boldfaced key words in the text and listed at the end of each chapter, and a glossary defines or explains these. All the chapters provide source citations. Also helpful to readers and researchers are the master bibliography and index that appear at the end of the book.

The book employs two general types of boxed features, which appear in most chapters:

- "How Things Work" touches on the intersection of process, politics, and policy and delves more fully into the rationale and implication of certain features of government and how things "work" in the real world.
- "History's Lessons" ties contextual history examples to the analytical framework.

The boxes help to highlight facts drawn from accounts of specific disasters or provide more detailed documentary evidence from the field of disaster policy and emergency management. Boxed material complements textual material and spotlights topics, issues, or documents in an engaging manner.

Researchers, including instructors and students, may find the Public Entity Risk Institute Web site, "All about Presidential Disaster Declarations" (see http://www.peripresdecusa.org), a useful tool. David Racca and I built and maintain the site at the University of Delaware. The site contains information on every presidential declaration of major disaster or emergency issued between 1953 and 2006, and it includes presidential turndowns of gubernatorial declaration requests; we hope to update the site in the near future. The site is designed so that researchers can easily build tables of information about the declaration history of every state and county in the United States, including the District of Columbia and U.S. trust and commonwealth territories. The nature of each declared disaster plus federal funding amounts by declaration are among several variables one can use in conducting research at the site.

The purpose of this book is to provide an introductory, although substantial, understanding of disaster policy and politics. The work synthesizes the ideas, methods, and approaches used by other scholars of the subject and offers my own observations and insights as well. I sought to produce a balanced work that was neither partisanly biased nor a political polemic. I am an unapologetic supporter of emergency managers and what they do. I am thoughtfully concerned about, but not necessarily an opponent of, military and national security involvement in disaster policy and emergency management. This work concedes that disaster policy and emergency management, like any field of public policy, has flaws and deficiencies. Government manages many disasters capably. However, some have been poorly managed, and occasionally, often in catastrophic circumstances, government disaster management has been abysmal. The field of disaster policy and politics is ever-changing.

ACKNOWLEDGMENTS

I owe debts of gratitude to a great many people. My doctoral advisees, Bruce Lindsay (now a disaster researcher with the U.S. Government Accountability Office) and Zoltan Buzas, provided invaluable help. Bruce dedicated some three to six hours every week for a year to critiquing my draft work. Chapter 8, "Globalization of Disasters," was coauthored with University of Delaware doctoral student and Villanova University assistant professor Cedric Sage, to whom I am immensely grateful.

I owe my home university and department much for permitting me to develop and teach a new, strange course back in 1988, called Politics and Disaster. The course won permanent listing and is offered once every academic year at the University of Delaware. That course should be considered the test bed for this book. One major reason I so much wanted to write this book is that for too long virtually no textbooks exclusively on disaster policy and politics have been available for graduate and undergraduate political science students.[4] My University of Delaware colleagues Joseph Pika, a scholar of the presidency, and Jason Mycoff, a scholar of the U.S. Congress, both CQ Press authors themselves, counseled me on several aspects of this study and I deeply appreciate their advisement.

I must thank the many graduate and undergraduate students who read and critiqued successive drafts of chapters for this book over the past three years. Although merely homework for some, many took it upon themselves to offer wonderful suggestions. I am especially grateful to Courtney Bordino, Meredith Bullamore, Christopher T. Campbell, Paul Connelly, Nicole deBrabander, Jeffrey Engel, Katie Rose Faherty, Daniel LoFaro, Carrol Luttrell, Lauren M. Ross, and Michele Sloan.

There is a small army of colleagues at the University of Delaware and at other universities and institutions to whom I am immensely grateful. I am blessed to have the University of Delaware Disaster Research Center on my home campus; its faculty and resources have been of invaluable help to me. I am happy to note the long-term support of John Byrne, director of the University of Delaware Center for Energy and Environmental Policy. I am very much beholden to William Cumming, a retired member of the FEMA General Counsel Office, for painstakingly critiquing many of the chapters of this book as a subject matter expert. I also owe much to Richard Buck, a brilliant and highly experienced career FEMA official now retired. B. Wayne Blanchard, director of FEMA's Higher Education Program at its Emergency Management Institute, has been a remarkable help to me and to the entire field of emergency management through the years. Many ideas in this work I owe to conversations with my friend and fellow hiker Malcolm Watts, now retired from AstraZenica International.

I wish to thank my longtime colleagues and friends William L. Waugh Jr., at Georgia State University; Frances Edwards, San Jose State University; Thomas Birkland, North Carolina State University; William Anderson, National Academy of Sciences, and William Hooke, American Meteorological Society, codirectors of the National Academy of Sciences Disasters Roundtable; George Haddow and Claire B. Rubin, George Washington University; Rutherford Platt, University of Massachusetts at Amherst; Sandra Sutphen, professor emeritus, California State University at Fullerton; William C. Nicholson, North Carolina Central University; James F. Miskel, formerly of the Naval War College; Louise Comfort, University of Pittsburgh; Beverly Cigler, Pennsylvania State University at Harrisburg; and Linneal Henderson, University of Baltimore. I am deeply thankful for the years of help and support provided to me by the late Thomas Pavlak at University of Georgia's Carl Vinson Institute. Although I did not impose on them to read this project work, I wish to acknowledge my lifelong thanks to my undergraduate mentor, Henry Steck, State University of New York, Cortland, and my graduate mentor, Barry Rundquist, University of Illinois. I would be remiss if I did not thank my wife, and lifelong "mental health" counselor, Claire, for her long-suffering support and patience throughout this project.

I am especially fortunate to have had tremendous and able help from CQ Press development editor Kristine Enderle and manuscript editor Joanne S. Ainsworth. I also thank the preliminary reviewers of this endeavor, all outstanding scholars of the field in their own right, for their sound advice and enthusiastic endorsement: Beverly Cigler, Pennsylvania State University; Charles Craig, Volusia County (Florida) Emergency Management; Eric

Holdeman, King County (Washington) Emergency Management; Jim Miskel, Naval War College; Dave Neal, Oklahoma State University; Chester Quarles, University of Mississippi; Carmine Scarvo, East Carolina University; Steven Stehr, Washington State University; William L. Waugh Jr., Georgia State University; and Robert Whelan, University of New Orleans. All, especially my friends at CQ Press, have saved me from many errors and omissions; yet, as ever, those that have snuck through are my responsibility alone.

NOTES

1. Dennis S. Mileti, *Disasters by Design: A Reassessment of Natural Hazards in the United States* (Washington, D.C.: Joseph Henry Press, 1999).
2. Thomas A. Birkland, *Lessons of Disaster: Policy Change after Catastrophic Events* (Washington, D.C.: Georgetown University Press, 2007), 2.
3. The secret and obscure program dubbed Continuity of Government (COG) evolved from a series of presidential executive orders and has at times been quite controversial. The program calls for the protection and safe evacuation of the nation's leaders during periods of imminent threat of nuclear attack. As one might expect, controversy surrounded defining who was in this exclusive leadership, how feasible the program actually was, and how much was actually spent on it. The fundamental premise of the program was to somehow reassure the nation that legitimate government would be maintained even in the event of a nuclear attack. Revelations that COG would include every senator and representative and their respective families, as well as the president and vice president, did little to defuse controversy over the program. The Biltmore Hotel in Tennessee was later reported to contain a huge basement and subbasement facility intended to house the leadership evacuees. As nuclear threat response time shrank, owing to submarine-launched missiles and to multiple, independently targetable warheads, COG became less feasible and more disputed. COG does continue for the president and vice president, and others, to this day, however.
4. Wonderful books have been available on the public administration of disaster management, on the political geography of disasters, on the sociology of disaster, and on law and disaster, but none has been produced as a core text for political science and public policy courses.

DISASTER
POLICY
AND POLITICS

CHAPTER **1**

DISASTER MANAGEMENT IN THE UNITED STATES

FROM THE NATION'S EARLIEST DAYS, COPING WITH DISASTERS and emergencies stemming from natural forces or from nonattack human causes was left to individuals, to charitable organizations, or to voluntary actions at the community level. For more than a century the prevailing social and legal view was that disasters were "acts of God." [1] As such, it was up to surviving disaster victims, perhaps aided by altruistic individuals, family members, or organizations, to recover from disaster circumstances. As the nation developed economically, as business and industry grew, as capital formation advanced, and as people came to perceive the world with more scientific rationality, Americans began to understand disaster in a different and more logical way. Earthquakes and volcanic activity were explained in geologic and seismologic terms. Severe storms, tornadoes, hurricanes, and their ensuing manifestations—floods, straight-line winds, storm surges, mudslides, landslides, erosion, droughts, and the like—were examined and largely explained by meteorologists, atmospheric scientists, and climate researchers.

The private sector sought to adapt to the occurrence of disasters through the use of insurance and reinsurance systems. By distributing the risk through private insurance, those suffering losses from a disaster had a better chance to rebound economically. Property-casualty insurance protected business owners as well as homeowners and other owners of property, such as cars and boats, but not everyone could afford the amount of insurance needed.

When certain forms of disaster wreaked havoc on certain regions and their economies, private insurers calculated that they could profitably sell policies to cover fire, theft, and wind damage only as long as thousands of policyholders did not file claims for loss all at once. Major earthquakes, hurricanes, and floods that devastate highly developed and heavily populated areas often generate a colossal number of claims in a very short time. In the late 1940s and early 1950s private insurers discontinued selling flood insurance. In addition, the insurance industry found it profitable to market commercial earthquake insurance but less so to sell residential earthquake insurance. And only days after the terrorist attack on New York and the Pentagon on September 11, 2001, private insurance companies eliminated provisions of their

On October 10, 2005, this photo was taken of stacked fishing boats on Highway 23 in Empire, Louisiana. Hurricane Katrina had struck the Gulf Coast on August 29, 2005, causing this devastation. The hurricane proved to be a catastrophic nightmare for people in the central Gulf region as well as for emergency managers and elected officials at all levels of government.

policies covering acts of terrorism. The failure of insurance to cover various types of disasters represented a market failure that by default demanded government action.

Disaster relief in America is closely enmeshed with nonprofit organizations, some of them secular and some of them religious. For many decades charitable organizations ministered to those who could not recover from disaster through private insurance. However, inadequate social giving and deficiencies in the methods of relief allocation used by some charities often failed to meet the full range of human needs created by disaster losses.

Because the United States is a democratic republic with a national constitution, and because it is composed of three countervailing branches of government, responsibility for protecting the polity from harms posed in emergency circumstances falls largely on government institutions operating in accord with certain laws. The U.S. Constitution clearly entrusts the president and Congress with the job of providing for the common defense. Preventing, repelling, responding to, and recovering from the effects of attacks on the American homeland perpetrated by other nations or by terrorists who are stateless has always been a cardinal responsibility of the federal government.

When the citizenry generally accepted that disasters were not simply acts of "God," and when the American private sector conceded that the insurance industry could not cope with the complete panoply of disasters, it was time to press for government action. The creation and maintenance of public emergency management agencies is a product of public policymaking.

As in many domains of public policy, disaster policy emerged at the local level first. Neighborhoods, local communities, and local governments were often forced to provide for both public safety needs and their own disaster recovery.

Governments, too, are property owners. Local and state governments not only own and operate public schools, public hospitals, and government office buildings but also often own and operate important public utilities, roads, bridges, ports, bus and light rail systems, airports, and other public infrastructure. Most local and state governments do not buy private insurance to protect themselves against damage caused by disasters. Consequently, local governments have often petitioned their state governments to provide financial help after disasters.

Governors, as well as mayors, city managers, or other local executives, have the power to declare or proclaim disasters or emergencies in their respective jurisdictions. Local and state taxes have been used to pay for significant shares of local and state government disaster loss. Owing to the damage caused by catastrophic multistate disasters and disasters that cover huge portions of single states, the federal government has gradually been expected to provide disaster relief to disaster victims and to local and state governments themselves. Since 9/11, disaster management has been more tightly linked to what is called terrorism consequence management. Even before 9/11, under **all-hazards emergency management,** all levels of government had been in the business of preparing for and responding to acts of terrorism inside the United States. The so-called Nunn-Lugar-Domenici Act (Title XIV of the 1996 Department of Defense Authorization Act) mandated that the federal government furnish major metropolitan jurisdictions with training and equipment that could be used to help local authorities thwart terrorist attacks of various types or respond to such attacks that actually occur.

The evolution of disaster policy across all levels of American government has helped create the field of emergency management. In this chapter, I first discuss what emergency management is as an occupation, as a field of study, and as policy and politics and then conclude with the fundamental challenges of emergency management, effective intergovernmental relations, and the phases of emergency management.

EMERGENCY MANAGEMENT AS A PROFESSION

Disaster management is seemingly an oxymoron.[2] Disasters are by definition destructive, calamitous, and often deadly or injurious events, so how is it possible to conceive of managing one? Some insist that disasters cannot be "managed" at all.[3]

From a national perspective, disaster management in the United States has its roots in civil defense. America practiced various forms of **civil defense** at least as long ago as World War I and perhaps as far back as the War of 1812. Civil defense was part of the domestic realm of the U.S. experience during World War II. After World War II, as America's Cold War with the Soviet Union emerged, local communities were pressed to continue civil defense. When the Soviet Union detonated its first atomic bomb in 1949, President Harry S. Truman, and later President Dwight D. Eisenhower, sought to mobilize the nation to prepare for civil defense against nuclear attack. To this day, many local emergency managers owe the origin of their positions to civil defense work.

Over the years, civil defense work moved through a very long "dual use" phase, in which federal support to local civil defense provided overlapping benefits to emergency management of natural disasters. Emergency management as a profession underwent gradual "civilianization." Preparedness and response to domestic natural disasters gradually supplanted and replaced a civil defense focused on national security.[4]

Thus, **emergency management** is the discipline and profession of applying science, technology, planning, and management to deal with extreme events that can injure or kill great numbers of people, do extensive property damage, and disrupt community life. Efforts are made to limit losses and costs through the implementation of strategies and tactics reflecting the full life cycle of disaster: **preparedness, response, recovery,** and **mitigation.**[5]

An **emergency manager** is someone who has the day-to-day responsibility for emergency management programs and activities. Emergency managers marshal and distribute resources to mitigate (lessen the effect of or prevent), prepare for, respond to, and recover from the effects of all types of hazards. They work in every level of government. Because disasters have the potential to affect almost every government agency or program, people with various emergency management duties can be found in almost every type of government agency. In the United States, local emergency managers may hold the title "emergency manager," but it is more likely that they hold a different title, such as director of public safety, sheriff, fire chief, or city or county manager. In some areas the job of emergency manager might be assigned to one of the following civil servants:

- A civil defense coordinator or director
- A civil preparedness coordinator or director
- A disaster services director
- An emergency services director
- A police or fire chief

Some local emergency managers are paid and some are not. State and federal emergency managers are paid civil servants, and those in the highest positions may be politically appointed to their posts. Many federal, state, and local emergency managers are full-time professionals. However, in many relatively low population counties and municipalities emergency managers are part-time volunteers, some of whom may have professional education or training.[6]

Owing to the breadth and complexity of many disasters, the field of emergency management requires multidisciplinary and cross-disciplinary approaches. It requires a wide variety of technical skills: social welfare, community and land-use planning, civil engineering, public works management, environmental science, supply chain management, and information technology, to name a few. Many emergency managers come from emergency responder occupations that are important in emergency management: the fire services, law enforcement, and emergency medicine. Most emergency managers must understand elements of public law, public management, environmental policy, and disaster sociology. At the local level emergency support services (ESS) are usually within the departments of local government. ESS units are expected to be staffed in a way that enables them to respond to emergencies twenty-four hours a day. ESS workers typically come from jobs in law enforcement, fire protection, rescue operations, environmental protection, and public works, and they are the backbone of local emergency response.

Advancing Emergency Management as a Profession

The organizations presented below represent a share of those with strong interest in emergency management. These organizations have helped make emergency management a full-fledged profession, but their variety connotes how multidisciplinary and interdisciplinary the field of emergency management actually is.

- *American Public Works Association, Council on Emergency Management.* The American Public Works Association (http://www.apwa.net/) is an international educational and professional association of public agencies, private sector companies, and individuals dedicated to providing high-quality public works goods and services.
- *American Planning Association.* The American Planning Association (http://www.planning.org/) is a nonprofit public interest and research organization. Members are involved, on a day-to-day basis, in formulating planning policies and preparing land-use regulations that will meet the needs of people and society more effectively.
- *International City/County Management Association.* The International City/County Management Association (http://www.icma.org/main/sc.asp) is the professional and educational association for appointed local government administrators throughout the world.
- *American Society for Public Administration, Section on Emergency and Crisis Management.* The American Society for Public Administration (http://www.aspanet.org/scriptcontent/index.cfm), established in 1939, is the largest and most prominent professional association in the field of public administration. The Section on Emergency and Crisis Management (SECM) was formed in 1985 largely through the efforts of William Petak of the University of Southern California. SECM has some 200 to 300 members and most of them are professors or practitioners of the field.

- *International Association of Emergency Managers (IAEM).* The IAEM (http://www.iaem.com/) is a nonprofit educational organization dedicated to promoting the goals of saving lives and protecting property during emergencies and disasters. IAEM is primarily composed of local emergency managers. It operates a Certified Emergency Manager program.
- *National Emergency Management Association (NEMA).* NEMA (http://www .nemaweb.org/) is the professional association of and for state emergency management directors.
- *International Sociological Association (ISA).* The ISA is a nonprofit association for scientific purposes in the field of sociology and social sciences. The ISA was founded in 1949 under the auspices of UNESCO. The goal of the ISA, is to represent sociologists everywhere, regardless of their school of thought, scientific approaches, or ideological opinion, and to advance sociological knowledge throughout the world. Its members come from 109 countries. The ISA's Research Committee on Sociology of Disasters has made many contributions to both the study and field of emergency management.
- *The International Emergency Management Society (TIEMS).* TIEMS (http://www .tiems.org/) has worldwide membership that includes emergency managers and social science researchers.[7]

An important contributing organization to the profession is the Emergency Management Accreditation Program (EMAP). EMAP maintains a voluntary assessment and accreditation process for state or territorial, tribal, and local government emergency management programs. EMAP conducts baseline assessments of all state and territorial emergency management programs. EMAP combines self-assessment in accord with accepted national standards; documentation of compliance; independent evaluation by trained assessors; and, for accreditation, committee and commission review. These reviews provide the following information:

- An evaluation of a jurisdiction's emergency preparedness and response system against established national standards
- A structure for identifying areas in need of improvement and benchmarking progress
- A methodology for organizing strategic planning and corrective actions and accountability in prioritizing resources
- A catalyst for improved interoperability and continuity
- Strengthened state, territorial, and local preparedness

The standards used in emergency management are collectively called the **EMAP Standard,** and these are based on the National Fire Protection Association (NFPA) 1600 standards (recognized as the national preparedness standard for the private sector) and were developed by state, local, and federal emergency management practitioners.[8]

DISASTERS AS A FIELD OF SCIENTIFIC RESEARCH

Disaster research has been done in many disciplines and fields. Meteorology, seismology, volcanology, engineering, architecture, and a host of other fields routinely contribute scholarship to the study of emergency management. The social sciences, particularly through sociology, political science, and economics, have also contributed to knowledge creation in emergency management. Today, a wide array of institutes, research centers, and clearinghouses, many working through universities and colleges, conduct research that advances knowledge in disaster studies and emergency management.

Journals like *The International Journal of Mass Emergencies and Disasters, Natural Hazards Observer, The Journal of Contingency and Crisis management* (Europe), *The Journal of Emergency Management,* and *The Journal of Homeland Security and Emergency Management* (an e-journal) have been platforms for presenting new research in the field. The National Science Foundation, the Federal Emergency Management Agency (FEMA), the U.S. Army Corps of Engineers, the U.S. Geological Survey, the National Oceanic and Atmospheric Administration, the U.S. Environmental Protection Agency, the National Institute for Standards and Technology, and other federal agencies have contributed research and research support to the field of emergency management as well.

The United Nations sponsored the International Decade for Natural Disaster Reduction over the 1990s and has assigned emergency management study and work to several of its component offices and organizations. The Organization for American States, serving virtually the entire Western hemisphere, has taken a keen interest in emergency management and disaster research. The World Meteorological Organization serves as an umbrella organization linking meteorologists around the world. The World Health Organization seeks to prevent the spread of disease globally and it, too, serves as a nexus of interchange for physicians and medical researchers worldwide.

Scientists now make daily contributions to emergency management. Earth Observation Satellites now track the advance of drought across West Africa. They make this information available to humanitarian relief organizations, which in turn pre-position food supplies in storage facilities in communities likely to experience drought six months to a year in the future. Satellite telemetry supplies U.S. Forest Service scientists with terrestrial data that make it possible for them to project the likely path of forest fires moving through mountainous terrain. The information they supply is used by smoke jumper teams to plan drop zone locations where the teams, once on the ground, can safely and effectively combat the advancing conflagration. U.S. Geological Survey scientists staff tsunami research centers in Alaska and Hawaii that use deep ocean sensors and seismologic equipment to detect suboceanic earthquakes likely to trigger sea waves, referred to as tsunamis, capable of traveling thousands of miles across the Pacific, ultimately smashing coastlines where they strike. They quickly broadcast their findings to governments and news organizations to provide an alert or disaster warning. The National Severe Storm Center uses Doppler radar, among other technologies, to detect the formation of tornadoes. It then notifies the National Weather Service and media organizations like the Weather Channel to forewarn people in the danger zones. Similarly, the National Hurricane Center tracks tropical depressions, tropical storms, and hurricanes wherever they occur in the world. Its ability to forecast points of likely hurricane landfall has done much to spur successful coastal evacuations and hurricane preparation.

Emergency management is usually associated with public service and government work. However, corporations have become interested in the field for many reasons. Insurance firms consider disaster probabilities in their models and calculations. Disasters and emergencies affect many lines of insurance, often in profound ways, such that insurers have a vested interest in studying and promoting new ways to reduce disaster risk and loss. Virtually every business or corporation needs to consider how disasters and emergencies will affect their workers, their physical assets, their rates of production or service deliveries, and their profitability. Consider for example how Hurricane Katrina's impact on Gulf Coast oil platforms and onshore oil facilities affected U.S. and world oil and gasoline prices. Major "disaster industry" trade shows and exhibits are now common, demonstrating the growth of a disaster services industry. The private sector has been drawn to the products of disaster research and the services emergency managers are able to provide.

PRESIDENTIAL DISASTER DECLARATIONS

Presidential **declarations of major disaster** or emergency are now so commonplace that they are becoming a routine mode of president-governor interchange. They are also evolving into a major conduit of interaction between federal, state, and local governments. Increased nationwide media coverage of disasters and emergencies of all types became the norm by the late 1980s.[9] This, along with other factors, may have discouraged presidents after Ronald Reagan from turning down gubernatorial requests for major disasters at the rate that earlier presidents did.

The rise of emergency management as a profession and changes in information technology have coincided with increased state and local administrative capacity to document disaster losses. In turn, this may be a factor in the greater number of presidential disaster declarations and subsequent policies and programs.[10] Improved disaster information management since the mid-1980s has aided FEMA in the past and the Department of Homeland Security (DHS) FEMA today, in ascertaining the worthiness of each gubernatorial major disaster declaration request sent to the president.[11] With advances in information technology, state emergency managers can document disaster loss more accurately through more expert damage assessments, and thus governors now have a stronger factual basis for requesting declarations of major disaster than they did earlier. In other words, governors have become better able to prove need before they request declarations.

Some disaster researchers have maintained that U.S. disaster policy is becoming more federalized, this ironically in an era of devolution and decentralization in many other realms of policy.[12] **Counterterrorism** initiatives may portend a complete nationalization of disaster management, but it is more likely that they indicate a much-expanded federal role in the intergovernmental relations of emergency management and disaster policy with the DHS counterterrorism mission given primacy.[13]

FUNDAMENTAL CHALLENGES OF EMERGENCY MANAGEMENT

Emergency managers must face many challenges in crafting emergency management policies and programs and in responding to potential disasters. They need to understand the challenges of issue salience, fragmented government responsibility, and technical expertise.[14]

Issue Salience

Issue salience, or the importance of the issue to the public and to their elected leaders, is a perennial political problem of emergency management. Disasters are by their very nature high-risk, low-probability events. Their infrequency makes it difficult to justify predisaster expenditures of public money in view of seemingly more pressing, ongoing public needs and issues. In the aftermath of major disaster, emergency managers, for a time, enjoy a high political profile and may be able to influence the public and their political representatives to undertake certain essential emergency preparedness or disaster mitigation efforts or projects. However, their salience is usually short-lived once the jurisdiction returns to normalcy. Hurricane Katrina not only opened a "policy window" to allow new issues to move on to the nation's policy agenda, but it "blew down a wall, and through the resulting hole came a raging stream of policy proposals." [15] Policy windows represent the confluence of three separate streams: problem, policy, and politics. Policy windows represent periods when solutions are coupled to problems, and both solutions and problems are connected to favorable political forces.[16] Simply put, Hurricane Katrina was a compelling event in which pronounced problems occurred; various solutions were available to address the problems highlighted by the event; and the event propelled these problems and solutions to the top of the policy agenda, where political officials acted on them.

One way to measure issue salience is through public opinion polling. Disaster policy suffers from what is called the **issue attention cycle.**[17]

This issue attention cycle is rooted both in the nature of certain domestic problems and in the way major communications media interact with the public. The cycle itself has five stages, which may vary in duration depending upon the particular issue involved, but which almost always occur in the following stages:

1. The pre-problem stage. This prevails when some highly undesirable social condition exists but has not yet captured much public attention, even though some experts or interest groups may already be alarmed by it. Usually, objective conditions regarding the problem are far worse during the pre-problem stage than they are by the time the public becomes interested in it.[18] For example, this was true of the U.S. vulnerability to terrorist attack before September 11, 2001, despite the bombing of the World Trade Center by terrorists in 1993. America's coastal vulnerability to hurricanes was understood by many experts before 2005 but poorly appreciated by the public until Hurricane Katrina and the failures of the levees protecting New Orleans and neighboring communities.

2. Alarmed discovery and euphoric enthusiasm. As a result of some dramatic event (like Hurricane Katrina in 2005, the 9/11 terrorist attack, or the *Exxon Valdez* oil tanker spill in 1989) or for other reasons, the public suddenly becomes both aware of and alarmed about a particular problem. This alarmed discovery is invariably accompanied by euphoric enthusiasm about society's ability to "solve this problem" or "do something effective" within a relatively short time. There is strong public pressure in America for political leaders to claim that every problem can be solved. This outlook is rooted in the great American tradition of optimistically viewing most obstacles to social progress as external to the structure of society itself. The implication is that every obstacle can be eliminated and every problem solved

without any fundamental reordering of society itself, if only we devote sufficient effort to it. In some cultures, an underlying sense of irony or even pessimism springs from a widespread belief that many problems cannot be "solved" in any complete sense. In American social and political culture pessimism about seemingly intractable problems like disaster is on the rise, but nevertheless, after every major disaster most Americans expect, and often demand, that government officials do something to address the disaster and its causes.[19]

3. Realizing the cost of significant progress. The third stage consists of a gradually spreading realization that the cost of "solving" the problem is very high indeed. Really doing so would not only take a great deal of money but would also require major sacrifices by large groups in the population. The public thus begins to realize that part of the problem results from arrangements that are providing significant benefits to someone—often to millions. For example, Americans realize it will cost huge sums of money and vast resources to rebuild Louisiana levees to withstand a category 5 hurricane. They may also come to understand the high cost of replacing Louisiana's vanishing wetlands, a major coastal defense against hurricane storm surge. However, Americans, especially many Gulf Coast residents, are likely to insist on resettling the same hurricane-vulnerable damage zones they occupied before. They will demand that all of the public infrastructure they relied on before the hurricane be rebuilt in virtually the same exact location as before.

   In certain cases, technological progress may eliminate some of the undesirable results of a problem without causing any major restructuring of society or any loss of present benefits by others (except for higher money costs). In the optimistic American tradition, such a technological solution is initially assumed to be possible for nearly every problem. Our most pressing social problems, however, usually involve either the exploitation, whether deliberate or unconscious, of one group in society by another or the prevention of one group from enjoying something that others want to keep for themselves.[20] (For example, before Hurricane Katrina struck in 2005 many of those who lived along the Gulf Coast in hurricane-vulnerable zones and who had the means to purchase National Flood Insurance to protect their homes but elected not to buy it nevertheless demanded that the national taxpayer bail them out through generous disaster relief. Correspondingly, development policy, both national and state, gave priority to dredging the Mississippi River and maintaining canal and channel navigability in the interests of commerce and water freight in the lower Mississippi and around New Orleans. This came at the expense of levee protection and wetland preservation that would have mitigated some of Katrina's devastating effects. There was in fact a trade-off between economic priorities and public safety.[21]) The increasing recognition that this type of relationship exists between the problem and its "solution" constitutes a key part of the third stage.

4. Gradual decline of intense public interest. The previous stage becomes almost imperceptibly transformed into the fourth stage: a gradual decline in the intensity of public interest in the problem. As more and more people realize how difficult, and how costly for them, a solution to the problem would be, three reactions set in. Some people just get discouraged. Others feel positively threatened by thinking about the problem, so they suppress such thoughts. Still others become bored by the issue. Most people experience some combination of these feelings. Consequently, public desire to keep attention focused on the

issue wanes. And by this time, some other issue is usually entering stage 2; so it exerts a more novel and thus more powerful claim upon public attention.[22]

5. The post-problem stage. In the final stage, an issue that has been replaced at the center of public concern moves into a prolonged limbo—a twilight realm of lesser attention or spasmodic recurrences of interest. However, the issue now has a different relation to public attention from that which prevailed in the pre-problem stage. For one thing, during the time that interest was sharply focused on this problem, new institutions, programs, and policies may have been created to help solve it. These entities almost always persist and often have some impact even after public attention has shifted elsewhere.[23] For example, the president and Congress established a Gulf Coast Recovery Authority to help victims of hurricanes Katrina and Rita recover from those 2005 disasters. Billions of federal dollars are now flowing to the region through a variety of federal and state programs. People have come to believe that the problem of hurricane vulnerability is being addressed. As other problems come to the fore, disaster preparedness tends to get less news media attention, less public attention, and less attention from policymakers.

Any major problem that once was elevated to national prominence may sporadically recapture public interest; or important aspects of it may become attached to some other problem that subsequently dominates center stage. Therefore, problems that have gone through the cycle almost always receive a higher average level of attention, public effort, and general concern than those still in the prediscovery stage.[24]

Fragmented Government Responsibility

Fragmented government responsibility is a political challenge for disaster managers. The United States has a highly decentralized, federal system of government, which under the U.S. Constitution affords the national government a range of authority. Some powers are reserved for the states under the Tenth Amendment. Similarly, in some states, local governments, although legally vestiges of their respective state government, possess certain powers under home rule provisions approved by their states, by their state constitution, or through enabling statutes. The federal system of layers of governments creates a form of vertical fragmentation among national, state, and local governments.

Moreover, there is also horizontal fragmentation, owing to a multitude of competing agencies with overlapping jurisdictional prerogatives on each level of government. Effective decision making and program coordination among all these agencies is difficult in the extreme. Here is one view of the system:

> Disaster relief is a system of complex and interdependent programs that work well most of the time. When it succeeds, the disaster relief system does so not because of the inspired operational leadership at the federal level, but because it is a system whose pieces have been built beforehand, over time in response to public preparedness policies, state and local government initiative, and private sector response to market incentives and regulation, as well as the dedication of private voluntary organizations, and the acumen of individuals and families.[25]

This underlines the need for multiagency and multijurisdictional coordination concerning emergency and disaster issues. The National Response Plan (NRP), put into effect in 2005 and massively revised that same year after Hurricane Katrina, aims to promote the coordination and integration of federal, state, and local emergency management. However, some complain that the Department of Homeland Security has used the NRP to overemphasize preparedness for terrorism to the detriment of preparing the nation for natural disasters.

Vertical fragmentation occurs when federal, state, and local officials fail to coordinate their respective actions with one another. For example, this happens when federal officials act independently or without consultation with their state and local counterparts. It may also occur when local or state officials fail to act in concert or when each fails to properly apprise federal authorities of their actions. The overcentralization of decision making on the federal level under the NRP and its National Incident Management System, often alleged by state and local emergency managers and their professional organizations, promotes vertical fragmentation.[26]

Disaster policy and emergency management both inherently involve intergovernmental relations. **Intergovernmental relations** involve the interaction and exchanges of public and private organizations across all layers of government. The growth of societal interdependence, in economic and technological terms, has created a webbed and networked world that depends on both the support and regulation of government.

The major power blackout suffered by the Northeast in the summer of 2004 stemmed in part from inadequate tree pruning around the power lines of a small private electric utility in northeastern Ohio. A cascade effect was produced that knocked down huge portions of the power grid of New York State, Ohio, and Pennsylvania. Millions were without power for a period of several days. To rectify the problem, private and public utilities had to cooperate and rebuild portions of the grid and power pool managers (those who manage the flow of electricity from utility to utility and over a regional power network) had to work in synchronization; state and local emergency managers meanwhile had to swing into action to direct traffic when no signals operated, rescue people trapped on elevators, and work with public and private nonprofit social welfare agencies, making sure people would not die of heat stroke in their un-air-conditioned residences. The Federal Energy Regulatory Commission (FERC) launched months of investigations. FERC sought to ascertain the source of the outage and to determine liability for costs of the power failure. The president even issued disaster declarations to New York, Ohio, and Pennsylvania, among other states. How could inadequate tree pruning in Ohio produce such dire consequences? The answer is "tightly coupled interdependence." [27]

Communities of Stakeholders

Emergency management has various communities of stakeholders. **Stakeholders** with political clout have often been influential in determining which state or local agency has lead jurisdiction during emergencies and disasters. Stakeholders are persons, groups, or institutions with interests in a project, program, or policy. Primary stakeholders are those ultimately affected by the policy or program, either positively or negatively. Key stakeholders are those who can significantly influence, or are important to the success of, the policy, program, or project. In some states and localities the political power of paid or volunteer fire service people, a key stakeholder group, dominates emergency management. In some states and localities law enforcement agencies have

| TABLE 1-1 | Needs of Stakeholders and Participants in Disaster Recovery |

	Immediate and long-term needs
Individuals and families	Housing Restoration of employment Health and welfare Restoration of schools and other educational facilities
Business and industry	Reconstitution of business, business recovery Rehiring of workers Insurance supplementation or coverage of uninsured losses Business altruistic activity
Communities and local government	Restoration of utilities and lifeline services Support of nonprofit charitable organizations Infrastructure repair and replacement Supervision of local recovery Debris removal Postdisaster planning
State and federal government	Repair or replacement of state-owned infrastructure or facilities Repair or replacement of federally owned infrastructure or facilities

Source: George D. Haddow and Jane A. Bullock, *Introduction to Emergency Management,* 2nd ed. (Boston: Elsevier, Butterworth-Heinemann, 2006): 136–140.

been entrusted with emergency management authority and responsibilities. In some local governments the medical community, another key stakeholder, has assumed lead jurisdiction in emergency management, through the services it provides in public and private hospitals and emergency medicine. In about half of the states top emergency management is a quasi-military responsibility led by the state adjutant general, an official who heads the state's National Guard. Because National Guard units are under the control of governors in each respective state, adjutant generals often have close relationships with their respective state governor.

State and local governments have moved into the realm of disaster policy and emergency management in different ways. Through the 1950s and 1960s, some have nurtured emergency management as an extension of their civil defense work. Others, which have had poor experience with previous disasters, often with highly negative political repercussions for those in office, have moved emergency management closer to the executive realm. In some localities disaster management was a political football fought over by police and firefighters, both of whom wanted primary jurisdictional authority in emergency and disaster circumstances. Some of the common concerns of emergency managers and stakeholders active in disaster recovery are presented in Table 1-1.

Who Has Jurisdiction over Emergency Management?

Until the Rudolph Giuliani mayorship in the mid-1990s, New York City emergency management was led by the city's police department (NYPD) for many years. Giuliani carried out a reorganization that took the city's Office of Emergency Management away from the NYPD and made it an arm of his executive office some two blocks away from the World Trade Center. Mayor Michael R. Bloomberg, who succeeded Giuliani in 2002, reversed his predecessor's action and moved city emergency management back under the lead control of the NYPD. Why all of these machinations? In New York City several city departments, more specifically the Fire Department of New York (FDNY) and the NYPD, have long fought for leadership control of city emergency management. As in most municipalities, the mayor of New York relies heavily on emergency managers. Mayors need notification about local emergencies and disasters for at least two reasons. First, certain emergency circumstances require mayor-level executive decisions. Second, owing to the newsworthiness of local disasters and emergencies, mayors need to be apprised of these events at least as early as the news media. In emergencies and disasters the mayor's public image may be at stake. Moreover, mayors are the personification of the municipalities they lead, and people expect them to respond to the calamities their cities experience.

In New York, one factor in the dispute between the NYPD and the FDNY was the 911 emergency call system. The NYPD operates and controls the city's 911 emergency telephone system. Police leaders have long insisted that emergency management authority should be located within the NYPD and adjacent to its 911 operations center, as it was before Giuliani's reorganization. The FDNY responds daily to a vast number of city calamities, including false alarms and non-fire emergencies, through its citywide system of fire-call boxes. For this reason and others, top city firefighters believe they are justified in insisting that control of city emergency management should reside with their department.[28] Another factor in the New York dispute may have stemmed from conflict between Mayor Giuliani and the New York police commissioner. On top of all this, New York police and firefighters have a long history of competition and disputes dating back to the mid-1800s. However, the terrorist attacks of 9/11 and the sad shared experience of loss by each department on that day served to temper the dispute between the NYPD and the FDNY over control of emergency management, and the two groups have formulated protocols, planned for, and practiced together many emergency management and homeland security scenarios and exercises since then.

The point of the example is that jurisdiction over some realms of emergency management is occasionally a subject of bureaucratic and political conflict. Government reorganizations are often manifestations of ongoing "battles" between different leaders, public departments, agencies, and offices. Sometimes emergency management is the object of reorganization. State and local emergency management involves so many different subjects and concerns that seldom can a local government agency claim complete dominion over it. This, too, adds to political and administrative disputes over who will have control of what in emergency management. The post-9/11 emergence of homeland security, introduced with relatively massive levels of federal funding, triggered waves of state and local reorganization, much of it involving emergency managers and emergency management.

Local Governments and Decentralization Issues

Disasters are usually localized geographically. Therefore, county and municipal authorities most often assume primary responsibility for emergency management. However, the policymaking, administrative, and fiscal capacity of many local governments is often questionable. Owing to competing demands and cross-pressures, many local officials are reluctant, unwilling, or unable to design, implement, and support effective disaster preparedness and response programs. As mentioned previously, vertical fragmentation transpires when federal, state, and local authorities fail to coordinate their emergency management responsibilities, when they act independently of one another, when they duplicate their efforts or work at cross-purposes, or when one level of government fails to carry out its obligations. The National Response Plan, officially put into effect in the spring of 2005, was supposed to prevent vertical fragmentation. Moreover, the plan was supposed to establish a system to help the nation manage "incidents of national significance," whether caused by terrorism or natural disaster.

HOW THINGS WORK

MULTIAGENCY AND MULTIJURISDICTION COORDINATION

Multiagency and multigovernment jurisdictions challenge emergency managers. Disasters and emergencies often:

- change the division of labor and resources in an organization;
- compel a sharing of tasks and resources among organizations;
- involve the crossing of jurisdictional boundaries both in terms of geography and responsibility;
- require completion of nonroutine tasks under abnormal circumstances;
- damage, make unavailable, or overwhelm normal emergency response tools and facilities;
- necessitate new organizational arrangements to meet the problems posed.

Emergency management is also challenged by a fundamental public distrust of government planning efforts, strong resistance to land-use and construction regulation, and a tendency, especially at state and local levels, to focus only on recent disasters. Levels of risk are also difficult to measure. Cause-and-effect relationships are elusive as well. Unfortunately, in some places there remain people and government officials who continue to believe that waiting for emergencies to occur and then dealing with their effects is more sensible than preparing for and mitigating potential effects before a disaster strikes. Furthermore, government relief assistance is politically popular and desired, whereas mitigation and preparedness are seldom politically popular. Because of this, "Mitigation is still not the sole or even the primary goal of federal disaster policy." [29]

In large measure, the federal system's division of powers accords local and state governments the lead role in responding to most types of hazards and disasters. The national government has assumed a facilitating role through FEMA, which was independent from 1979 to 2003 and has been positioned within DHS since then. State and local governments also develop emergency management procedures. America has a highly decentralized and elaborate array of emergency management procedures in which local emergency management is the base. There are some qualifiers. For some types—civil defense, nuclear accidents, and counterterrorism—the federal role in policymaking and administration is dominant. Unfortunately, the job of emergency manager often lacks clarity in law, regulation, and historical practice. Some of this lack stems from how people perceive disaster and the risk of disaster.

Horizontal fragmentation may be reduced if adjacent or nearby states and local jurisdictions establish mutual assistance agreements with one another "before" disasters and emergencies transpire. These agreements alleviate some of the jurisdictional confusion. Vertical and horizontal fragmentation complicates emergency management. Such fragmentation is not easily overcome even though "shared governance" holds some potential for achieving improvements in emergency management.[30] Vertical and horizontal fragmentation often contributes to the problems of insufficient technical expertise, inadequate fiscal resources, and unclear legislative mandates.

Over the past three decades, decentralization in government has become a mantra of political leaders, regardless of political party. **Decentralization,** with sound coordination, is how many authorities define successful emergency management. As noted earlier, emergency management has fundamentally been a local obligation, often undertaken with the help of private charitable organizations. However, local governments in most states are either considered "creatures" of their states or they are accorded certain "independent powers" by their states, sometimes under "home rule" laws or policies. States themselves enjoy limited areas of "reserved powers" under the U.S. Constitution, but the range of federal powers over the states is vast. Thus, although many people consider emergency management a "bedrock" local responsibility, both the state and the federal government are now actors, often with public endorsement, in local emergency management. Simply put, local officials may have recognized their own limitations in addressing disaster; local officials may have become accustomed to state and federal assistance after disasters; and local officials may have come to recognize their dependence such that the coordinated help of state and federal authorities is today ordinarily welcomed.

Federal and state policymakers and public managers often cannot easily grasp the emergency management organizational complexity of some thirty-five hundred county governments and thousands more municipal and special district governments. In fashioning disaster policy, federal and state authorities have endeavored to promote where possible consistency and, to a degree, professionalism in local emergency management. Part of this effort is evident in all-hazards emergency management. The essence of this concept is that common sets of emergency preparedness and response procedures and practices are applicable in any locality regardless of differences in geography or demography. It is also assumed that an economy of scale can be reached by planning and preparing for disaster in generic terms (thus, "all hazards") rather than by planning or preparing for each unique type of disaster.

Disaster management also requires strong cooperation and coordination among public, nonprofit, and private organizations. Emergency management is conducted in a fluid and often chaotic environment. Local government officials must interact ably with other local government officials and with people representing private or nonprofit organizations. A county government may offer assistance under a previously arranged mutual aid agreement. Private construction companies that have experience in meeting building code rules may offer emergency rebuilding or repair assistance. Area chemical companies may volunteer their services to clean up and detoxify hazardous substances accidentally released during the disaster. A host of local, state, or national charitable organizations may offer human services aid that local governments cannot. Help from the private and nonprofit sectors often augments successful emergency management, sometimes meeting needs or filling gaps that government is unable to address fully.

Disaster management recognizes the need to consider the types or categories of disaster. Each one of the different categories of disaster embodies different types of duties and responsibilities for disaster managers. These duties and responsibilities are not always compatible across categories of disaster incidents. For example, a terrorist attack, such as occurred on September 11, 2001, mobilized fire service personnel, police officers, emergency managers, law enforcement officials, military personnel, and many others. The sites attacked were a scene of human disaster, a crime scene, and of high national security interest. Search and rescue, public safety, firefighting, crime scene investigation, forensic and coroner work, all had to be pursued at the same site. In such situations conflicts are likely to occur over who is to do what and when.

Similarly, a coastal flood, such as the flooding that often occurs after nor'easters in New England and along the Mid-Atlantic, may be a human disaster and an environmental issue. Some authorities will press for rebuilding damaged onshore structures or replenishing lost beach sand, whereas others will seek to protect natural habitats and coastal marine resources by discouraging rebuilding and instead recommending ways to accommodate the changes produced by the storm. Different types of disasters embody different sets of concerns, political issues, authority, and jurisdiction.

Political Aspects of Disaster

Disasters have political features. Natural disasters and emergencies, in particular, provide excellent windows of opportunity for public officials.[31] Often these officials use disasters or emergencies to demonstrate their leadership capabilities and their willingness to tackle difficult problems. Their actions on these occasions usually draw media publicity and instant public notice. Moreover, it is extremely difficult to oppose or criticize an official who steps in and gives the appearance of taking charge in order to help disaster victims.

Natural disasters also produce conditions that allow political leaders to show their concern for citizens' needs and demands. Disaster victims often encounter problems that they have never before experienced and which they may be unprepared or ill equipped to handle on their own. Public officials are in a position to highlight needs and channel resources to help those in distress. Disaster gives elected or appointed leaders a perfect opportunity to demonstrate their responsiveness to the needs of the people. Disasters may create tremendous opportunities for elected officials to provide service to their constituents. Government leaders who successfully address disaster-related problems are likely to be rewarded politically, whereas those leaders who are unwilling or unable to act may suffer negative political repercussions.

Disasters embody "political dangers" for elected executives and for senior public managers. Bungle a disaster and political executives will pay a political price. Perceived incompetence during disasters often comes at a high price for political officials.[32]

The Problem of Disaster Insurance

It became apparent to policymakers as early as the 1950s that private sector insurance companies were either unwilling to provide residential insurance against flood or incapable of doing so. This created a major unmet need in several respects. Federal disaster relief programs only gradually came to extend relief directly to individuals and families, and much of this relief was at the time wholly inadequate to help victims who suffered losses from flooding or from any other disaster agent.

A massive share of presidential disaster declarations from 1950 to 1980 covered flood disasters, many associated with hurricanes, tornadoes, and severe storms. Presidents and lawmakers seemed constantly to revisit the problem of inadequate help for those individuals and families suffering flood loss.[33]

Presidents and Congress slowly and haltingly moved toward the creation of a National Flood Insurance Program (NFIP) that would invite localities to join if they promised to meet federal

---

HISTORY'S LESSONS

THE MATTER OF DISASTER INSURANCE

Owing to a 1958 study by the geographer Gilbert F. White and his colleagues entitled "Changes in Urban Occupance of Flood Plains in the United States," and due to the public education and advocacy efforts of White and others, many policymakers and others were made aware that land-use pressures and the failure to keep development out of potential flood zones were putting more people and structures in jeopardy.[34] The study even alleged that a condition of "moral hazard" was emerging because postflood federal disaster relief led many people to believe that should flood disaster occur the federal government would be there to set things straight. **Moral hazard** in the realm of insurance refers to an increase in the probability of loss caused by the behavior of a policyholder.[35] Another way to look at this is that federal disaster assistance "creates a type of Samaritan's dilemma: providing assistance after a catastrophe reduces the economic incentives of potential victims to invest in protective measures prior to a disaster. If the expectation of disaster assistance reduces the demand for insurance, the political pressure on the government to provide assistance after a disaster is reinforced or amplified."[36]

By 1960, the final year of Eisenhower's presidency, Congress had amended the Flood Control Act and authorized the U.S. Army Corps of Engineers to compile and disseminate information on floods and flood damages at the request of a state or responsible local agency. As a result of the act, the Army Corps of Engineers established a Flood Plain Management Service, a body that promoted flood mitigation and supplied advisory flood maps to local communities.

One of the reasons that the National Flood Insurance Program (NFIP) was established in 1968 was to encourage individuals who resided in hazard-prone areas to purchase flood insurance. The insurance was low priced—remember, a government insurance program is not necessarily required to show a profit—and policymakers hoped that the availability and low cost of this insurance would reduce the need to supply so much federal disaster grant and loan assistance after future floods. Yet, "[f]ew individuals voluntarily bought this coverage so that when Tropical Storm Agnes in June 1972 hit the northeast causing over $2 billion in damage, only 1583 claims totaling $5 million were paid under the NFIP. Even though flood coverage has been required since 1973 as a condition for a federally insured mortgage, it has been estimated that less than 40 percent of the victims of Hurricane Katrina in Mississippi and Louisiana had flood insurance to cover their losses."[37]

standards aimed at limiting development in floodplains and promoting flood-proof construction. People living in the communities that joined the NFIP would then be eligible to buy relatively low-cost flood insurance from the federal government. In effect, the federal government would use insurance as a key form of disaster assistance and as a tool of flood mitigation.

The National Flood Insurance Program was supposed to be a premier instrument of both disaster mitigation and disaster recovery. The program that continues today has been only modestly successful. Many local governments participate in the program and generally abide by its flood mitigation rules. Through the years, however, NFIP has only weakly penalized localities that disregarded its rules, owing to understaffing and limited sanction powers. Worse still, too few property owners purchase and maintain NFIP policies. People who refuse to buy national flood insurance, even those who experience recurring flood loss through the years, are rarely denied federal disaster relief after a federally declared flood disaster damages their property. On top of all of this, private insurers continue to cover wind damage (but not that caused by flood water) in their homeowner insurance policies. NFIP covers flood water damage but not wind-caused damage. Consequently, many homeowners have fallen into insurance "limbo" as private insurers contest claims for damage they believe is caused by flooding and NFIP denies claims for damage it concludes was caused by wind. For example, a vast number of NFIP policyholders in Katrina damage zones ended up having their claims denied by both NFIP and their private insurer. At this writing, this insurance "policy" failure remains unresolved.

Technical Expertise

Emergency management is conducted within a complex political, economic, and social environment. In part, this explains why emergency management has so long lacked a coherent, coordinated policy framework. Designing and implementing comprehensive emergency management procedures is easier said than done, principally because of the obstacles to effective action created by problems stemming from low political salience, fragmented government responsibility, and lack of emergency manager technical expertise.

Lack of technical expertise and confusion about the kind of expertise that is needed is another major impediment to effective emergency management. The technical expertise needed to identify and assess hazards adequately, predict the occurrence of disasters, and provide the requisite technical information for the design and implementation of effective programs is crucial to effective emergency management. Moreover, even when hazards have been identified, it is often unclear just how much risk is involved. In bygone eras, emergency management required little technical knowledge or expertise when compared with many other occupational specialties.

Today, emergency managers need to master a specialized body of knowledge, often involving many different disciplines. Accounting and budgeting skills are important. Public relations expertise and political savvy are necessary. Computing ability, for information management, decision support, geographic information systems, and so on, has become more a part of routine emergency management work. A working knowledge of disaster-related laws and programs is vital. FEMA's Emergency Management Institute regularly conducts conferences that examine the knowledge-skills-abilities (KSAs) needed to do emergency management.[38] There is no consensus thus far on precisely the skill sets needed. However, the Emergency

Management Accreditation Program, a private voluntary consortium, has been working to establish what credentials are needed for a person to be classified as a "qualified emergency manager." [39]

Decision making in disaster management encompass the following assumptions.

- Disaster planning is a continuous process. It should not be based on a single emergency but instead on several. Such planning must allow for the constant incorporation of new findings.
- Disaster planning should attempt to reduce uncertainty in crises by anticipating problems and projecting possible solutions.
- Disaster planning stipulates that the appropriateness of response is more important than speed of response.
- Disaster planning is based on what will probably happen; procedures need to address what people are likely to do in emergencies, not on myths or common nostrums about human behavior.
- Disaster planning involves the education of response and recovery people. They need to know that emergency procedures exist and that it is important that they understand and follow these procedures.
- Disaster management needs to be "sold" effectively to communities to be taken seriously.
- Disaster management requires exercises and practice or otherwise the best plans tend to become worthless.

PHASES OF EMERGENCY MANAGEMENT

The four phases of emergency management encompass mitigation, preparedness, response, and recovery.

Mitigation

Mitigation involves deciding what to do where a risk to the health, safety, and welfare of society has been determined to exist and then implementing a risk reduction program. It is sustained action to reduce or eliminate risk to people and property from hazards and their effects. The recovery phase of disaster also offers opportunity for mitigation actions.[40] In addition, mitigation may also be any cost-effective measure that will reduce the potential for damage to a facility from a disaster event. This includes identifying, measuring, and addressing hazard vulnerability; more and more often, it also includes activities undertaken after a disaster to lessen the likelihood of future disasters from both physical and social phenomena that are potentially dangerous.[41]

The formation of FEMA spotlighted the significance of hazard mitigation and preparedness, and by the 1990s FEMA gave impetus to a proactive, rather than a reactive, approach to emergency management. Instead of merely doing disaster recovery work, FEMA emphasized keeping people out of hazard-prone, high-risk areas through instruments such as zoning laws, building codes, and land-use regulations. In effect, FEMA began to encourage or induce local

HOW THINGS WORK

POLITY, POWER, AND RESPONSIBILITY

In the American polity, power and responsibility are dispersed by design. This poses a challenge to those who seek tighter and more coherent organization of federal emergency management. If the Department of Homeland Security helps integrate federal disaster management, it may work to diminish jurisdictional fragmentation. However, if the goal of "national disaster management" becomes the prevention or preparation for terrorist attacks inside the United States, to the detriment of conventional disaster management, new forms of jurisdictional controversy will result. According to a 1995 congressional report, spending percentages of federal disaster relief funding demonstrated the following shares: recovery (73 percent), mitigation (22 percent), and combined preparedness and response (5 percent).[42] These figures highlight the need to promote more mitigation, preparedness, and response. The Senate Bipartisan Task Force report of 1995 discloses that 54 percent of funding in the period measured has gone to grants for disaster victims and communities, as

well as to payment of operating expenses of federal disaster response programs.[43] The terrorist attacks of 9/11 and the resulting national reaction have infused preparedness and response with massive new funding. Therefore, the 1995 shares may be badly out of date today. However, Hurricane Katrina in 2005 may have counterweighted the disaster spending scale back to huge recovery expenditures.

In spite of the remarkable upturn in federal disaster spending since the 1980s, federal efforts are supposed to supplement, not supplant, the efforts of others. Most disasters and emergencies do not involve state or federal government, only local government, although the state and federal role has increased dramatically since 1950. Federal agencies, particularly FEMA, stimulate and guide emergency planning efforts, furnish substantial response and recovery funding, coordinate response efforts after (and sometimes before) a governor secures help from the president, and fund many disaster mitigation endeavors.

officials and individuals to adopt mitigative policies. Mitigation work opened up a perennial, highly political difference of opinion between FEMA and various local officials, developers, and citizens. As subsequent chapters explain, federal efforts to promote local disaster mitigation activity, especially through grant conditions and NFIP requirements, often ran afoul of local economic development interests, who objected with accusations that the federal government was interfering with local land use and building code powers. FEMA officials attempted to persuade community people to proactively protect themselves through hazard mitigation activities.

Tools for mitigation include the following:

- Hazard identification and mapping (for example, by the NFIP, the U.S. Geological Survey, the states, geographic information systems, Hazards U.S.-Multi-Hazard [HAZUS-MH] software program)
- Design and construction applications (code development, model codes, geographic

sensitivity, retrofit ordinances, elevation of homes, removal of flammable vegetation around homes, landscaping)

- Land-use planning (prevents development in floodplains or high-hazard zones, relocates structures), zoning rules, property acquisition
- Financial incentives (special tax assessments in the interest of mitigation or relocation aid), use of other federal program monies to pay for property acquisition and relocation
- Insurance (NFIP, federal subsidization of some other forms of insurance, such as terrorism insurance), indemnification requirements as a condition of loan approvals by the Department of Veterans Affairs (VA), the Department of Housing and Urban Development (HUD), or the Federal Housing Administration (FHA); other federal mortgage aid. The federal government provides insurers with maps of high-hazard zones. The Community Rating System rewards good performers with lower NFIP premiums for their people.
- Structural controls (public works, flood works, levees, dams, flood channels, shoreline structural protection).[44]

Preparedness

Preparedness involves developing a response plan and training first responders to save lives and reduce disaster damage, identifying critical resources, and developing necessary agreements among responding agencies, both within the jurisdiction and with other jurisdictions. Preparedness also entails "readying for expected threats, including contingency planning, resource management, mutual aid, . . . [and] public information."[45] Preparedness is a functional aspect of emergency management that contributes to sound emergency "response" and "recovery" from a disaster.

Emergency management has to rely on academic or analytical processes, especially those resting on a systems approach to management. Preparedness relies heavily on a systemic conceptualization. The standards used, collectively called the EMAP Standard, are based on the National Fire Protection Association 1600 standards (recognized as the national preparedness standard for the private sector) and were developed by state, local, and federal emergency management practitioners.[46]

Response

Response entails providing emergency aid and assistance, reducing the probability of secondary damage, and minimizing problems for recovery operations. In an emergency situation, emergency managers rarely direct actual response operations. There are exceptions, as when management of a crisis falls to a senior elected official or to the lead emergency services agency.[47] Disaster response objectives include protecting lives, limiting property loss, and overcoming the disruptions that disasters cause.[48] The response phase of disaster is often the most dramatic phase of the disaster cycle.

Recovery

Recovery involves providing the immediate support during the early postdisaster period necessary to return vital life-support systems to minimum operational levels and continuing to provide support until the community returns to normal.[49]

Recovery is the most expensive phase of the disaster cycle. Recovery involves restoration, rebuilding, and return to normalcy. The pool of players involved in recovery is huge and far exceeds the number of players usually involved in disaster response. Decisions regarding disaster recovery are fundamentally made at the local level of government.[50]

CONCLUSION AND SUMMARY

In some respects, disasters are socially and politically constructed phenomena. Who could imagine that the influx of Cuban immigrants from Fidel Castro's Mariel boatlift in 1980 would induce President Jimmy Carter to issue a disaster declaration for this event? How could the breakup of the *Columbia* Space Shuttle in 2003 cause President George W. Bush to use his disaster declaration powers to grant governors in states suspected to be in the shuttle's debris zone reimbursement of the costs related to their shuttle disaster response? Presidents have at times used their power to declare disasters in ways that have expanded the definition of disaster in political and public administrative terms.

Disasters sometimes cause major shifts in national priorities and significant changes in other policy domains. The August 2007 collapse of the Minneapolis area I-35 Mississippi River Bridge, a dramatic infrastructure disaster, may impel national policymakers to shift a portion of federal defense spending to the replacement, repair, and improved maintenance and inspection of the nation's bridgeworks. The 9/11 terrorism disaster induced policymakers to move federal emergency management into a holding company of agencies implementing policies ranging from immigration control, border security, coastal maritime work, aviation security, public health, domestic intelligence collection, right up to Secret Service protection of government leaders.

This chapter examined the essentials of emergency management and disaster policy. It covered emergency management as a profession. It explored stakeholder groups in the domain of disaster policy. The chapter also introduced an overview of disaster as a field of scientific research. Presidential disaster declarations were introduced, as were the major challenges facing emergency management. Among these challenges are the perennial low issue salience of disaster as a public and political phenomenon, the fragmentation of government responsibility for disaster-related concerns, the difficulties local governments face in addressing emergency management, the political aspects of the disaster phenomenon, the problem of disaster insurance, and the challenge of training and educating emergency managers for a field that is technically complex and highly multi-disciplinary. This chapter also introduced the four-phased cycle of emergency management: mitigation, preparedness, response, and recovery. Many of these essentials will be developed more fully in subsequent chapters. If you know these essentials you are off to a good start.

KEY TERMS AND CONCEPTS

all-hazards emergency management   4

civil defense   5

counterterrorism   9

decentralization   17

disaster management   5

EMAP Standard   7

emergency management   5

emergency manager   5

horizontal fragmentation   17

intergovernmental relations   13

issue-attention cycle   10

issue salience   10

major disaster declaration   9

mitigation   5

moral hazard   19

preparedness   5

response   5

recovery   5

stakeholders   13

vertical fragmentation   13

CHAPTER 2

DISASTER MANAGEMENT AND THEORIES OF PUBLIC MANAGEMENT

SCHOLARS HAVE DEVELOPED THEORIES AND CONCEPTS TO HELP themselves and us understand and explain governance and public policy generally. Theories and concepts have also been used to help understand and explain specific domains of public policy, such as health care, social welfare, environment, defense, and education. Disaster policy, although a relatively new domain of public policy, is also amenable to analysis through the development and application of theories and concepts. Theories and concepts often serve as tools one can apply to the study of specific subjects or problems.

As emergency management is evolving into a profession, we must rely on theories, concepts, and abstract knowledge as well as experiential learning and experimental research. Emergency management as an occupation increasingly demands the mastery of a body of professional knowledge, although it also depends on the skills and abilities of generalist managers. To understand their role in the policy process and to establish their profession, emergency managers need to grasp the significance of political and managerial theories relevant to their work.[1] They need to appreciate that government embodies actors and structures intended to facilitate the effective operation of democracy and political accountability.

This chapter provides a sampling of theories and concepts, many produced by political scientists, public administrationists, sociologists, and economists, applicable to the domain of disaster policy and to the field of emergency management. It also provides an overview of how and where theory knowledge fits in the evolution of emergency management as a profession and supplies some insight about how people new to the field can use theories and concepts to independently analyze disaster policy as a domain of public policy.

The chapter begins with a discussion of two relatively simple normative theories: one Jeffersonian and the other Hamiltonian. Matters of bureaucratic politics and administrative culture are then considered. From there it moves on to a look at the role of "best practice" contributions to the field. Intergovernmental relations theory is touched upon, followed by a brief examination of the relevance of principal-agent theory in disaster policy implementation.

Work at Ground Zero continues some eleven weeks after the September 11, 2001, attack on the World Trade Center. How can we understand and cope with such horrible events? Was 9/11 the first truly "national" disaster for the United States since Pearl Harbor in 1941? How does emergency management need to be understood as a field of knowledge? What kind of theory tools can be applied in disaster management?

After this is a special topics review of the new public administration approach and a brief discussion about how emergency management knowledge is produced and how it is learned by others.

NORMATIVE POLITICAL THEORIES: MANAGERS IN THE JEFFERSONIAN AND HAMILTONIAN STYLES

Consider two simple normative political theories that emanate from the contributions of two of America's important forefathers: Thomas Jefferson and Alexander Hamilton.[2] Jefferson, major author of the Declaration of Independence and the nation's third president, has been generally understood to insist that the job of public managers was to try to obtain "popular and stakeholder guidance" through political consultation or public deliberation before the fact. In other words, public managers should make their decisions as the product of grassroots public consultation and the consensus of interest group recommendations. This gives a public manager's decisions greater legitimacy for public purposes.

This so-called Jeffersonian approach requires that public managers possess not only skill in consultation, negotiation, and communication but also deftness in probing for public understanding and consent. Good **Jeffersonian public managers** are educated **generalists** (gentlemen [or gentlewomen], as Jefferson might put it) who know and understand personal relationships that exist between agents (workers) and their assigned tasks (their duties). Jeffersonian public managers are strictly accountable to the public and to their elected overseers. As communities bear the effects of a disaster, Jeffersonian managers must use their sociotechnical skills to meet the expressed needs of those in their communities. Strong community participation would be a hallmark of emergency preparedness and planning for Jeffersonian emergency managers.

Recent thinking about emergency management indirectly stresses the importance of Jeffersonian behavior at the local government level. One scholar's explanation of what emergency managers do captures Jeffersonian thinking superbly well:

> Emergency managers are public servants who help communities prevent and prepare for disasters. They issue warnings, oversee evacuation, and communicate with responders. They also assemble statistics on damages, share disaster knowledge with citizens through the media, and work with those in charge of shelters. Emergency managers also acquire resources. They make sure that departments are working together to address response and recovery challenges. They gather information about expenses. They help determine response and recovery priorities. Their contributions are crucial to post-disaster operations.[3]

Local emergency managers must serve local executives and at the same time respond to the needs of people in their jurisdiction. Should they fail badly on either or both counts, they risk losing their posts and they risk harming the reputation and welfare of their agencies. However, to most elected and appointed officials who control budgets and staffing allocations, emergency management is a low priority. One study quotes a police chief emergency manager as saying, "My number one priority is getting the uniforms out to response calls. The public judges me on that performance, not whether I'm planning for an earthquake that may never happen. If left alone, disaster planning would get even less attention from my office. It requires that the executive clearly make this a priority." [4]

Thus, for Jeffersonian emergency managers, their work and the success of their agencies reside in "maintaining community support from senior elected and appointed officials, the news media, and the public." [5] Local emergency managers often rely on local emergency management committees (LEMCs). An LEMC is a disaster-planning network that increases coordination among local agencies. [6] LEMCs succeed when they effectively receive and respond to community information requests, when they establish and maintain good working relationships with people of the news media, when they earn and maintain local support, and when they retain the confidence and backing of local officials. [7]

LEMCs are often composed of volunteers from municipal agencies representing organizations relevant to public safety or people from organizations vulnerable to certain hazards. Besides the customary police, fire, and emergency services organizations, LEMCs frequently include representatives from hospitals, public works, nursing homes, land-use departments, schools, building inspection agencies, environmental organizations, public health agencies, and local industries, to name a few. [8] The reason for this broad inclusiveness stems from the need for local emergency managers both to consult with representatives of these organizations as they draft emergency plans and proposals and to win the broad pluralistic consent and support they need to secure political or administrative approval of their plans and proposals. Such is the essence of Jeffersonian emergency management at the local level.

Jeffersonian principles apply at the state government level as well but less so than at the local level. Successful state emergency management depends on the active and sustained interest and support of the governor. However, state emergency management is conducted more in a world of bureaucratic politics, state legislative oversight, and intergovernmental relations such that this work is often far removed from direct public interaction. In federal emergency management, detachment from the general public is even greater and public participation in emergency management at that level is very circumscribed and frequently heavily co-opted. In federal emergency management, presidential support is vital, and the collective public perception of emergency management is of great political and managerial importance.

Alexander Hamilton, who was a Revolutionary War hero, a major architect of the U.S. Constitution through *The Federalist Papers,* and the first secretary of the U.S. Treasury, believed that public managers must put emphasis on getting results. In a **Hamiltonian approach,** public managers expect others, especially strong elected executives, to judge them by whether or not their efforts produce the desired results. They work under after-the-fact accountability, and their concerns are performance and evaluation under public law. **Hamiltonian public managers** must be expert decision makers, must be students of organization, and must possess executive talents in formulating plans and carrying out duties. Hamiltonian public managers know the substance, tools, and processes of their work.

A Hamiltonian public manager is in many ways a **technocrat** who possesses special knowledge and expertise most average citizens do not have and who works under norms of objectivity and political neutrality. The rise of a professionalized U.S. civil service system of government employment in the 1930s and its perpetuation today demands well-educated public managers. Moreover, the complexity and vast array of public problems and governmental responsibilities demands that managers possess specialized knowledge and technical abilities.

Emergency management is time- and knowledge-sensitive. Thus, Hamiltonian emergency managers can be trusted to act independently and with dispatch. Time pressures raised by the acute needs of emergencies and disasters often make it difficult and inefficient for Hamiltonian managers to work exclusively through a community- or public-participation model of consultation and decision making. One proponent of Hamiltonian-style emergency management wrote, "In order to design and deliver such a sophisticated learning management system, it means tapping into the greatest minds in the fields of emergency management, disaster research, public health, community development, computer technologies, online learning, multimedia, virtual community building and facilitation, and simulation gaming." [9]

Hamiltonian forces have over the last thirty or more years converted emergency management into an intellectual and scientific enterprise. Significant advances in hazards research—most particularly in meteorology, seismologic studies, and physical geography, as well as in the building sciences, climate change research, and environmental studies—gave further credibility to disaster research. [10] These advances coincided with, and often were made possible by, major technological innovations: advances in high-speed computing and massive data storage, the development of personal computers and sophisticated computer software, civilian use of satellite telemetry of data about the atmosphere and surface of the Earth, and geographic information system (GIS) technology.

The new technologies automate emergency planning, response, recovery, and mitigation. The combination of GIS software and global positioning system tools, including remote sensing, empowered emergency managers to do things they could only imagine a decade before. [11]

The social sciences also made major contributions to the field through the work of disaster sociologists, political scientists, economists, social geographers, demographers, and urban planners. Sociologists expanded knowledge about how people behave in disaster circumstances. They helped identify "mythological" and incorrect assumptions many people had about how individuals and groups behave before, during, and after disasters. They advanced understanding about how people receive, comprehend, and respond to warnings and alerts. Political scientists explained how disaster was emerging as a new domain of public policy, flush with major political actors, interest groups, and a political process. Economists took on the daunting task of studying and measuring the economic effects of disasters. They produced a copious body of work on how insurance may or may not be used as a tool of disaster mitigation. Social geographers, demographers, and urban planners produced many studies that promoted practical knowledge of emergency management. Owing to their contributions, new communities and residential developments could be better designed and built to be more disaster resistant and better able to keep people from occupying unsafe areas. [12]

Emergency management advanced as a Hamiltonian-style area of expertise in other ways too. In the 1990s, FEMA developed HAZUS, an earthquake simulation applicable and adaptable to most of the nation, and HAZUS-MH, a powerful risk-assessment software program for analyzing potential losses from earthquake, hurricanes, and more. FEMA distributed it free of charge on the Internet, thus making a huge contribution to seismic engineering science and disaster loss estimation. HAZUS-MH also models loss from wind and flood. [13]

Modern emergency managers are expected to be well educated and professional. They are expected to manifest knowledge, skills, and abilities that average citizens could not be expected to have. Moreover, they are often expected to make independent judgments and decisions drawing on their authority of expertise. This is the epitome of Hamiltonian-style emergency management.

However, emergency managers in the course of their work cannot easily behave as both good Jeffersonians and good Hamiltonians simultaneously. The two theories point to two fundamentally different ways to approach public management work. Although the two theories may be compatible in some rare circumstances, they ordinarily stand in basic counterpoise to one another. In a pioneering work of 1948, *The Administrative State,* it was argued that public administration scholarship revolved around a core set of beliefs, one of which was that "efficiency and democracy were compatible." [14] In many respects they are not. Jeffersonians press for making public administration advance democracy. Hamiltonians advocate a public administration that rests on efficiency, or in modern parlance, state-of-the-art professional expertise. Also criticized in the 1948 book were those who would advance a science of administration geared to maximizing efficiency. A "science of administration," the author said, tends to overlook and ignore the political ramifications of public administrative work. [15]

Emergency managers have much to learn from these two management approaches. Sometimes they need to behave in a Jeffersonian manner and at other times they must perform as a Hamiltonian. If managers understand these theories, they may be able to make more informed decisions in the course of their work. They also may be better able to cope with the competing demands of their work. The key is to know when each behavior, Jeffersonian or Hamiltonian, is called for.

ORGANIZATION STUDIES

Another good way to explore how political theory may contribute to the study and application of emergency management is to consider its contributions to organization studies and theories of public management.

But before considering these theories, first think about what defines something as a **profession.** A profession is an occupation that is esoteric, complex, and discretionary. It requires theoretical knowledge, skill, and judgment that others may not possess or cannot easily comprehend. Theory-grounded knowledge is the basis of most professions and it is acquired through higher education. A profession embodies self-directing work. A profession occupies a position of legal or political privilege, or both, that protects it from competing professions. [16] Professions sanction theory and application, something emergency managers must fully appreciate. Furthermore, a profession is regulated by a **professional body** that sets examinations of competence, acts as licensing authority for practitioners, and enforces adherence to an **ethical code.** Regulation enforced by statute distinguishes a profession from **occupations** represented by technocratic groups that aspire to professional status for their members. For example, medical doctors in the United States and elsewhere work in a profession that requires them to master a vast body of complex knowledge, to train and practice the application of that knowledge, to pass licensure examinations, to agree to uphold an ethical code, and to submit to oversight by professional boards of their profession in the course of their medical practice.

Has emergency management (and related homeland security work) evolved into a profession? To enter a profession one needs education and training in a professional program in order to achieve mastery of the necessary abstract concepts. Professions often rely on universities and colleges, since people at these institutions are expert at imparting and creating abstract knowledge. Almost every profession survives competition and encroachment by other professions through special knowledge systems governed by abstractions and accepted methodologies. A profession is able to distinguish itself from other professions by the content and characteristics of its knowledge system. Disputes between people of different professions often flow from what each considers meaningful knowledge in his or her respective profession. Many television dramas create scenarios in which doctors and lawyers clash over matters such as malpractice or end-of-life decisions. These disputes are often portrayed as a conflict between different knowledge systems. The setting in which these disputes occur (a court room versus a medical facility) often influences which profession appears to win any particular dispute.

Once people master a profession's abstractions those people enjoy more autonomy in the work they do. People in most professions must be suitably credentialed, and universities or colleges are often able to convey these credentials. Many people find it worthwhile to become a member of a profession, because along with greater freedom of action, they come to assume high-paying, high-status, and often powerful positions.

If those working in the field of emergency management want to establish their work as a profession, they have to do so by building and enriching theoretical knowledge of the field of emergency management. Lack of theory or weak theory undercuts emergency management's authority of expertise and contributes to its marginalization: something dangerous in an era of occupational competition within the realm of homeland security.

Why is abstraction important in a profession? **Abstract reasoning** helps produce testable propositions and knowledge that is generalizable and applicable in many contexts. **Generalized knowledge** furnishes reasoning tools or conceptual lenses. In other words, the generalized knowledge has explanatory power within or across a wide variety of cases and circumstances.

Abstraction and generalized knowledge help individual researchers transcend the world of single case studies. Disaster research is rife with case studies. Many case studies provide extraordinary historical information about specific events in time. However, many case studies imply that each disaster is a relatively unique event. Abstract reasoning and theory developed from the study of many cases provides disaster researchers and managers with some degree of predictive power about future disaster events. Such broad-gauged work also advances hazard risk and vulnerability analysis. However, case studies should not be the sole engine of disaster research and professional development.

Abstraction enhances the value of experiential learning and case studies by enabling those with field experience to collect empirical evidence amenable to analysis by themselves and by others, most particularly those experts working to add predictive power to the theories they are developing and testing. Abstraction provides a basis for improved qualitative and quantitative examinations of social and physical phenomena; this includes disaster phenomena. The logic and rationalism supporting abstract reasoning facilitates the co-production and exchange of knowledge between people of different scientific disciplines, something essential in emergency management work.

Emergency management as a field achieves greater academic legitimacy when its core theories and concepts have currency in the physical and social sciences. Conversely, physical and social scientists are likely to contribute to the theory and conceptual growth of emergency management and disaster studies if they conclude that emergency management is a knowledge-driven, research supportive realm.

The outcome of disputes regarding who may officially accredit emergency management education programs and who may certify people as qualified emergency managers will profoundly affect whether and how emergency management evolves as a profession.[17] Theories and concepts are engines of knowledge creation, but in emergency management the matters of developing and testing theories and deciding what constitutes knowledge may well be determined by the authorities and interests that win accreditation and certification powers.

HOW THINGS WORK

TO BE OR NOT TO BE A PROFESSION

Some tend to judge emergency management as a body of unsophisticated skill sets imparted to others through simplified, one-directional training. Worse still is that some might assume "anyone could do emergency management because the field is so ill-defined, diffuse, or based on easily learned behaviors." [18] People might then conclude that emergency managers are interchangeable functionaries who carry out relatively simple tasks with clerklike efficiency during episodic periods officially defined as disasters or emergencies.

This conceptualization may appeal to Jeffersonians because it rests on simplification, facilitates mobilization and participation of unskilled volunteers, and maximizes political control and grassroots political responsiveness. However, there is not much use for Jeffersonian emergency managers between disasters. Jeffersonian emergency managers have little or no role in mitigating disasters or reducing hazard vulnerabilities in any sophisticated way; and these emergency managers are neither well suited to address the causes of disaster nor are they likely to understand the complex, multifaceted ramifications of disasters and emergencies.

It would be reasonable to expect the recommendations of *professional* emergency managers to top political officials, including the president and White House officials, to be respected and taken seriously, owing to the substantive and technical merit of the recommendations themselves and because the recommendations were conceived by those with acknowledged expertise (extensive education, training, and experience). If political officials do not consider emergency managers as part of a specialized, knowledge-based profession, or if they consider emergency management skill sets interchangeable or indistinguishable from that of other professions, those political officials might conclude that their own judgments about disasters and emergencies are just as valid as those of their emergency managers.[19] In other words, emergency managers would lack an "authority of expertise" and (generalist) emergency managers might then be supplanted by political appointees who have little or no emergency management training or experience.

A caveat is in order. One scholar of disaster research has written, "Disaster is a term, which has been defined, understood and packaged by the so-called 'experts' to an extent that disaster reduction has become merely a problem solving exercise. The definers declare what they perceive as a problem and how they intend to solve it. . . ." He adds, "There needs to be a strong interface between 'reality' of disaster constructed by us 'the experts' and the one created by the victims based on their worldviews." [20] This is fair warning for those who seek to become professional emergency managers.

Organization Culture of Bureaucratic Politics

In a nutshell, **bureaucratic politics** theories strive to explain why public officials do the things they do. These theories suggest that the desire of public officials to protect or promote their own agency's special interests (as they compete with other agencies) forms a major motivating factor in shaping the timing and the content of their decisions. "Bureaucratic politics are conducted quietly, behind the scenes, in skillful ways, with strategic reversals possible, caution, and contentment with sharing credit for good results. A person needs these attributes in order to exhibit good statecraft." [21] The statecraft of political administration is how effectively people fulfill the obligations of the office they hold and how much they advance the welfare of the entire polity and state from the official position they hold.[22] Statecraft is defined as "using and risking political power through action." [23] It is political leadership times bureaucratic power.

In other words, each government division continually strives to maximize its budget and its authorized manpower, as well as to protect or extend its operating autonomy and discretion in decision making in the area of its assigned responsibilities. Often this can be most readily accomplished by lobbying for an expansion of the bureau's responsibilities. The policies and policy recommendations generated in the executive branch of the government and passed on to both the chief executive and the legislature are often better understood as the by-product of bureaucratic turf battles and expedient compromises between bureaucratic chieftains than as the product of reasoned analysis of how most effectively and efficiently to carry out the policy commitments of the elected chief executive or to serve the public interest.

Applying the study of bureaucratic politics allows us to think about emergency management theory. Let's think about emergency management by way of three models of bureaucratic politics: a **rational actor model,** in which the president makes his own decision; a **governmental (or bureaucratic) politics model,** in which the president follows the recommendations of senior political appointees and other elites; and an **organizational process model,** in which the decision largely rests with various disaster management officials (see the box "The Cuban Missile Crisis).[24]

Much of the world of emergency managers is made up of bureaucratic politics. Often emergency managers must work with elected executives (as a rational actor), must bargain and negotiate with very senior political or merit-appointed administrative officials (an organization process), and must be responsive to legislators (governmental or bureaucratic politics). To succeed they must demonstrate technical competence as well as lead or manage the coordination of people working in their own agency or department and bring about the coordination of work by other departments or agencies. Theirs is a world of high-tension intergovernmental relations and intense media coverage.

Best-Practices Approaches

At the intersection of public management and bureaucratic politics, we find what is referred to as best practices. The **best-practices approach** is a method of producing knowledge by observing (or recounting) field experience and then creating applicable principles. This is often described as "practice as the basis for scholarship," not scholarship as the basis for practice, and reflective practitioners are needed to make the best-practices approach work.[25] Here

HOW THINGS WORK

THE CUBAN MISSILE CRISIS

The political scientist Graham Allison used the Cuban missile crisis as a case example to demonstrate that there were analyzable alternative explanations for political events. Allison's work had a dramatic effect in clarifying and differentiating a bureaucratic politics conceptualization.

Each of Allison's models can be adapted to help explain presidential decisions to declare disasters in a different way. For example, the rational actor explanation holds that the president decides largely on his own, as a unitary actor, on behalf of the entire federal government. It also assumes that individual rationality surrounds that decision making. The rational actor model would assume that each president decides whether to approve or reject a governor's request for a presidential declaration of major disaster or emergency independently, perhaps after consultation with various advisers.

The governmental or bureaucratic politics model explains presidential decisions on disaster declarations as the outcome of negotiations between senior political appointees (agency heads, cabinet-level secretaries, state emergency management leaders, and so forth) and elected executives (governors, mayors, and the like). Allison refers to these players as elites. Their bargaining and negotiation activities culminate in persuading the chief executive to take some course of action or to make some type of decision. The bureaucratic politics model assumes that whether or not a president issues a declaration of major disaster or emergency is largely based on the recommendations of a combination of these major political actors. Certainly, in asking, a governor presses the president to

approve the governor's request by convincing the president of the worthiness of his or her request. Presidents are also advised, sometimes in group settings, by their staffs, by their confidants, and, as well as by lawmakers.

Allison's organizational process model would maintain that presidential decisions regarding declarations of disaster are essentially a routine administrative determination handled by a stovepipe-connected assortment of federal, state, and local disaster management officials. The organizational process model contends that emergency management professionals compile disaster damage information and they use it to review gubernatorial requests for declarations (the governor's request itself would be the product of state emergency management agency activity). In the organizational process model the executive has either largely delegated decision authority to someone else or rubber-stamps the official recommendation of his or her emergency management functionaries.

One would expect presidents to decide and act on very major, even catastrophic, disasters as a rational actor. One might also expect that disasters or emergencies that pose unusual or unanticipated political and management problems would encourage the bureaucratic model type of decision making. Finally, very routine disasters and emergencies (seasonal flooding, winter storms, metropolitan power outages, minor earthquakes in seismically active zones, and the like) that are neither major nor catastrophic and that involve few political costs or benefits for a president, would, one would think, elicit an organizational process model decision.

public management study becomes a kind of art form. The practitioner draws the picture for the observer. Rudolph Giuliani, former New York City mayor, and James Lee Witt, former director of FEMA, stand as good examples of best-practice knowledge offered by an emergency management reflective practitioner.[26]

AMERICA'S MAYOR
AND CITY MANAGEMENT

Is Rudolph Giuliani the new model of what city management by mayors should be? Consider, "In the aftermath of September 11, New York Mayor Rudy Giuliani eventually established himself as the front-line spokesman. He gathered around him the resources he needed, from all levels of government. And New York's response began to emerge. It didn't emerge because Giuliani clawed to the top of a pyramid. It emerged because he became the conductor of a large and hugely complex symphony. He built a network of horizontal partnerships." [27]

Giuliani's honesty and ability to comfort were just two of the qualities that he used to get New York City back onto its feet. He was portrayed as a commoner by the news media. He joined the people of New York on the street as the 9/11 attacks unfolded. As the entire nation watched media coverage of the event, Giuliani was filmed in large crowds walking (and sometimes running) to escape the carnage of Lower Manhattan. The mayor of New York would soon be labeled "America's Mayor."

Giuliani's quick response, confident demeanor, and firm hand won international praise in the New York 9/11 disaster.[28] Giuliani went on to write about some of his experiences on and after 9/11 in a book entitled *Leadership*. In that book, he talked about his method and style of mayoral leadership. During his mayorship he moved control of New York City emer-

gency management out of the New York City Police Department and created an Office of Emergency Management (OEM) that was located near his office. Giuliani wanted to assume more control over city emergency management and temper competitive police and fire service relations in his city. He appointed a series of OEM directors who advanced city preparedness for a variety of terrorist threats. However, as mentioned earlier, Mayor Michael Bloomberg, who succeeded Giuliani, elected to move leadership of city emergency management back to the NYPD.

In major disasters citizens need a "voice of confidence" from the scene. Following the 9/11 terrorist attacks, Mayor Rudolph Giuliani clearly was a "voice of confidence" from New York City and from there he provided steady leadership. "One of the things that worsened Katrina's aftermath was the sense that no one was in charge because the public did not have steady communication from an official who could speak confidently about what was being done." [29] This may be one of Giuliani's most important legacies. On the strength of his performance in the 9/11 disaster, Giuliani campaigned for the Republican Party presidential nomination in 2007–2008.

Giuliani, very much like James Lee Witt, represents through his publications and speeches the essence of best-practice knowledge in emergency management.

Another best-practices approach is to create knowledge based on empirical validations of useful propositions derived from models—in other words, building practice wisdom as a social scientific approach to scholarship as a basis for practice. This is the **applied heuristics approach.** Such analytical approaches help public managers deal with a messy reality. These approaches and models allow for experimentation, trial and error; they were the early basis of policy analysis. For public managers, heuristics are verbal explanatory sketches, or conceptual frameworks, that help them produce adequate explanations for puzzling things. Heuristics embody propositions subject to confirmation or disconfirmation; in other words, one can test the utility of the proposition. For example, one can test the proposition that increased federal funding to a state's terrorism preparedness program will improve its terrorism response capability. This can be done by evaluating the performance of state emergency managers via unannounced drills and exercises.

Detailed studies alleged to represent best practice in public management have been criticized because they are often not good guides to scholarship, teaching, or practice. However, some open-minded studies of cases, especially those showing how public executives shape the institutional frameworks for policymaking and execution, have been praised for their contributions to theory knowledge.[30] Executives are the molders of contexts that will affect public policy in both the short and long runs. Best practice research flows from a broad perspective on public executive leadership, one that draws from classic works on executive leadership inspired by practice.

Analytical Approaches vs. Social Constructivist Theories

Within subfields of various physical and social scientific disciplines there is an incredible range of **analytical approaches** to the study of disaster (for example, meteorology, climate science, seismology, volcanology, sociology, policy studies, economics, physical geography, epidemiology, emergency medicine, and engineering). Those advancing the analytical approach to the study of disaster have benefited from advances in high-powered computing and the development of sophisticated software programs (computer-based data analysis, GIS, HAZUS, and others).[31] Emergency managers and students of emergency management must embrace analytic approaches and tools in order to advance disaster study and research.

However, the generalization sought in analytical approaches overlooks the assertion that "Reality is a social construction rather than an objective construct that is the same for all observers." [32] Those following **social constructivism** might argue that it is the actions and persuasiveness of people, perhaps amplified through mass communications, that defines what is or is not a disaster. In other words, the "reality" of some disaster phenomenon may be more an issue than how people have conceived of and conveyed the "idea" that a disaster has occurred. Consider the claim, "whether an event constitutes a disaster, how probable and how damaging disasters are, and what can be done to reduce their impacts, are socially produced through organized claims-making activities." [33] Some social constructivist scholars working in the disciplines of sociology or political philosophy maintain that organizations (including government organizations) are systems of socially constructed and cognitively ordered meanings.[34] I once listened to a respected and brilliant economics professor glibly enquire, "So FEMA makes disasters?" What he was inferring was that the mere fact that the government has established a federal emergency management agency presumably composed of disaster management experts, suggests that those experts will look for opportunities to apply their skills and expertise. As FEMA officials they would have great incentive to find more and more phenomena they could persuade the president to declare as disasters or emergencies so their agency could prove its worth, serve public needs, and win more authority and larger budgets.

In contrast, empiricism is the collection of information about the physical and social "real" world, which is so essential to analytical approaches. Empirical research loses out if the social constructivist approach to disaster research dominates. This is because social constructivists are likely to routinely discount empirical information and scientific "facts" as mere products of individual or group constructions of social "reality" and personal belief systems. "A constructivist theory of social problems explains problems and policy issues by focusing on people's actions rather than on the putative 'conditions' that are the object of those actions." [35] "Conditions" are alleged to exist and to have harmful qualities owing to issue advocates and claims makers. For example, television news reporters disclose certain important human needs that they allege must be addressed by government. Also, political actors representing what they perceive to be the needs of various individual people or aggregations of people and interests issue clarion calls for action. Some of these people may be elected government officials, some may be officials representing an interest group, and some may be independent social advocates. The concern here is how issue advocates and claims makers define problems and their policy solutions and how they are able to persuade others to take their concerns seriously, even to the point of getting them to act on those problems.

Today, constructivist theory is widely popular in many academic realms, including disaster sociology and political science.[36] Social constructivist research has an important place in the intellectual sphere of emergency management. There is a growing body of scholarship, international in scope, predicated on social constructions of the disaster phenomenon. Much of it is insightful and much of it is relevant to political officials and their advisers. Political officials need to understand how people comprehend safety and danger, how they formulate judgments of risk and vulnerability, and how they gauge the effectiveness of disaster management (particularly given their role in the situation: disaster victim, unaffected observer, emergency responder, and so forth).

Social constructivism and its variants, however, do not represent the only intellectual paradigm through which to conduct disaster research. Several alternative theories and paradigms—such as scientific rationalism, empirical study, management theories, institutional studies, public policy analysis, and some interdisciplinary theories that link the physical and social sciences—offer more instrumental and application usefulness, for emergency managers than does social constructivism.

Principal-Agent Theory

Principal-agent theory assumes that managers function in an environment in which they cannot observe whether their agents in fact carried out the instructions they issued as principals. In addition, it assumes that agents hide information from principals and that agents may use the information to act in ways contrary to what principals intended. Principal-agent theory gives rise to performance-based government contracting studies.

For example, the study and use of principal-agent theory would not only help government emergency managers better understand the realm of contracting and grants management but would also press elected and appointed officials to work jointly toward achieving legal and policy goals. Thus they would better be able to oversee and steer contractors to do what they are expected to do. Principal-agent theory may also help them oversee and influence the behavior of their grantees working in state and local emergency management organizations.

Principal-agent theory helps integrate normative noneconomic concerns with structured economic analysis. This approach involves refining situational logic.[37] Principal-agent theory seems quite appropriate in the world of emergency management.[38] Government emergency managers work in a universe of federal, state, local, and private sector agencies. An immense amount of government emergency management work is contract management, involving private contractors and nonprofit volunteer organizations. In a sense, government officials are principals who retain agents, in this case contractors, who in turn carry out various duties, functions, and tasks. Information flows among agents and principals. This information is used by policymakers and government officials and influences their decisions in matters of fund distribution, budgeting, planning, program administration, and management in general. Emergency manager principals might be well served by using normative factors (that is, was the public happy with the job the contractor performed? How quickly was work completed and how satisfied were clients or customers with the products and services they received from the contractor?) and structured economic analysis to help ensure that contractor agents addressing disaster-related needs are better guided toward achieving the goals emergency manager principals are legally and officially obligated to meet.

"Working the seams" is part of principal-agent theory. Public managers must know how to work the edges of administrative-legislative interaction, intergovernmental relations, agencies, and interest groups.[39] Seams are gray zones. They are areas in which there is legal and administrative flexibility. Disasters and emergencies often require that emergency managers behave adaptively, bend or ignore rules that confound or delay their work, and establish new and often unusual modes of interaction with people and organizations they do not often encounter in normal periods. They need technical and analytical knowledge to do this. Their world is composed of agents, seams, and a technical core.

Partisan Mutual Adjustment

Partisan mutual adjustment seeks to explain how public managers behave in governing relations. Partisan mutual adjustment has many features of the bureaucratic politics model employed by Allison.[40] In partisan mutual adjustment public managers clash owing to their respective personal political motivations, their respective obligations to the law (laws differ from agency to agency) and to the agencies they lead, and their respective commitments to their elected executive and legislative overseers. This theory provides emergency managers a guide to surviving in a world of partisan political competition among political actors.[41] It also acknowledges the ongoing need for political appointees to interact with top civil servant administrators.[42] Political appointees and top civil servant administrators work in a system of organic interdependence, something commonly found in emergency management in the United States. In many respects the failure of federal, state, and local governments to perform well in the early aftermath of the 2005 Hurricane Katrina disaster relates to competition among political actors and the ensuing difficulties embodied in the relations between public managers and political officials.

Intergovernmental Relations Theory

Three models have commonly classified intergovernmental relations (IGR): inclusive authority, overlapping authority, and coordinate authority.[43] Although those relations in emergency management at one time more resembled a coordinate-authority model, they have moved through an overlapping-authority model finally to become an inclusive-authority model.

The **coordinate-authority model** assumes a sharp and distinct boundary between separate national and state governments. National and state governments appear to operate independently and autonomously, and they are linked only tangentially. Moreover, in the coordinate-authority model local governments are somewhat dependent on their respective state governments.[44]

Before 1950, disaster management in the United States conformed to the coordinate-authority model of **federalism** and **dual federalism.** The *Stanford Encyclopedia of Philosophy* defines federalism in the following way:

> Federalism is the theory or advocacy of federal political orders, where final authority is divided between sub-units and a center. Unlike a unitary state [system], [in a federal system] sovereignty is constitutionally split between at least two territorial levels so that units at each level have final authority and can act independently of the others in some area. Citizens thus have political obligations to two authorities. The allocation of authority between the sub-unit and center may vary, typically the center has powers regarding defense and foreign policy, but sub-units may also have international roles. The sub-units may also participate in central decision-making bodies.[45]

The period from 1789 to 1901 has been called the era of dual federalism, "characterized as an era during which there was little collaboration between the national and state governments." However, in the period 1865 to 1901, the national government began to move into several policy areas that had previously been the purview of the states.[46]

In the coordinate-authority model, local governments often handled major disasters and emergencies on their own with only intermittent state government help and with very little federal help. When local governments could not cope they sought state government help, usually petitioning the governor or state legislature. State governments coped with disasters and emergencies that largely affected state government assets, infrastructure, and interests. U.S. policy has long assigned the responsibility for disaster management to the government jurisdiction(s) that experienced the disaster. As Clinton-era FEMA director James Lee Witt used to say, "All disasters are local." [47] The responsibility for public safety is a local government role under American federalism.

From 1950 to about 2003, U.S. disaster management could be categorized as an **overlapping-authority model.** In the overlapping-authority model substantial areas of governmental operations involve national, state, and local governments simultaneously. In the overlapping model, areas of autonomy or single-jurisdiction independence and full discretion are relatively small. Power and influence for any one jurisdiction is substantially limited and authority patterns involve heavy bargaining.[48]

From a disaster studies viewpoint, if a disaster or emergency exceeded the response and recovery capacity of the local government, the local government executive officer (mayor, city manager, county executive, or the like) and the city or county council declared a "local disaster." This was often followed by a local request for state and federal assistance. The governor may respond to the request by issuing a state declaration of disaster or emergency. Once the governor declares a state of emergency the local government may then receive personnel, goods, services, and funding from the state to deal with the disaster. If the governor believes that the disaster may overwhelm the capacity of the state to manage the emergency effectively, the governor then sends the president a request for a presidential declaration of major disaster or emergency. A presidential declaration of major disaster mobilizes a multi-departmental, multi-program federal response conducted in coordination with state and local officials and agencies.

This overlapping, layered approach to local, state, and federal relations correlates with the overlapping-authority model. In this model, no one level of government is dominant and no level intervenes in the affairs of another without the permission of that government.

The era of overlapping authority in U.S. disaster policy came to an end after the 9/11 terrorist attacks and with the ensuing enactment of the Homeland Security Act of 2002, the establishment of the U.S. Department of Homeland Security in early 2003, and a succession of Bush administration presidential homeland security directives.

These changes—including the creation of a National Response Plan and National Incident Management System—brought on an era of inclusive authority. Under the **inclusive-authority model,** each level of government has a diminishing proportion of responsibilities, from the national to the state to the local government level.[49] Under the inclusive-authority model the federal government plays a key coordinating role as the states and federal government cooperate and interact in certain critical areas. The inclusive-authority model assumes the sharing of power and responsibility, with the various participants working toward shared goals.[50] The model also conveys the essential hierarchical nature of authority. In some respects, the new homeland security paradigm has made states and localities "mere minions of the national government." The role of the state as the "service delivery arm" continues as it has since 1950. However, the federal government provides "its vast resources" as a new backstop for state and local governments.

In this inclusive-authority era, homeland security presidential directives, several new federal laws, and a battery of new federal grant programs were introduced. Collectively, these measures dictated to local governments the exact steps they were expected to take in emergency management. These measures placed terrorism preparedness above preparedness for all other types of disaster agents. The effect of these reforms was to move both emergency management and homeland security toward "nation-centered" federal dominance within an inclusive-authority model. DHS authorities told states and localities that they would be heavily consulted and welcomed "partners." Yet the profusion of "top-down" directives and the vast sums of federal money used to steer states and localities in various directions have left little space for state codetermination and even less local freedom of action.[51]

Disaster Victims and Clients as Customers

This chapter opened with a review of Jeffersonian-oriented emergency management. Owing to the professionalization of emergency management, the Hamiltonian perspective was shown to be gaining ascendance over the Jeffersonian approach. Regardless, the rise of the **reinventing-government movement** in the 1990s and the modern management consultant conclusion that organizations need to rediscover the importance of customer satisfaction, have given Jeffersonian emergency management reinvigoration.

Increasingly, customer satisfaction has become a focus of emergency management.[52] The Clinton-era reinventing-government effort offered low-level administrators more power.

However, low-level administrators must have the training and experience necessary to assume more responsibility. Under James Lee Witt, FEMA assiduously embraced the reinvention movement. Customer satisfaction in government work has a ring of Jeffersonianism. Clearly, no agency or profession can afford to ignore customer satisfaction very long without losing credibility. However, although customers may help professionals identify unmet needs, in no profession do customers actually define the nature of professional work.

Still, if emergency managers are judged to have failed in meeting the legitimate needs of people seeking postdisaster government aid, then they have also failed in the criterion of customer satisfaction. Policy analysts have been slow to recognize the utility of customer satisfaction studies in measuring the effectiveness of government disaster assistance programs. The failures of FEMA and a host of other state and local emergency management organizations in the days and weeks after Hurricane Katrina struck in 2005, impelled Congress to launch a host of investigations about why victims' needs were not addressed faster and more effectively. One lesson relearned by emergency managers after the Katrina debacle is the importance of public responsiveness and customer satisfaction. Catastrophic disasters produce a vast array

HOW THINGS WORK

TURF WARS AND SHIFTING FOCUS

In disaster policy, emergency management has been a combatant of bureaucratic "turf" wars. New problems, calamities, or emergencies, sometimes defined as "disaster" by public opinion, media influence, and political forces, often produce new policies. Which federal executive branch departments, agencies, or offices will get the jurisdiction and resources to implement these new policies? Simply put, Who's in charge?

FEMA, throughout the 1980s and 1990s, was the only federal agency with large-scale disaster recovery monies and budget authority. The nature of FEMA's work has long manifested both "humanitarian" and "technical" characteristics. Throughout its twenty-three-year history as an independent executive branch agency, those who appointed FEMA officials and those FEMA officials who had to define the agency's public service positions, qualifications, and work assignments (as well as engage in recruitment and selection of workers) have faced a dilemma. Should FEMA be managed and staffed by generalist public managers, often schooled in the

social sciences or the humanities? Or should FEMA be managed and staffed by technical specialists, educated in the physical or biological sciences or in engineering fields?

If FEMA leaders opted to rely mostly on generalists, generalist managers might be capable of serving humanitarian goals well. They might also be highly politically responsive in periods when elected officials demanded expedited emergency services or recovery resources. However, putting generalists ahead of technical specialists might also mean that policymakers would assign technical management of the problem, with commensurate jurisdictional authority and resources, to another federal agency possessing the appropriate scientific and engineering expertise, not to FEMA. Conversely, if FEMA leaders chose technical specialists rather than generalists, the agency's scientific and engineering recommendations and training might be more credible and its in-house emergency response better suited to manage disasters in accord with scientific rationalism. However, of citizen (and subnational government) needs. Meeting those needs expeditiously and competently is a daunting challenge to emergency managers.

KNOWLEDGE CODIFICATION AND KNOWLEDGE DIFFUSION ISSUES

The experience and actions of any organization are based on a blend of tacit, or uncodified, knowledge and structured, or codified, knowledge. **Tacit knowledge** is vague and ambiguous and depends on sharing expectations and values through social relationships. **Codified knowledge** is impersonal and learned through thinking and reasoning, not social relationships. To manage well, do emergency managers need to operate in face-to-face forums (that are consensual, democratic, Jeffersonian, and based on tacit knowledge)? Or might they achieve their goals by imparting technocratic knowledge, which is produced from data analysis, repeated experimentation, scientific study, Hamiltonian behavior, and codified knowledge?

technical specialists, when compared with generalists, may be less able to address humanitarian disaster assistance, less able to work compatibly in the intergovernmental world of domestic disaster management, and less able to fulfill presidential obligations of public responsiveness.

After the formation of the Department of Homeland Security the focus of emergency management shifted from the more frequent emergencies of natural disasters to terrorism. With this shift came a new focus on prevention and diminished attention on response and mitigation, the hallmarks of successful emergency management of the past. Pseudo-intelligence and pseudo-defense officers co-opted emergency managers, highly militarizing their positions and casting them into unfamiliar environments filled with "turf" battles and wrestling matches over who would gain or lose DHS funds and programs.

Federal emergency management officials found it difficult to adjust to the new DHS terrorism-dominated environment. Similarly, state and local emergency management officials, an imputed interest group and intergovernmental partners of FEMA, were now thrust into the field of homeland security. During the shuffling, FEMA was swallowed up within a massive department. Other agencies dwarfed the new FEMA, which was forced to work through new layers of administration to accomplish the same tasks that a single telephone call might have taken care of in years past. Moreover, according to James Lee Witt, under the DHS system, "FEMA's grant making authority was sharply eroded. Taking away this function and instead giving it to other divisions within DHS has also contributed to the nation's slip away from all-hazard preparedness. While homeland security is an important aspect of our nation's readiness, we have seen all too clearly the price that can be paid in not striking an adequate balance between natural and man-made hazard preparedness." [53]

This may depend on whether codified knowledge is diffused or undiffused knowledge.[54] Diffused codified knowledge is written down and openly available so that audiences outside government can use it. If knowledge is codified but not diffused, it sits contained within the bureaucracies. Someone could master this knowledge only if he or she worked inside the bureaucracy and learned internal rules and unique types of information. If knowledge is diffused but not codified, those entering public management positions from the outside stand little chance of coordinating the work of others, unless they receive help from those inside or they have the time to learn the uncodified information as government employees. To succeed under conditions of diffused, tacit knowledge, a public manager needs to "learn the agency." Managers would have to learn from mentors.

Unfortunately, a considerable share of federal emergency management knowledge, if recorded at all, is partially codified but not sufficiently diffused beyond the agency. The *U.S. Code of Federal Regulations* sets forth the core rules of federal emergency management, but it does not elucidate the essence of what emergencies and disasters are and it does not explain how to actually do emergency management work.[55]

Some federal emergency managers have codified their expertise, but much of this information resides within the bowels of various agency offices; a possible exception is the National Emergency Training Center within DHS-FEMA, which disseminates codified emergency management knowledge and trains state and local authorities and managers. However, according to former FEMA attorney William Cumming, "the real disaster tradition was oral, not in writing, and ad hoc rather than procedural." [56] Moreover, FEMA and its progenitor agencies lacked "history divisions" (common at the Department of the Army, Department of Energy, Nuclear Regulatory Commission, NASA, and other departments and agencies) or institutional memories that were more than merely the recollections of employees who have worked there.

A fiefdom or cult of personality results when management knowledge is both uncodified and undiffused (inaccessible) or kept secret by government classification. Such may have been the case in J. Edgar Hoover's FBI many years ago. Management control then becomes highly personalized, unreviewable, and unappealable. Some fear that the advancement of emergency management largely depends on high-profile, charismatic figures chosen to lead agencies like FEMA or state and local emergency management agencies. If emergency management knowhow depends heavily on a cult of personality, there is little hope emergency management will be professionalized.

In uncodified but diffused situations, clans are the norm and people learn by being socialized. Those selected to join the U.S. Diplomatic Corps face this type of situation. Diplomatic histories are many but inadequate to train potential diplomats. Before they are officially entrusted to do U.S. diplomatic work new diplomats must be socialized to the State Department's way of doing things.[57] Certain first responder emergency management occupational specialties (fire services and law enforcement), too, put great emphasis on socialization and mastery of tacit knowledge and of codified knowledge not widely diffused to those outside the occupational specialty.

If emergency management is basically learned through apprenticeships within emergency management agencies, few in the academic profession will be drawn to the field. If that is the case, the growth of the field of emergency management will be a function of in-house training, not of broadly based advancement of emergency management education and published research.

CONCLUSION AND SUMMARY

This chapter furnished an overview regarding how and where theory knowledge fits in the evolution of emergency management as a profession. It also demonstrated how people new to the field can draw from this chapter's theories and concepts to independently analyze disaster policy as a domain of public policy.

The chapter began by laying out two simple normative theories: one Jeffersonian and the other Hamiltonian. Hamiltonian theory and assumptions hold out the best prospect for professionalizing the work of emergency management. Jeffersonian theory has many laudatory features in that it rests on public participation, public assent, and democratic principles. However, Hamiltonian emergency management embodies an authority of expertise for emergency managers. They must learn and apply a growing body of knowledge, some of it practical knowledge and some of it academic knowledge.

Bureaucratic politics and matters of administrative culture permeate emergency management and disaster policy in the United States. Understanding models and concepts of bureaucratic politics helps one analyze power relationships in disaster policy and management. Also hugely important is intergovernmental relations theory. Owing to the U.S. system of relations between federal, state, and local governments and because other parties outside of government are heavily involved in "governance" of this policy domain (for example, nonprofit organizations active in disasters, corporately owned utilities, special district governments, and armies of trained volunteers), intergovernmental relations is one of the most critical components of disaster policy. This is true both in the formulation and implementation of that policy.

Principal-agent theory and other theories were briefly examined and proposed as worthwhile tools for both analyzing and conducting emergency management. The chapter also included a review of topics ranging from customer satisfaction to partisan mutual adjustment. The chapter closed with a commentary about how emergency management knowledge is produced and how it is learned by others.

KEY TERMS AND CONCEPTS

abstract reasoning   32
analytical approaches   37
applied heuristics approach   36
best-practices approach   34
bureaucratic politics model   34
codified knowledge   43
coordinate-authority model   40
dual federalism   40
ethical code   31
federalism   40
generalists   28
generalized knowledge   32
governmental politics model   34
Hamiltonian approach   29
Hamiltonian public managers   29

inclusive-authority model   41
Jeffersonian public managers   28
occupations   31
organizational process model   34
overlapping-authority model   40
partisan mutual adjustment   39
principal-agent theory   38
profession   31
professional body   31
rational actor model   34
reinventing-government movement   41
social constructivism   37
tacit knowledge   43
technocrat   29

CHAPTER 3

HISTORICAL TRENDS IN DISASTER MANAGEMENT

ORDINARILY, THE POLICY PROCESS ASSUMES THAT POLICYMAKERS identify a problem. If they choose to define it as a "public problem," lawmakers begin a process of policy formation in which various solutions to the problem are put forward, often in the form of legislative measures. Various political interests establish positions on these measures and a process of coalition building takes place among legislators. The president and some officials of the executive branch may engage in this policy formation and policy adoption process by exercising political influence or by contributing to the hearing process. Legislators ultimately vote on proposed measures to address the problem, and once a policy is adopted, often through enactment of a law, institutional resources and spending authority are provided to implement the law. This is the "textbook" idealization of the policy process. Many federal disaster laws have emerged by way of this general process over the years.[1]

However, history demonstrates that the president and other policymakers regularly have to decide how to manage different types of disaster and what the subsequent role of the federal government will be. In some acute and unforeseen new type of disaster or in certain emergency circumstances when a legislative determination proves to be too slow, cumbersome, and costly to rely on, presidents are entrusted with deciding whether a national interest exists and if so how the federal government will respond. Presidential executive orders sometimes provide the president and the federal government a high-speed, highly responsive alternative to the conventional policy process. The president's creative use of disaster declaration authority is an important and available tool.

Thus, presidents often lead in the formulation and legitimation of disaster policy. Presidents are chief executives and many presidents have either by choice or by the press of

Flood disaster has been the nation's perennial and arguably most common disaster agent. The history of emergency management in the United States has been profoundly shaped by flood, and virtually every state has experienced flood disaster in some form. This aerial photograph of Mississippi flooding in 1937 illustrates the nation's effort to protect against flood using engineered structures, such as levees. The levee failure here is actually human-caused, because the U.S. Army Corps of Engineers blew up this portion of the levee to protect a large and more populated community downstream from predicted levee-failure flooding there.

emergency circumstances used their executive authority to move the federal government to address new emergencies, disasters, and exigencies.

This chapter tracks the role and actions of presidents in the formation and implementation of disaster policy. Specific disaster-related laws and policy trends, as well as actual major disasters that have been factors in the enactment of these laws or contributors to these policy trends, are examined. The theme of federal-state and intergovernmental relations in disaster issues is another matter worthy of attention, as are matters of civil defense and civil-military relations. In many ways the continuum set forth in this chapter reveals the antecedents of twenty-first-century homeland security.

THE COLD WAR AND THE RISE OF CIVIL DEFENSE

Continued testing of atomic weapons by the United States after the end of World War II and the Soviet Union's successful test of an atomic bomb in 1949, the Soviet occupation of Eastern Europe, and a growing rivalry and competition between the United States and the Soviet Union opened a cold war that lasted forty-four years. Civil defense against nuclear attack became a principle focus of U.S. disaster management. President Harry S. Truman's administration (1945–1953) and congressional lawmakers prepared Americans for the possibility that the nation might be attacked by atomic weapons, and they pressed for improved civil defense preparedness. Ironically, the escalation of the Cold War drew federal policymakers to the issue of disaster preparedness for the civilian population. Several landmark federal disaster laws and policies originate, for better or worse, from the Cold War and the related concern of civil defense against nuclear attack.

The Civil Defense Act of 1950

Congress enacted the Civil Defense Act of 1950, a measure that placed most of the civil defense burden on the states. The act created the Federal Civil Defense Administration (FCDA), which was to formulate national policy to guide the states' efforts.[2]

Congressional resistance to paying for a comprehensive program, and concerns about establishing public dependency on government, led to adoption of a doctrine of **self-help:** individual responsibility for preparedness to minimize (although not eliminate) risk. The idea of decentralized, locally controlled, volunteer-based civil defense was not new; in fact it was the foundation of the successful British civil defense effort in World War II. Still, the decision to make self-help the basis of civil defense was a political compromise, a way to balance conflicting views over the size, power, and priorities of the emerging postwar nation.

The Civil Defense Act of 1950 allocated significant funding to a shelter initiative. The FCDA led shelter-building programs, sought to improve federal and state coordination, established an attack warning system, stockpiled supplies, and started a well-known national civic education campaign.

The political, fiscal, and emotional crosscurrents were reflected in civil defense funding. Despite ambitious funding requests, actual appropriations to civil defense remained low throughout the Truman administration and throughout the 1950s.

The Federal Disaster Relief Act of 1950

The Federal Disaster Relief Act of 1950 was a companion measure of the FCDA. As typical after major disasters that grab national attention, the Disaster Relief Act of 1950 was passed as a **limited federal response,** in this case to flooding in the Midwest. However, this law was anything but "ordinary." The new law set forth a framework and process that carried the nation through more than fifty years of disaster experience. Much of that framework and process is embedded within or underpins major federal disaster laws that followed and that are still in effect today. The act provided "an orderly and continuing means of assistance by the Federal government to States and local governments in carrying out their responsibilities to alleviate suffering and damage resulting from major disasters," including floods. Essentially the law created the first permanent system for disaster relief without the need for congressional postdisaster action. It also clearly stated for the first time that federal resources could and should be used to supplement the efforts of others in the event of a disaster. The new law made federal disaster assistance more immediately accessible, because it no longer required specific congressional legislation to address each new disaster but instead simply allowed the president to decide when federal disaster assistance was justified and necessary.

Policymakers of the era did not consider the Disaster Relief Act of 1950 as precedent setting. They did not intend the measure to go beyond earlier disaster legislation efforts. Only later did congressional leaders begin to see the 1950 act as precedent setting and as an early, general, national-level disaster policy model.

The Disaster Relief Act of 1950 put in place a standard process by which governors of states could ask the president to approve federal disaster assistance for their respective states and localities. It set precedents by establishing a federal policy for providing emergency relief, by laying out national governmental responsibility in disasters and by transforming the intergovernmental context of disasters. In effect, it set up a framework for government disaster assistance that invests immense and broad authority in the president.

Dual-Use Preparedness Programs

Through the 1950s, **civil defense preparedness** continued to evolve. Civil preparedness emergency management and the policy options associated with it were in great measure influenced by foreign policy and weapons technology matters. Certain foreign policy conflicts between the United States, its allies, and the Soviet Union, and its allies, that came to diplomatic or military boiling points pressed American presidents to take various civil defense countermeasures on the home front. Moreover, as atomic weapons of the 1940s became thermonuclear weapons of the 1950s and beyond, their destructive capacity increased by many orders of magnitude. Over the years nuclear weapons became smaller and more easily delivered to their targets by ever more sophisticated ballistic missiles carried on submarines and military aircraft or launched from hidden land-based silos. Over time certain civil defense options proved ineffective or infeasible and new ones were proposed. President Dwight D. Eisenhower (1953–1961) advanced a mass evacuation policy, instead of the shelter program initiated under Truman.[3] President John F. Kennedy (1961–1963) emphasized the importance of home, school, or workplace fallout shelters as a means to save lives.[4] Owing to the escalation of the war in Vietnam, President Lyndon B. Johnson (1963–1969) put civil defense against nuclear attack on a back burner.[5] Attention to civil defense in the Johnson administration was also undermined by a series of major natural disasters that rattled the nation. Hurricane Hilda struck New Orleans in October 1964, and Hurricane Betsy devastated the Southeast in August 1965; a catastrophic Alaskan earthquake transpired in 1964, and a lethal tornado swept through Indiana on Palm Sunday in 1965.

In response, Sen. Birch Bayh of Indiana sponsored legislation that granted emergency federal loan assistance to disaster victims. The bill passed in 1966, and Bayh urged Congress over the next few years to provide even more disaster assistance to citizens. The concept of all-hazards assistance was gaining adherents at the expense of civil preparedness for attack.[6]

In the late 1960s President Richard M. Nixon (1969–1974) introduced National Security Decision Memorandum (NSDM) 184.[7] NSDM 184 recommended a **dual-use approach** to federal citizen preparedness programs and the replacement of the Office of Civil Defense with the Defense Civil Preparedness Agency (DCPA). Nixon implemented these recommendations, placing the new DCPA under the umbrella of the Department of Defense. Congress played a role in formulating "dual use" policy through the Disaster Relief Act of 1966, a measure that linked civil defense warning systems with threats from natural disasters.[8] In 1973 the Department of Defense determined that civil defense activities could also be used to prepare for natural disasters, "and the parallel tracks of civil defense and natural disaster management merged," into what became known as dual-use policy.[9]

After Nixon resigned from office in August 1974, President Gerald R. Ford (1974–1977), his successor, initially supported the dual-use approach to disaster preparedness.[10] However, Ford, only seven months in office, rescinded the Defense Department's use of civil defense funding for natural disaster mitigation and preparedness.[11] Civil defense returned to what it was in the Truman and Eisenhower years, primarily a nuclear attack preparedness program.[12]

Ford's concern about perceived Soviet progress in civil defense, compared with modest American efforts, contributed to his concern that the United States was falling behind. Developments in Cold War diplomacy also contributed to the temporary suspension of all-hazards planning. Gradually the idea of limited nuclear strikes against strategically important military and industrial targets, rather than population centers, replaced earlier notions.

By 1978 Congress had amended the Civil Defense Act of 1950 so that it authorized funding on a dual-use basis: "to prepare for the threat of enemy attack *and* for natural disasters." [13] For the first time in the history of U.S. civil defense, federal funds previously allocated for the exclusive purpose of preparing for military attacks could be shared with state and local governments for natural disaster preparedness. This dual-use initiative assumed that preparations for evacuation, communications, and survival were common to both natural disasters and enemy military strikes on the homeland.[14] From a practical perspective, the dual-use approach allowed planners to prepare for a broader range of disasters and emergencies.

Through the 1970s the concept of dual-use gained acceptance as the perception of threats changed and federal resources stimulated state and local planning efforts. Over the next decade, the ideas of flexible targeting and limited retaliation developed into the policy of "flexible response." Flexible response was based on the idea that both the Soviet Union and the United States had the capability for small-scale nuclear attacks that could be answered by similarly sized acts of retaliation by the other side. Theoretically, instead of massive retaliation against population centers, targets would be specific, highly strategic sites. Since some of these sites could be civilian in nature, some level of civil defense and nuclear attack preparedness was deemed necessary. Thus, U.S. policymakers again emphasized civil defense as a means of protecting against targeted highly strategic attacks.[15]

One result was a new initiative called the **Crisis Relocation Plan (CRP).** CRP evacuation planning was conducted at the state level with federal funds and encompassed all of the necessary support for relocation, food distribution, and medical care. Under the CRP, urban residents would be relocated to rural host counties.

Vocal critics from Congress and the public doubted the feasibility of such large-scale evacuations as they envisioned horribly bottlenecked transportation routes. However, as in previous administrations, civil defense still competed for funding against more traditional military expenditures, and the 1975 increases were nullified the following year in favor of spending on offensive military capabilities. As a harbinger of things to come, in June 1976 the Working Group of the Cabinet Committee to Combat Terrorism was assigned Federal Preparedness Agency responsibility for coordination of federal and federal-state responses to terrorism.[16]

NATIONWIDE EMERGENCY MANAGEMENT

By the time President Nixon entered office in January 1969, public and government interest in civil defense had fallen precipitously from its peak in the early 1960s. President Nixon helped "redefine civil defense policy to include preparedness for natural disasters." [17] Nixon was profoundly affected by his administration's poor experience in managing the Hurricane Camille disaster of August 1969. The haphazard and bungled federal response to Camille and its aftermath was a public relations debacle for the new president.

During the Nixon era and over the course of the 1970s, the basic governmental approach to disasters began to shift from an exclusive preoccupation with **structural hazard mitigation** (for example, building flood works, coastal infrastructure, dams, and other "hard" engineered structures) to greater emphasis on the use of **nonstructural mitigation** (for example, using wetlands to buffer against flooding, protecting coast lines and barrier islands from erosion and development, encouraging the use of landscaping that protects structures from flooding or wildfires, and other "soft" engineering approaches).

In the late 1960s and early 1970s the American environmental movement was widely popular among the public and many federal policymakers. Conserving wetlands, reducing humanity's impact on the natural environment, protecting natural habitats, and removing human structures and pollution contamination from areas where they were producing environmental damage, were all tenets of American environmentalism. In many ways American environmentalism and disaster mitigation complemented one another. Often, political alliances between environmental and disaster mitigation interests produced mutual victories. For example, the U.S. Environmental Protection Agency, which began operation in 1970, had an environmental emergency response division, conducted land and water environmental research that helped reduce disaster effects, and carried out an elaborate environmental impact statement process that was relevant to disaster mitigation efforts.

Federal policy changed from merely initiating projects designed to build physical barriers to emphasis on keeping people and structures out of hazard-prone, high-risk areas through zoning laws, building codes, and land-use regulations. Thus, national environmental and disaster policies combined to press more people and officials of state and local government to assume greater responsibility for where and how people lived. Such lifestyle-changing policies, however, often created disputes between levels of government and between the government and the public. At one end of the spectrum was a growing sentiment among many federal, and various state, officials that their governments should not have to "bail out" localities that do not proactively protect themselves from known hazards through the use of zoning laws, building codes, and land-use restrictions. At the other end were resentful local officials and citizens who saw such measures as unnecessarily burdensome. They sometimes argued that these measures invaded their personal freedom, conflicted with their private property rights, and were financially burdensome to them. Some state and local officials also feared federal encroachment into a policy domain they perceived as within traditional local government jurisdiction or as a matter of powers reserved to the states under the U.S. Constitution. A perennial worry of American local government officials has been fear of **federal zoning.** In a great many pol-

HISTORY'S LESSONS

TOO MANY COOKS?

From the 1950s to the end of the 1970s, problems arose because many federal disaster management responsibilities were parceled out to different federal agencies and offices. Disaster policy was fragmented and this often generated complaints and criticisms when megadisasters challenged federal authorities. The ensuing lack of leadership and coordination was compounded because responsibility for disaster relief at the federal level seemed at times to bounce from one agency to another. These problems had a tendency to complicate and confound state and local emergency management.

For example, between 1951 and 1973, disaster assistance and relief activities were the responsibility of four different federal agencies (see Table 3-1).

Some of this paralleled what would happen later. The terrorist attacks of 2001 impelled policymakers to again reorganize emergency management. The enactment of the Homeland Security Act of 2002, a series of Bush administration presidential homeland security directives, and other policy changes squeezed a relatively

tiny FEMA into a giant "holding company" of big and small organizations, few with explicit emergency management duties. Before 1979, federal emergency management was fragmented and lacked an integrated identity; yet in 2003, when FEMA, an independent federal agency, was folded into the Department of Homeland Security, federal emergency management lost much of the integrated essence that it had acquired in the intervening years. It was not simply that FEMA was absorbed into DHS. In point of fact, FEMA was pulled apart as top DHS officials tried to bind and refashion all of the DHS so-called legacy agencies into one administrative whole whose primary mission would be preventing acts of terrorism and helping the nation prepare for and respond to a terrorist attack. For DHS officials, the term "legacy agency" was meant to infer that the agencies absorbed into the new department were outmoded and obsolete. DHS top-level administrators saw their job as one of dismantling these units and reassembling them into a new bureaucratic structure aligned to address the mission of preventing or icy domains federal involvement tends to gradually, and sometimes spectacularly, increase over time. Protectors of local land-use authority fiercely contest federal encroachment into matters of local land use, zoning, and building regulation. Consequently, federal (and state) government disaster policy has had to find subtle and uncontroversial ways to impel local government officials to recognize their disaster vulnerability and to act responsibly to address it.

Meanwhile, the Nixon administration made a host of organizational changes in federal disaster management. In addition to replacement of the OCD with the Defense Civil Preparedness Agency, Nixon Reorganization Plans 1 (1970) and 2 (1973) abolished the Office of Emergency Planning, an agency established in 1961. The Office of Emergency Planning had managed programs, functions, and activities previously housed in the Office of Emergency Preparedness, Executive Office of the White House. Nixon Reorganization Plan 1 reassigned preparedness tasks, doling them out to the Department of Housing and Urban Development (HUD) (which created the Federal Disaster Assistance Administration to assume this jurisdiction), the General Services Administration (GSA), and the departments of

TABLE 3-1	Federal Emergency Management Organizations
Organization	**Dates**
Housing and Home Finance Administration	1951–1953
Federal Civil Defense Administration	1953–1958
Office of Civil Defense and Mobilization	1958–1961
Office of Emergency Planning (renamed Office of Emergency Preparedness)	1961–1973
Federal Disaster Assistance Administration, Defense Civil Preparedness Agency, and Federal Preparedness Agency	1973–1979
Federal Emergency Management Agency	1979–2003
Department of Homeland Security	2003–

coping with terrorism in the homeland, first and foremost. What this reasoning may have dismissed out of hand was that each of these "legacy" agencies was never relieved of their original legal and program responsibilities.

Before 1979 no federal agency embraced as its core mission disaster management in all of its phases and manifestations. After 2002 the only

agency whose core mission was disaster management, FEMA, was relegated to "legacy agency" status in a superdepartment whose officials would attempt to transform it, along with the many other administrative agencies and offices moved into DHS, into a combination whose primary mission was protecting the nation from terrorism and its effects.

the Treasury and Commerce. In total, the new Nixon's emergency management bureaucratic structure placed responsibility for disaster relief with more than 100 federal agencies.[18] All these shifts of administrative authority may seem trivial and confusing. What is important is that there was no central administrative identity for federal emergency management over the Nixon and Ford years. Various stakeholders and interest groups associated with policies other than natural and human-caused disaster policy managed to keep their respective pieces of disaster policy where they wanted them, and did so ostensibly with White House and congressional consent. Housing, defense, insurance, business regulation, transportation, and other interests jealously retained control of their disaster-relevant jurisdictions.

Flood Insurance Policy History

Another realm of domestic emergency management involved flood insurance, a domain that heavily involved intergovernmental relations. In 1968 President Johnson signed the National Flood Insurance Act (Title XII of the Housing and Urban Development Act of 1968), a measure that created the National Flood Insurance Program (NFIP) and the Federal Insurance Administration (FIA) within HUD. As noted earlier, its purpose was to provide flood insurance in communities that voluntarily adopted and enforced floodplain management ordinances consistent with NFIP requirements. Communities had until June 30, 1970, to comply if they wanted to join the program. Residents would be eligible for flood insurance after the NFIP identified local flood-hazard areas and established actuarial rates. Occupants of structures in floodplains would have their premiums federally subsidized. Structures built in floodplains after the act's passage would have to pay actuarially based (higher risk and more expensive) premiums.[19] The law stipulated that as a condition of future federal financial assistance, states and communities must "participate in the flood insurance program and adopt adequate floodplain ordinances with effective enforcement provisions consistent with federal standards to reduce or avoid future flood losses." [20]

The Disaster Relief Act of 1974

In May 1974 President Nixon signed into law the Disaster Relief Act of 1974, a measure that sought to remedy the bureaucratic confusion created by the administration's earlier reorganizations. The new law also, for the first time, created a program that provided direct assistance to individuals and families following a disaster. Although preceding laws had provided temporary housing aid and other modest forms of individual assistance, the Individual and Family Grant program finally bridged the gap that had existed between public and individual assistance. From 1950 to 1974, federal postdisaster relief had been more generous to state and local governments than it had been to victims of disaster.

Budgeted funding for these programs remained low, however. The original Disaster Relief Act of 1950 had the effect of minimizing congressional involvement in federal postdisaster relief. However, inadequate annual funding of the **President's Disaster Relief Fund,** a main repository of federal postdisaster spending authority, meant that Congress would often be forced to approve emergency supplementary appropriations within a budget year to replenish the fund's spending authority. This often had the effect of repoliticizing disaster policy and implementation.

The Disaster Relief Act of 1974 brought state and local governments into all-hazards preparedness activities and provided matching funds for their emergency management programs. The act also authorized in law the **emergency declaration** category; a measure triggered by the federal government's experience with Tropical Storm Agnes.[21] Presidents Eisenhower, Kennedy, and Johnson, serving before 1974, could only issue declarations of major disaster. Remember, when governors ask the president to issue their state and localities an emergency declaration, they do not have to conduct a damage assessment or otherwise document need as they do when they ask the president to issue them a major disaster declaration. Granting the president authority to issue emergency declarations opened the door to president-approved proactive federal mobilization for disasters that had not yet transpired but appeared imminent. It also increased the temptation of presidents to issue declarations for events that would ordinarily not meet damage thresholds administratively set for major disaster declarations.

The 1974 law recognized the need for improved disaster mitigation. It required states and communities receiving federal disaster assistance to "agree that the natural hazards in the area in which the proceeds of the grants or loans are to be used shall be evaluated and appropriate action shall be taken to mitigate such hazards." These provisions represented the first congressional mandate for hazard mitigation as a precondition for federal disaster assistance. Many hoped that the emphasis on disaster mitigation would save lives and protect both public and private property.

The 1974 act was precedent-setting in its own right. Among its features were the following:

1. Instituted the **Individual and Family Grant (IFG) program,** which supplied 75 percent of the funding for state-administered programs providing cash help for furniture, clothes, and essential needs

2. Formalized efforts to mitigate, rather than simply respond to, disaster events

3. Mandated that local, state, and federal agencies develop strategies aimed at preventing disasters in the future

4. Stressed a **multihazard approach** to disasters, in which the government would manage all kinds of hazards, rather than maintaining unique and separated capacities to deal with different types of disaster agents. In effect, disaster management would be all-hazard generic to the extent possible so that capacities to address one type of disaster agent could be applied to address a variety of types. An all-hazards approach would help reduce duplication and redundancy in emergency management. It would encourage cross-training of emergency responders and it would encourage adaptability. It would also integrate functions and disaster types, providing more coherence for the field and the profession.

The 1974 law also advanced multihazard, or all-hazards, approaches to emergency management. This implied that before 1974 emergency management was fragmented and preoccupied with confronting individual disasters or specific types of disasters as if each disaster were unique or as if each category or type of disaster had its own independent set of response needs. Also, by emphasizing a multihazard approach, the Disaster Relief Act of 1974 signaled the diminution of civil defense issues, funding, and concerns in the realm of domestic emergency management. However, the bureaucratic rivalry between civil defense and emergency management officials would not end for twenty more years, when the Federal Civil Defense Act was repealed in 1994.

THE BIRTH OF FEMA

Few presidents are more associated with disaster policy than President James Earl Carter (1977–1981).[22] He is justifiably credited with establishing the U.S. Federal Emergency Management Agency. As a former governor of Georgia, Carter knew natural disasters well, and he was anxious to respond to the calls of other governors and the National Governors Association for improvements in the organization of federal disaster management.

The Federal Emergency Management Agency (FEMA) had its origins in proposals put forward by the National Governors Association in the late 1970s and a 1978 working group formed by President Carter. In 1978, civil emergency management programs and activities were scattered among five principal federal departments and agencies. Using authority allowing him to reorganize the executive branch, President Carter presented Reorganization Plan No. 3 of 1978 to Congress for its approval in June.[23] President Carter had specific aims in Reorganization Plan No. 3:

1. To establish a single entity (FEMA), headed by an official directly responsible to the president that would serve as the sole federal agency responsible for anticipating, preparing for, and responding to major civil emergencies

2. To develop an effective civil defense system, integrated into the programs and operations of nonfederal entities, to improve communications, evacuations, warnings, and public education efforts to prepare citizens for a possible nuclear attack as well as for natural and accidental disasters (an all-hazards approach)

3. To rely on federal agencies to undertake emergency management responsibilities as extensions of their regular missions and on FEMA to coordinate these resources

4. To incorporate federal hazard mitigation activities, linked with state and local activities, into preparedness and response operations

In the reorganization FEMA absorbed the Federal Insurance Administration (implementer of the National Flood Insurance Program), the National Fire Protection and Control Administration, the Federal Preparedness Agency of the General Services Administration, and the Federal Disaster Assistance Administration that had resided in HUD. The Department of Defense Civil Preparedness Agency had its civil responsibilities transferred to FEMA as well.[24]

The Carter plan proposed transferring civil preparedness programs, fire prevention and control, flood insurance, crime insurance, dam safety, earthquake hazard reduction, terrorism, and national emergency warning systems to this new agency and giving it primary responsibility for mobilizing federal resources, coordinating federal efforts with those of state and local governments, and managing the efforts of the public and private sectors in disaster responses. [25]

Following congressional acceptance of Reorganization Plan No. 3, the new agency opened for business on the inauspicious date of April 1, 1979.[26] President Carter then issued an executive order in July that delegated most of the authority granted to the president under the Disaster Relief Act of 1974 to the director of FEMA. The order also transferred to FEMA various functions previously carried out by the Department of Defense, HUD, and the General Services Administration, as well as by other federal entities. Also, the director of FEMA was delegated authority to establish federal policies for all civil defense and civil emergency planning, management, mitigation, and assistance functions of executive branch agencies. One section stipulated, "The Director shall be responsible . . . for the coordination of preparedness and planning to reduce the consequences of major terrorist events."[27] In August 1979 John W. Macy won Senate confirmation as FEMA's first director.[28]

The new agency ultimately absorbed civil defense, certain elements of national emergency preparedness, fire prevention and assistance, disaster relief, flood insurance, earthquake hazards reduction, and dam safety. However, disaster loan programs operated by the Department of Commerce Small Business Administration and by the U.S. Department of Agriculture Farmers Home Administration were not transferred into FEMA and both continue operation today.

Under Carter, the new FEMA did not fully consolidate all federal disaster and emergency functions and programs. Consequently, federal agencies continued to compete for jurisdiction over disaster and emergency management.

By May 1980 FEMA had adopted a fund-matching policy that required state and local governments to agree to pay 25 percent of the eligible costs of public assistance programs (other than Individual and Family Grants, today called Individual and Household Grants). Prior to this time, the required nonfederal contribution was subject to negotiation between FEMA and the affected state and local governments. Still, since 1950, presidents have remained free to waive part or all of the "state-local" match for any declaration they issue, despite the 25 percent fund-matching rule.

DISASTER DECLARATION ISSUES

Over the period 1981 through 2001 the federal government increased its subsidization of state and local disaster response and recovery costs. It has been claimed that federal disaster outlays spiraled upward over the decades of the 1980s and 1990s.[29]

In April 1986 FEMA proposed changing the process of declaring disasters, the criteria for eligibility for federal assistance, and the nonfederal responsibility for major disasters.[30] The proposed regulations would have decreased the federal share of disaster costs to 50 percent from 75 percent. Furthermore, states would have been required to meet certain economic criteria before they would be eligible to receive federal assistance and to increase their cost-sharing responsibilities, along with that of local governments, for disaster assistance. Due to strong opposition in Congress, FEMA subsequently withdrew the proposed rules.[31] In 1993 Congress amended the law to prohibit the use of only arithmetic formulas in making declarations. Since then, in implementing the statute, FEMA has considered arithmetic factors as well as measures of economic impact.

The domain of national security and national defense overlapped the policy domain of disaster management. Because disaster management is so centrally linked to the institution of the

HOW THINGS WORK

"CIVILIANIZING" FEMA?

An intriguing political issue that arose during FEMA's gestation involved the transfer of civil preparedness activities from the Pentagon to FEMA. Many questioned how important civil defense would be within FEMA. If civil defense were to be under the umbrella of the new FEMA, how would national security aspects of civil defense, particularly preparedness for nuclear attack, be addressed? Nuclear attack civil defense officials and domestic emergency management officials regularly fought or disagreed over management, funding, operations, and personnel issues. At times FEMA's public image suffered as various lawmakers and journalists alleged that the agency maintained an overly large and influential "secret" side: a side dedicated to certain national security concerns, such as continuity of government, national emergency communications, and maintenance of a set of secret underground facilities to be made available to the president and Congress during national emergencies.

As mentioned previously, in the late 1970s, state and federal officials, as well as governors and their National Governors Association, began to acknowledge the need to plan for dis-

asters generically, rather than as separate incident types or as unique events. Many advocated an all-hazards approach to emergency management. Many hoped that the consolidation of so many important disaster management duties and functions in FEMA would achieve federal all-hazards emergency management. Yet, in combining national security work and traditional domestic emergency management work, each often working together awkwardly or not at all, the young FEMA gravitated toward an all-hazards approach to emergency management in a somewhat schizophrenic way.

The nuclear accident in late March 1979 at Metropolitan Edison's Three Mile Island Unit 2 nuclear power plant, located south of Harrisburg, Pennsylvania, changed federal emergency management. Although the incident did not result in a presidential declaration of a major disaster, it did persuade President Carter to quickly put FEMA into operation. The slow response, miscommunications, lack of decisive leadership, and poor coordination of the federal Nuclear Regulatory Commission (NRC) with the utility, the state of Pennsylvania, and affected localities, demonstrated to policymakers the

presidency, and because preparations for the destructiveness of a possible nuclear attack in some ways corresponds with preparedness for catastrophic natural or nonwar disasters, it was not unreasonable to expect presidents of the 1950 to 1980 era to make one purpose also serve the other. Although dual-use policy had to await "official" approval in law in the 1970s, Presidents Truman, Eisenhower, Kennedy, and Johnson all found ways to make their civil defense programs, which were interlocked with state and local emergency management, provide some form of double duty as disaster management activities.[34]

The jumble of federal disaster agencies that existed from 1950 until 1979 connoted presidential and congressional failure to recognize the need for cohesiveness and sound organization in federal disaster management. Yet, the limited range of federal disaster relief available to subnational governments and disaster victims in 1950 was gradually expanded, usually owing need to improve disaster response, coordination, and planning. Reacting to vociferous public criticism of the NRC, Carter assigned to FEMA some of NRC's emergency planning duties for areas surrounding nuclear power plants, a duty previously under NRC's exclusive jurisdiction.[32]

At the time, the creation of FEMA represented the single largest consolidation of civil preparedness efforts in U.S. history. Practical plans continued to reflect traditional civil defense programs, although Carter did urge FEMA to direct more of its efforts to coping with peacetime disasters. Evacuation continued to be the focus of federal planners, and Secretary of Defense Harold Brown maintained crisis relocation strategies. When FEMA assumed responsibility for citizen preparedness, the agency called on civil defense planners nationwide to create area-specific crisis relocation plans. The Carter administration's focus on evacuation was very much affected by Cold War diplomacy of the late 1970s. The continuing Strategic Arms Limitation Talks with the Soviet Union created a conflict between the president's desire to advance U.S. civil defense and his desire to avoid

upsetting the delicate strategic balance required for successful threat-reduction negotiations. President Carter continued to support evacuation policies, believing that this offered the best option for the nation.[33]

Thus, owing to continuing civil defense against nuclear attack concerns and the Three Mile Island nuclear power plant accident, President Carter concluded that it made sense to allow the new Federal Emergency Management Agency to include nuclear attack and nuclear power plant incident response and preparedness in its mission. FEMA was fundamentally a civilian agency that included a variety of national security duties and responsibilities. Many FEMA officials held security clearances that allowed them to do double duty. In other words, they could work in both civilian and national security domains. Sometimes natural disasters would pull FEMA's national security program staff into handling necessary civilian tasks. Conversely, sometimes national security incidents or crises would pull FEMA's security-cleared civilian workers into working for the agency's national security programs.

to controversial experience with megadisasters, escalating disaster losses over many areas of the nation, and political pressure to increase federal government involvement in disaster response and recovery.

CIVIL DEFENSE AGAIN, AND CHANGES IN FEMA

Disaster policy, regardless of laws and rules in force, has been very much a function of what each presidential administration decided it wanted to do in this domain. For President Ronald R. Reagan (1981–1989), FEMA was for a brief period an uncomfortable holdover remnant of the Carter administration.[35] Regardless, Reagan recruited FEMA into his strategic and tactical battle with Soviet communism.

In November 1988 President Reagan signed into law the Robert T. Stafford Disaster Relief and Emergency Assistance Act, amending the Federal Disaster Relief Act of 1974. The Stafford Act, as it came to be called, added many wholly new provisions, superseded many old ones, and revised others. The effects of the Stafford Act were so profound for emergency managers that this law came to demarcate the beginning of modern-era national disaster management.

In sum, the Stafford Act authorizes the president to issue major disaster or emergency declarations, sets broad eligibility criteria, and specifies the type of assistance the president may authorize. The definition of "emergency" has been a politically charged issue. "Emergency" refers to "any occasion or instance for which, in the determination of the president, federal assistance is needed to supplement state and local efforts and capabilities to save lives and protect property and public health and safety, or to lessen or avert the threat of catastrophe in any part of the United States." [36] This refinement of the definition of "emergency" clearly affords the president a great deal of political subjectivity in determining what is or is not an emergency. In effect, this subjectivity often leaves governors guessing about whether emergencies their states have experienced or are about to experience qualify for federal disaster aid and whether they should seek a presidential declaration of emergency or not.

In the Reagan years, state and local government officials, recognizing the rising importance of emergency management and seeking to find ways to stretch dual-use civil defense to the limit, began to establish their own state and local variations of FEMA. Moreover, nonprofit organizations active in disaster, the nation's fire services, private property insurers, the nation's public safety and police officials, and others began to lobby on behalf of government emergency management interests as stakeholder groups.

From 1981 nearly to the end of his administration, Reagan gave civil defense against nuclear attack priority in its disaster policy. In part, Reagan built up America's defense against nuclear attack by Soviet ICBMs through an expensive antiballistic missile program. Reagan refused to take a vow of "no first use of nuclear weapons," thus reserving the right to use limited or medium-scale nuclear weapons (neutron bombs, tactical nuclear weapons, or the like) to confront or rebuff a conventional Soviet military attack or invasion of Western Europe. Through all of this, the Reagan administration tapped FEMA for help, and FEMA's directors in the period were happy to oblige the president. Population sheltering and crisis relocation again became FEMA priorities. A Pentagon official created a public relations gaffe for the Reagan White House when he publicly remarked that Americans should be prepared to dig holes in their backyards and cover them with boards to survive a Soviet nuclear attack.

Civil defense issues were moved to a back burner toward the end of the Reagan administration as U.S.-Soviet relations improved, as Presidents Reagan and George H. W. Bush (1989–1993) built improved relations with the Soviet leader Mikhail Gorbachev, and as Soviet communism collapsed.[37] Nonetheless, the threat of terrorism grew during the 1980s as the United States grappled with successive and sometimes tragic airline hijackings and other terrorism incidents that sometimes killed Americans. The civil war in Lebanon and a deadly suicide bomber attack on the Marine barracks in that nation in the mid-1980s was a harbinger of future terrorist threats to the United States.

In March 1989 an executive order issued by President Bush delegated Stafford Act authority, with some exceptions (principally disaster and emergency declarations), to the director of

FEMA. The Stafford Act authorizes the president to issue those two types of declarations when an incident overwhelms state and local resources.

President Reagan and each of his successors had to learn to cope with a new stressor in emergency management: improved television news coverage of disasters and emergencies. In the early 1980s, Ted Turner's Cable News Network (CNN) showed that television news had achieved the ability to cover disasters and emergencies quickly, owing to major technological advances in electronics, satellite communications advances, miniaturization of cameras and other equipment. News commentators could do voice-overs of live video from the field and could ask questions like, "What is the President and his administration doing about this?" **Camcorder politics** came to be a television staple. Television news now covered cities, states, or any region of the nation. Broadcasts could go global and take live feed of reportage and video virtually anywhere in the world. Fueled by media coverage, the major and minor disasters of the era were often quickly politicized, or at the very least political officials were expected to be more immediately visible and responsive to them. In 1981, CNN, owing to its around-the-clock news broadcasting, was the first to break the story that a would-be assassin had shot President Ronald Reagan. In 1986 millions were watching CNN when the space shuttle *Challenger* exploded shortly after liftoff. CNN had been the only network carrying the launch live. "By then, some were calling the channel the 'Crisis News Network' and it consistently pulled in large audiences when major stories broke." [38] CNN coverage of the *Challenger* disaster drew President Reagan into weeks of official pronouncements; he impaneled the Rogers Commission to investigate the incident and was filmed by CNN in several commemorations. Reagan, and each succeeding president, learned to cope with, and sometimes use to their political advantage, CNN coverage. Owing to CNN and other twenty-four-hour TV news channels, disasters and emergencies came almost immediately to the White House just as they did to the homes of millions of other viewers.

On the matter of federal-state relations, President Reagan's record of approvals and turndowns of governor requests for declarations of major disasters and emergencies says much about his philosophy of federal-state relations. A tough judge of declaration deservedness, Reagan turned down a larger share of gubernatorial requests for major disaster and emergency declarations than almost any other president, before or since. The exception was, ironically, President Jimmy Carter. He matched Reagan in the percentage of turndowns of governors' requests for major disaster declarations, but Carter approved a much larger share of emergency declaration requests than did Reagan. Emergency declaration requests do not require that governors submit damage estimates, as do their requests for major disaster declarations.

In reality, however, the nation experienced few megadisasters and no catastrophic disasters during Reagan's eight years in office. Nevertheless, disasters outside the United States, such as the 1984 poison chemical release in Bhopal, India, and the 1986 Chernobyl nuclear power plant disaster in the Soviet Ukraine produced major changes in U.S. law and disaster policy. George H. W. Bush, serving only one-term in office, suffered through a series of megadisasters both at the beginning and at the end of his administration. The northern California Loma Prieta earthquake and Hurricane Hugo (which devasted much of the Carolinas), both transpiring in 1989, plus Hurricane Andrew in 1992, disclosed FEMA's limitations under Bush and revealed significant flaws in the nation's system of disaster management.

FEMA as an Instrument of Presidential Power

In the early Reagan years, FEMA was directed to: (1) prepare federal response plans and programs for the emergency preparedness of the United States, and (2) sponsor and direct plans and programs to coordinate with state efforts. FEMA quickly became an instrument of presidential power. In times of disaster or emergency, or when certain relatively unique calamities arose, presidents, as they had done in the past, sometimes chose to use their emergency powers to address new or unique problems. The President's Disaster Relief Fund, administered by FEMA, provided the president a useful emergency spending account. Presidents could and did use it to fund unexpected problems not otherwise anticipated or not adequately funded in other programs established by Congress.[39] The president invoking his authority through the issuance of a declaration of major disaster or emergency, may require that FEMA draw money from the fund to pay for some type of incident or event the president judges worthy of assistance. If another federal agency besides, or other than, FEMA, is responsible for addressing the event, FEMA makes fund money available to that federal department or agency through "mission assignment" authority (discussed in Chapter 4). In other words, the President's Disaster Relief Fund is, in effect, a first-layer financial safety net open to the president; his federal disaster agency may pay itself, state and local governments, program eligible disaster victims, and other federal agencies (under mission assignment) for costs associated with events the president chooses to declare disasters or emergencies.[40]

Although FEMA possesses authority, funding, and limited assets that enable it to do some disaster management work independently, it must depend on other federal departments and agencies to provide additional resources to ensure a complete federal response. In the event of a presidentially declared disaster, a mission assignment may be issued to a federal agency by the FEMA director, associate director, or regional director. A mission assignment is a work order given to a particular agency. It directs an agency to complete a specified task and confers funding, managerial controls, and guidance.

The main reason why FEMA has been and remains deeply beholden to whoever is in the Oval Office is that FEMA has always had a small, politically weak, and occasionally divided clientele and community of advocates. FEMA has a base of support in Congress, but that base is usually only mobilized after disasters in which large sums of federal money need to be dispensed to meet a great many needs, needs often championed by various congressional lawmakers. Congress often exhibits great ambivalence toward the agency; they need it to do what it does but they sometimes need to criticize it when their constituents complain about slow or inadequate disaster relief. If FEMA officials are highly responsive to presidential wishes and if they succeed in maintaining a positive image in the minds of most of the public, FEMA leaders judge themselves favorably.

Through the Reagan and George H. W. Bush era, FEMA was an independent federal agency with few regulatory powers.[41] The organization came to be exceptionally good at mobilizing contractors and temporary volunteer workers to meet most of the nation's fluctuating disaster management needs. Although FEMA's full-time workforce never exceeded three thousand, the agency relied on paid reservists and also on volunteers, various disaster-knowledgeable private contractors, and certain nonprofit organizations when circumstances dictated.[42]

Moreover, the independent agency's emergency response and recovery capabilities were dramatically enhanced by its ability to mobilize and work cooperatively with the people and resources of other federal agencies, including working under various emergency response plans in effect between 1981 and 2001.

Stakeholders in Disaster Policy

The nation's pool of emergency managers, public safety directors, and firefighters, working mostly at the state or local level, usually supports FEMA strongly.[43] Less committed but still likely to promote federal emergency management are many of the nation's governors, mayors, and county executives. In addition, the people of nonprofit organizations active in disasters, who often work shoulder to shoulder with FEMA personnel and whose organizations often qualify for FEMA funding in declared disasters or emergencies, can usually be counted on to back the agency.

Additionally, property insurance officials, almost uniformly enthusiastic about federal efforts in disaster loss reduction but always suspicious that the federal government might nationalize certain lines of insurance, have sometimes found it advantageous to promote certain aspects of government emergency management. In addition, major construction firms, the building trades, and economic development interests have all benefited from postdisaster, federally subsidized reconstruction. However, these same groups sometimes perceive FEMA as a de facto regulator or inhibitor of development and construction in times between disasters. Although these sources of political support are important and necessary in the maintenance of FEMA's organizational and political life, between 1981 and 2003 the collective political power of these interests was not strong when compared with the political clout of interest groups and clientele groups associated with other federal policy areas and agencies. Consider, for example, the domain of health policy and the program offices of the U.S. Department of Health and Human Services (HHS). Clearly, the interest groups and clientele of health policy and HHS (that is, the American Medical Association, the American Hospital Association, Health Maintenance Organizations, and the like) have vastly greater political influence in Congress than FEMA's backers do.[44]

Disasters, as prevalent as they may seem nationally, are by definition intermittent and, at least for any specific locality, infrequent. People who survive disasters and who receive aid from FEMA, or from any government agency at any level, do not necessarily go on to champion emergency management. Disasters unquestionably affect the perceptions of voters, regardless of whether or not they directly experienced a disaster themselves. However, disasters rarely affect how people cast their votes in elections, and even more rarely do disasters influence election outcomes. According to the political scientists Kevin Arceneaux and Robert M. Stein, "whether citizens blame the government depends on their level of political knowledge" and how severely the disaster affected their lives. "Although many individuals attribute blame to the government, it does not affect their voting decision for mayor unless they blame the city in particular." [45] Still, there have been some notable exceptions in a few states and cities, as when elected or appointed government officials bungle management of a disaster and so experience the political consequences.

From State and Local to Federal Emergency Management

When examining the evolution of emergency management from 1981 through 1992 one is inevitably led to ask, why does it seem that disaster management is moving away from being a function that is state and locally centered to one that is federally centered? How was it that the president and Congress expanded the federal role in disaster management and how was it that governors, as well as state and local authorities, were willing to submit to this enhanced federal role? In many ways the trend toward "nationalizing disaster" management and toward creating a national response plan in which federal, state, and local authorities worked in unison, or at least in more coordinated ways, was something well under way before the 9/11 attacks and before the era of homeland security.

President Reagan, a former two-term California governor, espoused a new federalism policy that may have discouraged governors from requesting presidential declarations as frequently as they had in the 1970s. Reagan's political ideology held that states too often relied on the federal government for help in matters they could easily address on their own. Reagan philosophy also maintained that the federal government needed to be less intrusive in matters traditionally left to state and local government. A catchword of the Reagan era was "devolution" of certain federal responsibilities back to the states and localities.

However, from 1989 through 1992, when George H. W. Bush held office, the number of disasters increased and the scale of disaster devastation began to mount. Thus, many more presidential disaster declarations were issued than in the Reagan years. Natural and human-caused disasters, many routine and several catastrophically large, challenged the government's system of disaster management. Governors grew accustomed to regularly requesting declarations for major and minor disasters and emergencies. In addition, Bush and the federal policymakers themselves seemed more receptive to greater federal involvement in emergency management, a realm long understood to be a local and state responsibility.

In April 1992 the Federal Response Plan (FRP) was issued. This plan established a process and structure that promised more systematic, coordinated, and effective delivery of federal assistance to address the consequences of any major disaster or emergency. Also stated in the FRP is that sometimes a major disaster or emergency may affect the national security of the United States. "For those instances, appropriate national security authorities and procedures will be utilized to address the national security requirements of the situation." [46]

From Civil Defense to Homeland Security

As mentioned previously, civil defense against nuclear attack was a significant part of the Reagan administration's Cold War foreign policy. Reagan had initially campaigned on a promise to do away with Carter's FEMA. Once elected, however, he called on the agency to ramp up its nuclear attack crisis relocation plans and preparedness. FEMA was directed to undertake ambitious civil defense work to parallel Soviet civil defense activity. The Reagan administration also persuaded Congress to increase defense spending, particularly for new generations of nuclear weaponry and for an antiballistic missile defense system.

The Reagan White House issued an executive order titled "Assignment of Emergency Preparedness Responsibilities," which defined a national security emergency as any occurrence that seriously degraded or threatened the national security of the United States. Terrorist incidents were not directly addressed but only listed as Department of Justice responsibilities. The National Security Council was assigned responsibility for developing and administering this national security emergency policy. The director of FEMA was to assist in the implementation of and management of national security emergency-preparedness policy by coordinating with other federal departments. FEMA was also to be responsible for coordinating, supporting, developing, and implementing civil national security emergency preparedness and response programs, continuity of government functions, and civil-military support. This executive order was in effect for five years.[47]

However, by the late 1980s and early 1990s, civil defense against nuclear attack proved less essential as the Cold War came to a relatively rapid end. Consequently, civilian emergency management addressing other hazards in the United States benefited accordingly. Federal, state, and local emergency managers were gradually freed of the restraints imposed by civil defense dual-use requirements—in which civilian use of federal emergency management funding had to have an acceptable civil defense justification—that had previously confounded and frustrated emergency managers at all levels.

ALL-HAZARDS MANAGEMENT

President William Jefferson Clinton's administration (1993–2001) represented a watershed in U.S. disaster policy history.[48] Clinton had twice been governor of Arkansas and he had had good and bad experiences with FEMA through the years. Clinton was governor when President Carter issued a major disaster declaration to help Florida address the influx of fleeing Cubans during the so-called Mariel boatlift in 1980. Arkansas was selected as a place to host a type of detention facility to house many of these evacuees. FEMA and other federal agencies were to separate average Cubans from the convicted criminals Fidel Castro had funneled in among evacuees. Long processing times and poor living conditions impelled some in the detention camps to riot, thus producing a political controversy for both President Carter and Governor Clinton.

Arkansas, like many states, experienced its own share of floods, tornadoes, severe storms, and other disasters through the years. Clinton knew what federal help meant to states and their governors. Clinton was also keenly aware of the Bush administration's disaster management problems after Hurricane Andrew, an arguable catastrophic disaster that produced widespread human suffering. Andrew took place a mere two months before the 1992 presidential election and this gave Clinton the opportunity to use FEMA's mismanagement and slow response under Bush as a strategic weapon in his campaign.

Between 1993 and 2001, several megadisasters and a great many smaller disasters transpired, including the Great Midwest Flood (1993), California's Northridge earthquake (1994), and a series of highly destructive hurricanes. Moreover, the World Trade Center truck bombing of 1993 and the Murrah Office Building bombing in Oklahoma City in 1995 signaled an escalation in the scale of terrorist attacks inside the United States.

Nonetheless, during the Clinton administration, FEMA enjoyed its "golden years," although agency staff probably did not realize it at the time.[49] Under President Clinton, FEMA was directed by an experienced emergency manager, James Lee Witt. FEMA continued as an independent agency much beholden to presidential support. President Clinton and Director Witt did much to diminish FEMA's civil defense activities. Witt created three functional directorates corresponding to the major phases of emergency management: Mitigation; Preparedness, Training, and Exercises; and Response and Recovery. The shift in emergency preparedness toward an all-hazards approach allowed FEMA to focus on addressing natural disasters without having to fear negative political reactions from advocates of civil defense. The agency's Mitigation Directorate, for example, focused many of its early programs on such hazards as flooding and earthquakes.

At the same time, however, recognition of the threat of terrorist attacks inside the United States was beginning to emerge. In 1993 Congress included a joint resolution in the National Defense Authorization Act that called for FEMA to develop "a capability for early detection and warning of and response to: potential terrorist use of chemical or biological agents or weapons; and emergencies or natural disasters involving industrial chemicals or the widespread outbreak of disease." As evidenced by this resolution, Congress was becoming increasingly concerned about the threat posed by terrorist organizations and technological disasters. Much of this concern resulted from the World Trade Center bombing earlier that year, committed by a group of Islamic fundamentalist terrorists (later determined to have been led by Osama bin Laden), in which 6 people were killed and 1,042 were wounded. The blast left a five-story deep crater and caused $500 million in damages.[50]

By early 1993 President Clinton and Congress helped divest FEMA of many of its responsibilities in planning and preparing for nuclear attack by Russia, which had shed communism in the early 1990s. In November 1994 the National Defense Authorization Act for Fiscal Year 1995 stipulated that the policy of the federal government was for FEMA to provide necessary direction, coordination, guidance, and assistance, so that a comprehensive emergency preparedness system would emerge for *all* hazards in the United States.[51]

In January 1994 the FEMA National Security Steering Group, chaired by FEMA's national security coordinator, was established to serve as the focal point for intra-agency and interagency coordination of national security–related activities. It was to ensure that national security matters were integrated into FEMA's overall "all-hazards" approach to emergency management.

In November 1994, the Civil Defense Act of 1950 was repealed and all remnants of civil defense authority were transferred to Title VI of the Stafford Act. The all-hazards approach to preparedness, much favored by state and local emergency managers, had finally broken free of the confines of "civil defense against nuclear attack" dual-use restrictions. FEMA now had the statutory responsibility for coordinating a comprehensive emergency preparedness system to deal with all types of disasters. Title VI also ended all Armed Services Committee oversight over FEMA and significantly reduced the priority of national security programs within FEMA. Money authorized by the Civil Defense Act was reallocated to natural disaster and all-hazards programs, and more than 100 defense and security staff members were reassigned.[52]

Support for traditional civil defense declined, but in the 1990s terrorism was increasing. FEMA had just undergone a complete reorganization early in the Clinton administration and FEMA's leadership had no appetite for additional responsibilities and obligations in matters of terrorism.[53]

The Rise of Terrorism

During the Bill Clinton administration, terrorism gradually emerged as a new and major concern of federal emergency management. The United States has a long history of dealing with terrorists and terrorism, but the first presidential disaster declaration for a terrorist-caused incident occurred only after the 1993 truck bomb attack on the World Trade Center in New York City.

This attack was followed in 1995 by a much deadlier truck bomb attack, committed by domestic terrorist Timothy McVeigh and his co-conspirators, on the Murrah Federal Building in Oklahoma City, killing more than 178 people. The Oklahoma City bombing was the first disaster in which FEMA officials had to work closely with FBI officials. The attack, although committed by Americans, drew FEMA further into the business of managing the consequences of terrorism. The Oklahoma City bombing impelled the president and other policymakers to seek clarification of FEMA's role in terrorism consequence management.[54] Also, this was one of the very few times that a president had used his authority under the Stafford Act of 1988 to issue an emergency declaration before a governor requested one. Ordinarily, presidents do not issue an emergency or major disaster declaration in the absence of a governor's request unless the disaster or emergency involves a direct federal concern.

A presidential decision directive issued by Clinton in June 1995 stated that it is the policy of the United States to use all appropriate means to deter, defeat, and respond to all terrorist attacks on our territory and resources, both people and facilities, wherever they occur. It assigned main responsibility for crisis management to the Department of Justice and main responsibility for consequence management to FEMA.[55]

So even before September 11, 2001, domestic disaster management began to be eclipsed by the nation's growing concerns about terrorism.[56] Some policymakers and emergency management professionals worried that the devastation from human-made disasters, particularly terrorist-caused disasters, would match or exceed the scale of damage caused by natural disasters.

In November 1994, the National Defense Authorization Act repealed the Federal Civil Defense Act. In the new Title VI of the Stafford Act of 1988, FEMA was to provide the necessary direction, coordination, guidance, and assistance to create a comprehensive emergency preparedness system based on all-hazards emergency management. FEMA was to prepare federal response plans and programs for the emergency preparedness of the United States, in cooperation with state and local emergency preparedness efforts. The FEMA director could request reports on state plans and operations for emergency preparedness as may be necessary to keep the president, Congress, and the states advised of the status of emergency preparedness in the United States. Interstate Emergency Preparedness Compacts were authorized to assist and encourage the states to negotiate and enter into interstate emergency preparedness compacts; facilitate uniformity between state compacts and consistency with federal emergency response plans and programs; assist and coordinate the activities under state compacts; and aid and assist reciprocal state emergency preparedness legislation advancing mutual aid between states and with the federal government.[57]

Disaster Mitigation Becomes Law and Policy

Disaster mitigation is defined as sustained action to reduce or eliminate risk to people and property from hazards and their effects. The recovery phase of disaster offers opportunity for mitigation actions. In December 1993, following the Great Midwest Flood of the previous summer,
the Volkmer Amendment contained within the Hazard Mitigation and Relocation Assistance
Act of 1993 amended some parts of the 1988 Stafford Act. The Volkmer Amendment increased
FEMA's funds dedicated to community assistance disaster funding for relocation or hazard mitigation activities from a subsidy of 10 percent (in the Stafford Act) to 15 percent.[58] What this
means is that once FEMA has paid out a sum total of federal disaster relief to a state under a
presidential declaration of major disaster, the state then is entitled to receive additional federal
money equivalent to 15 percent of the total funds the state received from the federal government
under the declaration. The state may use this additional federal money to subsidize state and
FEMA-preapproved disaster mitigation projects. Such projects pay for relocating buildings vulnerable to flooding, improving storm-water systems in various municipalities, bridge retrofitting, seismic reinforcement of public structures, or other purposes.

The Volkmer Amendment also increased from 50 percent to 75 percent the federal share of
the cost of specific mitigation activities or projects. This increase greatly benefited states and localities that put forward worthy mitigation projects and that were willing to come up with the
remaining costs. The amendment also stipulated federal rules and conditions under which FEMA
could "buy-out" damaged homes and businesses vulnerable to recurring disaster loss owing to
their presence in high-hazard zones; it required the complete removal of such structures in certain circumstances; and it dictated that the purchased land be dedicated "in perpetuity for a use
that is compatible with open space, recreational, or wetlands management practices." [59] One reason why so many U.S. cities today have open space, bikeways, river walks, parks, and other recreational amenities adjacent to rivers and streams running through their jurisdictions is because of
their disaster mitigation efforts, many of these subsidized by FEMA mitigation funding.

By early 1995 Witt's vision for FEMA was to strive for a cooperative effort among the different levels of government and agencies, through the Partnership for a Safer Future for America.
The initiative included a wide assortment of FEMA stakeholders. Witt wanted to ensure that
more people were dedicated to protecting their families, homes, workplaces, communities, and
livelihoods from the sometimes devastating effects of disasters. FEMA wanted builders and
developers to construct hazard-resistant structures located out of harm's way. The agency's leaders hoped that governments and private organizations would set forth plans, compile necessary
resources, and rigorously train and exercise for disaster responses. Another goal was community
preparation and planning for recovery and reconstruction before disasters struck.

Central to Witt's vision was an increased emphasis placed on disaster mitigation. FEMA
had housed a collection of modest mitigation programs before Witt's regime, but Witt made
mitigation the foundation of emergency management and the primary goal of the agency.[60]
The reasoning was that mitigation activities and strategies may substantially reduce the impact
of disasters and, in some cases, prevent disasters altogether.

Through highlighting mitigation efforts and securing more program resources, FEMA
could substantially enhance its capacity and presence in intergovernmental relations on a continuous basis, rather than merely after a disaster. Whether such invigorated FEMA mitigation
efforts would elicit adequate state and local responses, however, was uncertain. Local officials

sometimes assume that they have little to gain from mitigation efforts, because in the event of a disaster, the federal and state government will pay the major share of their local disaster losses.[61] Moreover, mitigation efforts often have to compete with the far more alluring concerns of economic growth and development on the local level. Because local officials, developers, and citizens often view mitigation efforts as financially costly and restrictive of personal freedom, mitigation efforts were bound to become politically controversial.

In October 1997 the Clinton-Witt FEMA launched Project Impact, an effort that sought to build disaster-resistant communities through public-private partnerships.[62] The endeavor included a national public awareness campaign, the designation of pilot communities, and an outreach effort to community and business leaders. FEMA encouraged communities to assess the risks they faced, identify their vulnerabilities, and take steps to prevent disasters. The first three pilot communities were Deerfield Beach, Florida; Pascagoula, Mississippi; and Wilmington, North Carolina. Soon after, communities in the states of California, Maryland, Washington, and West Virginia joined Project Impact. FEMA's goal was to have at least one Project Impact community in every state by September 30, 1998. The program resonated well with U.S. lawmakers, and Congress appropriated $30 million for Project Impact for the federal fiscal year (FY) 1998 and $25 million for FY 1999.

Project Impact was a relatively small-scale but widely popular "distributive" politics program. It was distributive in the sense that benefits were allocated to an interested pool of local government applicants aided by their respective states. The costs of the program were shouldered by the national taxpayer, but the funding amounts were so modest relative to the size of the federal budget that any one taxpayer was spending only a fraction of a cent on the program. The logic behind the project was that the small federal subsidy could leverage ambitious local and community-level mitigation activity while at the same time raising community awareness of disaster vulnerability.

Project Impact paved the way for enactment of the Disaster Mitigation Act of 2000, a law that amended the 1988 Stafford Act and gave FEMA authority to establish a program of technical and financial assistance for enhanced predisaster mitigation to state and local governments. FEMA was to help state and local governments develop and carry out predisaster hazard mitigation measures that were cost effective and designed to reduce injuries, loss of life, and damage to and destruction of property, including damage to critical services and facilities under the jurisdiction of the states or local governments. The law also upgraded the 1974 requirement for postdisaster mitigation plans by requiring that states prepare a comprehensive state program for predisaster emergency and disaster mitigation before they could receive postdisaster declaration mitigation funds from FEMA. It also required local governments to identify "potential mitigation measures that could be incorporated into the repair of damaged facilities" before being eligible for pre- and postdisaster funding. The aim of this policy was to encourage local governments to engage in such mitigation activities as "hazard mapping, planning, and development of hazard-sensitive building codes." [63] The predisaster mitigation efforts that grew out of Project Impact built community partnerships and sought to increase community support for actions proposed. By 2001, more than two hundred local governments were participating in Project Impact.[64]

Nevertheless, the success of the Disaster Mitigation Act of 2000 and Project Impact has been modest at best. It is difficult for the federal government to compel county and municipal governments to take mitigation steps.[65] Disaster mitigation work at the local level is often difficult and controversial. Community opposition to mitigation may result from the costs mitigation imposes on residential and commercial property owners, from countervailing local development pressures, from a lack of the political will or the funding needed to retrofit existing government-owned facilities, and from controversy surrounding private property rights and government "takings" issues.

TERRORISM REMAKES DISASTER MANAGEMENT

On September 11, 2001, terrorists hijacked four commercial jetliners and used them in suicide attacks. The first aircraft struck the north tower of the World Trade Center. Within a period of minutes a second hit the south tower of the Trade Center. In the skies above the Mid-Atlantic area terrorists piloting two more hijacked airlines prepared for their attacks. One of those planes was flown into the Pentagon. A fourth plane, United Airlines Flight 93, may have also struck a critical Washington target had it not been for the heroic efforts of passengers who fought to regain control of the plane. Hijackers of Flight 93, realizing they would be overwhelmed by a group of passengers deliberately brought the plane down. Flight 93 crashed outside of Shanksville, Pennsylvania, killing all on board.

President George W. Bush (2001–2009) issued an emergency declaration to New York immediately upon Governor George Pataki's request, and six hours later the president issued a major disaster declaration to the state for New York City (approximately six hours after the initial attack at 8:43 a.m. Eastern Daylight Time).[66] On September 14, 2001, President Bush signed a Declaration of National Emergency, anticipating other possible terrorist attacks. By September 15, 2001, Congress had approved a $40 billion emergency supplemental appropriation to pay for disaster relief and further antiterrorism and counterterrorism actions.

Months later, several congressional leaders advocated creating a department of homeland security. President Bush at first resisted the idea on grounds that another new, large federal bureaucracy was not the way to prevent or prepare for future possible attacks. However, he relented in the face of growing political pressure to establish the new department. In late 2002 the Homeland Security Act was passed by Congress and signed by the president. On January 24, 2003, the Department of Homeland Security began operation.

The creation of the Department of Homeland Security (DHS) was one of the largest federal reorganizations since President Truman created the Department of Defense in 1947. DHS incorporated all or part of twenty-two federal agencies, forty different federal entities, and approximately 180,000 employees.[67]

The reorganization merged together agencies (or parts of agencies) with very diverse organizational structures, missions, and cultures, and, importantly, diverse ideas about the management of domestic threats and emergencies. In the emergency management arena, the overall effect of the reorganization has been to expand the role of defense and law enforcement–oriented agencies concerned exclusively with terrorism while diminishing the role and decreasing the prestige of organizations conducting all-hazards emergency management (Figure 3-1).[68]

HOMELAND SECURITY PRESIDENTIAL DIRECTIVE

Major events in U.S. history have often triggered major changes in the governmental process.[69] A great political impetus to act on terrorism was provided by the investigations and reports of

FIGURE 3-1 Department of Homeland Security

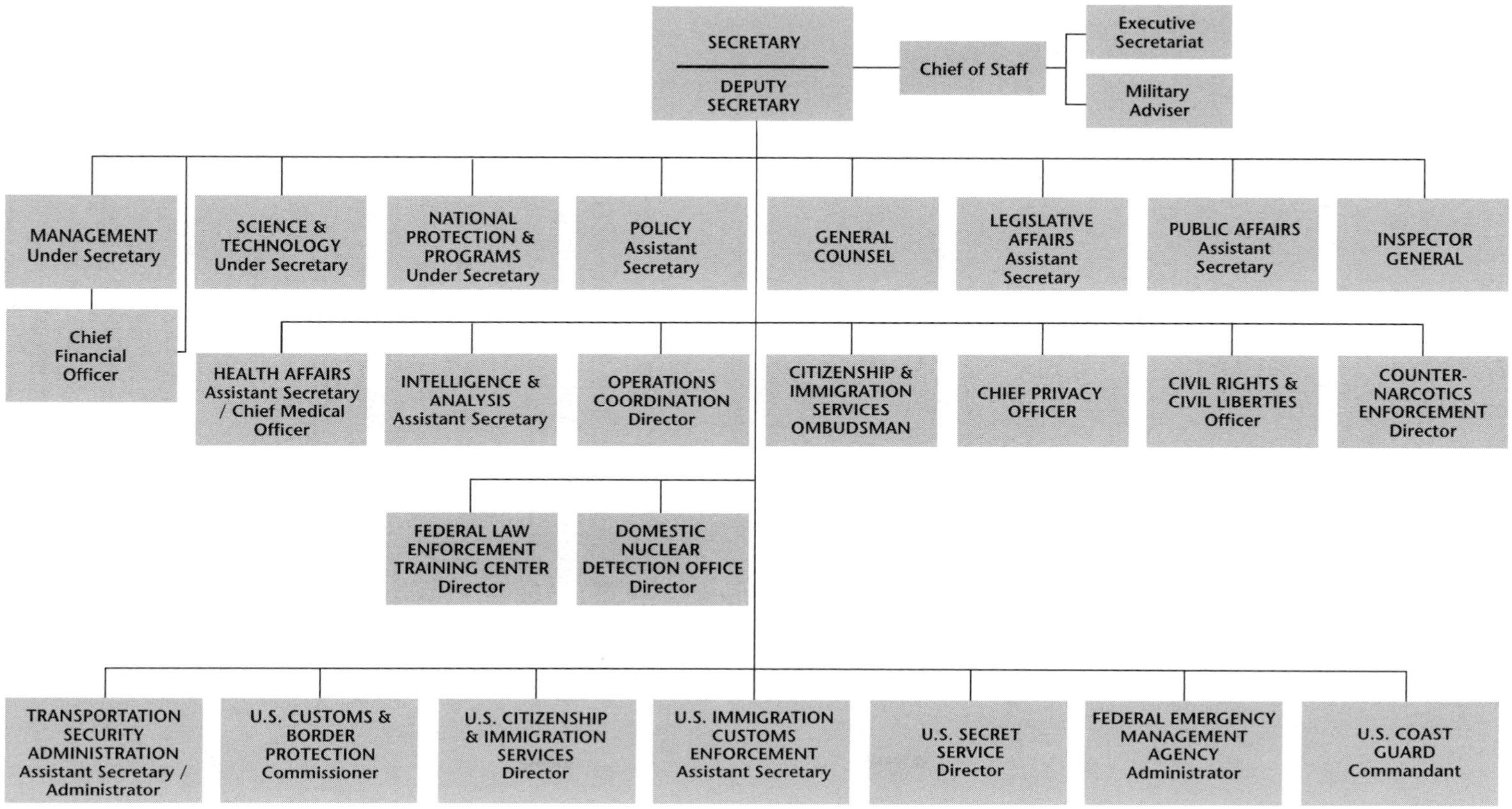

SECRETARY / DEPUTY SECRETARY

Executive Secretariat
Military Adviser
Chief of Staff

MANAGEMENT Under Secretary
Chief Financial Officer

SCIENCE & TECHNOLOGY Under Secretary

NATIONAL PROTECTION & PROGRAMS Under Secretary

POLICY Assistant Secretary

GENERAL COUNSEL

LEGISLATIVE AFFAIRS Assistant Secretary

PUBLIC AFFAIRS Assistant Secretary

INSPECTOR GENERAL

HEALTH AFFAIRS Assistant Secretary / Chief Medical Officer

INTELLIGENCE & ANALYSIS Assistant Secretary

OPERATIONS COORDINATION Director

CITIZENSHIP & IMMIGRATION SERVICES OMBUDSMAN

CHIEF PRIVACY OFFICER

CIVIL RIGHTS & CIVIL LIBERTIES Officer

COUNTER-NARCOTICS ENFORCEMENT Director

FEDERAL LAW ENFORCEMENT TRAINING CENTER Director

DOMESTIC NUCLEAR DETECTION OFFICE Director

TRANSPORTATION SECURITY ADMINISTRATION Assistant Secretary / Administrator

U.S. CUSTOMS & BORDER PROTECTION Commissioner

U.S. CITIZENSHIP & IMMIGRATION SERVICES Director

U.S. IMMIGRATION CUSTOMS ENFORCEMENT Assistant Secretary

U.S. SECRET SERVICE Director

FEDERAL EMERGENCY MANAGEMENT AGENCY Administrator

U.S. COAST GUARD Commandant

the National Commission on Terrorist Attacks Upon the United States, commonly referred to as the 9/11 Commission.[70] From this, the Bush administration was pressed to prepare a comprehensive national response plan.

On February 28, 2003, President Bush issued Homeland Security Presidential Directive-5 (HSPD-5).[71] Its purpose was "[t]o enhance the ability of the United States to manage domestic incidents by establishing a single, comprehensive national incident management system." The secretary of homeland security was given responsibility for implementing HSPD-5 by developing a **National Response Plan (NRP)** and a **National Incident Management System (NIMS).**[72] To this end, HSPD-5 mandated the development of a "concept of operations" for disasters that would incorporate all levels of government as well as crisis and consequence management functions within one unifying management framework to manage **domestic incidents.** Under the HSPD-5 directive, all federal agencies were required to adopt NIMS and to make its adoption a requirement for other governmental entities receiving federal assistance. Specifically, sections 3 and 4 revealed how the marriage of conventional disaster management and terrorism consequence management would work. Section 3 sets out the objectives of the department.

> To prevent, prepare for, respond to, and recover from terrorist attacks, major disasters, and other emergencies, the United States Government shall establish a single, comprehensive approach to domestic incident management. The objective of the United States Government is to ensure that all levels of government across the Nation have the capability to work efficiently and effectively together, using a national approach to domestic incident management. In these efforts, with regard to domestic incidents, the United States Government treats crisis management and consequence management as a single, integrated function, rather than as two separate functions.

Section 4 states the general responsibilities of the secretary of the department.

> The Secretary of Homeland Security is the principal Federal official for domestic incident management. Pursuant to the Homeland Security Act of 2002, the Secretary is responsible for coordinating Federal operations within the United States to prepare for, respond to, and recover from terrorist attacks, major disasters, and other emergencies. The Secretary shall coordinate the Federal Government's resources utilized in response to or recovery from terrorist attacks, major disasters, or other emergencies if and when any one of the following four conditions applies: (1) a Federal department or agency acting under its own authority has requested the assistance of the Secretary; (2) the resources of State and local authorities are overwhelmed and Federal assistance has been requested by the appropriate State and local authorities; (3) more than one Federal department or agency has become substantially involved in responding to the incident; or (4) the Secretary has been directed to assume responsibility for managing the domestic incident by the President.

Additionally, section 15 calls for a National Emergency Management System which is to include a core set of concepts, principles, terminology, and technologies covering the incident command system, multiagency coordination systems, unified command, training, qualifications, certification, and incident information collection, tracking, and reporting.

However, in calling for the development of a new national response plan, HSPD-5 seemingly ignored the fact that the United States already had a plan for coordinating the federal response to major disasters. The existing Federal Response Plan, which had been developed in the late 1980s and adopted in the early 1990s, had proved effective for coordinating federal resources in many major disasters and emergencies. It had even worked well in managing the effects of the 9/11 attacks. Although the NRP did not supplant that framework, it did make several important modifications. Under the NRP, the primary responsibility for managing domestic crises was now to rest with the secretary of homeland security. The plan also contained language strongly suggesting that the federal government would in the future assume more responsibility for directly managing some crises. This significantly modified the "bottom-up" emergency management and "shared governance" policies that had existed before.[73]

The National Response Plan, updated and reissued as the National Response Framework (NRF) in early 2008 is constantly subject to revision, established a comprehensive all-hazards approach intended to strengthen and improve the ability of the United States to manage domestic incidents. In the NRP, **incidents of national significance** encompassed major disasters or emergencies declared by the president. However, the secretary of the Department of Homeland Security also "can use limited pre-declaration authorities to move initial response resources closer to a potentially affected area." [74]

To be considered an "incident of national significance," four criteria had to be met:

- A federal department or agency acting under its own authority has requested the assistance of the secretary of homeland security.
- The resources of state and local authorities are overwhelmed and federal assistance has been requested by the appropriate state and local authorities, such as in major disasters and emergencies (covered by the Stafford Act) or catastrophic incidents.
- More than one federal department or agency has become substantially involved in responding to an incident, as in conditions of credible threats, indications, or warnings of imminent terrorist attack, acts of terrorism directed domestically against the people, property environment, or political or legal institutions of the United States or its territories or possessions—or threats or incidents related to high-profile, large-scale events that present targets such as National Special Security Events and other special events as determined by the secretary of homeland security, in coordination with other federal departments or agencies.
- The secretary of homeland security has been directed to assume responsibility for managing a domestic incident by the president.[75]

On December 17, 2003, President Bush issued Homeland Security Presidential Directive-8 (HSPD-8).[76] This directive gave the secretary of homeland security broad authority in establishing **national preparedness** and implementing programs to improve "prevention, response, and recovery" operations. Although the directive explicitly calls for actions that address all hazards within a risk-based framework, its major focus is on preparedness for terrorism-related events. Similarly, although HSPD-8 was intended to address issues related to preparedness, a broad term that is generally conceptualized as an integrative and comprehensive process, the directive is mainly concerned with training and equipping emergency response agencies.[77]

HOW THINGS WORK

WHITHER FEMA?

The Federal Emergency Management Agency was formerly an independent agency within the executive branch of government. Owing to an initiative of President Clinton, the FEMA director was accorded ex officio cabinet status for almost the whole of the Clinton administration. In 2003 FEMA was incorporated into DHS as lead agency for emergency preparedness and response. FEMA, which is the only agency within DHS that is charged specifically with reducing the losses associated with non-terrorism-related disasters, lost significant visibility and financial and human resources in the reorganization. As a small agency within a massive bureaucracy, its activities became overshadowed by much larger and better-funded entities within DHS.

The decline in FEMA's prestige and influence in the wake of 9/11 caused great concern among U.S. emergency management experts. Public policy now demands putting more resources into law enforcement and counterterrorism activities, and preparedness for other disasters, natural or technological, are viewed as less important. In addition, as the disaster sociologist Kathleen J. Tierney puts it, "as agencies based on command-and-control principles assume greater importance in local preparedness efforts, the influence of organizations that focus on hazards other than terrorism and that operate in a broadly inclusive fashion and on the basis of coordination, rather than control, has waned." [78]

Testifying before Congress in March 2004, former FEMA director James Lee Witt warned that the nation's ability to respond to disasters of all types has been weakened by some post–September 11 agency realignments. In written testimony regarding the loss of cabinet status for the FEMA director and the position of FEMA within DHS at the time, Witt stated, "I assure you that we could not have been as responsive and effective during disasters as we were during my tenure as FEMA director had there been layers of federal bureaucracy between myself and the White House." [79]

CONCLUSION AND SUMMARY

This chapter was an ambitious distillation of almost sixty years of disaster policy history. It revealed that presidents often make creative use of their disaster declaration authority. Presidents from Truman to Carter, within limits set by Congress, tethered civil defense to a nascent and evolving state and local emergency management of nonwar disasters and emergencies. Still, the theme and thread of civil defense continued for decades, often confounding or complicating conventional emergency management. Disaster policy is not simply emergency management shaped by presidents and other policymakers and carried out by government workers. Disaster policy is a hybrid of conventional emergency management, civil defense, and, since 2001, homeland security.

This chapter documents the history of presidential domination of disaster policy formulation and implementation. Congress has afforded the president considerable and unfettered discretion to define for the nation what is or is not a disaster or an emergency. This chapter demonstrated that emergencies and disasters are in some ways "political" constructs. The president is even entrusted with a fund he can use to pay for various disaster-related costs.

Congress periodically must replenish these funds with new spending authority under emergency supplemental appropriations.

Presidents from Truman to Carter conducted disaster policy implementation through an assemblage of federal organizations. Some of these organizations resided in the White House, some operated as major and minor arms of federal departments, and some labored in obscurity as back offices of independent agencies. It was not until nearly the end of the Carter administration in 1979 that disaster policy was granted a formal and largely integrated home in the form of a small independent federal emergency management agency. FEMA officials always understood that they survived and succeeded as a function of their closeness to the presidency. The agency lacked a strong pool of stakeholders that could assiduously lobby for it on Capitol Hill. It was too small to go toe-to-toe with the much larger departments like defense, HUD, justice, or transportation. Whatever clout FEMA possessed had to be backstopped by the White House.

Specific disaster-related laws and policy trends and several major disasters that have been factors in the enactment of these laws or contributors to these policy trends have been discussed. The theme of federal-state and intergovernmental relations is evident throughout the chapter. Similarly, matters of civil defense and homeland security have been discussed in conjunction with conventional all-hazards disaster management. Subsequent chapters delve more deeply into matters of presidential disaster declarations, the role of science and engineering in the field, how intergovernmental relations work in emergency management, how civil-military relations influence disaster policy, and how disaster policy has global relevance. This chapter may seem overwhelming, but it is an attempt to paint an accurate, although not comprehensive, picture of U.S. disaster policy history inside a modestly small frame.

KEY TERMS AND CONCEPTS

camcorder politics   61
civil defense preparedness   49
Crisis Relocation Plan   51
domestic incidents   72
dual-use approach   50
emergency declaration   55
federal zoning   52
incidents of national significance   73
Individual and Family Grant
    program   55

multihazard approach   55
limited federal response   49
National Incident Management
    System   72
national preparedness   73
National Response Plan   72
nonstructural mitigation   51
President's Disaster Relief Fund   54
self-help   48
structural hazard mitigation   51

CHAPTER 4

UNDERSTANDING
DISASTER POLICY
THROUGH PRESIDENTIAL
DISASTER DECLARATIONS

IN THE UNITED STATES THE PRESIDENT HOLDS THE CHIEF JOB of leading public management in times of catastrophic disaster. Since 1950, presidents have possessed the authority to define and officially declare disasters and emergencies ranging from catastrophes to more routine and much less devastating events.

Each president's declaration decisions reveal something about that president as a person, as a public servant, and as a political leader. The record of disaster declarations also says something about each president's view of federal-state relations, his position with regard to disaster policy and emergency management, his use of declarations as an instrument of political power, and his view of disasters within the broader context of the era in which he has governed. And more recently, the threat of terrorism has dramatically increased the range of presidential discretion in determining incidents of national significance, again ranging from suspected small-scale threats to megadisasters and catastrophes. This too has allowed the president to make policy determinations regarding how events of almost any type will be addressed by homeland security and emergency management agencies and officials.

This chapter looks at how the role of the president has evolved in declaring disasters, what may influence the president in declaring emergencies and disasters, and how the actual declaration process occurs. It concludes with some theories of presidential decision making.

THE PRESIDENT'S CONSTITUTIONAL EMERGENCY POWERS

Presidential emergency powers are the actions that the president may exercise in extraordinary circumstances: rebellion, epidemic, labor strike, or disaster. The president's oath of office requires that he "preserve, protect, and defend" the Constitution and uphold its provisions. Although no specific emergency powers were included in the Constitution, principal authorization of emergency powers resides in article 2, section 3, which states in part that the president

Three days after the 9/11 attack on the World Trade Center, in a quintessential moment for President Bush and his administration, the president stands with New York firefighter Bob Beckwith on a burnt fire truck at Ground Zero. Using his handheld loudspeaker, the president vowed that "the people who did this will soon hear from us." President Bush would soon use his presidential power to declare major disasters and emergencies as a tool in homeland security counterterrorism.

"shall take care that the laws be faithfully executed," and section 2, which grants the president power as commander in chief of the armed forces. In times of crisis, presidents can declare that the Constitution authorizes them to exercise powers usually granted to the legislative or judicial branches of government, thus fusing all governmental power in the executive branch for the duration of the crisis. President Abraham Lincoln justified the actions he took after the outbreak of the Civil War by claiming that the emergency made it necessary for him to exercise legislative powers until he could call Congress back into session. During World War II, President Franklin D. Roosevelt declared that unless Congress repealed a certain provision in a war-related economic measure, he would treat the law as if it had been repealed for the duration of the emergency, in effect threatening Congress with the loss of its legislative powers.[1]

Actual disasters and emergencies through history have helped to develop, refine, and expand the range of presidential emergency powers beyond what is alluded to in the Constitution.[2] Congress and the president have enacted a series of disaster relief laws, and a great many of these have essentially expanded the president's role in matters of disaster policy over time.

FEDERAL DISASTER RELIEF LEGISLATION AND DECLARATION AUTHORITY

Congress passed the first permanent statutes authorizing federal disaster assistance in 1947 and 1950. The 1947 legislation provided surplus property and personnel as needed, and its 1950 counterpart gave the president authority to determine what type of aid was required. These measures changed the nature of disaster relief in the United States. Only later did congressional leaders begin to see the 1950 act as precedent setting and as an early, general, national-level disaster policy model.

The Disaster Relief Act of 1950 clearly stated for the first time that federal resources could and should be used to supplement the efforts of others in the event of a disaster. The new law made federal disaster assistance more accessible, since it no longer required specific congressional legislation to address each new disaster but instead simply allowed the president to decide when federal disaster assistance was justified and necessary. The Disaster Relief Act of 1950 provided "an orderly and continuing means of assistance by the federal government to states and local governments in carrying out their responsibilities to alleviate suffering and damage resulting from major disasters." Congress built on the 1950 act by passing a number of laws in the 1970s that expanded the scope of federal government responsibility in disasters. For example, the Disaster Relief Act of 1974 created a program that provided direct assistance to individuals and families following a disaster. Importantly, the act gave the president the power to declare an emergency as well, whereas previously only a major disaster could be declared.

Under this federal law an emergency was defined as "any occasion or instance for which, in the determination of the president, federal assistance is needed to supplement state and local efforts and capabilities to save lives and to protect property and public health and safety, or to lessen or avert the threat of catastrophe in any part of the United States." An emergency is often of less magnitude and scope than a **major disaster.** However, the president may issue an emergency declaration to address an ongoing event that may later be declared a major disaster.

Congress passed the Stafford Act in 1988. This act enhanced presidential declaration authority in the sense that it imposed fewer restrictions on the types of disasters for which the president could issue a declaration. The measure opened the possibility that a president could issue a disaster declaration for a disaster caused by terrorism or by some unforeseen human or technological calamity.

Along with the authority to issue a major disaster declaration, the president has the authority to direct that the following types of federal disaster assistance be provided: general federal assistance for technical and advisory aid and support to state and local governments to facilitate the distribution of consumable supplies; essential assistance from federal agencies to distribute aid to victims through state and local governments and voluntary organizations, perform life- and property-saving assistance, clear debris, and use resources of the Department of Defense before a major disaster or emergency declaration is issued; hazard mitigation grants to reduce risks and damages that might occur in future disasters; federal facilities repair and reconstruction; repair, restoration, and replacement of damaged facilities owned by state and local governments, as well as private nonprofit facilities that provide essential services or commodities. In addition, the Stafford Act allows presidents to add new categories of emergency as deemed necessary.

Both the 1950 law and the Stafford Act of 1988 stipulate that the governor of an affected state must formally ask the president to declare a major disaster or emergency. If the request is granted, the federal government will then provide disaster assistance "to supplement the efforts and available resources of state and local governments in alleviating the disaster." The governor must provide certain information on the severity and magnitude of the disaster and on the amount of state and local resources to be committed to the disaster or emergency. The president is given wide discretion to determine whether the disaster or emergency is of sufficient severity and size to warrant federal disaster or emergency assistance. The authority to declare a disaster carries with it the power to determine the types of federal disaster assistance that will be made available to state and local governments and to individuals and families. Presidents have always reserved this authority to declare a major disaster or emergency and have never delegated it.

Post-9/11 Disaster Declaration Authority

Since 1950, natural and nonterrorism-related human-caused disasters were rarely considered matters of national security policy, with the notable exception of civil defense plans against nuclear attack. Owing to the 9/11 terror attacks, the administration of George W. Bush, with the assent of Congress, defined presidential disaster declaration authority as a national security instrument, thus drastically changing federal emergency management. The 9/11 disaster further centralized presidential authority, as did war and many catastrophic disasters before, but most of the governmental changes made in response to 9/11 significantly increased the president's range of authority.[3]

The Bush administration was pressed to prepare such a comprehensive national response plan by the *9/11 Commission Report*.[4] The Homeland Security Act of 2002, Homeland Security Presidential Directive-5, and the Stafford Act of 1988 justify and provide, according to the National Response Plan (NRP), a comprehensive, all-hazards approach to domestic

HOW THINGS WORK

THE STAFFORD ACT

This extract from a portion of the Robert T. Stafford Disaster Relief and Emergency Assistance Act of 1988 is a congressional statement of purpose regarding the federal role in disasters.

> It is the intent of the Congress, by this [Stafford] Act, to provide an orderly and continuing means of assistance by the Federal Government to State and local governments in carrying out their responsibilities to alleviate the suffering and damage which result from such disasters by,
> - revising and broadening the scope of existing disaster relief programs;
> - encouraging the development of comprehensive disaster preparedness and assistance plans, programs, capabilities, and organizations by the States and by local governments;
> - achieving greater coordination and responsiveness of disaster preparedness and relief programs;
> - encouraging individuals, States, and local governments to protect themselves by obtaining insurance coverage to supplement or replace governmental assistance;
> - encouraging hazard mitigation measures to reduce losses from disasters, including development of land-use and construction regulations; and
> - providing Federal assistance programs for both public and private losses sustained in disasters.[5]

The Stafford Act also provides federal assistance but under either fixed dollar limits or a percentage of eligible costs. The categories below explain these limits and also convey some information about the programs themselves.

Essential assistance: The federal share must be at least 75% of eligible costs.
Public Assistance, which is federal-to-state/local government aid.
Repair, restoration, or replacement of public facilities: In general, at least 75% of eligible costs must be provided, but this threshold may be reduced to 25% if a facility has previously been damaged by the same type of disaster and mitigation measures have not been adopted to address the hazard. Federal aid generally will be reduced if facilities in flood hazard areas are not covered by flood insurance. Cost estimation requirements must be adhered to, but the President may approve costs that exceed the regulatory limitations. "Associated costs," such as the employment of national guard forces, use of prison labor, and base and overtime wages for employees and "extra hires," may be reimbursed. The President must notify congressional committees with jurisdiction before providing more than $20 million to repair, restore, or replace facilities.
Debris removal: The federal share must be at least 75% of the eligible costs.
Individual and household assistance: Temporary housing units may be provided directly to victims of disasters, without charge, for up to 18 months, unless the President extends the assistance "due to extraordinary circumstances." Fair market rents may

Presidents regularly turn down gubernatorial requests for major disasters or emergencies. However, presidents sometimes approve requests for major disaster declarations when damage in the state is relatively light and the state may have been able to recover from the event without federal assistance.[25]

Sometimes disasters, particularly those that are catastrophic in magnitude, have transformed presidents and their administrations. Hurricane Camille (1969), and an ensuing weak and highly criticized federal response to that disaster, pressed President Nixon to assign various emergency management duties to an archipelago of federal agencies. The federal-state debacle in managing the response in Florida to Hurricane Andrew in 1992 damaged President George H. W. Bush's image, and, although he narrowly won the state's electoral votes in 1988, it may have contributed to his defeat in the November 1992 presidential election. Once in office, President Clinton responded to the Hurricane Andrew failure by appointing a qualified and experienced state emergency manager to head his FEMA. In spite of controversial problems in some realms of his administration, Bill Clinton left office perceived as a president capable of managing domestic disasters, although perhaps less so terrorism. The terrorist attack disaster of September 11, 2001, moved President George W. Bush to quickly redefine his administration's primary mission as one of countering terrorism. Hurricane Katrina and the excoriated federal response to that disaster moved Congress to reconstitute FEMA as a full-service emergency management agency, but one still embedded within the gigantic Department of Homeland Security.

ANOMALOUS PROBLEMS INVITE NEW DECLARATION PRECEDENTS

HISTORY'S LESSONS

Occasionally, certain anomalous events invite presidents to use the discretion they have in disaster declaration authority to issue declarations for unprecedented phenomena. An example is the presidential response to Cuban president Fidel Castro's Mariel boatlift of Cuban evacuees to the United States in 1980. President Jimmy Carter issued an emergency declaration to reimburse Florida for the costs incurred in working with Cuban refugees from the boatlift.[26] This action handed FEMA a unique management task that had to be performed in cooperation with various federal and state agencies, most particularly corrections agencies, which were assigned the job of separating convicted criminals from the pool of refugees.

Sometimes presidents single-handedly, or in conjunction with Congress, transform or expand what officially constitutes a disaster. In 1979 President Carter issued a controversial presidential declaration of a major disaster covering the western New York State Love Canal hazardous waste incident. In 1999 President Clinton's decision to approve New York governor George Pataki's West Nile virus emergency request (to cover pesticide spraying and public health costs) created a new category of federal emergency aid. Some analysts allege that federal activity in support of West Nile virus spraying was a precursor of modern antipandemic or bioterrorism federal preparedness initiatives.[27] These decisions set precedents that led governors to believe they could ask for presidential declarations to cover similar problems and calamities.

FACILITATING THE PRESIDENT'S WORK

Disaster policy is very much event driven.[28] Certain disasters, often catastrophes, not only stress the nation's disaster management system but force massive reforms that produce a "new normal" in the domain of disaster policy and homeland security.[29] FEMA, whether independent or within DHS, is fairly good at managing "routine" disasters.[30] However, no federal agency is invested with sufficient authority to adequately or proficiently cope with a catastrophe. It becomes the job of the president and his staff to orchestrate and oversee the work of many federal disaster agencies in catastrophic circumstances. Such work has to be carried out with the help and cooperation of governors, mayors, and other elected executives. A host of other players are involved as well, and these include state and local emergency managers, emergency responders, nonprofit organizations active in disasters, and private corporations, large and small.[31]

Presidents have help in addressing disasters and emergencies and in making judgments as to whether to approve or reject gubernatorial requests for presidential declarations of major disaster or emergency. Just as mayors are the personification of the cities they lead, and just as governors are the personification of the states they serve, each serving president is the personification of the nation as a whole. Presidents need help in determining when to intercede in matters of disaster and emergency. They need help in judging the worthiness of the declaration requests they receive. Since 1979, a FEMA director has advised each president about whether to approve or reject governor-requested declarations of major disaster. FEMA directors may well have advised various presidents about governors' requests for emergency declarations too, but because governors do not need to elaborately demonstrate need in their emergency declaration requests, presidents and their White House staffs, perhaps in consultation with the FEMA director, often make emergency declaration decisions quickly and on the basis of life and safety considerations.

Who are the White House organizational players in matters of disaster policy and disaster management?

The White House Staff

The White House staff consists of key aides whom the president sees daily—the chief of staff, congressional liaison people, the press secretary, the national security adviser—and a few other political and administrative assistants. Actually about six hundred people work on the White House staff, most of whom see the president rarely but provide a wide range of services. Some of these people play a role in helping the president consider governors' requests for declarations of major disaster or emergency.

Most presidents rely heavily on their staffs for information, policy options, and analysis. Different presidents have different relations with, and means of organizing, their staffs. President Carter was a "detail man," toiling ceaselessly over memoranda and facts. President Reagan was the consummate "delegator," who entrusted tremendous responsibilities to his staff. President George H. W. Bush fell somewhere between the Carter and Reagan extremes and was considerably more accessible than President Reagan. President Clinton, like Carter, was a detail man but someone who also ran an open White House with fluid staffing.[32]

be charged at the conclusion of the 18 month period. Up to $5,000 (adjusted annually) may be provided for housing repair or hazard mitigation measures, and up to $10,000 (adjusted annually) may be provided for the replacement of private residences. The federal share of housing assistance is 100%.

Financial assistance is also provided for uninsured medical, dental, funeral, transportation, personal property, and other needs; the federal share for this assistance is capped at 75% of eligible costs; the total amount that may be provided under the Individuals and Household Program (IHP) cannot exceed $25,000 (adjusted annually).

Small project grants: If the estimated costs of assistance for facility repair or replacement (Section 406), essential assistance (Section 403), debris removal (Section 407), or emergency assistance (Section 502) do not exceed $35,000 (adjusted annually), a small project grant may be issued.

Emergency declaration assistance: Federal assistance must constitute at least 75% of eligible costs. Expenditures made under an emergency declaration are limited to $5 million per declaration unless the President determines that there is a continuing need; Congress must be notified if the $5 million ceiling is breached.[6]

The passage below is a clearer summary:
- assistance to individuals and households including financial grants to rent alternative housing, direct assistance through temporary housing units (mobile homes), limited financial assistance for housing repairs and replacement, and financial assistance for uninsured medical, dental, funeral, personal property, transportation, and other expenses;
- unemployment assistance to individuals unemployed as a result of the major disaster, for up to 26 weeks, as long as they are not entitled to other unemployment compensation or credits;
- grants to assist low-income migrant and seasonal farm workers to be provided by the Secretary of Agriculture (total limited to $20 million annually) 'where the Secretary determines that a local, state or national emergency or disaster' has resulted in a loss of income or inability to work; food coupons and food distribution for low-income households unable to purchase nutritious food;
- food commodities for emergency mass feeding;
- legal services for low-income individuals;
- crisis counseling assistance and training grants for state and local governments or private mental health organizations to provide associated services or to train disaster workers.[7]

incident management.[8] Disaster declarations in the post-9/11 era are now conceived as matters of domestic incident management. All major disasters, emergencies, and catastrophic incidents declared by the president are incidents of national significance. Incidents of national significance now encompass major disasters or emergencies declared by the president and under the NRP are defined as "[a]n actual or potential high-impact event that requires coordination of Federal, State, local, tribal, nongovernmental and/or private sector entities in order to save lives and minimize damage." [9]

Catastrophes Enter the Mix, National Special Security Events, and More

The NRP added a new category of incident beyond major disaster and emergency. **Catastrophic incidents** became

> [a]ny natural or manmade incident, including terrorism, that results in extraordinary levels of mass casualties, damage, or disruption severely affecting the population, infrastructure, environment, economy, and national morale and/or government functions. A catastrophic event could result in sustained national impacts over a prolonged period of time; almost immediately exceeds resources normally available to State, local, tribal, and private sector authorities; and significantly interrupts governmental operations and emergency services to such an extent that national security could be threatened. All catastrophic incidents are considered incidents of national significance.[10]

National Special Security Events (NSSEs) are another category of incidents of national significance; they include "high-profile, large-scale events that present high probability targets" such as various summit meetings of world leaders inside the United States, the Republican and Democratic national political party conventions, and any other event the president believes may be vulnerable to terror attack.[11]

Annexes to the NRP stipulated that the president has formal declaration authority to cover bioterror, cyber terror, food and agricultural terror attacks, nuclear or radiological incidents, and oil and hazardous materials pollution incidents of national significance. Nonetheless, not every incident of national significance "necessarily results in a disaster or emergency declaration under the Stafford Act." [12]

The Significance of the Changes

Why are these changes important? The cumulative outcomes of these changes in presidential declaration power are several. Presidents now possess almost unencumbered authority to mobilize federal, state, and local resources if they conclude that an event of some kind represents either a terrorism threat or an assumed act of terrorism. The NRP puts various federal, state, and local agencies to work under the National Incident Management System. In addition, the Homeland Security Act of 2002, related laws, and a series of homeland security presidential directives created changes in FEMA and the domestic and international world of emergency management. Because the president and DHS-FEMA officials define major disasters and emergencies of any type as incidents of national significance, emergency management is today very much a matter of national security at home and abroad. U.S. emergency managers on every level of government must now learn more about disasters and emergencies, especially those involving terrorism, that occur outside, as well as inside, the United States.[13]

Federal emergency management is predicated on terrorism as a paramount threat, whereas other types of disasters or emergencies occupy diminished positions within the federal emergency management and homeland security community.[14] Until the mid-1980s, when concerns about terrorism arose within the Reagan administration, natural and nonwar human-caused disasters have rarely been considered matters of national security. This has been underscored in the testimony provided by Michael Brown, the former FEMA director forced to resign in the weeks after Hurricane Katrina struck in 2005, before the Select Bipartisan Committee to Investigate Preparation for and Response to Hurricane Katrina.[15]

Owing to the president's and federal government's problems in the 2005 Hurricane Katrina catastrophe, presidents facing potential mega-disasters may be tempted to federalize the government's response to certain disasters under presidential declarations of "catastrophic disaster." Although the Stafford Act of 1988 remains law, the processes by which the president and FEMA/DHS consider gubernatorial requests for declarations of major disaster and emergency and the nature of what constitutes a disaster agent have been altered. Most of these changes reflect a shift toward homeland security, and this has had ramifications at the state and local levels.

PRESIDENTIAL DISCRETIONARY POWER

Ever since presidential disaster declaration authority was enshrined in law, the president has been afforded the discretion and flexibility to decide what is and what is not a disaster or emergency. Under the Stafford Act of 1988 and several of its predecessor laws, as discussed, presidents are free, within limits, to interpret broadly or narrowly what is declarable as a major disaster or emergency.[16] Each president makes declaration decisions on a case-by-case basis.[17] Before 1950, when Congress considered unique relief legislation for each disaster, awkwardness, delay, pork barreling, and administrative confusion often resulted.[18]

By 1950, lawmakers had decided that it made more sense to entrust declaration decision making to the president as an executive responsibility.[19] Ironically, presidential authority to address domestic disasters won political support because many Americans grew concerned that there was no domestic equivalent of the post–World War II foreign aid sent to countries ravaged by war and famine disaster.[20] Taxpayers complained that they were supporting rebuilding and recovery efforts abroad but not at home.

A presidential declaration of major disaster or emergency has far-reaching consequences because it opens the door to federal assistance and aid by legitimizing the disaster for affected populations.[21] The declaration specifies one or more political jurisdictions and thereby delineates by location exactly who is eligible for relief. Each declaration is issued to a state or the District of Columbia or an American trust territory or commonwealth. Each declaration identifies the counties eligible to receive federal disaster assistance. Some declarations issued by the president make every county in a state eligible for some form of federal disaster assistance, but usually presidential declarations apply only to the counties that governors have asked them to cover. The president, perhaps advised by federal disaster managers, may choose to include some but not all of the counties recommended by the governor. Moreover, FEMA may add counties to an in-force presidential disaster declaration without the need for presidential preapproval.

Presidential declarations of major disaster and emergency are intriguing because authority to make the essential decision rests with the president himself. Most federal laws require implementation decisions by legions of government officials, many of whom operate some distance from the president.[22] Admittedly, once the president issues a declaration, federal agency and program officials, usually in concert with their state and local counterparts, undertake an elaborate and extensive assortment of implementing decisions. Yet the president's decision to push either the "approval button" or the "turndown button" is often highly consequential.[23]

Every presidential declaration contains an initial statement about the kinds of assistance people may request. This is extremely important because it determines whether disaster victims will receive direct cash grants, housing supplements, emergency medical care, disaster unemployment assistance, and so forth. It also specifies whether or not state and local governments themselves are eligible to receive federal disaster assistance to replace or repair public facilities and infrastructure. Certain nonprofit organizations may also qualify for federal disaster aid of various types. Federal disaster relief may flow to subcounty incorporated municipalities but only those that are in counties included in the presidential declaration.

A presidential declaration is vitally important to those directly affected by the disaster or emergency. It confers on them an "official" victim status needed to qualify for federal aid. Individuals and households may qualify for various forms of federal disaster assistance under a declaration. Many declarations make aid available through the Public Assistance program, which provides government-to-government (federal-to-state or local) disaster relief to subsidize much of the cost of repairing, rebuilding, or replacing damaged government or utility infrastructure.

To the public, including those not directly affected by the disaster, the president's declaration is significant for other reasons. At a basic level, a declaration signifies that a major event has occurred, requiring the attention and resources of the federal government. The content of the presidential declaration structures popular perceptions about the nature and scope of the disaster.

As of January 2007, presidents from Eisenhower (May 1953) to G. W. Bush (January 2007) have issued a total of 1,674 major disaster declarations.[24] This is a remarkable total because it represents an average of 31 major disaster declarations a year, or about 2.5 declarations per month. Moreover, from January 1993 through September 2005, about a thirteen-year span, the average number of major disaster declarations per year jumped to 48.2 a year, or 4 per month. The increasing volume and changing variety of presidential disaster declarations reveals in some respects the nation's history of disaster experience and the nation's increasing vulnerability to disaster agents and forces. The record of disaster declarations also connotes change in public attitudes about disaster, changes in federal-state relations, changes in various presidents' perception and use of disaster declaration authority, and changes in disaster law and management over time.

Presidents regularly turn down gubernatorial requests for major disasters or emergencies. However, presidents sometimes approve requests for major disaster declarations when damage in the state is relatively light and the state may have been able to recover from the event without federal assistance.[25]

Sometimes disasters, particularly those that are catastrophic in magnitude, have transformed presidents and their administrations. Hurricane Camille (1969), and an ensuing weak and highly criticized federal response to that disaster, pressed President Nixon to assign various emergency management duties to an archipelago of federal agencies. The federal-state debacle in managing the response in Florida to Hurricane Andrew in 1992 damaged President George H. W. Bush's image, and, although he narrowly won the state's electoral votes in 1988, it may have contributed to his defeat in the November 1992 presidential election. Once in office, President Clinton responded to the Hurricane Andrew failure by appointing a qualified and experienced state emergency manager to head his FEMA. In spite of controversial problems in some realms of his administration, Bill Clinton left office perceived as a president capable of managing domestic disasters, although perhaps less so terrorism. The terrorist attack disaster of September 11, 2001, moved President George W. Bush to quickly redefine his administration's primary mission as one of countering terrorism. Hurricane Katrina and the excoriated federal response to that disaster moved Congress to reconstitute FEMA as a full-service emergency management agency, but one still embedded within the gigantic Department of Homeland Security.

ANOMALOUS PROBLEMS INVITE NEW DECLARATION PRECEDENTS

HISTORY'S LESSONS

Occasionally, certain anomalous events invite presidents to use the discretion they have in disaster declaration authority to issue declarations for unprecedented phenomena. An example is the presidential response to Cuban president Fidel Castro's Mariel boatlift of Cuban evacuees to the United States in 1980. President Jimmy Carter issued an emergency declaration to reimburse Florida for the costs incurred in working with Cuban refugees from the boatlift.[26] This action handed FEMA a unique management task that had to be performed in cooperation with various federal and state agencies, most particularly corrections agencies, which were assigned the job of separating convicted criminals from the pool of refugees.

Sometimes presidents single-handedly, or in conjunction with Congress, transform or expand what officially constitutes a disaster. In 1979 President Carter issued a controversial presidential declaration of a major disaster covering the western New York State Love Canal hazardous waste incident. In 1999 President Clinton's decision to approve New York governor George Pataki's West Nile virus emergency request (to cover pesticide spraying and public health costs) created a new category of federal emergency aid. Some analysts allege that federal activity in support of West Nile virus spraying was a precursor of modern antipandemic or bioterrorism federal preparedness initiatives.[27] These decisions set precedents that led governors to believe they could ask for presidential declarations to cover similar problems and calamities.

FACILITATING THE PRESIDENT'S WORK

Disaster policy is very much event driven.[28] Certain disasters, often catastrophes, not only stress the nation's disaster management system but force massive reforms that produce a "new normal" in the domain of disaster policy and homeland security.[29] FEMA, whether independent or within DHS, is fairly good at managing "routine" disasters.[30] However, no federal agency is invested with sufficient authority to adequately or proficiently cope with a catastrophe. It becomes the job of the president and his staff to orchestrate and oversee the work of many federal disaster agencies in catastrophic circumstances. Such work has to be carried out with the help and cooperation of governors, mayors, and other elected executives. A host of other players are involved as well, and these include state and local emergency managers, emergency responders, nonprofit organizations active in disasters, and private corporations, large and small.[31]

Presidents have help in addressing disasters and emergencies and in making judgments as to whether to approve or reject gubernatorial requests for presidential declarations of major disaster or emergency. Just as mayors are the personification of the cities they lead, and just as governors are the personification of the states they serve, each serving president is the personification of the nation as a whole. Presidents need help in determining when to intercede in matters of disaster and emergency. They need help in judging the worthiness of the declaration requests they receive. Since 1979, a FEMA director has advised each president about whether to approve or reject governor-requested declarations of major disaster. FEMA directors may well have advised various presidents about governors' requests for emergency declarations too, but because governors do not need to elaborately demonstrate need in their emergency declaration requests, presidents and their White House staffs, perhaps in consultation with the FEMA director, often make emergency declaration decisions quickly and on the basis of life and safety considerations.

Who are the White House organizational players in matters of disaster policy and disaster management?

The White House Staff

The White House staff consists of key aides whom the president sees daily—the chief of staff, congressional liaison people, the press secretary, the national security adviser—and a few other political and administrative assistants. Actually about six hundred people work on the White House staff, most of whom see the president rarely but provide a wide range of services. Some of these people play a role in helping the president consider governors' requests for declarations of major disaster or emergency.

Most presidents rely heavily on their staffs for information, policy options, and analysis. Different presidents have different relations with, and means of organizing, their staffs. President Carter was a "detail man," toiling ceaselessly over memoranda and facts. President Reagan was the consummate "delegator," who entrusted tremendous responsibilities to his staff. President George H. W. Bush fell somewhere between the Carter and Reagan extremes and was considerably more accessible than President Reagan. President Clinton, like Carter, was a detail man but someone who also ran an open White House with fluid staffing.[32]

President George W. Bush is a delegator who follows a chief executive officer model of management and who prefers a less open White House.

In any disaster or emergency, many offices are likely to engage in facilitating the president's work. Clearly, the White House Political Affairs Office and the Communications Office would be tasked to help the president address a disaster or emergency, especially in cooperation with the White House press secretary. The White House Homeland Security Council and perhaps the National Security Council would also be involved.[33]

The Domestic Policy Council and Office of Cabinet Liaison would most likely help the president address various emergency or disaster management activities. Within the White House staff, schedulers, speechwriters, and travel planners would also join in this effort, especially if the president were to make arrangements to visit the disaster area. Secret Service officials, Military liaison, and medical personnel may also play roles, as would the Office of the Vice President.[34]

The Secretary, Department of Homeland Security

The secretary of homeland security is the head of the Department of Homeland Security and a member of the president's cabinet. The Homeland Security Act of 2002 authorized creation of DHS, a superdepartment with 180,000 employees. It was formed by transferring some twenty-two federal agencies or offices into the new department. The secretary of homeland security, and the deputy secretary, are managerial supervisors of the FEMA director. The secretary also holds authority to declare incidents of national significance independently or in conjunction with the president.

The FEMA Director

The FEMA director is a politically appointed official who is often handpicked by the president, and typically that person is one of his political confidants. Since FEMA's creation in April 1979, some FEMA directors have had previous experience in emergency management and some have not.

The FEMA director is in effect the chief executive officer of the agency, although some who have been appointed to the post have been satisfied in delegating day-to-day management of the agency to the assistant director. Under the Post-Katrina Emergency Management Reform Act of 2006, the FEMA director has been given a more direct line of access to the president, albeit with expected consultation of the secretary of the Department of Homeland Security, during periods of disaster response and when carrying out his or her responsibility to help in the processing of emergency and major disaster declaration requests submitted by governors.

Typically, the route of a governor's request starts with the regional FEMA director, who receives a request, reviews it, and sends a recommendation to FEMA headquarters in Washington. There, a declaration processing unit prepares documents pertaining to the request, and the director of FEMA, after compiling information for the president about the event and, often, consulting with the governors who have requested the declarations, adds a memorandum

HOW THINGS WORK

THE PRESIDENTIAL DISASTER DECLARATION PROCESS IN BRIEF

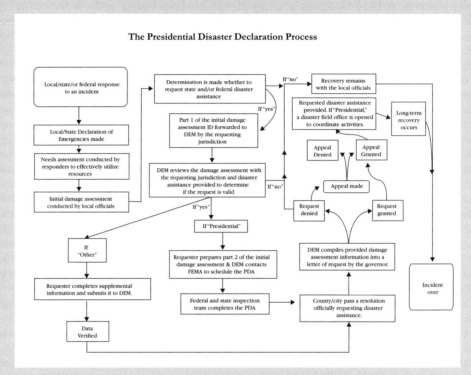

The Presidential Disaster Declaration Process

Source: State of Minnesota, Department of Homeland Security and Emergency Management, http://www.hsem.state.mn.us/uploadedfile/recovery_handbook/Chapter01/Toolkit/Pres_Disaster_Decl_Pro.pdf.

The Stafford Act (sec. 401) requires that "[a]ll requests for a declaration by the President that a major disaster exists shall be made by the Governor of the affected State." A state also

recommending to the president a course of action: approve or reject. All the information FEMA sends to the president, including the director's recommendation, is protected by rules of executive privilege and therefore unavailable for public scrutiny. The president is neither bound by FEMA's recommendation nor obligated to follow the agency's declaration criteria. The president alone determines whether to approve or reject every governor's request.

Following are some common factors FEMA officials consider before they make their recommendation:

- Number of homes destroyed or sustaining major damage
- The extent to which damage is concentrated or dispersed

includes the District of Columbia and American Samoa, the Commonwealth of the Northern Mariana Islands, Guam, Puerto Rico, and the Virgin Islands. The Marshall Islands and the Federated States of Micronesia are also eligible to request a declaration and receive assistance.

The governor's request is made through the regional FEMA/EPR office. State and federal officials conduct a preliminary damage assessment (PDA) to estimate the extent of the disaster and its impact on individuals and public facilities. This information is included in the governor's request to show that the disaster is of such severity and magnitude that effective response is beyond the capabilities of the state and local governments and that federal assistance is necessary. Normally, the PDA is completed prior to the submission of the governor's request. However, when an obviously severe or catastrophic event occurs, the governor's request may be submitted prior to the PDA. Nonetheless, the governor must still make the request.

As part of the request, the governor must take appropriate action under state law and direct execution of the state's emergency plan. The governor must furnish information on the nature and amount of state and local resources that have been or will be committed to alleviating the results of the disaster, provide an estimate of the amount and severity of damage and the impact on the private and public sector, and provide an estimate of the type and amount of assistance needed under the Stafford Act. In addition, the governor needs to certify that, for the current disaster, state and local government obligations and expenditures (of which state commitments must be a significant proportion) will comply with all applicable cost-sharing requirements.

Based on the governor's request, the president may declare that a major disaster or emergency exists, thus activating an array of federal programs to assist in the response and recovery effort.

Not all programs, however, are activated for every disaster. The determination of which programs are activated is based on the needs found during damage assessment and any subsequent information that may be discovered.

Some declarations will provide only individual assistance or only public assistance. Hazard mitigation opportunities are assessed in most situations.

Source: The material for this feature section, excluding the chart, was taken from the U.S. Department of Homeland Security, Federal Emergency Management Agency, http://www.fema.gov/hazard/dproc.shtm.

- The estimated cost of repairing the damage
- The demographics of the affected area
- State and local governments' capabilities

The Stafford Act does not prescribe exact criteria to guide FEMA's recommendations or the president's decision. As a prerequisite to federal disaster assistance under the act though, a governor must take "appropriate action" and provide information on the nature and amount of state and local resources committed to alleviating the disaster's impacts. Other relevant considerations include the following:

- The demographics of the affected areas with regard to income levels, unemployment, concentrations of senior citizens, and the like
- The degree to which insurance covers the damage
- The degree to which people in the disaster area have been "traumatized"
- The amount of disaster-related unemployment the event has produced
- The amount of assistance available from other federal agencies, such as the Small Business Administration and its disaster loans to homeowners and businesses
- The extent to which state and local governments are capable of dealing with the disaster on their own
- The amount of disaster assistance coming from volunteer organizations and the adequacy of that assistance given the magnitude of the disaster
- The amount of rental housing available for emergency occupancy
- The nature and degree of health and safety problems posed by the disaster and its effects
- The extent of damage to essential service facilities, such as utilities and medical, police, and fires services[35]

FEMA also evaluates the impacts of a disaster at the county, local government, and tribal levels. It considers whether critical facilities are involved; how much insurance coverage is in force that could provide affected parties reimbursement for various losses; the degree of hazard mitigation a state or local government has undertaken prior to the disaster; recent disaster history; and the availability of federal assistance aside from that to be provided by a presidential declaration.

Factors that reduce the chances that a governor's request for a presidential declaration of major disaster or emergency will be approved are several. Obviously, major infrastructure loss and widespread or intense human suffering advances deservedness, whereas ample insurance coverage that helps alleviate loss and advance recovery diminishes worthiness. Also, when there is evidence that the requesting governments failed to take reasonable steps to mitigate against the disaster before it transpired, or when state or local negligence is apparent, deservedness goes down.

Sometimes other federal agencies besides FEMA host disaster programs that may sufficiently address the needs of the disaster in question, such that a presidential declaration of major disaster or emergency is unnecessary. Governors contemplating or actually in the process of filing requests for presidential declarations may be dissuaded from doing so by FEMA or White House officials, who steer them to federal agencies better suited to assist them in their response and recovery given the nature of the event. For example, when the I-35 bridge disastrously collapsed in Minneapolis in August 2007, a presidential disaster declaration was unnecessary because the Department of Transportation, aided by the Army Corps of Engineers, the FBI, and other federal agencies, made available help and resources such that a presidential disaster declaration was unwarranted.

When a governor seeks a presidential declaration for an incident that does not conform to standard eligibility requirements, FEMA may recommend to the president that the governor's request be denied.

FEMA relies most heavily on how the assessment of a state's capability compares with the costs imposed by the disaster. Each governor requesting a declaration is expected to demonstrate to FEMA and the president that the state is "unable to adequately respond to the disaster or emergency," of whatever nature, and that federal assistance is therefore needed. The "unable to adequately respond" condition is often highly controversial. Some governors claim that state budget limitations make it impossible for them to "adequately respond." Some claim that they do not have reserve funds sufficient to pay for the costs of the response. Some governors indicate that their state has no disaster relief program in law to match FEMA's and so in the absence of a presidential declaration many victims will be without government assistance. FEMA's, and the president's, ability to judge "unable to adequately respond" is often complicated by news media coverage of the event, political pressures imposed on both FEMA officials and the president by legislators and other officials in the damage zone, and the difficulty of calculating state (and local) disaster response and recovery capacity.

Under the Public Assistance program (the government-to-government aid program that pays for infrastructure repair and reimburses certain disaster expenses of nonprofit organizations), FEMA examines the estimated cost of the assistance, using such factors as the cost per capita within the state. In 2007 FEMA used a figure of $1 per capita damage costs as an indicator that the disaster is of sufficient magnitude to warrant federal assistance. This figure is to be adjusted annually based on changes in the Consumer Price Index. In addition, FEMA established for each county a cost-indexed threshold of $2.50 per capita.[36]

However, it is difficult and sometimes impossible for FEMA officials to ascertain that an event warrants a presidential declaration unless preliminary damage assessments are first conducted and analyzed (often through photographs or video recordings) or unless media coverage of the event makes it obvious a major disaster has occurred. Moreover, it is difficult to judge whether state and local areas are capable of recovering on their own if disaster damage has not been assessed beforehand. Consequently, sometimes the president issues declarations of major disaster or emergency without documentary evidence that the disasters have met FEMA's criteria.

The Role of Congress

Lawmakers care deeply about disasters, emergencies, and the substance and process of presidential declaration issuance. When the Disaster Act of 1950 became law, Congress was tacitly conceding that it should not be in the business of legislating disaster relief for every disaster or emergency that transpires in the United States. Nevertheless, Congress as an institution and congressional lawmakers themselves enter into the politics and policy of disasters in myriad ways. When a disaster or emergency is threatened or is imminent, lawmakers representing jurisdictions in the threatened zone often press the president to mobilize federal help or issue a declaration of emergency. Some researchers have discovered in presidential library documents evidence that presidents considering a disaster declaration request submitted by a governor receive, as a matter of routine, a list of the names of the lawmakers whose districts are affected by a disaster event.[41]

Senators and representatives often petition the president as an entire state delegation to confer a declaration. Moreover, lawmakers frequently contact the White House about matters of disaster or emergency. Sometimes individual lawmakers seek audiences with the president or with White House staff to press for federal help.

THE ROLE OF NEWS
AND PUBLIC RELATIONS

Over the past thirty or more years, presidents have taken a greater interest in disasters, particularly major ones. Disasters have become targets of camcorder politics in which political officials seek opportunities to be filmed at disaster sites in order to exhibit compassion and at the same time demonstrate responsiveness to the public, actions that may yield them political benefits.[37] President Carter issued a presidential disaster declaration in Air Force One while flying over the volcanic eruption of Mount Saint Helens in Washington State. President Reagan was once photographed shoveling sand into a gunnysack on the banks of a flooding Mississippi River after issuing a presidential declaration of major disaster. President George H. W. Bush was filmed commiserating with victims of the Loma Prieta earthquake in a heavily damaged San Francisco neighborhood, weeks after having issued a declaration for the quake. Television cameras showed President Clinton at shelters and inspecting freeway damage in the days after he issued a declaration for the Northridge earthquake. Similarly, President George W. Bush visited the Pentagon and the World Trade Center "ground zero" in the days after the 9/11 terrorist attacks to exhibit compassion, concern, and resolve to prevent future events. He did likewise after Hurricane Katrina in September 2005 when he visited Louisiana and toured flood-damaged areas inside New Orleans. Today, Americans expect their president both to dispatch federal disaster help and to personally visit damaged areas. It is now customary for most of the president's cabinet, especially officials heading disaster-relevant departments, to visit major disaster sites.[38]

How presidents manage disasters and how responsive they are perceived to be to the needs of victims have far-ranging political and electoral consequences, which underlines the

importance of the role of the FEMA director. How well the FEMA director manages the agency's response to disaster is of great political importance to the president and his staff.[39]

The Clinton administration appreciated the role of the news media in covering disasters. Both President Clinton and FEMA director Witt emphasized postdisaster public relations, in part because they believed the president's public image was at stake in disaster circumstances. The public requires reassurance that a president is doing all he can to help disaster victims. The need for the president to provide reassurance, backed by action, was underscored after Hurricane Katrina. Not only was President Bush perceived to have performed poorly in managing the early stages of the disaster, but he actually went on national television to apologize for his own behavior and for the failures of the government's disaster response. Again there were political consequences. Heavy Republican losses in House and Senate races in the midterm elections of November 2006 were attributed to public dissatisfaction with the war in Iraq and with the Bush administration's poor performance in the Katrina catastrophe as well.

How the FEMA director and staff manage the federal response, and how they portray this effort to the media, shapes public opinion of both the presidency and the agency. Major disasters customarily, but not always, pull the nation together, encourage a centralization of authority, and often improve the president's approval ratings in public opinion polls.[40] Such activity promotes public awareness of the disaster across the state, nation, and world. It underscores the legitimacy of the government's response and of the presidency, and it may convey a greater sense of urgency to responders and to those considering the offer of help.

FEMA has many overseers within Congress. Before FEMA was folded into the Department of Homeland Security, it had a wide variety of House and Senate committees and subcommittees with jurisdiction over its programs in whole or in part. Since FEMA entered the Department of Homeland Security, Congress has reorganized these committees such that there is now a House Committee on Homeland Security. Moreover, the former Senate Governmental Affairs Committee elected to expand its title to become the Committee on Homeland Security and Governmental Affairs. However, many of the twenty-two federal agencies folded into DHS retain their traditional jurisdiction and so retain their traditional House and Senate committee and subcommittee overseers, the vast majority of which are not within the two House and Senate homeland security committees. This situation significantly complicates management of DHS units and risks muddled congressional oversight of those units.[42]

Lawmakers are key players in matters of furnishing federal money for disaster relief. The President's Disaster Relief Fund, administered by DHS-FEMA today, is replenished by "no-year" appropriations monies. "No year" simply means that there is no time limit attached to the spending authority of an appropriation law. The fund receives an annual congressional appropriation, but it is often insufficient to cover federal payouts for declared disasters and emergencies during the federal fiscal year. Congress has the power to approve emergency supplemental appropriations to recapitalize the fund. Congress never lets the Disaster Relief Fund exhaust its spending authority. Even if that possibility existed, however, the president has permission to borrow money from the Treasury to pay federal expenses on disasters lacking congressionally approved spending authority.[43]

The tendency is for each administration and its disaster agency to ask for the maximum emergency supplemental appropriation they think necessary. It is always better to estimate high rather than low, as no administration wants to have to return to Congress to seek an additional emergency supplemental for the same disaster (although this sometimes happens). Because these appropriations come with no spending expiration date, and because the disasters they are aimed at often end up costing the federal government less than the total spending authority conferred, spending authority in the fund often accumulates and so pays for other, smaller disasters and emergencies. However, megadisasters or catastrophes periodically swallow up all of the fund's spending authority. It is then that Congress goes to work on emergency supplemental appropriations.

The politics of congressional enactment of emergency supplemental appropriations often makes it obvious why Congress should continue to entrust the president with the bulk of routine declaration authority. **Emergency supplementals** must, like all legislation to be enacted into law, pass both the House and Senate. Whether or not an emergency supplemental is open to "riders" (nongermane legislation attached to a bill) in either body is often both controversial and consequential. Individual lawmakers often add to emergency supplementals riders that could never win majority support were they not attached to "must pass" emergency supplementals for disasters. Presidents have come to detest emergency supplementals because those measures often come to the Oval Office laden with riders that confer pork-barrel or special interest benefits he would never otherwise approve. As the president has no line-item veto to remove what he judges to be undeserved riders, he is more or less compelled to sign the emergency supplementals into law or otherwise be judged heartless and unresponsive to the needs of disaster victims who are awaiting the federal help the supplemental will provide. Emergency supplementals pose other problems. They often drive up the federal deficit and so may damage fiscal policy. The legislative process is often slow and cumbersome, even if riders are not permitted on the emergency supplemental. Some Republican and Democratic lawmakers have come to view emergency supplementals for disaster as a form of redistributive politics in which a zero-sum game applies. One part of the nation gains at the expense of another part of the nation. States with large congressional delegations that frequently experience disasters or emergencies have been alleged to have "gamed" the system in a way that funnels sizable federal resources to their postdisaster redevelopment.

On top of this, presidential and congressional political considerations are alleged to affect "the rate of disaster declaration" issuance and the allocation of FEMA disaster expenditures across states.[44] Researchers have shown that states politically important to the president have relatively higher rates of disaster declaration request approvals than other states. They have also discovered that federal disaster relief expenditures are relatively larger in states having congressional representation on FEMA oversight committees than in states unrepresented on FEMA oversight committees. Remarkably, one pair of political economists have a posited **congressional dominance model**, which predicts that nearly half of all disaster relief is motivated politically rather than by need.[45] The same researchers assert that there is a possibility that political influence may affect the outcome of gubernatorial requests for presidential disaster declarations at two distinct stages: during the initial decision to declare a disaster or not and in the decision of how much money to allocate for the disaster.[46] Here they assume that bureaus, like FEMA, follow congressional preferences and that the responsible congressional committees, FEMA jurisdictional overseers, make sure that they do so. Here legislators are assumed to behave as wealth maximizers seeking to direct federal resources to their home states or districts.[47]

However, the political geography of declaration issuance demonstrates that FEMA's alleged effort to reward legislators (the congressional dominance model) on its authorizations or appropriations oversight committees is far-fetched and arguable. This is because the ultimate decision to approve or reject a governor's request for a declaration is made by the president, not by FEMA officials. In effect, FEMA officials have little leeway in matters of presidential declaration decision making. FEMA officials compile a recommendation to the president regarding whether a governor's request for major disaster declaration should be approved or denied. Presumably, FEMA officials have considered the worthiness of a governor's request in accord with thresholds of loss at the state and county levels. The FEMA director (since 2002 in consultation with the DHS secretary) provides the president with his own recommendation on whether the president should approve or reject the governor's declaration request. It is highly unlikely, although difficult to prove, that any FEMA director would engage in strategic behavior aimed at placating the desires of lawmakers on FEMA oversight committees by endorsing unworthy or undeserving requests for presidential approval. It is difficult to prove this because the FEMA director's memorandum to the president is a matter of executive privilege and so is not open to public scrutiny. Moreover, every president is free to disregard the FEMA director and agency recommendation on any governor's request for a presidential declaration of major disaster or emergency.

Still, presidents, on their own, may use their declaration issuance discretion to reward states that are the political homes of key House and Senate legislators and to advance electoral strategies beneficial to themselves, to their fellow party members on Capitol Hill, and to other political actors they judge to be important, including the requesting governors themselves. The Stafford Act (1988) allows the president to unilaterally declare a disaster without the approval of Congress. Hence, the president may use this power to punish or reward legislators who support or oppose his policies. He may also want to "simply tarnish the image of opposing party legislators in hopes of reducing their probability of reelection." [48] Owing to the vague language of the Stafford Act and preceding federal laws since 1950, the president is free to decide what constitutes a disaster or emergency and free to decide whether or not he wants to issue a presidential declaration for the event." [49] This is even more the case since the 9/11 terror attacks, since enactment of the Homeland Security Act of 2002, and since the issuance by President George W. Bush of a series of homeland security presidential directives. Since 9/11, Congress has accorded the president powers that have vastly increased presidential discretion in matters of disaster. Disasters and emergencies are within a spectrum of possible "incidents of national significance." [50] However, not every declaration of major disaster or emergency is declared an incident of national significance. The determination of "national significance" resides with the president and the Homeland Security secretary.

The Role of Governors

Many governors, as state chief executives, possess emergency powers applicable to disasters or emergencies within their respective states. They have at their disposal state emergency management agencies, other state agency assistance, and the state's National Guard (along with reserve and active duty forces made available by the president, if needed).

Through state legislative work and often governor assistance, state governments enact emergency management laws. A variety of state agencies fashion codes and regulations subject to supervision by the governor and oversight by the state legislature. State government is a conduit through which extensive federal-local interchange takes place. In turn, state governments are responsible for implementing and enforcing a great many federal laws, among them federal emergency management laws. States are obligated to assist their respective local governments in development and maintenance of emergency management responsibilities.

Governors play a key role in the presidential declaration process. They need to mobilize and supervise their state agencies as those agencies address the emergency or disaster. They need to ensure that disaster loss information has been compiled and included in their request to the president. They need to consult and work cooperatively with local elected executives and other local government officials who are in the areas affected by the disaster or emergency. When a disaster strikes, local authorities and individuals often request help from their state government as well as private relief organizations. Local governments sometimes seek federal disaster assistance, often with state encouragement. Customarily, the process begins when county or municipal leaders, or both, ask their governor to declare a state emergency. These same local officials may ask the governor to request a presidential declaration. Governors may issue, if they believe it is warranted, a state declaration of disaster. They typically do this through an executive order or proclamation. The order usually describes the nature of the emergency, where it occurred, and the authority under which the governor makes the declaration.

Often, governors request presidential emergency declarations when a disaster seems imminent and federal aid would help in the pre-event response stage of a disaster. Many of these emergency declarations cover events that do not later earn a presidential declaration of major disaster.

Customarily, a governor must ask the president to declare a major disaster or emergency. However, the Stafford Act of 1988 and several preceding laws empower the president to

HOW THINGS WORK

VAGUE CRITERIA AND POLITICAL SUBJECTIVITY

For many years, the process and criteria of disaster declaration has been purposely subjective to allow the president discretion to address a wide range of events and circumstances. Former FEMA director Witt once remarked that there are no definitive objective evaluators that could be used in the declaration process, although he recommended that FEMA endeavor to establish some. Without such objective criteria, governors and their state disaster officials have little to guide them in estimating whether to go ahead with a request for presidential declaration of major disaster or emergency. They have little basis for concluding in advance whether their petition for a presidential declaration will be approved or denied.

However, as long as a governor or other state officials know that the state can afford to shoulder the 25 percent share of the 75/25 federal aid formula contained in a presidential disaster declaration, they have an incentive to request a federal declaration. State officials have an incentive to "cry poor" in petitioning for federal help, minimizing their own capacity and capability to address disaster. Some argue for reducing presidential discretion in the review of governors' requests for disaster declarations and often point to the disaster declaration systems used by Canada and Australia. Canadian provinces and Australian states and territories rely less upon federal assistance during disasters than do U.S.

states. Both in Canada and Australia (nations with federal systems), "there is no requirement for an explicit disaster declaration" by the prime minister and "the decision to authorize federal reimbursement is essentially automatic." [52] Canadian provinces and Australian states and territories must pay out sums in disaster relief that exceed certain deductible levels before they qualify for their respective nation's federal assistance. It should be noted that the provinces, states, and territories of these two nations are expected to shoulder the brunt of disaster management and relief duties, in service to their local governments. [53]

Some recommend making declaration judgments more of an administrative determination under which states would have to experience preset thresholds of damage to qualify; states would be expected to pay an upfront deductible sum of money and pay a much larger share of the total cost than the 25 percent that is now the state share in the United States. Such proposals are interesting but they tend to overlook the fact that American states come in all shapes and sizes. Some states cover huge expanses of land but contain relatively few people (Alaska, Idaho, Montana, North Dakota, Utah, Wyoming), some have relatively small populations and small land area (Delaware, New Hampshire, Rhode Island, Vermont). Conversely, the United States has heavily populated declare a major disaster (since 1950) or emergency (since 1974) before a governor asks for one or in the absence of a governor's request altogether. All governors have the authority to request a declaration. Sometimes in the interest of speeding mobilization a governor may short-circuit or expedite the usual process of submitting the request through FEMA and petition the president directly. In addition, federal law permits presidents to issue declarations of major disaster or emergency in the absence of a governor's request when there is a major federal interest

states that cover a wide range of land area sizes. The issue here is that American demographics make it difficult if not arbitrary to impose disaster deductibles on states and territories. American disaster declaration history shows that presidential discretion may take the degree of human suffering into account even if losses are relative light and damage is confined to a small area. There are many examples of a presidential disaster declaration issued to a single county in a single state, the most notable perhaps being the declaration that went to New York State and New York City after the first World Trade Center bombing in 1993.

Americans would be expected to oppose the idea of disaster deductibles for their states for a variety of reasons. First, using deductibles as thresholds for issuing federal declarations limits presidential flexibility to address disasters and emergencies. Second, it makes deservedness depend on loss accounting rather than on other indicators of need. Third, Americans, unlike a few of their elected representatives, probably do not generally perceive presidential disaster declaration spending as redistribution of taxpayer monies from one state to another. Few would conceive of federal disaster spending as a zero-sum game in which one part of the nation gains unfairly at the expense of another part of the nation. Fourth, the massive economic integration of the nation and the pervasiveness of glob-

al trade and economic transactions create a national interdependence. A small disaster in Florida may have significant economic consequences for interests in California, Massachusetts, Michigan, or Texas. Some may find it ironic that giant European reinsurance companies worry deeply about hurricanes threatening strikes along the U.S. Gulf or Atlantic coasts. A major earthquake in California could easily, though temporarily, wipe out the liquidity of American auto insurance firms, protracting the claim settlement of a fender-bender accident in Massachusetts. Some disasters affect entire regions of the United States and it would be foolish to discriminate between states in a massive damage zone on the basis of a deductible payment system of loss.

Many emergency declarations, more than major disaster declarations, are likely to stretch the rule that states must lack the capacity to recover on their own to qualify for a presidential declaration. In times of tight state and local budgets, or when they are in deficit, an emergency offers governors a flexible path for securing federal help. FEMA records disclose that snowstorms, windstorms, minor flooding, and drought are the most common types of emergency declarations. Emergencies also allow politically subjective determinations to come into play.

(the federal government is a directly involved party in the event) or when a governor is unable officially to request a presidential declaration.

Although the president has legal authority to issue a declaration of major disaster or emergency in the absence of a governor's request, presidents are reluctant to do so, and usually do so only in truly extraordinary circumstances, unless they choose to completely waive the state's matching share of declaration costs. Obviously, presidents do not want to commit a state and its localities to paying the state's share without first receiving a request from the governor that stipulates that the state is willing take on such a burden.

Governors customarily consult their respective state emergency management officials before requesting a presidential declaration. The governor may authorize a state-level preliminary damage assessment if state officials are not already assessing damage with local authorities. Sometimes, if the disaster appears to be beyond state and local response capacity, the governor can ask FEMA to join state and local personnel in conducting a preliminary damage assessment.

Governors, in requesting emergency declarations, do not have to prove to the president that the emergency disaster is beyond state and local response capabilities. Instead, they have to demonstrate that federal assistance is needed to save lives; protect property and public health; or lessen or avert the threat of catastrophe. Under federal law, FEMA's expenditures under an emergency declaration may not exceed $5 million.[51] However, when an emergency declaration is in effect and federal spending approaches the $5 million limit, the president need only notify Congress in a letter that the $5 million cap will be exceeded and this allows spending on the emergency declaration to exceed the limit. Many events that have earned emergency declarations have exceeded $5 million and the president has routinely notified Congress that spending would exceed the cap in these incidents. Governors appreciate presidential declarations of emergency because they supply federal funds and other assistance quickly, do not require the collection of state and local information to document need, and often furnish help when the full scope of the emergency or disaster is either not yet understood or is still unfolding.

FEMA'S ROLE IN THE DECLARATION PROCESS

The federal declaration process usually follows these steps. If the governor requests a major disaster declaration through FEMA the agency prepares a White House package. The package contains documents prepared for the president's action on a governor's request. The package includes the governor's request and the FEMA director's memorandum, made up of the following items:

- A summary of significant aspects of the event
- Statistics relative to damage and losses
- Outlines of the contributions made by federal, state, local, and private agencies
- A list of the unmet needs for which the governor seeks federal assistance
- A recommended course of action for the president

The package also contains appropriate letters and announcements related to the action, including the FEMA director's recommendation to the president regarding whether to approve or deny the governor's request.

In many cases the FEMA Regional Office initially receives the governor's request first; officials there prepare a regional summary, analysis, and recommendation. The summary contains only factual data concerning the disaster event, whereas the analysis and recommendation sections may contain opinions and evaluations. The FEMA Regional Office forwards the governor's request along with the regional summary, analysis, and recommendation to FEMA national offices. At headquarters, the director and senior FEMA staff evaluate the request, prepare the White House Package, and then forward it on to the president accompanied by the FEMA director's recommendation. The president is free to accept or reject the governor's request. Finally, the president makes a decision to either grant or deny the request.

Today, when a situation threatens human health and safety, and a disaster is imminent but not yet declared, the secretary of the Department of Homeland Security may preposition employees and supplies. DHS monitors the status of the situation, communicates with state emergency officials on potential assistance requirements, deploys teams and resources to maximize the speed and effectiveness of the anticipated federal response and, when necessary, performs preparedness and preliminary damage assessment activities.[54]

Early after its inception FEMA developed a general set of criteria by which the president may judge gubernatorial requests for declarations of major disasters or emergencies. However, the president is not legally bound to use or follow those criteria. A governor's request for disaster or emergency relief is not necessarily granted. As mentioned, presidents can issue a turndown. A turndown is the action authorized by the president and signed by the director of FEMA that denies a governor's request for a major disaster or emergency declaration. Every president from Truman to George W. Bush has turned down some gubernatorial requests for declarations (see Table 4-1). The president is as free to turn down emergency declaration requests as he is to turn down requests for presidential declarations of major disaster. Declarations, even if approved, may embody denial of certain kinds of assistance and may deny inclusion of certain areas. In other words, declarations stipulate approval and disapproval of certain requested program assistance.

In addition, sometimes presidents approve governors' requests submitted as emergencies but then go on to declare the events major disasters later. The president initially approved as emergencies the bombing of the Oklahoma City Murrah Office Building and the 9/11 attacks on the World Trade Center and the Pentagon, but within hours the president declared each a major disaster. Presidents do not need a second gubernatorial request to elevate an emergency to a major disaster. The decision may flow logically from official recognition that the emergency phase of life saving and property protection is at an end and a major disaster declaration is needed to mobilize the additional federal agencies, spending, and resources necessary in disaster recovery.

Moreover, governors may request that certain localities (usually counties or the state's equivalent of counties) be added to a presidential declaration already in force.[55] Since 1988, the federal coordinating officer (FCO) assigned to respond to the disaster, not the president, has possessed the authority to add counties to a presidential declaration of major disaster.[56] If

| TABLE 4-1 | Presidential Approvals and Turndowns of Governor Requests for Disaster Declarations, 1953–2005 |

President	Time span	Approvals			Turndowns			Turndown percentage		
		Major[a]	Emerg[b]	Total	Major[c]	Emerg[d]	Total	Major	Emerg	Total
Eisenhower	5/2/53–1/21/61	106	0	106	55	0	55	34	0	34
Kennedy	1/21/61–11/20/63	52	0	52	22	0	22	30	0	30
Johnson	11/23/63–1/21/69	93	0	93	49	0	49	35	0	35
Nixon	1/21/69–8/5/74	195	1	196	102	15	117	34	94	37
Ford	8/5/74–1/21/77	76	23	99	35	7	42	32	23	30
Carter	1/21/77–1/21/81	112	59	171	91	37	128	45	39	43
Reagan	1/21/81–1/21/89	184	9	193	96	16	112	34	64	37
G. H. W. Bush	1/21/89–1/21/93	158	2	160	43	3	46	21	60	22
Clinton	1/21/93–1/21/01	380	68	448	103	13	116	21	16	21
G. W. Bush	1/21/01–9/22/05	247	98	345	46	12	58	16	11	14
Total		1,603	260	1,863	642	103	745	29	28	28

Sources: FEMA, Declaration Information System (DARIS), June 1997, and Federal Emergency Management Information System (FEMIS), Dec. 2001, Department of Homeland Security, Emergency Preparedness and Response Directorate; and DHS Justification of Estimates FY04, March 2003; 9/11/01–9/22/05 turndown data: Sen. Thomas R. Carper, D-Del., to author.

Note: Date of declaration checked for each administration to the day.
a. Represents approved presidential declarations of major disasters, which began in 1953.
b. Represents approved presidential declarations of emergencies. Emergency declarations began in 1974.
c. Represents president's turndown of a governor's request for a presidential declaration of major disaster.
d. Represents president's turndown of a governor's request for a presidential declaration of emergency.

the president denies a governor's request for a declaration, that governor has the right to appeal. In rare instances, a governor may win a declaration on appeal.

History demonstrates that from May 1953, the time of the first presidential disaster declaration, until September 2005, the president has approved about seven in every ten (71.5 percent) gubernatorial requests. Since 1989, following adoption of the Stafford Act, the odds that the president will approve a governor's request have risen to about a four in five (80.3 percent) chance (see Table 4-1). Certainly, the broader authority to judge what is or is not a disaster under the Stafford Act has provided presidents since 1988 with more latitude to approve unusual or "marginal" events as disasters or emergencies. This may be one reason for the higher rate of gubernatorial request approvals since 1988.

PRESIDENTS AND DISTRIBUTIVE POLITICS

Over the years federal disaster officials have attempted to establish definitive and quantitative requirements for disaster declaration eligibility. One such effort would have tied declarations to damage translated into dollars per capita.[57] These efforts proposed rigorous declaration criteria, but presidents have resisted and Congress has vehemently opposed such measures.[58] Presidents do not want their range of declaration discretion further circumscribed or ceded to federal disaster officials.[59] Legislators want assurance that they may use their legitimate political influence to press for declarations directly from the president when their home states and districts experience incidents or events they consider emergencies or disasters.[60]

Presidents, assisted by their staffs and top disaster agency officials, must judge each governor's request for a declaration based on need. However, both managerial and political factors may enter the president's judgment. Clearly, initial damage assessments, imminent disaster threat (for example, a hurricane about to make landfall), and news media coverage of an event, and the like may make it obvious to the president that a governor's request deserves approval.[61] There are also many instances when presidents, and perhaps their advisers, are unconvinced of the need or worthiness of the request. Still, the president makes these determinations in a political environment.[62]

Disaster declarations have been called an easy-to-use political tool of the president. Using data provided in Table 4-1, from 1989 through 2005, presidents (G. H. W. Bush, Clinton, G. W. Bush) have turned down as a collective group 19.65 percent of the major disaster declaration requests they have received. Table 4-1 data for the same period shows that about 20.9 percent of emergency declaration requests have been denied by the president. When the requests are accepted, FEMA, not the president, decides how much money to allocate.

During his four years in office, President George H. W. Bush averaged thirty-nine disaster declarations annually. The seven years of the Clinton presidency that Reeves studied averaged seventy-two disasters per year.[63] In his 2007 paper, Reeves reports that for presidential disaster declarations issued from 1981 through 2004, "electoral considerations have come to shade a policy," referring to presidential disaster declaration issuance, "that should be firmly based on need." [64] Reeves maintains that "[p]rior to the Stafford Act (1988), there was virtually no relationship between the competitiveness of a state and disaster declarations." [65] He is referring to statewide presidential election contests in which an incumbent president is competing to win state electoral votes, especially in certain battleground states. He asserts that "voters react and reward presidents for presidential disaster declarations." [66]

Political parties view particular states as "friends," "enemies," or "competitive," based on their likelihood of voting for the party's presidential candidate.[67] When it comes to disaster declarations and presidential political strategizing, "the size of the state (in terms of electoral votes) and whether the political parties view it as 'competitive' matters quite a bit." [68]

Large states friendly to the president appear to be more successful in winning declarations than large, unfriendly states. Reeves declares, "The incumbent president (or his party) is rewarded by voters for providing relief in the wake of natural disasters to the tune of over 1.5 points in the statewide popular vote." [69] For Reeves, "the Stafford Act transformed the disaster declaration process into a highly political exercise." [70] Studies by Reeves, Garrett and Sobel, and Dymon infer that the pattern of presidential declaration approvals is consistent with the "politically driven, distributive politics" model. When declarations are examined in terms of political geography and elections, it seems that presidents, at least since 1988, are acting "on the basis of political motives, political pressures, and political responsiveness more than they are issued on the basis of objective need." [71] Governors of large and heavily populated states enjoying a sizable number of electoral votes and previously supportive of the incumbent president may seek to capitalize on this advantage and ask for declarations more often than they normally would. From this perspective, we would expect political factors to influence the odds of receiving a presidential disaster declaration.

HOW THINGS WORK

OVERWHELMED OR OVER BUDGET?

The word "overwhelmed" is subject to different interpretations. It is extremely difficult to determine whether a municipality, county, or state is overwhelmed by a disaster or emergency. The word "overwhelmed" connotes "incapacity." A dictionary definition of "overwhelm" is to surge and submerge, to engulf, to overcome completely, either physically or emotionally, to overpower, to turn over or upset.[72] Presumably, if a municipality, county, or state can respond to and recover from a disaster or emergency using their own resources, they are not overwhelmed. However, the term "overwhelmed" is not easily defined within the realm of intergovernmental relations. Even the worst disasters seldom terminate or suspend the operation of state and local government. In many disasters, state and local governments suffer significant economic losses and government aid to disaster victims is fully justified and deserved, but state and local governments are rarely overwhelmed.

Therefore, "overwhelm" is a disputatious term. Some governors have requested presidential declarations of disaster on the grounds that they must maintain a balanced budget or because they have no "rainy day" money to pay for the recovery costs. Municipalities and counties have grown accustomed to having the huge costs of public employee overtime and debris removal paid for by the federal government under presidential declarations. Governors are tempted to ask for declarations in advance of the onset of disaster because they reason that county and municipal disaster response will be more robust if federal subsidization of response costs is assured ahead of time. Senators and representatives have frequently pressured various presidents to approve declaration requests submitted by the governors of their home states.

A governor's temptation to "cry poor" before, during, or after some state-level misfortune is often, pardon the pun, "overwhelming." FEMA's deservedness criteria could provide a guide for governors, but only if the president makes declaration decisions in conformity with FEMA's recommendations. As noted, the president is not compelled to do so.

Assuming the president does generally follow the recommendations, governors may find that asking for declarations when losses or damage are less than the recommendations runs the embarrassing risk of having a request turned down. Yet, most governors would not judge a turndown as great embarrassment, particularly in an era when presidential disaster declarations seem to be more freely issued and when a request may provide significant federal benefits to the state.

As mentioned earlier, once the president approves a governor's request for a declaration it is the job of FEMA, not the president, to actually determine how much money is to be allocated to states, counties, and other eligible entities under specified conditions (that is, damage assessment), laws, and rules—all subject to audit by a variety of government offices. Political discretion exercised by the president is likely to be evident when the president approves gubernatorial requests on low-damage, marginal incidents, involving relatively low federal payouts. This means the relationship is an "inverse one." In other words, the lower the federal payouts are for various declarations the higher the probability that political considerations at the presidential level played a role in a president's approval of a declaration.[73] Nonetheless, the federal government is not pushing disaster relief money out of planes. People must apply for it, must prove eligibility, must document their losses, must show that their insurance is not duplicating federal disaster relief, and must submit to inspection and audit. State and local governments are expected to do even more than that in securing federal funds to repair infrastructure. State and local governments also must shoulder a share of the cost of rebuilding under many disaster declarations.

Important politically subjective determinations come into play in the matter of "marginal" disasters. Marginal disasters are those events that are far less than catastrophic, that are not matters of national security, and that are near or within the response and recovery capacity of the state or states in which they occur.[74] Analysis of a half century of presidential disaster declarations discloses that there have been hundreds of marginal disasters, some granted a presidential declaration and some turned down. Specific case examples indicate that there are definite losers in the competition for presidential declarations. For example, in 1980, Florida experienced flooding after a dam failure and President Carter denied the Florida governor's request for a declaration. In the same year, he turned down two requests from Oklahoma within a two-week period for a declaration to cover devastation from severe storms and flooding.

The record of approvals and turndowns raises questions about how gubernatorial requests for presidential declarations are considered, particularly for marginal disaster denials. For many years there have been no objective criteria governing approvals and turndowns, and as stated earlier, only the president who received the governor's request knows the basis upon which a request is approved or denied. Nor is it possible to ascertain statistically from government records whether or not fatalities played a role in a president's decision. FEMA does not keep records of fatalities and injuries sustained in declared disasters or emergencies.

Governors also play the game by seeking presidential declarations for drought, crop failures, minor wildfires, small floods, beach erosion, and a wide range of other calamities that cannot be considered catastrophes, major disasters, or emergencies under the "overwhelm" or "beyond the capability of the state/local government to adequately respond" condition.

CONCLUSION AND SUMMARY

"People look to the President for reassurance, a feeling that things will be all right, that the President will take care of his people." [85] This is an important management responsibility for presidents. As the nation has come to face increasing numbers, wider varieties, and often relatively larger scale disasters and emergencies, changes in law have given presidents more latitude in deciding what actually constitutes a disaster or emergency. Because the United States chose not to significantly limit presidential discretion in judging the deservedness of governors' requests, the system tolerates a degree of subjectivity, and sometimes political bias, in how presidents decide whether or not to approve or turn down any single gubernatorial request. Hence, some presidents have created new categories of disaster type. Moreover, the availability of the President's Disaster Relief Fund provides a pool of spending authority presidents may draw on to pay the federal costs of major disasters and emergencies they so declare.

HOW THINGS WORK

FUNCTIONAL FEDERALISM VERSUS PORK-BARRELING

The theory of **functional federalism** identifies distinctive areas of competence for each level of government. It assumes that local governments are the ones that are best able to design and implement developmental programs, especially those programs that involve the physical and social infrastructure. This is because local service providers know best the quality and level of public services and thus can best respond to citizen choice.[75] Furthermore, emergency management is best conducted on the local government level, although there must be some state involvement for the purpose of coordination across local jurisdictions.

To use economic language, in order to prevent disasters from having negative economic spillover effects in other places and to ensure that all local governments possess emergency management capability that is at least consistent with a national minimum standard, the federal government can promote local emergency management through grants. Emergency management aims to "sustain or restore a community's pre-disaster condition, not to alter the distribution of wealth."[76] Consequently, functional federalism applies in emergency management if local government pursues developmental endeavors, such as those in disaster response and

recovery, whereas the national government must be more limited and aimed at efficient redistribution and possibly research, technical advancement, disaster mitigation, and national standards development. Thus, functional federalism can be defined as a "need-based, means-tested" model of presidential decision making.

Another theory applied to emergency management holds that "emergency management is promulgated by actors who are elected or appointed in the context of a representative democracy, and thus these actors can be expected to respond to various pressures exerted by their constituents."[77] In short, this legislative theory model is characterized by "politically driven, distributive politics" in which elected local public officials are likely to respond to disasters not on the basis of whether or not their local government has the ability to respond and recover on their own but on the basis of demanding federal and state assistance to meet constituent needs. These officials want to be reelected and thus they wish to curry favor with their electorate by providing tangible benefits for which they can claim credit.[78] Simultaneously, elected local and state officials attempt to shield their constituents from the costs of disaster response and recovery by funding these costs at the national level, which diffuses

A tolerated political dilemma continues. On the one hand presidents are accorded the freedom to disregard recommendations of FEMA in making decisions about whether to approve or turn down governors' requests for presidential declarations of major disaster or emergency. U.S. disaster policy maintains that the president should not be restricted in using declaration authority to address calamities, some expected and others quite unforeseen, that the nation may face. On the other hand, the president's freedom to decide what is and what is not a disaster or emergency invites subjectivity. Congress and taxpayers sometimes suspect that political motives and factors as well as the temptation to distribute various forms of federal largess occasionally draw presidents into issuing declarations to states for undeserving events. Some the fiscal burden over the largest possible population.[79] Under legislative theory the national government inappropriately assumes developmental responsibilities, often resulting in pork-barrel spending and encroachment into local response and recovery activities. Local government officials, meanwhile, tend to shape their behavior to conform to federal criteria in order to secure as many resources as possible.

If the "need-based, means-tested" model of presidential decision making applies, then presidents are likely to defer to the professional judgment and recommendations of their top disaster managers, who themselves are judging the governor's request against a general set of qualification criteria.[80] Requesters would ask for declarations only if they were genuinely unable to respond and recover from an emergency or disaster on their own. Decision making would rest upon administrative consideration of "need" for the declaration, not upon political responsiveness to the interested parties. The president would tend to behave as a chief executive who carefully considers the latitude the law affords him, the federal government's involvement in state and local affairs, whether states and localities have the capacity to recover from a disaster using their own resources given the case present-

ed, and the effects of his decisions on the national taxpayer and the federal budget.

Under the "politically driven, distributive politics" model, presidential decisions and requester behavior would be very often politically motivated. Presidents would tend to issue approvals generously. The few turndowns they issue would stem from their political differences with requesting governors or from their conclusion that an approval would carry too many political negatives. According to one scholar, "The president may weigh the documented need for assistance, the political costs of providing aid, the political advantage associated with giving aid, and a variety of other political and economic factors before issuing a presidential disaster declaration." [81] Another states, "The decision as to whether or not to issue a declaration is a political choice by the president, often influenced by congressional and media attention." [82] Still others conclude that FEMA itself has undergone a politicization of its administrative mechanisms.[83] I would add that the politicization of disaster should come as no surprise, since "[m]ajor disasters customarily pull the nation together, encourage a centralization of authority, and often improve the president's approval ratings in public opinion polls." [84]

allege that governors sometimes ask for presidential declarations when their states and localities could respond to and recover from the "disaster" on their own. At times governors may exploit the political subjectivity of the system in a way that garners for their state more presidential declarations, and hence generous federal subsidization of costs associated with the calamity they face, than they actually deserve. Such undeserving calamites were defined as "marginal disasters."

According to the need-based, means-tested model, presidential disaster declarations tend to reflect obvious need based on scales of damage, the degree of human suffering, and the inability of subnational governments to address the circumstances they face.[86] In other words, under this model the president's approval of governors' requests for declarations may be very much based on indisputable objective need first and foremost in almost every case. Catastrophic disasters invariably manifest the characteristics required for such approval: large-scale damage, immense human suffering, and the inability of subnational governments to address the need. Presidential political subjectivity in reviewing governors' requests for federal disaster relief is not in play when a state has experienced catastrophic disaster damage. However, catastrophic disasters still demand presidential management skills and responsiveness.

Homeland security law and policy has affected presidential authority in the matter of declaration issuance. The "incident of national significance" categorization has both expanded the range of presidential declaration issuance to include various events related to terrorism or terrorist threats, and it has subsumed many aspects of conventional declaration issuance for non-terror disasters under a broader rubric. The addition of "catastrophic incidents" formally signifies that some megadisasters have national security implications and the potential to damage the nation's economy. Presidents, advised by homeland security and federal emergency management officials, today have the power both to decide what a catastrophe is and to declare such events "catastrophic incidents." The addition of the power to make declarations for "incidents of national significance" and "catastrophic incidents" has dramatically expanded presidential discretion and has altered president-governor, federal-state relations.

For disasters that are less than catastrophic, particularly those that are marginal and that require close scrutiny of their deservedness for a presidential declaration, the "politically driven, distributive politics" model applies when the president approves those declaration requests. When presidents turn down specific gubernatorial requests for a declaration, the president is clearly opting to apply need-based, means-tested criteria. It is also reasonable to conclude that the need-based, means-tested model largely explains declaration approvals that take presidents weeks or months to decide.

Clearly, news media coverage is highly important in the realm of disasters and emergencies, as is presidential participation or coproduction in the making of the news. News media coverage of disasters has helped the politically driven, distributive-politics model assume ascendancy at the expense of need-based judgments. In addition, each president's relationship with his top federal emergency manager is a factor in how that president handles emerging disaster circumstances and governors' requests for federal assistance. So many top federal disaster managers' owing their appointments to political spoils more than to qualified disaster management expertise has helped to elevate further the distributive politics of presidential declaration decision making.

KEY TERMS AND CONCEPTS

catastrophic incidents   82

congressional dominance model   94

emergency supplementals   93

functional federalism   104

major disaster   78

National Special Security Events
(NSSEs)   82

CHAPTER 5

THE ROLE OF
SCIENTISTS AND
ENGINEERS

FOR MANY YEARS, DISASTER RESEARCH HAS HELPED GROW AND inform the profession of emergency management. Theories and concepts developed by scholars studying the physical and social dimensions of hazards and disasters have built and continue to build the foundations of the field of emergency management.

Disaster research is conducted by a broad array of experts. Scientific and engineering communities that focus on such research exist within the federal government, within academia, and within the private sector.[1] Meteorologists and atmospheric researchers are assiduously examining weather phenomena, among them hurricanes, tornadoes, severe storms, and drought, as well as global climate change. Flood phenomena are the focus of many dedicated geoscientists, engineers, meteorologists, and land-use and physical geography experts. Biomedical researchers are hard at work tracking the spread of disease, striving to prevent pandemics, and testing and developing new vaccines, some intended to protect people from bioterrorist attack. Researchers developing homeland security technology have made advances in high-speed computing and massive data storage, sophisticated computer software, and the use of satellite data and geographic information system technology.[2]

This chapter covers scientific and engineering groups who study disaster and who are developing a body of theoretical and applied knowledge aimed at improved disaster prediction, mitigation, preparedness, response, and recovery. Additionally, the chapter includes discussions of how science informs and shapes disaster policy and politics and how related intergovernmental and civil military issues play a part.

This menacing tornado photographed from a skyscraper in Tampa, Florida, moves over southern Tampa Bay, headed toward Pinellas County, in one of the state's most densely populated metropolitan areas. Fortunately, the July 1995 twister did little damage in the region and there were no injuries. The photo connotes the combination of heavy coastal settlement and tornado, severe storm, and hurricane vulnerability. Americans have placed their trust in the scientists who study disaster agents and in the engineers who design structures to mitigate the effects of disaster agents, but have Americans yet understood how their own behavior may increase their vulnerability to disaster?

RESEARCHING HAZARDS AND DISASTERS

From the 1950s onward, federal emergency management grew as an intellectual, scientific, and engineering enterprise. By the 1980s and 1990s, great advances in hazards research, most particularly in meteorology, seismology, and physical geography but also in the building sciences, climate change research, and environmental science, gave credibility to disaster research.[3]

Disaster research serves emergency management but also generates funding needs policymakers are asked to address. To pursue many lines of disaster study, researchers need expensive technical equipment. Special types of aircraft are needed to fly through hurricanes and tropical storms; uniquely outfitted ships are needed to deploy and maintain vast arrays of high-technology ocean buoys from which to monitor changes in water temperatures, currents, and chemistry; high-speed computing technology is needed to process and store prodigious information flows. And there are many other technical needs as well. Securing budget authority to pay for these needs puts many disaster researchers into the world of government lobbying. Thus, owing to the need for government funding to pay for expensive research equipment and facilities, some domains of disaster research engage what has been referred to as **"big science."** [4] The world of big science has its own politics and policy.[5] Indeed, many segments of the nation's academic community, often in cooperation with scholars outside the United States, have received government support for their research through federal agencies such as the National Oceanic and Atmospheric Administration (NOAA), the U.S. Environmental Protection Agency (EPA), the U.S. Geological Survey, the National Institute of Standards and Technology (NIST), the U.S. Army Corps of Engineers (USACE), and FEMA.

Additionally, the National Science Foundation funds a great variety of academic research endeavors, a portion pertinent to disaster studies. Many private foundations either subsidize disaster research or pursue this research using their own experts in-house. Major corporations, including giant utility companies and insurance firms, routinely pursue research aimed at the study of hazards and disasters. The National Academies—made up of the National Academy of Sciences, the National Academy of Engineering, and the Institute of Medicine, facilitated by their National Research Council—conduct numerous disaster-related research studies for various sponsors, among them federal agencies that contract with them to form panels and conduct studies. The research reports of the National Academies have been known to greatly influence makers of public policy who are struggling to find solutions or policy approaches to the complex problems they must address. For example, in 2002 the National Research Council published a report that addressed how science and technology could help the nation facilitate counterterrorism work.[6] Two years earlier the council published a study on risk analysis and flood damage reduction.[7]

In 2000 the National Academies formed the Disaster Roundtable, a body led by a group of experts from academia, scientific professional societies, federal scientific research agencies, and private industry. The quarterly disaster-related workshops sponsored by the Disaster Roundtable bring together many of the top authorities in the world. In some respects these workshops represent a peak association of disaster-interested science and engineering experts.

After the 9/11 attacks, the National Laboratories of the U.S. Department of Energy (DOE) began to dedicate more of their research endeavors to examining disaster threats posed by terrorism. The National Laboratories owe their origin largely to the Manhattan Project of World War II. Today they comprise an expansive system of research facilities in which university, government, and private sector scientists and engineers grapple with basic and applied research endeavors, many intended to address defense, security, and other societal needs.[8] The Homeland Security Act of 2002 transferred a portion of DOE laboratory research expertise to the new Department of Homeland Security.

The intellectual and technological advances achieved in the 1980s and 1990s gave rise to a disaster services business sector composed of consultants, contractors, for-profit businesses, and nonprofit organizations. Many business executives recognized the importance of maintaining business continuity before, during, and after disasters. Some types of businesses recognized their increased importance in periods of disaster. Home Depot, Lowe's, and other hardware and building supply firms created an ability to scale up their operations at times of need in areas where their stores could be used to help their customers prepare for impending hurricanes or tropical storms. In the same respect, these and many other businesses able to survive disasters often gave many of their critically needed wares to disaster victims at no charge. Major store chains, franchise businesses, and other firms improved their capacity to help the owners and managers of disaster-ravaged facilities re-establish themselves.

The 9/11 attacks impelled American policymakers to support private sector and government contractor research on new types of counterterrorism technologies. Vast sums of federal funding went to firms producing vaccines that would be needed in the event of various types of bioterrorism attacks. The need to improve port security and interdict shipments of cargo hiding weapons of mass destruction impelled policymakers to fund both conventional and exotic lines of screening devices. Aviation and airport security was another top post-9/11 policy priority. Major firms won federal contracts to X-ray baggage, to detect explosives being carried by passengers, to set forth massive computer databases that could be used to verify the identities of air travelers, to check passengers against "watch lists," and to match every item of a plane's checked luggage to an actual passenger on that plane.

The threat of terrorism inside the United States also induced Presidents Clinton and G. W. Bush as well as Congress to support new types of security research and technologies. Data mining, improved intelligence collection via analysis of Internet traffic and transmissions, improved surveillance technologies, new forms of bomb disposal and explosives monitoring, computer-assisted visual identification technologies, X-ray and electromagnetic resonance technology to examine the contents of containers shipped through airports and shipping ports, technologies used in hard-line and wireless telecommunications, and other innovations all gave rise to a **securitization** of the field of emergency management. The anthrax attacks in the fall of 2001 motivated policymakers to dedicate vast resources to counter the chemical or biological weapons that terrorists might use to contaminate, poison, or destroy food, water, medicines and even the air we breathe.

SOCIAL SCIENCES AND EMERGENCY MANAGEMENT

Not to be overlooked is the work of social scientists, who work inside many of the organizations mentioned above.[9] Disaster sociologists, political scientists, economists, social geographers, demographers, and urban planners have made major contributions to the study of hazards and disasters.[10] The disaster sociology community laid the foundations of the entire field of emergency management as we know it.[11]

The social sciences play a key role in helping emergency managers understand human behavior and the phenomena of disaster. Disaster sociologists have produced a massive body of scholarship and research results about the community-level disaster experience. They have helped identify common misconceptions (myths) about how people behave in disasters.[12] Moreover, by taking into account cultural, age, ethnic, racial, and gender factors, they have helped explain human behavior before, during, and after disasters.[13] Social science researchers have also explored such questions as to whether human-made disasters are becoming indistinguishable from "natural disasters" and whether both types of disaster are being made worse by tolerated and growing disaster vulnerability.

Most Americans believe they understand risks and many believe they are behaving prudently in the face of risk. However, according to disaster sociologist Dennis Mileti, everyone he's interviewed "always thinks they are safe." [14] It is only human for a person to assume that disasters happen to other people, never to them. Unsurprisingly, many Americans fail to anticipate or prepare for the possibility of disaster. Research analysis, some of which is conducted in the field at or near disaster sites, has been the stock-in-trade of the University of Colorado's Hazards Research Center and the University of Delaware's Disaster Research Center for decades.

Social scientists who focus on disaster research appreciate that "policy makers have sought ideas to improve the nation's preparedness for and response to natural and other types of disaster," and they understand that the products of their work carry the potential to influence public policy in ways that may reduce disaster vulnerability and promote hazard mitigation and preparedness.[15] The National Science Foundation has supported the social science research community "to pursue a long term program of research on hazards and disasters, to train cohorts of graduate students, and to pursue strategies to disseminate knowledge." [16]

Social scientists working in academic settings have often been able to examine controversial dimensions of disaster study. For example, several social scientists have argued that Hurricane Katrina was actually a **social catastrophe** in which deeper forces of structural racism and social inequality caused the poor and people of color to suffer disproportionately.[17] Some social scientists contend that there is no such thing as a "natural disaster" but only a natural event for which humans have inadequately prepared. This is a strong assertion intended to convey a lesson. Moreover, social scientists posit that disasters are very much defined as types of extraordinary social events experienced by people and often in a variety of ways.

Social scientists have helped the field of emergency management as well. They have demonstrated that human-caused disasters and natural disasters logically require an all-hazards emergency management approach. Social scientists sometimes explore the political interests and legal issues associated with each type of disaster. In this respect, philosophers would hold that **volition** is important. A common assumption is that most people who experience natural disasters are innocent victims. These victims did not freely choose to put their lives and their loved ones' lives at risk. They were unfortunate victims of circumstance. However, both natural and human-caused disasters often involve some form or degree of culpability on the part of some party or parties, and they sometimes involve **voluntary risk** taking by people who may become victims. Did those people who chose to build homes on the periphery of known, fire-vulnerable dry-brush-covered or chaparral areas of southern California voluntarily assume a disaster risk before the fires of 2003 and 2007? Disaster sociologists remind us that there is a tendency to "blame the victim" for disaster calamities. Yet, disaster researchers fully appreciate that human settlement patterns, commercial and government building decisions and infrastructure construction, and known geophysical and meteorological phenomena often combine to create a realm of **tolerated disaster vulnerabilities.**

In 2006 a committee of the National Research Council of the National Academies published a major report on how over the last twenty-five years the social sciences have contributed to disaster research. Below is a short summary of its major findings.

- The origins, dynamics, and impacts of hazards and disasters [have] become much more prominent in mainstream as well as specialty research interests throughout the social sciences;
- Traditional social science investigations of postdisaster responses [have become] more integrated with no less essential studies of hazard vulnerability, hazard mitigation, disaster preparedness, and postdisaster recovery;
- Disciplinary studies of the five core topics [hazard vulnerability, hazard mitigation, disaster preparedness, emergency response, and disaster recovery] within the social sciences [have] increasingly become complemented by interdisciplinary collaborations among social scientists themselves and between social scientists and their colleagues in the natural sciences and engineering.
- There is continuing attention throughout the hazards and disaster research community on resolving interdisciplinary issues of data standardization, data management and archiving, and data sharing;
- There is continuing attention throughout hazards and disaster research on the dissemination of research findings and assessments by social scientists of their impacts on hazards and disaster management practices at local, regional, and national levels;
- Each generation of hazards and disaster researchers makes every effort to recruit and train the next generation; and
- The funding of hazards and disaster research by social scientists, natural scientists, and engineers is a cooperative effort involving the NSF, its partner agencies within the National Earthquake Hazard Reduction Program, the Department of Homeland Security, and other government stakeholders.[18]

THE SCIENCE INFORMING THE POLICY AND POLITICS OF DISASTERS

Science and engineering play integral roles in mitigation, preparedness, response, and recovery. Although FEMA has many scientists and engineers, there are far more whose jobs involve disaster in some form and who work in other federal agencies. The examples and cases that are presented within the discussions of each of the four phase categories demonstrate the importance of science and engineering in disaster policy and politics.

Mitigation

Since the 1970s, emergency managers have sought to reduce disaster loss, or prevent a disaster or emergency altogether, by identifying and attempting to reduce hazard risks and vulnerabilities capable of producing disasters or emergencies. This is known as mitigation and is seen by many as the cornerstone of emergency management. Mitigation involves "keeping homes away from floodplains, engineering bridges to withstand earthquakes, creating and enforcing effective building codes to protect property from hurricanes." [19] There are small armies of geoscientists and engineers across the nation, and the world, who are dedicating their expertise to the study of seismic events. Similarly the U.S. Forest Service invests sizable efforts in researching wildland and other types of fire disasters. Such research leads to programs and plans for mitigation and informs policy.

From its origin to the present, FEMA has made great strides in examining the practice and in performing disaster loss estimation. [20] FEMA's Federal Insurance Administration (FEMA-FIA) managed the National Flood Insurance Program (NFIP), established by Congress in 1968. The administration's Unified Program for Floodplain Management established national goals and set strategies to reduce losses and to protect natural resources. [21] For property owners to qualify for NFIP's low-cost flood insurance, their respective local government has to agree to participate in the program and abide by its rules, which includes instituting laws and ordinances to discourage unsafe construction in flood zones. Homeowners whose domiciles were subject to recurring flood loss sometimes petitioned FEMA to buy their properties or relocate them (at government expense) to safer locations. The subsequent era of FEMA residential home buyouts may have had its origins in assistance provided to those displaced by the abandoned waste contamination of Love Canal, in Niagara Falls, New York, and later to the relocation undertaken in the small Missouri community of Times Beach, which was affected by dioxin contamination and subsequently relocated using FEMA funds. [22]

The NFIP, mentioned in other chapters, is noteworthy here because the success of the program rests very much on the ability of FEMA-FIA officials to analyze the science and geography of flood risk. NFIP is in the business of calculating flood risk information and factoring findings into actuarial calculations that determine rates to be charged to those who seek to buy NFIP insurance on their homes and businesses. The basis of the NFIP program is to advance flood disaster mitigation through encouraging local governments to engage in sound land-use practices and in pressing NFIP buyers through the instrument of insurance to do the same thing.

Disaster mitigation has assumed increasing and enduring importance in emergency management across all levels of government. Disaster mitigation is recognized as important "between disaster" emergency management work. Emergency management officials continue to stress that disaster mitigation or prevention is everyone's responsibility. An important element in disaster mitigation is to motivate Americans to engage in disaster prevention activity in their homes, schools, and workplaces. In many ways, the diffusion of disaster mitigation knowledge has done much to advance public awareness of emergency management and catalyze public action. Nevertheless, some communities and states have chosen to take few if any mitigation steps.

Preparedness

Preparedness involves anticipating and developing a variety of resources for response and recovery.[23] For emergency managers at the local level, a preparedness strategy "is the mechanism by which the community builds its capacity to respond" to an emergency or disaster.[24] A preparedness strategy involves tactical planning, in which plans and procedures are developed to support the strategy; logistics management, which examines resources needed, resources available, shelter planning, and how resource shortages will be addressed; and training of personnel.[25] Preparedness identifies key functions to be performed after a disaster. Preparedness also involves warning systems and predisaster actions taken to promote safety and facilitate community disaster response.[26] Toward the end of this chapter is the case of the year 2000 (Y2K), a major emergency preparedness effort. Below is an example of homeland security-related preparedness and mitigation. Homeland security officials have long advocated that "prevention" be added to the four-phased disaster cycle of mitigation, preparedness, response, and recovery. The "prevention" example below embodies, though focused on interdiction, features of preparedness, mitigation, and response, and it will be presented here for its preparedness relevance.

One example of disaster preparedness at the national level involves how the nation has engaged in preparations to detect nuclear weapons being fabricated, transported, or deployed by enemies of the United States. For more than a decade federal policymakers have worried about the threat posed by a smuggled nuclear weapon or radiological dirty bomb. Since September 11, 2001, the Bush administration, with congressional assent, has spent more than $5 billion on homeland security detection systems.[27] The Bush administration faced major challenges choosing among contractors who could develop "a new generation of rugged and precise radiation monitors and imaging scanners designed to sniff out radioactive material at the nation's borders. Authorities had to choose in part between older, reliable technology of limited effectiveness and new, more costly, less proven devices that promise greater accuracy." [28] The stakes were high in every regard. Any technology that promised to mitigate or prevent detonation of a radiological bomb of any type, and actually delivered on its promise, would be of colossal value to the nation. Moreover, government contractor scientists and engineers who develop proposals and who work on such technologies would be helping their firms compete for and acquire a share of $3 billion in government contract funding.

In many respects the challenge posed by the need to develop more sophisticated radiation monitors and screening technologies demonstrates how the nation puts scientists and engineers to work in the service of homeland security and emergency management. Makers of public policy often use government funds for the purpose of "technology forcing." For example, one aim of federal policy has been to install 3,000 next-generation radiation detectors by September 2009. The cost of this initiative is estimated to be $1.2 billion. Homeland security secretary Michael Chertoff called this effort a "mini-Manhattan Project" and it represents a preparedness and interdiction effort to address the threat of weapons of mass destruction in an era of terrorism.[29]

Political scientist Graham T. Allison, an expert on nuclear proliferation, believes that research and engineering on next-generation detection technologies is justified because, although intelligence efforts provide the nation a first line of defense, the intelligence community may not be able to ferret out every terrorist threat.[30] On April 15, 2005, President Bush signed the fourteenth homeland security presidential directive. It consolidated within the new Domestic Nuclear Detection Office the development of countermeasures to a smuggled radioactive weapon. The effort had previously been split among the Pentagon, the Energy Department, and other federal agencies. That new office is now designing a national detection system and a global strategy. Key parts of the directive follow:

> The Secretary of Homeland Security, in coordination with the Secretaries of State, Defense, and Energy, and the Attorney General, shall establish a national level Domestic Nuclear Detection Office (DNDO) within the Department of Homeland Security. The DNDO shall include personnel from the departments of Homeland Security (DHS), Defense (DOD), Energy (DOE), State (DOS), Justice (DOJ), and other Federal departments and agencies as appropriate. The Secretary of Homeland Security shall have authority, direction, and control over the DNDO as provided in section 102 (a) (2) of the Homeland Security Act of 2002. The DNDO shall:
>
> * Establish, with the approval of the Secretary of Homeland Security and in coordination with the Attorney General and the Secretaries of Defense and Energy, additional protocols and procedures for use within the United States to ensure that the detection of unauthorized nuclear explosive devices, fissile material, or radiological material is promptly reported to the Attorney General, the Secretaries of Defense, Homeland Security, and Energy, and other appropriate officials or their respective designees for appropriate action by law enforcement, military, emergency response, or other authorities;
> * Develop, with the approval of the Secretary of Homeland Security and in coordination with the Attorney General and the Secretaries of State, Defense, and Energy, an enhanced global nuclear detection architecture with the following implementation: (i) the DNDO will be responsible for the implementation of the domestic portion of the global architecture; (ii) the Secretary of Defense will retain responsibility for implementation of DOD requirements within and outside the United States; and (iii) the Secretaries of State, Defense, and Energy will maintain their respective responsibilities for policy guidance and implementation of the portion of the global architecture outside the United States, which will be implemented consistent with applicable law and relevant international arrangements;
> * Conduct, support, coordinate, and encourage an aggressive, expedited, evolutionary, and transformational program of research and development efforts to support the policy.[31]

The effort led by the federal government to better detect nuclear weapons that might be detonated inside the United States carries with it several lessons. First, policymakers sometimes steer government funding and resources to contractors who are expected to invent or adapt new technologies for use in homeland security monitoring schemes. Some of these efforts dovetail with other national security and defense interests, and so defense contractors have been eager to go after high-technology homeland security contracts and funding. Second, the president and DHS are conducting a policy to support and subsidize "technology forcing" work that produces new types of detection equipment and systems. Again, national security and homeland security therefore intertwine here. Third, the federal government and private contractors together possess massive scientific and technical expertise that can be brought to bear on certain problems, but endeavors such as this one have a chance of success only if they receive the endorsement of the president and other policymakers and if federal funding flows generously to the purpose.

Researchers from within America's academic community also play a role both in educating policymakers to the potential of new types of technologies and in competing for project funding, just as defense and other private contractors do. Finally, it has become apparent that policymakers, owing to the perceived catastrophic consequences of failing to detect or prevent use of a weapon of mass destruction (WMD), have been willing to steer many billions of dollars to this agent of disaster, whereas other agents of disaster, such as hurricanes, earthquakes, floods, and wildfires, draw only a relatively small share of federal research funding.

Response

Science and engineering play a major role in disaster response. Consider the example of firefighting. Because fires are a constant threat to communities it has become a customary public safety and emergency management obligation of local governments. They must establish and provide for local fire services able to respond quickly and capably. The local emergency manager develops emergency response plans, and firefighters must be trained to carry out these plans so as to save lives and reduce damage. They must respond to both routine emergencies and major disasters.[32] First-responder units, such as firefighters, emergency rescue, and hazardous materials teams, must have various kinds of specialized education and training to do their work.[33] Training shows new recruits what is expected of them and training allows for the creation of unified teams. Firefighters must be trained and educated to grasp the problems they confront, to operate or handle equipment, to work in groups, and to help serve their community. Fire service people also work to educate the public on matters of fire safety and prevention.

Over the years national policymakers in Congress have enacted laws, established organizations, and created programs that have facilitated local and state emergency response to fire disasters. The U.S. Fire Administration (USFA), the National Fire Academy, FIRE grant programs, and the First Responder Initiative are key components of the federal contribution to the fire services. The USFA was developed out of the former Fire Prevention and Control Administration of 1974 and is now a part of the Federal Emergency Management Agency.[34] "The mission of the USFA is to reduce life and economic losses caused by fire and related emergencies, through leadership, advocacy, coordination, and support." [35] Through public education, training, technology, and data initiatives, the USFA hopes to reduce fire calls and at the same time improve firefighting response operations so as to reduce the amount of damage that fires cause.

The USFA provides training to fire service personnel on a national level. By augmenting existing state and local fire service training programs, it hopes to improve and maintain high fire company standards of capacity and performance across the nation. Also, the USFA helps develop the technology that fire services must obtain to help them promote fire prevention and to improve response. The USFA assists state and local groups in collecting and interpreting data on fires in their respective areas; using this information, USFA scientists and researchers develop customized solutions and programs tailored to the needs of the community. This work promotes a partnership between people at the community level and their local fire service people.[36]

The USFA director reports directly to the FEMA director. The USFA conducts hazardous materials training courses for emergency responders at its National Fire Academy, in Emmitsburg, Maryland.[37] The National Fire Academy provides firefighters sophisticated education and training, all intended to improve their expertise as emergency responders.[38]

Since early 2001, Fire Investment and Response Enhancement (FIRE) grants have been awarded to local fire departments for equipment, protective gear, training, and prevention programs. This congressionally approved FEMA program provided $100 million in small grants in its first year. By 2002 that amount had risen to $300 million, and in 2006 FEMA provided over $1.8 billion to U.S. local fire services.[39] Most of this money is directed to companies that lack the basic tools and resources needed to protect their community and the fire service personnel that respond to disasters. FIRE grants may be used to hire or train personnel, buy more equipment, or develop prevention plans, all aimed at improving response.[40]

The Assistance to Firefighters Grant Program is aimed at promoting mitigation and preparedness in fire departments across the country. The Assistance to Firefighters Grant Program, like the FIRE grants program, provides assistance to fire companies at state or local levels, enabling them to identify and obtain the necessary public safety resources. These one-year grants go directly to fire departments.[41] It is through programs and organizations such as the USFA, FIRE grants, and the Assistance to Firefighters Grant Program that state and local fire services are better able to respond to disasters or emergencies.

Federal fire programs make a significant contribution in national preparedness and response to terrorism. Congress and DHS understand that firefighters will be called first once a terrorist attack occurs and they must be ready. As much as $3.5 billion to $4 billion a year in federal spending has been devoted to the first responder community. Fire grants, as well as Urban Area Security Initiative funding, has gone toward equipping and training first responders to prepare for various forms of terrorist attack.[42]

The Medical Sciences and Disaster Response

Biological and chemical warfare has been a reality for years. In 1988 Saddam Hussein ordered the use of chemical weapons against Iraqi Kurds—five thousand people were killed in that attack. In March 1995, members of the Aum Shinrikyo cult, using sarin nerve gas, launched an attack on the Tokyo subway system. Twelve were killed, fifty were injured, and some five thousand people experienced temporary vision problems. The United States had considerable experience dealing with hazardous materials incidents and chemical contamination from abandoned hazardous wastes well before 2001. However, the anthrax-laced letter attacks of fall 2001, coming only weeks after the 9/11 terrorist attacks, deeply alarmed Americans and their elected representatives. The prospect of terrorist biological and chemical attacks inside the United States was becoming a reality.

At that time one expert said the United States was unprepared to respond to a chemical or biological attack at the state and local levels because the U.S. public health infrastructure had been "decimated" over the previous two decades. The public health community helps track the incidence of disease, maintains records of morbidity and mortality, helps combat the outbreak of epidemics, monitors the adequacy of local health services, and promotes food and drug safety. The anthrax incident in 2001 helped move public health to the top of the federal policy agenda for a time. In the years after 2001, the federal government, aided by

HOW THINGS WORK

PRESIDENTIAL ACTION AND PROJECT BIOSHIELD

On July 21, 2004, President George W. Bush signed into law **Project BioShield.** Bioshield seeks to develop and make available modern, effective drugs and vaccines to protect against attack by **chemical, biological, radiological, or nuclear (CBRN) weapons.** The president first proposed Project BioShield in his 2003 State of the Union address and Congress sent him legislation to make it a reality in mid-July 2004. Project BioShield is a comprehensive effort overseen jointly by the secretary of health and human services and the secretary of homeland security. Other federal agencies also serve the project.

The purpose of Project BioShield is the following:

- Expedite the conduct of National Institutes of Health research and development on medical countermeasures based on the most promising recent scientific discoveries.
- Give the Food and Drug Administration the ability to make promising treatments quickly available in emergency situations.
- Ensure that resources are available to pay for "next-generation" medical countermeasures. Project BioShield is intended to allow the government to buy improved vaccines or

drugs. The fiscal year 2004 appropriation for the Department of Homeland Security included $5.6 billion over ten years for the purchase of next generation countermeasures against anthrax and smallpox as well as other CBRN agents.

Project BioShield launched a process for acquiring several new medical countermeasures:

- Seventy-five million doses of a second-generation anthrax vaccine were to become available for stockpiling beginning in 2005.
- New medical treatments for anthrax were to be directed at neutralizing the effects of anthrax toxin.
- Polyvalent botulinum antitoxin was to be developed and stockpiled
- A safer second-generation of smallpox vaccine was to be developed.
- Initial evaluation was to be made of treatments for radiation and chemical weapons exposure.

BioShield sponsors initiatives aimed at developing advanced treatments and therapeutics for exposure to biological agents and radiation poisoning. President Bush considered BioShield to be a major component of the War on Terrorism.[44]

state and local governments, went on to vastly rejuvenate the nation's system of public health services.[43]

In many respects it was U.S. military research on biological and chemical weapons of decades past, some of this impelled by the threat or fear of biochemical attack from other nations and some driven by military interest in using biochemical weapons as tools of war, that raised awareness of the possibility of anthrax terror attack. U.S. international treaty commitments of the past ten to twenty years are driving forward an American program to destroy all remaining stocks of U.S. chemical weapons. The military is a central stockpiler and producer of biochemical vaccines and medications.

As mentioned, the U.S. Public Health Service and a variety of other federal health response agencies enjoyed a major and sustained infusion of federal funding in the long-term aftermath of the anthrax attacks of 2001. This has helped overhaul the nation's public health system. The federal government scaled up its capacity to address bioterrorism in spectacular and expensive ways. Project BioShield, launched in 2004, is a major example. Nevertheless, it remains to be determined how adequate our response would be in a future biological or chemical attack.

Recovery

Disaster recovery is often the most expensive and most protracted phase of the disaster cycle. Science and engineering issues permeate a vast array of disaster recovery issues. For example, a major environmental health issue surrounds disaster recovery for those affected by Hurricane Katrina. Flooded areas, especially in and around New Orleans, created toxic or viral collections of mold and mildew. As after many floods, owners of flooded structures face the often daunting task of identifying all the areas of contamination. Those who seek to repair flooded structures must take care not to ignore the environmental health threats posed by mold and other contaminants.

Disaster recovery involves a host of other scientific and engineering problems emergency managers and policymakers can ill afford to ignore. The Great Midwest Flood of 1993 covered a vast area from April to October. Nine states, ranging over the Mississippi and Missouri river basins, suffered flood inundation sufficient to obtain presidential declarations of major disaster. At one point every county in the state of Iowa was covered under a presidential declaration of major disaster. Direct federal assistance exceeded $4.2 billion, plus an additional $621 million in disaster loans to individuals and businesses.[45]

However, this expansive multistate flood generated the highest flood crests ever recorded at some ninety-five widely dispersed measuring stations.[46] President Clinton declared 505 counties in nine states to be federal disaster areas. Estimates of the total damage ran as high as $16 billion. Only about one in ten structures affected by the flood were covered by flood insurance policies.[47]

FEMA was widely praised for its handling of the flood response. The disaster was one of the first major challenges of Clinton's revamped FEMA. Director Witt made sure FEMA people proactively addressed the disaster under his new policy of no longer waiting for states to ask for damage assessment teams. Before the flooding became a major disaster,

Witt sent out FEMA regional staffs to help states apply for disaster assistance. In the Midwest flood disaster, FEMA responded quickly to requests from states and anticipated requests. FEMA's handling of the Midwest floods won praise from both Republicans and Democrats in the Senate and House.[48] Still, the Midwest floods were predicted by weather forecasters almost twelve weeks in advance, thus giving Witt and FEMA considerable time to consult with governors and to mobilize federal response people and assets before the flooding climaxed.

The St. Charles County case demonstrates well that technical and engineering decisions made in the disaster recovery phase often have profound effects on disaster victims. The case also makes it obvious that disaster recovery and disaster mitigation are tightly linked, if not coincident at times.

CASE STUDIES OF SCIENCE AND ENGINEERING APPLIED TO DISASTER

Disaster policy and politics are embedded in many realms of scientific and engineering research. Below are a series of examples. These are presented outside this chapter's mitigation, preparedness, response, and recovery framework.

The first case demonstrates that earthquake engineering research and seismological study have long been core concerns in U.S. disaster policy and emergency management. The steady and major decline in fatalities from earthquake in the United States over the last half-century is in part a credit to significant public and private investment in the building sciences, better engineered structures, improved **seismic building codes,** and **earthquake retrofitting** of homes and businesses.

The second case takes up tornadoes. Tornadoes are extreme weather events that have killed many people and have destroyed or damaged a sizable amount of structures and property through the years. Much tornado activity is seasonal or is associated with severe storms, and tornado activity continues from year to year. The quest to provide threatened communities with reliable forecasts and longer intervals of advanced warning after a tornado is identified has been the mission of many atmospheric scientists. Just as in earthquake engineering, improvements in tornado and severe storm research have through the years saved lives. Successful mitigation is seldom newsworthy and attention grabbing, hence the contributions of both earthquake and tornado research often go unheralded.

The third case represents a computer-age fear that is gradually fading in the public's collective memory. The Y2K phenomena was a major national, and international, concern in the late 1990s. In some respects, Y2K was a "socially constructed" disaster in the sense that public imagination—about the calamities computers might cause when their internal two-digit software time code moved from 19(99) to 20(00)—anticipated countless nightmare scenarios. Y2K preparation was also a massive mitigation effort. In many respects, Y2K was the disaster that never happened. However, the case is notable because it underscores our ever-increasing dependence on computing and on the resources that keep computer connectivity and communication in operation. We rely on scientists and engineers to protect us from the hazards and vulnerabilities that come with this dependence.

The Policy and Politics of Earthquake Research and Engineering

Earthquake research and engineering issues overlap many dimensions of emergency management. In the United States, earthquake research receives considerable attention and regular political support. The earthquake research and engineering community is both mature and

HISTORY'S
LESSONS

THE GREAT MIDWEST FLOOD OF 1993

In 1993 the Upper Midwest, comprising 30 percent of the total basin, experienced massive flooding. Some nine different states were affected. There were forty-eight flood-related deaths and about $16 billion in overall damage. Federal outlays related to the flood amounted to $4.3 billion in direct expenditures and about $1.3 billion in federal insurance payments composed of $297 million in NFIP claims, and $1.03 billion in USDA crop insurance payouts.

St. Charles County, Missouri, posed significant flood recovery problems for FEMA.[49] About 43 percent of the county is floodplain and the county sits at the intersection of the Missouri and Mississippi Rivers. The county is a bedroom locality for St. Louis and it was the fastest growing county in Missouri in 1992.

President Clinton twice declared St. Charles County a major disaster in 1993. Some homes in the county were under floodwaters for six months. At flood crest, 30 percent of St. Charles County was under water. Many farmers lost homes, outbuildings, their crops, and a planting season. Termination of barge traffic on the rivers also hurt farmers. A great many levees in and around St. Charles County failed during the floods.

The flood damaged 4,300 structures in the county, forced 2,000 families from their homes and farms, including 400 families who had resided in mobile home parks. The county's losses exceeded $160 million.

The recovery process involved damage assessment, damage inspection, and homeowner review of decision options. Negotiating with homeowners over whether their damaged structures, including homes, should be repaired or demolished proved to be controversial. For each property owner the total cost of flood damage was compared with the market value of the structures as listed in county tax records. Adjusters from FEMA's National Flood Insurance Program inspected damaged structures, as did charities. However, the county inspection was most critical.

As is common after many disasters, county inspectors acting as a type of emergency management authority had to issue structures a colored tag. Inspections work routinely requires structural engineering expertise and judgments. An orange tag, denoting "condemned," was issued if a structure was damaged greater than 50 percent of its preflood market value. A white tag designated that the house or structure was uninhabitable and the criteria for white tagging was damage between 25 percent and 50 percent of preflood market value. A green tag signified "safe" and meant that damage was less than 25 percent of preflood market value. County planners were to enforce NFIP rules. The county was the final authority in setting damage levels and reconstruction options.

For property owners, the seemingly innocuous technical decision regarding which color tag a structure should get produced tremendous politically influential. The United States is dotted by large and small earthquake research centers.

Earthquakes, like other disasters, may temporarily overwhelm the emergency response and recovery capacity of individuals, businesses, and state and local governments. The human and economic losses inflicted by an earthquake and its consequences may be so great that people,

stress and anxiety. This engineering judgment often produced profound social and economic outcomes for them. Complicating the situation further, FEMA allocated rebuilding aid before the county had determined whether structures would be "demolished and rebuilt" or simply "repaired." A county permit was needed before any repair or rebuilding could proceed. Owners who were forced to replace or rebuild their structures owing to an orange tag ruling had to build new structures in accord with NFIP standards. This often required elevation of the structure to a required base height, an expensive proposition.

Many people had an incentive to maximize loss estimates in order to qualify for more NFIP claim money. However, if they minimized their losses for FEMA and the county they might be able to remain under the 50 percent threshold that forced demolition. Many disasters produce these types of dilemmas for victims.

Recurrent loss is another endemic problem of disaster recovery and one encountered in the St. Charles County case. The federal government did not then or even now have a database for all of its disaster outlays, all of its loans, all of its defaulted loans, and all of its interest subsidies. Nor was it possible for federal officials to discover how many private insurance payouts duplicated federally insured loss payouts. Federal agencies such as the NFIP do track their policyholders' flood loss payouts and do seek to identify and prohibit recurrent flood loss. Buyout programs are one tool emergency man-

agers may be able to use in order to stanch the problems of recurring flood loss claims. However, technical judgments about who is most vulnerable to flood loss are enmeshed with the economic and social problems these decisions pose for those affected. One reason why **buyout programs** are almost never compulsory is because people who are the targets of buyouts have political and legal avenues through which to block or contest such administrative action.

A second variety of recurring loss involves both residents and local governments. The Galloway Report, a product of a presidential commission's study of the Great Midwest Flood of 1993, warned of possible moral hazard, whereby individual incentives to guard against disaster are undercut by overzealous government assistance programs. The huge sums the federal government paid out for infrastructure repair after the flood, often with 100 percent federal subsidy, may have encouraged river counties to increase, rather than decrease, their vulnerability to flooding. The report insisted that national taxpayers should not be obligated to bail out uninsured flood victims. Relief should be linked to responsibility. The report queried whether federal disaster relief was an "addiction."

The federal government has very little control or influence over local land-use and building practices The bulk of federal relief to St. Charles County went to infrastructure replacement or repair, payments for lost crops, social services, or reimbursement for loss of local tax revenue.

businesses, and governments outside the damage zone must provide a great deal of help. Consequently, earthquake threat and destruction have been addressed in national policy and federal law for many years.[50]

Earthquakes often strike with few or no measurable precursors. In spite of major scientific advances in both the science and technology of seismology, it remains extremely difficult for seismologists to provide accurate advance warning of the month, week, day, or hour a major earthquake will strike. Beyond their decadal or longer probabilistic timescales, it is difficult for them to provide the public with sufficient advance warning of when a major quake will hit. Regardless, seismic and geologic research has advanced dramatically over the past half century. Seismic research has led to **seismic mapping.** Those who engineer built structures, everything from one-story homes to skyscrapers, have made major, life-saving contributions to the field. They have helped design and build seismic-resistant structures and they have disseminated model building codes appropriate for the seismic risk communities face.

With the possible exceptions of Hawaii and Alaska, few American states are more prone to earthquake activity than California. Consequently much of the history of U.S. earthquake policy is intertwined with California's earthquake experience. In many ways, that state's earthquake politics and policies have been carried forward into national earthquake policy. In 2007 California had almost 36 million people, and the state's delegation to the U.S. House of Representatives numbered fifty-four, more than 12 percent of the chamber. Thus the state, along with the earthquake vulnerable states of Alaska, Hawaii, Oregon, and Washington, as well as a group of Midwest states that fear catastrophic seismic activity from the New Madrid fault between St. Louis and Memphis, have had considerable political influence in shaping U.S. earthquake policy.

In 1977 Congress determined that almost all fifty states are vulnerable to earthquakes and that a national policy to address earthquake as a major natural hazard was necessary.[51] As a result, Congress passed the National Earthquake Hazards Reduction Act of 1977 (NEHRP). This measure supports federal, state, local, and private research and planning to reduce the risk of earthquake losses in seismic risk areas. The goal of the law and its implementing program was to reduce the risks to life and property in the United States resulting from earthquakes.[52]

The NEHRP has provided the framework for a national earthquake policy, and FEMA, after its formation in 1979, was designated the lead agency charged with coordinating that program. However, the National Institute of Standards and Technology was assigned lead agency responsibility for the NEHRP when FEMA joined the Department of Homeland Security in 2003. Under the NEHRP, FEMA worked with other federal agencies—the USGS, NSF, and NIST—the states, academia, and the private sector to minimize risk to life and property from future earthquakes. The primary goals of the program have been to make structures safer, better inform the public of earthquake threat, and advance better seismic mitigation. This entails the following:

- Better understanding, characterizing, and predicting of seismic hazards
- Improving model building codes and land-use practices
- Learning risk reduction through post-earthquake investigation and analysis
- Developing improved design and construction techniques
- Promoting the dissemination and application of research results[53]

The NEHRP supports research, planning, and response activities conducted within each of the four participating agencies. It also sets forth external grant programs funded through FEMA, the USGS, and NSF. When FEMA was formed in 1979 it was assigned lead agency responsibility for the young NEHRP program. FEMA retained lead agency status for NEHRP until 2003. From 1979 to 2003 FEMA provided project grants through its state cooperative agreements program. The state matching requirement ultimately rose to 50 percent, and a share of federal-state funding had to be used for mitigation activities; some states used these funds to support seismic hazard loss reduction.

In the 1990s FEMA developed an earthquake simulation applicable and adaptable to most of the nation. It was called **HAZUS,** and FEMA distributed it free on the Internet. HAZUS is a powerful risk assessment software program for analyzing potential losses from earthquake. Its successor, HAZUS-MH, also models losses from hurricane, wind, and flood disaster agents.[54] The results of this research were used to mitigate the effects of disasters and to improve preparation for, response to, and recovery from such events. Not long ago FEMA announced the availability of a third generation of **HAZUS-MH** software.

One of the significant accomplishments of the NEHRP has been the development of seismic resistance standards for new construction and for strengthening existing buildings in earthquake-prone areas. FEMA's work under the NEHRP facilitated creation of the Federal Response Plan. As mentioned, the FRP provided the basic framework for coordination of federal disaster relief work among the federal departments and agencies until it was replaced by the National Response Plan in late 2004.

Before its absorption into the Department of Homeland Security, FEMA had a National Earthquake Mitigation Program Office within its Mitigation Directorate. FEMA produced manuals, seismic safety provisions, and guidance documents that were the basis for U.S. seismic safety codes. For its part, the USGS produces earth science data, calculates earthquake probabilities, and supports land-use planning and engineering design, as well as emergency preparedness. The NSF promotes earthquake mitigating construction and siting, fundamental geotechnical engineering design, and structural analysis, in part through the Multidisciplinary Center for Earthquake Engineering Research (MCEER) housed at the State University of New York at Buffalo.[55] NIST and FEMA together work with state and local officials, model-building code groups, architects, engineers, and others to be sure that scientific and engineering research flows into building codes, standards, and practices.

The NEHRP Reauthorization Act of 2003 moved NEHRP lead agency authority from FEMA to NIST, but the law continued to hold FEMA responsible for earthquake emergency response and management, estimation of loss potential, and implementation of mitigations actions.[56]

The Policy and Politics of Tornado Research

Vast areas of the United States are vulnerable to tornadoes and severe storms. Government officials at the federal, state, and local levels are responsible for providing public warnings of tornado and severe thunderstorm threats. How they do this and how well they do this are matters of controversy. Also controversial is the role of government in tornado mitigation activity. Moreover, not all tornado-damaged jurisdictions win presidential declarations of major disaster or emergency. Such determinations are sometimes a function of damage assessment after the fact.

Most people can recall previous tornado disasters reported by the media. This gives tornado disaster events broad, but thin, public attention over the nation. Sometimes new laws or policies have stemmed from tornado disasters. Some have argued that there is actually a tornado politics, very much intertwined with matters of how science comes to influence politics.[57]

Three issues are paramount in tornado policy: the degree of preparedness, the definition of disaster, and the amount of federal aid that should go to individuals, state, and local governments after a tornado or severe storm disaster.[58]

Political issues and factors have influenced all three issues. Many state and local governments are not as prepared to meet the threat of tornadoes as they could be. Local elected officials have difficulty determining the costs and benefits of spending public funds on tornado preparedness measures. They often seriously discount the probability that a tornado will strike their jurisdiction.

Meteorologists rely on weather radar to provide information on developing storms. The National Weather Service has strategically located **Doppler radar** facilities across the country, which are capable of detecting air movement toward or away from the radar. Early detection of increasing rotation aloft within a thunderstorm may allow authorities to issue life-saving warnings before the tornado forms. Not all tornadoes, however, are detectable or traceable on radar, regardless of the type of radar technology used.

Nevertheless, the increased use of Doppler radar by the National Weather Service and other organizations has done much to improve public warning time in advance of tornado strikes. It is ironic that improvements in the handling of tornado watches and in the timely broadcast of tornado warnings issued by federal agencies and by radio and television news organizations have inadvertently alleviated some of the burden of emergency notification handled by local governments. Local governments that do not maintain adequate tornado warning systems for their people because of overdependence on tornado tracking by others may be derelict in fulfilling their public responsibility.

An unusual problem facing many local governments in more rural areas has been the loss of local privately owned radio stations owing to consolidations, mergers, and acquisitions in the radio industry. As independent local radio stations have been absorbed by much larger radio broadcast corporations, many rural or remote localities have lost an avenue for issuing unique tornado warnings to their local populace. However, local emergency management officials may access and use radio broadcast facilities in their environs under the Emergency Alert System (EAS). EAS equipment is a core element of the country's first response effort. According to Clear Channel's senior vice president of engineering, Steve Davis, "Our responsibility as a broadcaster is twofold—to deliver the equipment to local authorities (in many cases, we subsidize the equipment also), and to ensure that the EAS equipment at each of our stations is fully operational so that local or Federal authorities can automatically interrupt our broadcasts with public-safety messages." Local emergency management officials must now understand and be prepared to use EAS equipment residing at transmission facilities of private radio broadcasters. The National Weather Service is the most frequent user of this feature, for things like tornado warnings, but it is available to all local and federal authorities.[59]

Since tornado and severe storm disasters have such low probability, they do not have high political salience. People residing in areas recently hit by these disaster agents may for a time accord these agents high political importance. Still, the infrequency of tornado experience for

WHEN TECHNOLOGY MAY FAIL US: THE CASE OF Y2K

Human-caused disasters or emergencies, or calamities, sometimes resulting from failures of various technologies (dam failures, nuclear reactor malfunctions, hazardous substance releases, and the like) involve most all of the same controversies as encountered in natural disasters. But human-caused disasters, including technology failures, often pose problems of identifying liability and possible negligence; confronting terrorism, sabotage, arson, or other crimes; and addressing matters of environmental protection. Disasters from technology often reveal excessive human dependence on vulnerable infrastructure, much of it serving "lifeline" needs.

Disaster policy in the Clinton administration involved the matter of the year 2000 computer date-changeover problem. The Clinton administration (1993–2001), with congressional support, engaged in a massive federal preparedness effort in expectation that when two-digit-year 19(99) internal computer clocks struck 20(00) at midnight, December 31, 1999, major disruptions would occur across the nation. To avert these possible calamities, the federal government pressed every federal agency to study the possible problems computing systems and computer-operated devices would have when the changeover occurred. Many of these efforts were paralleled by others in the private sector. One report at the time declared, "Estimates are that

Y2K expenditures represent the largest civil preparedness funding effort to date." [60]

Y2K emergency preparedness in the United States, and in many other nations of the world, was vast. Federal, state, and local government agencies, as well as many thousands of corporations and other private organizations responded to the Y2K threat by replacing, upgrading, or reconfiguring their computing systems. Preparedness and mitigation for the potential Y2K calamity had both positive and negative outcomes. Negatively, fears of disaster and other nightmare scenarios ultimately proved to be largely unfounded and exaggerated. Positively, measures taken to avert a Y2K debacle had the silver lining effect of modernizing both government and private sector computing technology and software on a grand scale. This improvement aided government efficiency and served to increase both private sector productivity and economic growth. The nationwide effort to prevent Y2K calamities may have partially fueled the so-called dot.com revolution that for a time spurred the growth of computer manufacturing, services, and software companies.

Y2K was an information technology challenge as well as a massive disaster-related social phenomenon. Had Y2K produced disaster effects, this would have represented a form of human-caused disaster.

each single locality encourages local governments collectively to underprepare for tornado disasters. Many state and local officials who have not had recent experience with a devastating tornado or tornado outbreak (which is a rash of many tornadoes over a region) have decided that the risk of a touch down is simply not great enough to warrant allocating funds to better prepare for one.

There are some steps that local jurisdictions can take to prepare for and mitigate the effects of tornadoes and severe storms. They include installing siren-warning systems, building reinforced structures near mobile home communities, and supplying NOAA self-activating radios to residents.

According to the National Weather Service, the most tornado-vulnerable structures are permanent homes and mobile homes. Some 77 percent of tornado fatalities are among those in mobile homes. One mitigation measure that would probably save lives is to limit the use of mobile homes. However, it is extremely expensive to provide alternate housing, and it is politically infeasible to win approval of such a measure in law. Nonetheless, many mobile homes cannot withstand the high winds associated with tornadoes. Despite the increased risk, the 5 to 6 percent of the population who live in mobile homes and the manufactured-housing industry would aggressively fight any attempt to limit the sale or location of mobile homes. As a result, much of the federal government's tornado mitigation policy rests on a program of public education. One of the options for local municipalities, as mentioned above, is the building of reinforced shelters in mobile home communities where residents may go to better protect themselves in the event of a tornado.

The National Weather Service, the National Severe Storm Laboratory, and the Emergency Alert System, in cooperation with state and local emergency management agencies, shoulder much of the burden for providing public warning of tornado threat. Privately owned television and radio news organizations, particularly the Weather Channel, provide extensive tornado tracking, severe storm tracking, and public warning coverage. The National Weather Service continuously broadcasts updated weather warnings and forecasts that can be received by the NOAA Weather Radios sold in many stores. The average range of the radios is forty miles, depending on topography. The National Weather Service recommends purchasing radios that have both a battery backup and a tone-alert feature that automatically alerts people when a watch or warning is issued. Inadequate advanced warning time, wind vulnerable structures, and an unaware or heedless public may result in many people being unnecessarily exposed to tornado or severe storm threats. Public education, drills, practices, siren warnings, and feasible structural mitigation (there is no such thing as a perfectly windproof building) could all help in reducing the public's vulnerability to tornadoes. However, strong national, state, and local leadership is needed to reach such goals.

Critical scientific and technical issues in tornado disasters include effective forecasting, credible public announcements of tornado watches and tornado warnings, tracking the general path of sighted tornadoes, and public evacuation in advance of tornado hazards, appropriate sheltering of evacuees. The matter of demobilization—that is, issuing of an all clear notice—standing down responders, and facilitating the return of people to their homes and offices, is an additional responsibility. As in most disasters, emergency response to damaged areas, search and rescue operations, emergency medical services, utility repair, business and residential insurance against wind and rain damage, disaster relief from public sources, and long-term recovery efforts may all be part of tornado emergencies and disasters.

ENGINEERING AND PUBLIC INFRASTRUCTURE POLICY

If emergency management is becoming more federal-centered, one might also ask if U.S. disaster policy has become a modern and growing **public works** subsidy program for state and local governments.[61] How is infrastructure defined, and who pays for its postdisaster repair? Are buyouts and relocations replacing engineered disaster mitigation (that is, flood levees or flood control works)? The U.S. Army Corps of Engineers is an agency with a very long history of work in construction, operation, and maintenance of infrastructural works (dams, levees, revetments, and the like), and nonstructural, disaster mitigation works. USACE also owns, operates, and maintains other massive infrastructure (lock systems, navigable waterways, bridges, ports, and the like). Consequently, USACE became an important player in the nation's system of emergency management, particularly in the 1980s and 1990s.[62]

The federal government had been in the business of building flood control works since at least the 1920s; however, by the 1980s, U.S. emergency management became more extensively involved in restoring disaster-damaged public infrastructure.[63] Such infrastructure included highways, roads, streets, bridges, ports, airports, flood control works, utilities such as water and sewer systems, electrical systems, natural gas distribution networks, and telephone and cable systems, plus government-owned buildings.

Communications infrastructure became a huge new concern of emergency management. The astounding growth of the Internet and the World Wide Web made possible colossal advances in the range and depth of information technology. Maintenance of routers and hubs, protection of transmission vehicles (from hard lines, to fiber optic cables, to cell towers, to wireless instruments), and most particularly perpetuation of connectivity all became concerns of emergency managers. This involvement by emergency managers, public and private, came about because of they had come to depend on the availability of the Internet before, during, and after disasters.

Economic and social dependence on these communications and information pathways convinced political leaders that "cyber security" was essential. Computer hackers who disrupted Internet usage came to be recognized as potential "terrorists" and purveyors of disaster. By the 1990s, disasters and emergencies that damaged or threatened to damage any of these critical systems and facilities became a growing concern and a new core area of responsibility for FEMA. The vulnerability of these systems and facilities to both terrorism and natural disaster forces encouraged policymakers to fund scientific and engineering endeavors aimed at advancing the fortification and resilience of these systems and structures. In 1997 a report by the Presidential Commission on Critical Infrastructure and Protection convinced Clinton of the need to issue a presidential directive (number 63) in 1998, pressing federal agencies to act on these vulnerabilities. George W. Bush went much further on this subject when he issued Homeland Security Presidential Directive-7 in 2004.[64]

In many respects, one of the main criteria by which disaster management effectiveness has been judged is how quickly government agencies restore lifeline services and public infrastructure after a disaster. Repairing or replacing damaged public infrastructure often costs millions if not billions of dollars. Americans have become accustomed to virtually uninterrupted delivery of lifeline services. Interruptions of electricity service, even for only a period of hours, are considered "disasters" or "emergencies." Loss of Internet availability and connectivity has grown to have massive economic and social implications. Hence, the president, Congress, and all federal agencies engaged in public infrastructure operations or publicly subsidized construction have come to recognize government's key role in the aftermath of disasters.[65] Since the mid-1950s, state and local political executives and lawmakers have come to appreciate the importance of federal postdisaster subsidies to repair or replace public infrastructure.

Although disaster mitigation had become a policy goal set forth in law in 1974, it was not until the Northridge earthquake in Los Angeles in January 1994 that FEMA was authorized to fund public infrastructure repairs so that they were more than restoration of original structures.[66] For example, California Freeway overpasses that collapsed owing to the Northridge quake and its aftershocks were rebuilt, at great public expense, to meet more powerful seismic shocks.[67] The U.S. Department of Transportation (DOT) funds a major share of the federal highway system and has programs and resources in place to repair or replace disaster-damaged segments of its national system, as became necessary after the tragic collapse of a bridge and major segment of an elevated eight-lane interstate highway in Minneapolis in August 2007. However, FEMA subsidizes state and local government postdisaster highway repair.

CONCLUSION AND SUMMARY

Science and engineering have helped grow and professionalize the field of emergency management. Moreover, the scientists and engineers who study hazards and disaster phenomena have found ways to engage the political process in order both to promote the public interest and to solicit the funding resources they need to do much of their work. Big science applications of disaster research especially require subtle forms of political lobbying of lawmakers. It is clear that disaster study informs, but also transcends, emergency management.

This chapter posited that different types of disaster agents are of interest to different types of scientific and engineering clientele groups.[68] The scientific and engineering interests dedicated to the study of earthquakes are not identical to the scientific and engineering interests focused on hurricanes. Those who focus on tornadoes and severe storms, as meteorological phenomena, lobby often as a group separate from the two just mentioned. In turn, the scientific and engineering groups concerned with flood control and water resources only partially overlap the other groups.

What this means is that these communities of interest sometimes conflict with one another when they seek to secure government support and funding of their respective scientific endeavors. However, these communities also have a great deal in common. They often form alliances, or at least tolerate their differences, in the interest of showing a united front to policymakers, who are often rapaciously looking for ways to reallocate government funding to purposes they judge more important than basic or applied scientific and engineering research. For example, each year the federal budget request for climate research is fashioned as a joint package of requests cooperatively fashioned by federal officials whose agencies are researching different features or aspects of climate change or global warming. This package is reviewed by various White House offices, including the Office of Management and Budget. The logic of this research budget request is that the package is better justified and defended as a whole rather than as separately and independently submitted budget requests.

An unfortunate aspect of U.S. disaster policy is that most of the government scientific and engineering agencies, offices, and programs important to emergency managers are neither in FEMA nor in the Department of Homeland Security. Some of these organizations are capable of making predictions of disaster frequency and magnitude, some design various countermeasures or advance disaster mitigation research and engineering, some work to improve government disaster preparedness and response, and some are capable of facilitating disaster recovery. The National Oceanic and Atmospheric Administration, the U.S. Geological Survey, the National Institute of Standards and Technology, the National Aeronautical and Space

Administration, the U.S. Environmental Protection Agency, and the National Science Foundation all operate very much independently of FEMA and DHS. Scientists of the National Hurricane Center, the U.S. Tsunami Warning Center, the National Severe Storm Laboratory, the National Center for Earthquake Engineering, the Center for Disease Control and Prevention, the National Center for Atmospheric Research, and the National Climate Data Center have major ongoing research responsibilities, only some of which draw them into disaster policy and management. Not to be overlooked is that in 2006 DHS-FEMA established a National Preparedness Directorate, which includes a technological hazards branch. However, many of the experts in this directorate are largely focused on terrorism prevention.

The public works engineering side of emergency management is critical in disaster policy's intergovernmental relations. In many homeland security realms, research involves sizable pools of government contractors and universities working on security-related technologies. This has moved emergency management deeper into the world of national security and defense-related contracting. Although the president rarely personally engages in matters of disaster-related science and engineering, certain techno-scientific problems do percolate to the presidential level. Decisions regarding the U.S. Army Corps of Engineers' rebuilding of the levees around New Orleans, decisions to allow the rebuilding of the Northridge-earthquake infrastructure to exceed original design in the interest of disaster mitigation, and decisions to go forward with Project BioShield are a few examples of the types of decisions that have drawn presidents into this realm.

KEY TERMS AND CONCEPTS

big science   110
buyout programs   123
chemical, biological, radiological,
   or nuclear (CBRN) weapons   119
disaster research   109
Doppler radar   126
earthquake retrofitting   121
HAZUS   125
HAZUS-MH   125

Project BioShield   119
public works   128
securitization   111
seismic building codes   121
seismic mapping   124
social catastrophe   112
tolerated disaster vulnerabilities   113
volition   112
voluntary risk   112

CHAPTER **6**

WHAT HAPPENS WHEN PEOPLE ON DIFFERENT LEVELS OF government must work together to address a disaster or emergency? Emergency management is by its very nature intergovernmental and intercommunity—it requires government agencies and officials to coordinate and cooperate with each other on the same level and across levels. It also requires that communities cooperate and coordinate in preparing for, and responding to, a disaster.

In the United States many policies are implemented through intergovernmental relations. As a term, "intergovernmental relations" defines the interaction of federal, state, and local officials and officials of the private and nonprofit sectors, as they collectively implement public policy. The term includes special district governments as well as general-purpose governments. General-purpose governments are cities, counties, towns, or other municipal jurisdictions that collect broadly based taxes to pay for a wide variety of public services. Special district governments, usually spun off from cities or counties, customarily operate to provide one or two specialized services funded from an earmarked (dedicated) single tax or sometimes user fees.[1] In modern usage, as mentioned above, the phrase intergovernmental relations also encompasses the interaction of these bodies with groups and organizations of the nonprofit and private sectors. There are some 87,000 substate governments of all forms in the United States.

This chapter examines the interaction of people working within specific levels of governmental and between levels through intergovernmental program management. This chapter also provides an overview of the policy and politics of federal-state-local interchange, mutual aid agreements, interstate assistance compacts, and preparedness and response agreements in disaster management. The National Response Plan, recast in early 2008 as the National Response Framework (NRF), and its tactical application, the National Incident Management System, are discussed.[2] Also considered are two hugely important nongovernmental players in disaster management: voluntary organizations active in disasters and government contractors

This spectacular August 2007 photo of some of the remains of the I-35 bridge collapse, an elevated roadway spanning the Mississippi River in Minneapolis and St. Paul, Minnesota, draws attention to the need to monitor and maintain the safety of American infrastructure, often taken for granted by their owners and users. The federal, state, and local governments and private corporations that own vitally necessary infrastructure and utilities all share responsibility for maintaining and protecting it. How they do that is a matter of intergovernmental relations and emergency management.

that engage in emergency management work for governmental units. Finally, the current impact of counterterrorism or domestic terrorism consequence management on the nation's system of all-hazards emergency management is investigated.

INTERGOVERNMENTAL PROGRAM MANAGEMENT

America has a highly decentralized federal system, which under the U.S. Constitution affords the national government a range of authority, with some powers reserved for the states under the Tenth Amendment.[3] The federal and state governments share authority concurrently in some domains, such as in the regulation of business, education policy, health care, and corrections.

In U.S. emergency management, shared authority is not supposed to be a **top-down command and control system.**[4] The Department of Homeland Security's FEMA cannot, and the

HOW THINGS WORK

FIRST RESPONSE AND MANAGEMENT BY LOCALS

When a disaster or emergency transpires, local governments are expected to manage the response. State and local governments have been delegated by history, tradition, and their own laws the authority and responsibility for disaster response.[5] It is also true that members of the general public, and sometimes people working for private or nonprofit organizations, respond. A private prehospital-care provider may dispatch ambulances carrying emergency medical workers. The American Red Cross or other relief organization may send help to victims.

When local government leaders conclude that the nature or magnitude of the emergency or disaster is beyond their capability, they may ask their respective state governor for help.[6] Governors, like presidents, are free to approve or deny these requests. If the governor agrees to provide state government help, he or she may issue a state declaration or proclamation. This mobilizes various state agencies and makes available state resources, including workers and equipment, which are dispatched to augment local response and recovery. If a governor judges that the emergency or disaster is beyond the full capability of

his or her state and local government(s), that governor may decide to ask the president directly, or through FEMA (or both), for a declaration of major disaster or a declaration of emergency. The federal government comes to the assistance of a state government when the president determines that it is overwhelmed by, or incapable of, addressing a disaster.

If the president approves the governor's request for a declaration of major disaster or emergency, the National Response Framework is activated. The purpose of the NRP was "to align federal agencies, capabilities, and resources into a unified, all-discipline, all-hazards approach to disasters. The plan was developed jointly by federal, state, local, and tribal governments and the private sector."[7] The National Response Framework is a revision of the NRP developed primarily by the White House homeland security adviser and Department of Homeland Security officials, in cooperation with representatives of state, local, and tribal governments as well as the private sector. The NRF carries forward much of the essence of the NRP.

previously independent FEMA before it could not, actually "command" state and local officials in matters of emergency management.[8] Instead, there is supposed to be a **bottom-up approach,** wherein local political subdivisions (cities, towns, and counties) are primarily responsible for emergency management, unless those governments have been overwhelmed by the disaster or emergency. Similarly, in some states, local governments, although they are legally vestiges of their respective state governments, are sometimes accorded certain powers under home rule provisions under the state constitution, or through enabling statutes. This underscores the need for multiagency and multijurisdictional coordination in emergency management work. However, many presidential and DHS initiatives in this homeland security era have reintroduced **command and control strategies** under which federal officials get to assume top-down leadership positions, and state and local authorities are expected to submit.[9] Owing to competition between homeland "defense" interests and homeland "security" interests, both

Part of the official response to a disaster may involve use of **private for-profit government contractors.** Customarily, government contractors are allowed to build into their contracts with the federal government a 20 percent rate of profit. Federal, state, and local government officials may choose to retain contractors in the early response phase of a disaster with the expectation that they will address short-term response needs. Sometimes governments have in place predisaster contracts with private firms that may be activated when those governments deem it necessary.

Nonprofit voluntary organizations active in disasters are often part of both the official and unofficial response to a disaster or emergency. Such organizations often go to work providing for the basic needs of disaster responders as well as for the needs of disaster victims. A great many nonprofit organizations active in disasters rely on donations from the general public, from corporations, or from an established pool of regular donors. Voluntary organizations come in all shapes and forms. Some are **emergent organizations** that form spontaneously after a disaster. Some organizations are **faith-based voluntary organizations** and some are not. Some conduct humanitarian operations and missions geared to addressing disaster or emergency needs that are not met, or that cannot by law be met, by government disaster response and recovery organizations. Some of these organizations operate internationally and inside the United States. Nonprofit voluntary organizations may respond to human suffering on any scale; they do not need to wait for an official declaration of disaster to respond. In other words, these organizations may send representatives to a single house fire that makes a family temporarily homeless or they may send representatives to the scene of a catastrophic disaster affecting many thousands of people.

Often government emergency preparedness and response planning is done cooperatively with contractors and representatives of nonprofit voluntary organizations. The pool of actors involved in the intergovernmental relations of disaster management is immense, and some of these participants organize and respond to disasters independently of government and outside the framework of government-supervised disaster preplanning.

seeking political attention and resources, military command-and-control type organizational arrangements have found their way into many realms of emergency management.

A well-coordinated and well-managed intergovernmental approach to disaster often involves a vast number of government-to-government arrangements, agency-to-agency memorandums of understanding, interstate compacts, and predisaster preparedness and response agreements. Coordination of all of these public, private, and nonprofit organizations is a core purpose of emergency management.

Federal-State Agreements

From 1979 to 2003, FEMA's relationship with states and localities was primarily through agreements with state offices of emergency management and then, by extension, with local emergency management offices. FEMA allocated certain program grant funds to state offices of emergency management, and those offices in turn passed some or most of this funding onto local offices of emergency management. States, for better or worse, were the chief points of contact for most local governments seeking federal emergency management funding. This remained so even after 9/11 and into the era of homeland security.

Today, much as in the past, FEMA's success in carrying out its missions is directly related to its success in interagency and intergovernmental coordination. Today's FEMA has authority, funding, and some assets but must depend on other federal departments and agencies to provide additional resources to ensure a complete federal response. Many assume that it is FEMA's job to physically deliver most or all forms of federal assistance in a president-declared major disaster or emergency. This is incorrect. FEMA's job is to plan, prepare, and respond to disasters in a way that functionally coordinates, or helps to coordinate, the provision of federal resources, human-power, and equipment possessed by "other" federal departments, agencies, and offices.

In the 1990s, FEMA generated many new **federal-state agreements** under the agency's response to the second-round National Performance Review, a Clinton administration effort spearheaded by Vice President Al Gore aimed at reinventing federal government so that it would work better and cost less. Director James Lee Witt declared, "A centerpiece of our reinvention is changing the way in which we do business with the States by empowering them through **Performance Partnerships.**" [10] FEMA asked state officials to integrate disparate programs into multiyear, risk-based agreements signed by the president and their respective governors. FEMA funding to the states was to be consolidated into two streams, one predisaster and the other postdisaster. FEMA authorities expected this to reduce state agency reportage to the federal agency. State officials also hoped that this might reduce what they perceived as FEMA's micromanagement of existing grant processes.

Governors and state emergency managers need FEMA program financial resources and most particularly FEMA's postdisaster technical assistance. However, governors cannot afford to commit state resources to emergency management on an open-ended basis when federal emergency management budgetary support to their state emergency management agencies is meager and vacillating. Governors do have some degree of political influence on the policies and operations of the federal government. Governors, who often believe they are being obligated by FEMA to do too much for too little support, may press their arguments directly to the president or Congress. Correspondingly, in the 1990s, FEMA officials could only expect to leverage the resources they received from the Congress in modest ways. In other words, the resources FEMA provided to states and localities often shaped the nature and degree of governor and state commitments to emergency management. The success or failure of FEMA's programs before the 9/11 terror attacks rested on negotiated partnerships with states sweetened only by very modest infusions of federal funds "between" disasters for certain preparedness and mitigation activities.

The FEMA of 1979–2003 had, and the DHS-FEMA since 2004 has, specific intergovernmental relations goals. FEMA is expected to establish and maintain an emergency management partnership with other federal agencies, state and local governments, volunteer organizations, and the private sector (for example, government contractors, corporate-owned public utilities, and disaster service industry firms) to better serve customers. Federal agencies are expected to establish, in concert with their state and local partners, a national emergency management system that is comprehensive, risk-based, and all-hazards in approach. They are expected to make hazard mitigation the foundation of the national emergency management system.[11] They are supposed to provide a rapid and effective response to, and recovery from, declared disasters. They are asked to strengthen state and local emergency management.

Homeland Security is today, and FEMA was previously, geographically divided into ten standard federal regions, and each regional office is directed by a politically appointed regional director. See **FEMA's ten standard federal regions** in Table 6-1.

Regional offices allow FEMA to decentralize operations geographically. Officials in these regional offices have an opportunity to become familiar with their state and local counterparts who engage in emergency management. The working relationships of the individual directors and the governors in their respective regions often help facilitate emergency preparedness and response to disasters and emergencies. Capable **regional directors** and personnel sometimes

TABLE 6-1	States, Territories, and the District of Columbia, by Respective FEMA Standard Federal Region

Region	State
I	Connecticut, Maine, Massachusetts, New Hampshire, Rhode Island, Vermont
II	New Jersey, New York, and Puerto Rico, Virgin Islands
III	Delaware, Maryland, Pennsylvania, Virginia, West Virginia, and District of Columbia
IV	Alabama, Florida, Georgia, Kentucky, Mississippi, North Carolina, South Carolina, Tennessee
V	Illinois, Indiana, Michigan, Minnesota, Ohio, Wisconsin
VI	Arkansas, Louisiana, New Mexico, Texas, Oklahoma
VII	Iowa, Kansas, Missouri, Nebraska
VIII	Colorado, Montana, North Dakota, South Dakota, Utah, Wyoming
IX	Arizona, California, Hawaii, Nevada, and American Samoa, Guam, Commonwealth of the Northern Mariana Islands, Republic of the Marshall Islands, Federated States of Micronesia
X	Alaska, Idaho, Oregon, Washington

Source: FEMA, "Regional Operations," available at http://www.fema.gov/about/regions/index.shtm (accessed November 12, 2007).

REVISITING WHO GETS WHAT
UNDER A PRESIDENTIAL DECLARATION

What can states and localities expect in the way of federal disaster relief? "The Stafford Act designates the universe of eligible applicants (for example, states, local governments, owners of certain private nonprofit facilities, individuals, or families). However, not all persons or entities affected by a disaster are guaranteed Stafford Act assistance when the president issues a declaration. FEMA officials must determine the categories of assistance made available after the president issues a major disaster or emergency declaration. Persons and organizations (including state and local governments) must make application to FEMA and other federal agencies for certain aid made available in the approved categories.

It is the job of FEMA and other federal agencies to ascertain that the applicant is eligible for the categorical aid for which they have applied. FEMA and other federal agencies accepting and processing applicant requests must determine that these requests are valid. FEMA, like many federal agencies tasked with issuing federal assistance on an expedited basis, is challenged to process applications as quickly as possible but at the same time authenticate claims made so as not to issue funds to undeserving applicants or to applicants making **fraudulent claims.** Obviously, application is not necessary when FEMA and other federal agencies furnish directly, or through voluntary organizations or contractors, food, water, clothing, medicines, first aid, emergency transport, and other services or in-kind commodities directly to disaster victims.

For example, a family with adequate insurance and alternative housing options might not be considered eligible to receive some forms of FEMA financial aid. A unit of local government that suffers damages to some of its public facilities or infrastructure, but damage judged by FEMA officials to be insufficient under FEMA regulations and guidelines, might not receive federal funds to help subsidize rebuilding of those facilities and infrastructure. Certain nonprofit organizations (for example, owners or operators of educational or nonemergency health care facilities) may have to rely on Small Business Administration loans, not FEMA Stafford Act grants, to restore services." [12]

Under **major disaster assistance** the president is authorized to direct that the following types of federal disaster assistance be provided:
- General federal assistance for technical and advisory aid and support to state and local governments to facilitate the distribution of consumable supplies
- Essential assistance from federal agencies to distribute aid to victims through state and local governments and voluntary organizations, perform life- and property-saving assistance, clear debris from roadways, and use resources of the Department of Defense before a major disaster or emergency declaration is issued

contribute mightily to emergency management work in their regions, particularly when they work well with federal coordinating officers assigned by the president to manage active major disasters and emergencies declared in their respective regions. Correspondingly, weak, inept, or incompetent regional directors and officials who make little effort to engage governors, mayors, and other key elected or administrative officials of their region sometimes bungle federal response and sour federal relationships with state and local elected officials and emergency managers.

- Hazard mitigation grants to reduce risks and damages that might occur in future disasters
- Federal facilities repair and reconstruction
- Repair, restoration, and replacement of damaged facilities owned by state and local governments, as well as private nonprofit facilities that provide essential services, or contributions for other facilities or hazard mitigation measures in lieu of repairing or restoring damaged facilities
- Debris removal through the use of federal resources or through grants to state or local governments or owners of private nonprofit facilities
- **Individual and household assistance,** including financial grants to rent alternative housing, direct assistance through temporary housing units (mobile homes), limited financial assistance for housing repairs and replacement, and financial assistance for uninsured medical, dental, funeral, personal property, transportation, and other expenses
- **Unemployment assistance** to individuals unemployed as a result of the major disaster, for up to twenty-six weeks, as long as they are not entitled to other unemployment compensation or credits
- Food coupons and food distribution for low-income households unable to purchase nutritious food
- Food commodities for emergency mass feeding

- Legal services for low-income individuals
- Crisis counseling assistance and training grants for state and local governments or private mental health organizations to provide associated services or to train disaster workers.[13]

Emergency declaration assistance to state and local governments usually makes available fewer types of assistance and less funding than major disaster declarations do. The types of assistance authorized to be provided under an emergency declaration include the following:

- Activities to support state and local emergency assistance
- Coordination of disaster relief provided by federal and nonfederal organizations
- Technical and advisory assistance to state and local governments
- Emergency assistance through federal agencies
- Debris removal through grants to state and local governments
- Grants to individuals and households for temporary housing and uninsured personal needs
- Distribution of medicine, food, and consumables.[14]

The declaration process for emergencies is similar to that used for major disasters, but the criteria (based on the definition of "emergency") are less specific.[15]

The Impact of 9/11 on Federal-State Relations

The attacks of September 11, 2001, had profound and surprising effects on FEMA's federal-state relations. Under new laws enacted for homeland security and under the a new Department of Homeland Security, which constantly made managerial and organizational changes, FEMA both suffered and prospered in unexpected ways. A major national policy response to the 9/11 attacks on the United States was to fuse twenty-two federal agencies (one

of them FEMA), into a new department that would incorporate about 180,000 federal workers. Many of these federal organizations had vastly more personnel and much larger budgets
than did FEMA.[16] When FEMA was plunged into a sea of larger and more politically influential federal agencies, it suffered and so did its relations with states.

The federal government recruited state and local governments into the War on Terrorism.[17]
This may stem from the fact that the first emergency responders to almost every disaster are
state and local emergency responders. In the United States there are about 2.2 million professional and volunteer fire service people and some 800,000 state and local police, as well as a
huge number and assortment of physicians, nurses, and other emergency medical personnel.
This intergovernmental integration was to be accomplished through massive federal, state, and
local planning efforts, through information sharing, and through a profusion of heavily funded antiterrorism Department of Homeland Security programs, a small fraction of which
involved FEMA.

In theory, many of the War on Terrorism initiatives should have worked to the advantage
of FEMA, in part because FEMA was one of the few DHS "legacy agencies" to have worked
closely and often with governors and local leaders and with state and local emergency managers, many of the latter experienced in law enforcement, firefighting, emergency medicine,
and public works. However, the DHS rush to yoke and refashion all of its component organizations into a massive antiterrorism assemblage had the effect of stripping FEMA of some of
its most capable people. Many of FEMA's senior officials were reassigned to other posts in
DHS, and many of these posts had little to do with emergency management.

The reorganization failed to fully consider the varied legally mandated **nonterrorism missions** of many of these agencies. Such mistakes are not without precedent. Many presidential
administrations and Congresses have had a penchant for meeting new acute policy needs by
retasking and realigning federal administrative entities. Policymakers give the impression that
a new problem, need, or threat has been addressed but at "little or no additional cost" to the
national taxpayer.[18] This tactic also supplies the public reassurance that the federal workforce
will not actually have to grow in order to meet the challenge. Among the implications of this
ploy are added work burdens for federal employees and an increase in government contracting to help meet new and old needs simultaneously.

Before 9/11, federal and state emergency managers bonded through very modest "between
disaster" federal grant programs and through their occasional, or sometimes regular, work on
presidentially declared major disasters and emergencies (where federal funding and other aid
was often substantial). After 9/11, many states were heavily tempted to form state homeland
security departments. These typically competed for staff and funding with state emergency
management offices and other state-level organizations. The National Guard is the umbrella
organization for emergency management in twenty-six states, and on account of this, emergency management has long been dominated by military approaches in many of these states.
The result is that many of these states were somewhat better prepared for military-oriented
federal homeland security than were states whose emergency managers worked outside the
National Guard–dominant model. Nonetheless, the promise of massive federal grants, many
far eclipsing the between-disaster funding the federal government had offered in the past,
impelled governors and state legislatures to marginalize or subsume state emergency management and in turn prioritize state homeland security.

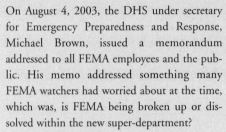

HOW THINGS WORK

MEMO OF THE MONTH, RE: FEMA

On August 4, 2003, the DHS under secretary for Emergency Preparedness and Response, Michael Brown, issued a memorandum addressed to all FEMA employees and the public. His memo addressed something many FEMA watchers had worried about at the time, which was, is FEMA being broken up or dissolved within the new super-department?

> It is with great pride that I announce today that we will be retaining the name Federal Emergency Management Agency and the acronym FEMA to identify us within the Department of Homeland Security (DHS). This decision, on the part of DHS Secretary Tom Ridge and other DHS officials, clearly shows the respect our new colleagues have for us and our work on behalf of the American people. As part of DHS, we will continue to meet our mission while working to help the entire department show that it merits the trust given to it by President Bush and the country.
>
> Retaining the FEMA name will assure the public that we remain ready to assist them before, during and after any disaster they might face—natural or manmade. Its use, in conjunction with the DHS seal, allows FEMA's past successes and future contributions to come together in a visible, tangible way.[19]

The title, Federal Emergency Management Agency, was not simply a federal agency name; it was a symbol important to emergency managers across the nation. It represented a kind of nationally and internationally recognized embodiment of the entire field of emergency management. Eliminating FEMA would be akin to eliminating the name "U.S. Environmental Protection Agency" or "Federal Bureau of Investigation." At the time, the morale of emergency managers was already low owing to FEMA's absorption into DHS; eliminating the brand name FEMA would have been devastating for them. Brown and other DHS officials were wise not to eliminate FEMA as it represented at the time a respected "trade name" for those in the field. Conversely, owing to the highly deficient Hurricane Katrina response in 2005, for which Brown shouldered considerable blame and was pressed to resign, the FEMA name was vilified and the FEMA acronym made an object of humor and derision. The agency is destined to ride this public relations rollercoaster for many years to come, sometimes due to its own failures and successes and sometimes due to unrealistic expectations of policymakers and the public after catastrophes.

Source: BNET Research Center, "Memo of the Month, FEMA," *Washington Monthly,* December 2003, available at http://findarticles.com/p/articles/mi_m1316/is_12_35/ai_111897436.

The absorption of FEMA into the Department of Homeland Security did not represent the end of FEMA. Instead, the small, previously independent, federal agency had to find its place in a new department and had to defend itself in **bureaucratic "turf wars"** with other, bigger organizations within DHS. For a time during 2003–2004 it seemed as if FEMA would be carved up within DHS and that "FEMA" as both an organization and brand name would disappear. Michael Brown, as DHS undersecretary for emergency preparedness and response

HISTORY'S LESSONS

THE BRIDGE TO GRETNA INCIDENT AS A FAILURE OF INTERGOVERNMENTAL DISASTER MANAGEMENT?

A controversial and regrettable incident took place on the bridge to Gretna from New Orleans several days after Hurricane Katrina had collapsed levees, flooded neighborhoods to the rooftops, and sent thousands seeking higher ground. Here is an extracted account of the event taken from a CBS News *60 Minutes* written account regarding correspondent Ed Bradley's investigation of the incident in 2005 and from Douglas Brinkley's 2006 book, *The Great Deluge*.

The incident involved people who sought to escape New Orleans shortly after Hurricane Katrina by trying to walk over a bridge out of New Orleans into Gretna, Louisiana. Since most of the police officers were white and most of the evacuees were black, the incident quickly took on racial overtones. Many wondered why, under any circumstances, people who were only trying to walk out of a devastated city would be prevented from reaching relative safety. The bridge where the incident took place is called the Crescent City Connection and it links the city of New Orleans with the city of Gretna on the west bank of the Mississippi River.[24]

Wednesday, three days after Katrina had struck, thousands of people started to walk across the bridge. Some 6,000 would eventually be put on buses. The exodus continued the next day when a group of tourists who had been staying in the French Quarter started heading in the direction of the bridge to Gretna. Investigators at *60 Minutes* found eight people who were on the bridge that day, among them Cathey Golden, Larry Bradshaw, and Lorry Beth Slonsky.[25] As they left their hotel they were told that buses awaited them on the far side of the bridge. With that assurance, they joined hundreds of other people, most of them African Americans and residents of New Orleans, and

walked to the bridge to Gretna.[26] But when the group tried to cross the bridge, they were met by a line of armed Gretna policemen who fired shotguns over their heads. Those police told them Gretna was closed and turned them back.[27]

Golden said that when her group reached the police line, they were told there were no buses, and they were stopped with a shotgun blast. Also present was Shauron Holloman who also saw police officers fire their guns. "We were close enough to them. They'd rack their shotguns and let off a warning shot."[28] Bradshaw, who was at the front of the group, said he tried to get an explanation as to why they were being turned back. He said, "The only two explanations we ever received were 'We're not going to have any Superdomes over here,' and, 'This is not New Orleans.'"[29] Bradshaw commented, "To me, that was code language or code words for, 'We're not having black people coming into our neighborhood.'"

With nowhere to go, the group set up a makeshift camp in the middle of the highway on the bridge; they would try to cross again the next day. But then a Gretna police vehicle drove up. "He sped down in his cruiser and over the loudspeaker he just continuously said, 'Get the f*** off the bridge,'" according to a male eyewitness who spoke with correspondent Ed Bradley. The individual added that the officer pointed his gun at some people.[30] Soon after, a helicopter dropped close to the encampment and its downdraft blew things everywhere, forcing the evacuees off the bridge. When the eyewitness was asked why he thought they were turned away he answered, "I think because the group was 95 percent African American."[31]

The Counter Argument:

Gretna mayor Ronnie Harris felt strongly that the Gretna police department's actions on the bridge had nothing to do with race and had been greatly misunderstood. On the *60 Minutes* program, he commented, "Our community is one that understands compassion, one that understands that we have to give where we can. But when there is none, you have to take care of your own population first. And that is what we were faced with." [32]

Gretna is a middle-class suburb of 17,500 that is mostly white but that has a substantial black minority comprising 35 percent of the population. According to Mayor Harris, from "day one" after the hurricane, Gretna was in no position to help outsiders. He said, "The city of Gretna was completely on its own. Our entire services were disrupted. No city services. No electricity. We had no shelter. We had no medical services. We were hit by a category four hurricane. What were people expecting us to do?" Harris said he saw brief reports of the looting in New Orleans. "Quite frankly, I was embarrassed to see a free-for-all of not taking food and water but goods and items. Vandalism. Civil unrest. Civil disobedience. And it sickened me." The mayor's image of New Orleans came from media reports that emphasized chaos, looting and violence. [33]

"So, this environment of police officers being shot, citizens lying dead in the street, images of looting going on in the city of New Orleans made me realize that our community was in a crisis of far greater proportion than just of the hurricane," Harris exclaimed. His concern increased on Wednesday when thousands of people from New Orleans, mostly desperate poor African Americans, started walking across the bridge towards Gretna. [34]

Mayor Harris explained, "It started as a trickle, then it began quite heavily. From our estimates, between five thousand and six thousand people

amassed on the west bank of the river. Now, that's our side of the river, the Gretna side." [35] The number of people fleeing the city was so large that the Gretna police commandeered transportation to bus them out of town. Over the next twenty-four hours, the police say they bused 6,000 evacuees from New Orleans. At the same time, police were on guard against reports of looting and stolen guns. "All of this was crashing down on all of us who were in charge, had to make decisions in a crisis mode," says Harris. [36] Brinkley wrote that the mayor and his chief of police "seemed to resent the fact that no one at City Hall in New Orleans had even tried to coordinate the movement of people with them." [37]

What led to the police chief's decision to seal off Gretna? "Something had to be done," says Harris. The mayor stated that it was the police chief's decision, a decision which he supported "wholeheartedly." Arthur Lawson, Gretna's chief of police was reported to have said, "We had to make a decision because we did not have the wherewithal to continue and to evacuate thousands and thousands of more people." He added, "Our job was to secure our city. We did our best to evacuate those that came over, but we could not continue to evacuate the entire city of New Orleans." [38]

Mayor Harris said he sealed off the city because he wanted to protect the lives of Gretna's residents. He remarked, "You had to be there to understand and witness total chaos, total mayhem, the lack of information." Harris defended against accusations of racism by claiming that "everyone" was turned around, including the elderly and children. Harris declared, "What we did was seal that location off just like a dead end, because there was no safety or security available to wherever they were going. It did not exist. Was not there." [39]

(continues)

THE BRIDGE TO GRETNA INCIDENT
(continued)

Gretna chief of police Arthur Lawson had said: "We had no more to offer here than they did in New Orleans. We did not have food. We did not have water. We did not have shelters here." Evacuee Bradshaw's response: "We weren't asking for food, water or shelter. We were asking for the ability to walk out of New Orleans." Lawson insisted, "We did secure our community. I do not apologize for shutting the bridge down. You know my job and responsibility to this community is to make sure that it's safe, the people and their property are safe in this community." People in Gretna were not apologizing either. Signs thanking the police chief and his department were displayed in many of Gretna's front yards for a time. And the city council unanimously passed a resolution saying, "Allowing individuals to enter the city posed an unacceptable risk to the safety of the citizens of Gretna." The people of Gretna seem to be saying that there's a limit to compassion, that there is only so much you can do in circumstances like this to help people.[40]

One set of conclusions one might draw about this incident could begin with the question, how could a local government deny people in abject conditions the chance to evacuate a flood zone and a city that had "shoot-to-kill" nighttime curfew orders? Turning these evacuees away seems inexcusable, despite the insistence of Gretna authorities that the action was necessary. Because many of the evacuees were African American, the incident appears to be an act of racism committed by local authorities. Gretna, perhaps as other U.S. local governments, possesses legal authority to use local law enforcement to block the entry of unwanted people into their jurisdiction under certain circumstances. However, in many respects the Gretna bridge incident stands as a failure of American intergovernmental relations, a failure of emergency management, and a failure of civil rights law and policy.

Another set of conclusions might be that Gretna authorities were working under immense stress; Gretna itself had experienced traumatic effects and substantial damage from Katrina and its aftermath; for Gretna officials government-to-government information sharing about people fleeing New Orleans was grossly inadequate; and Gretna people were heavily influenced by television images of the pandemonium taking place on the opposite side of the bridge in flooded New Orleans. Brinkley disclosed that at the time of the incident, the Louisiana governor, Kathleen Blanco, had "ordered National Guardsmen to other bridges and points of exit around new Orleans in order to keep people from walking out." [41]

Regardless of the conclusion one reaches, the entire incident carries lessons and warnings for local and state authorities and their respective emergency managers about the proper treatment of people who are evacuees. How can all local governments, including Gretna's, prevent a recurrence of such incidents in future disasters?

in 2003, could have presided over the dissolution of FEMA. However, Brown issued a pronouncement that the Emergency Preparedness and Response Directorate would retain use of the name Federal Emergency Management Agency. Nevertheless, from 2003 to 2005, FEMA under DHS lost much of its jurisdiction over mitigation and recovery disaster management functions.

Memorandums of Understanding

In the Clinton era and before, FEMA worked out new **memorandums of understanding (MOU)** with each respective state emergency management agency. At the same time the agency endeavored to reduce the administrative burden it imposed on state programs and officials. Moreover, the Clinton FEMA routinely dispatched a representative to the staff of any governor whose state faced imminent disaster or whose state had experienced a major disaster. This was an attempt to smooth out FEMA-state relations and to assure coordination and cooperation in their intergovernmental activities.

Officials of various government agencies usually negotiate and abide by memorandums of understanding. Unless approved through a formal rule-making process as a regulation, they usually do not have the force of law behind them and stand as voluntary agreements.

An example of an MOU might be the case of California's Santa Clara County. There "each municipality in the county agreed to engage in planning and training together in normal periods and to exchange information and provide resources in the event of disaster," although each provides for its own routine emergency services.[20]

Mutual Aid Agreements

Mutual aid agreements are usually mandated in law and negotiated as legal contracts. Mutual aid is a prearranged agreement, which may or may not have a financial component, to provide essential resources when local resources are inadequate to meet the needs of a disaster.[21]

Agencies may draw up agreements for reciprocal assistance under certain conditions or may set out contingent acquisition agreements between providers, vendors, and contractors. California and Florida have elaborate mutual aid agreements and systems among their state and local governments. The Emergency Management Assistance Compact (discussed later in this chapter) provides for state-to-state mutual aid.[22]

An example of a mutual aid agreement might be a local multiagency plan regarding how the residents of a nursing home are to be evacuated during an emergency. Consider this example: "To ensure coordination among nursing homes, the committee provided mutual aid agreements to evacuating and hosting nursing homes, to be completed and included in each nursing home's disaster plan. These agreements outlined understandings between facilities operators with respect to transfer of patients and medical information, transportation costs, and so on." [23] An agreement, however expressed, identifies which agency controls certain resources in the field and how and when they may be reassigned. Agreements help create working relationships between agencies and governments and may facilitate trust. Mutual aid agreements are common both in conventional emergency management and in homeland security matters.

State-to-State Relations and Interstate Assistance Compacts

On October 9, 1996, Congress approved the **Emergency Management Assistance Compact (EMAC)** initiated by the Southern Governor's Association. EMAC was an agreement between fourteen states and territories made during 1995–1996 that committed them, through their respective governors, to cooperate in planning for state-to-state extension of emergency management help. The compact was open to any state or territory that chose to join, and today all the states belong to EMAC. FEMA testified in favor of EMAC before Congress and is a participant endorser of the compact. FEMA, however, decides funding of EMAC operations on a case-by-case basis. The National Emergency Management Association, an organization representing the interests of state emergency managers, through its Emergency Management Assistance Committee, moved the compact forward. EMAC represents a strong collective effort of the states to facilitate state-to-state mutual aid when major disasters and emergencies take place. In general terms, a **compact** represents an important intergovernmental agreement and it also indicates how political authorities provide consent for, and legitimacy to, such arrangements.

Predisaster Preparedness and Response Agreements

Emergency management in the United States has evolved into a complex and, since 9/11, federally dominated latticework of preparedness and response agreements. The original Federal Response Plan that emerged in the early 1990s arrayed a set of emergency support functions (ESFs); various federal agencies were expected either to lead the coordination of these functions or to serve within them.[42] The system of ESFs continues to apply today in the National Response Framework.

Emergency support functions and other components of the NRF and the National Incident Management System (both discussed more fully later in the chapter) constitute predisaster preparedness and response agreements. Table 6-2 presents emergency support functions contained in the NRP, and since December 2007, in the NRF. The original Federal Response Plan, as the title connotes, involved only federal agencies and the American Red Cross. Owing to the 9/11 terror attacks and ensuing federal laws and reorganizations, states and local governments are today integral participants in the NRF.

It is one thing to study U.S. government layer-by-layer, although some question whether the layers are as distinct as they seem.[43] It is another matter to consider how governments function when they must interact. Intergovernmental relations have both vertical and horizontal features. As shown in this chapter, when states fashion disaster mutual aid agreements and interstate disaster assistance compacts, they operate on a horizontal line. When federal, state, and local disaster agency officials establish predisaster preparedness and response agreements to facilitate the coordination of their respective agencies during future disasters, they do so along a vertical line. The new War on Terrorism has implications on the domestic front that affect intergovernmental relations on both dimensions.

THE NATIONAL RESPONSE PLAN, THE NATIONAL RESPONSE FRAMEWORK, AND THE NATIONAL INCIDENT MANAGEMENT SYSTEM

Homeland security policymakers have engaged in massive government planning efforts aimed fundamentally at a broad pool of federal, state, and local disaster responders. Since 9/11, it has largely been the president and federal agency officials who have steered home-

TABLE 6-2

Emergency Support Function Teams and ESF Coordinators

ESF #1—Transportation
ESF Coordinator: Department of Transportation
- Federal and civil transportation support
- Transportation safety
- Restoration/recovery of transportation infrastructure
- Movement restrictions
- Damage and impact assessment

ESF #2—Communications
ESF Coordinator: DHS (National Communications System)
- Coordination with telecommunications industry
- Restoration/repair and temporary provisioning of communications infrastructure
- Protection, restoration, and sustainment of national cyber and information technology resources
- Oversight of communications within the Federal incident management and response structures

ESF #3—Public Works and Engineering
ESF Coordinator: Department of Defense (U.S. Corps of Army Engineers)
- Infrastructure protection and emergency repair
- Infrastructure restoration
- Engineering services, construction management
- Critical infrastructure liaison

ESF #4—Firefighting
ESF Coordinator: Department of Agriculture (U.S. Forest Service)
- Firefighting activities on Federal lands
- Resource support to rural and urban firefighting operations

ESF #5—Emergency Management
ESF Coordinator: DHS (FEMA)
- Coordination of incident management efforts and response efforts
- Issuance of mission assignments
- Resource and human capital
- Incident action planning
- Financial management

ESF #6—Mass Care, Emergency Assistance, Housing and Human Services
ESF Coordinator: DHS (FEMA)
- Mass care
- Disaster housing
- Human services

ESF #7—Resource Support
ESF Coordinator: General Services Administration
- Resource support (facility space, office equipment and supplies, contracting services, etc.)

ESF #8—Public Health and Medical Services
ESF Coordinator: Department of Health and Human Services
- Public health

- Medical
- Mental health services
- Mortuary services

ESF #9—Search and Rescue
ESF Coordinator: DHS (FEMA)
- Life-saving assistance
- Search and rescue operations

ESF #10—Oil and Hazardous Materials Response
ESF Coordinator: Environmental Protection Agency
- Oil and hazardous materials (chemical, biological, radiological, etc.) response
- Environmental safety and short- and long-term cleanup

ESF #11—Agriculture and Natural Resources
ESF Coordinator: Department of Agriculture
- Nutrition assistance
- Animal and plant disease and pest response
- Food safety and security
- Natural and cultural resources and historic properties protection
- Safety and well-being of pets

ESF #12—Energy
ESF Coordinator: Department of Energy
- Energy infrastructure assessment, repair, and restoration
- Energy industry coordination
- Energy forecast

ESF #13—Public Safety and Security
ESF Coordinator: Department of Justice
- Facility and resource security
- Security planning and technical and resource assistance
- Public safety and security support
- Support to access, traffic, and crowd control

ESF #14—Long-Term Community Recovery
ESF Coordinator: DHS (FEMA)
- Social and economic community impact assessment
- Long-term community recovery assistance to States, local governments, and the private sector
- Mitigation analysis and program implementation

ESF #15—External Affairs
ESF Coordinator: DHS
- Emergency public information and protective action guidance
- Media and community relations
- Congressional and international affairs
- Tribal and insular affairs

Source: Department of Homeland Security, "Quick Reference Guide for the National Response Plan," version 4.0, May 22, 2006, available at http://www.dhs.gov/xlibrary/assets/NRP_Quick_Reference_Guide _5-22-06.pdf.

land security policy. Congress has provided them new authority and regular infusions of funding for purposes set forth in law and policy. Homeland security policy manifests itself as a colossal intergovernmental, multiagency, multimission enterprise fueled by widely distributed, but often highly conditional, federal program grants to state and local governments. Planning in homeland security is more than simply reorganization or realignment of existing functions; it is a formal embodiment of the federal government's official response to the terror attacks of September 11, 2001.

Development of a National Response Plan was mandated in the Homeland Security Act of 2002 and Homeland Security Presidential Directive-5 (HSPD-5). The basis for the NRP flowed from the Federal Response Plan that had preceded it; however, as mentioned, the NRP was a "national" plan that would now include "state and local government," rather than exclusively federal organizations. The NRP was to embody a single, comprehensive national approach; advance coordination of structures and administrative mechanisms; provide for direction for incorporation of existing plans with emphasis on concurrent implementation of existing plans; and set forth a consistent approach to reporting incidents, providing assessments, and making recommendations to the president, the DHS secretary, and the Homeland Security Council.

The NRP set forth a national template leaders may use to determine the appropriate level of federal involvement in response to domestic incidents. The plan was supposed to harmonize intergovernmental and interagency incident management. It was also tailored to handle "incidents of national significance," the definition of which is directly based on the criteria established in HSPD-5:

> Incidents of National Significance transpire,
>
> 1. When another Federal department or agency has requested DHS assistance;
> 2. When State/local capabilities are overwhelmed and Federal assistance is requested;
> 3. When an incident substantially involves more than one Federal department/agency;
> 4. When the (DHS) Secretary has been directed by the President to assume incident management responsibilities.[44]

A basic premise of the NRP was, and of the NRF is, that incidents need to be handled at the lowest governmental level possible. Reflecting its antiterrorism mission, DHS becomes involved through the routine reporting and monitoring of threats and incidents, and when notified of an incident or potential incident. Based on the severity, magnitude, complexity and threat to homeland security posed by the incident, DHS, its secretary, and possibly even the president, decide whether the incident warrants a designation of "incident of national significance." DHS uses various organizations at its headquarters, region, and field levels to coordinate efforts and to provide support to responders on-scene, who themselves are using a system long used by local responders, the Incident Command System (ICS). Other federal agencies carry out their incident management and emergency response authorities within this overarching framework.

The revised NRP, called the National Response Framework, is composed of seven layers, depicted in Figure 6-1.

The schematic shown in Figure 6-2 demonstrates in simplified, graphic form how DHS and FEMA officials expect the planning and preparedness process to work.

FIGURE 6-1 | Organization of the Framework

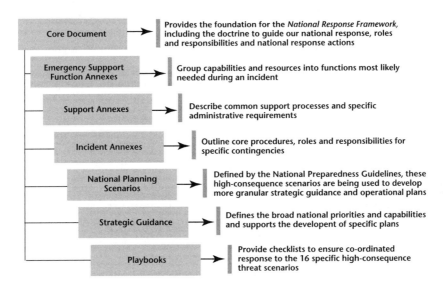

Source: U.S. FEMA, National Response Framework. Available at http://www.fema.gov/pdf/emergency/nrf/nrf-base.pdf. Last accessed November 9, 2007.

FIGURE 6-2 | National Response Network

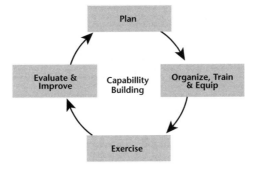

The Preparedness Cycle Builds Capabilities

Source: U.S. FEMA, National Response Framework. Available at http://www.fema.gov/pdf/emergency/nrf/nrf-base.pdf. Last accessed November 9, 2007.

Implementation of the NRP, the NRF, and the NIMS

The National Response Plan, and its successor, the NRF, was supposed to improve local capabilities and not diminish local ability to respond to more routine, localized emergencies. The federal, state, and local bonding element that emerged from Homeland Security Presidential Directive-5, was the National Incident Management System (NIMS). HSPD-5 states: "Beginning in Fiscal Year 2005, Federal departments and agencies shall make adoption of the NIMS a requirement, to the extent permitted by law, for providing Federal preparedness assistance through grants, contracts, or other activities. The Secretary shall develop standards and guidelines for determining whether a State or local entity has adopted the NIMS." [45] Under the directive, federal agencies were required to adopt, conform to, and apply the National Incident Management System.

State and local governments were not "preemptively" compelled to adopt and use the NIMS but were "encouraged" to work within the NIMS concept of operations. However, state and local officials understood that their prospects of winning many types of homeland security federal grants would be much improved if they agreed to join in and comply with the requirements of the NRP and the NIMS.

The NIMS was a product of the collaboration of DHS with state and local government officials and representatives.[46] Many in the group were from public safety organizations. The NIMS incorporated many existing emergency management "best practices" into a comprehensive national approach to domestic incident management, applicable at all jurisdictional levels and across all responder occupational fields. The aim of the NIMS was to help responders at all jurisdictional levels and across all disciplines to work together more effectively and efficiently.

A core component of the NIMS was the Incident Command System (ICS), a standard, on-scene, all-hazards incident management system already in use by many firefighters, hazardous materials teams, rescuers, and emergency medical teams. DHS officials declared that the ICS would henceforth be the standard method for addressing all incidents.

Local emergency managers were expected to learn the ICS, to participate in ICS exercises, and to acquire various certifications under NIMS, NRP, and later NRF protocols. Many local officials had to devise new, or modify existing, mutual aid agreements to suit NRP and NIMS requirements. Many state and local emergency management organizations were expected to modify their standard operating procedures as well. The NRP was to overlay existing response systems. DHS added three new emergency support functions and made some modifications to other ones. Three new structures were added to the NRP as well —the Homeland Security Operations Center, the Joint Field Office, and the Interagency Incident Management Group—all federal entities.

The NRP was issued as an unfunded mandate. States were expected to use a portion of the annual Emergency Management Performance Grant funds they received from FEMA to subsidize both state and local costs associated with meeting NRP and NIMS requirements. At the outset, the (now defunct) DHS Office of Domestic Preparedness and FEMA's Emergency Management Institute (still in operation) were to provide training, educational materials, and practice exercise opportunities. The institute developed an online independent study course to help emergency managers and others gain familiarity with the NRP, and today its successor the National Response Framework.

FIGURE 6-3 | Incident Command Structure

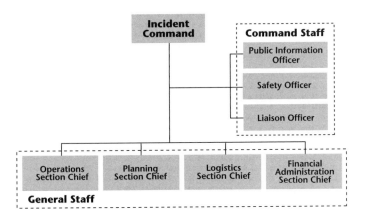

The NIMS constitutes a core set of doctrines, principles, terminology, and organizational processes. The NIMS is supposed to be based on a balance between flexibility and standardization. The recommendations of the National Commission on Terrorist Attacks upon the United States (the *9/11 Commission Report*, 2004) further highlight the importance of the Incident Command System.[47] The commission's report recommends national adoption of the ICS to enhance command, control, and communications capabilities.

In 2004 the fire and police departments of some cities had worked together using the ICS for years. In other municipalities, only the fire department used the ICS. Although law enforcement, public works, and public health officials were aware of the concept, many of these officials regarded the ICS as a fire service system. HSPD-5 required state and local adoption of the Homeland Security Department's approved NIMS definition of the ICS as a condition for receiving federal preparedness funding. According to DHS officials, although the ICS was first pioneered by the fire service, it was and still is, at its core, a management system designed to integrate resources to effectively attack a common problem.[48]

DHS officials attached great significance to the NIMS. They envisioned that the NIMS and the ICS would be necessary to address future terror attacks of the 9/11 type or scale. For them it was imperative that all responding agencies be able to interact and work together. The ICS component of the NIMS was supposed to make this possible. Not only would every state and local government be expected to establish an ICS-based system of emergency or disaster response, but they were expected to stay up to date and in conformity with the DHS-approved version of the ICS.

Figure 6-3 is a chart of the ICS structure. The ICS structure and response system has become standard in countless fire departments, police emergency operations, and emergency management systems across the nation. Many thousands of emergency responders in the United States not only know the ICS but use it as a practice, exercise, and training system frequently.

The NIMS contains a Joint Field Office component, depicted in Figure 6-4. Figure 6-5 graphically presents the federal incident planning structure under the NIMS.

HOW THINGS WORK

KEY CONCEPTS OF THE NATIONAL INCIDENT MANAGEMENT SYSTEM

The National Incident Management System (NIMS) is not easy to summarize in brief. However, it contains some core ideas and assumptions, which its authors define as concepts. Below is a rudimentary list of some of those ideas and assumptions.

Key Concepts

NIMS provides a core set of common concepts, principles, terminology and technologies in the following areas:

- Incident Command System (ICS). Much of *NIMS* is built upon the ICS, which was developed by the Federal, State and local wildland fire agencies during the 1970s. ICS is normally structured to facilitate activities in five major functional areas: command, operations, planning, logistics and finance/administration. In some circumstances, intelligence and investigations may be added as a sixth functional area.
- Multi-agency coordination systems. Examples of multi-agency coordination systems include a county emergency operations center, a State intelligence fusion center, the DHS National Operations Center, the DHS/Federal Emergency Management Agency (FEMA) National Response Coordination Center, the Department of Justice/Federal Bureau of Investigation (FBI) Strategic Information and Operations Center and the National Counterterrorism Center.
- Unified command. Unified command provides the basis from which multiple agencies can work together effectively with a common objective of effectively managing an incident. Unified command ensures that regardless of the number of agencies or jurisdictions involved, all decisions will be based on mutually specified objectives.
- Training. Leaders and staff require initial training on incident management and incident response principles, as well as ongoing training to provide updates on current concepts and procedures.
- Identification and management of resources. Classifying types of resources is essential to ensure that multiple agencies can effectively communicate and provide resources during a crisis.
- Situational awareness. Situational awareness is the provision of timely and accurate information during an incident. Situational awareness is the lifeblood of the incident management and effective response operations. Without it, decisions will not be informed by information on the ground and actions will be inefficient and inef-

More broadly, the push toward universal adoption of the NIMS and the ICS reflects the highly questionable assumption that once a consistent management structure is adopted, preparedness and response effectiveness will automatically improve. Such an assumption ignores many other factors that contribute to effective disaster management, such as ongoing contacts among crisis-relevant agencies during nondisaster times, common understandings of community vulnerability and the likely consequences of extreme events, realistic training and exercises, and sound public education programs.[49]

fective. Situational awareness requires continuous monitoring, verification and integration of key information needed to assess and respond effectively to threats, potential threats, disasters or emergencies.

- Qualifications and certification. Competent staff is a requirement for any leader managing an incident. During a crisis there will not be time to determine staff qualifications, if such information has not yet been compiled and available for review by leaders. To identify appropriate staff to support a leader during a crisis, qualifications based on training and expertise of staff should be pre-identified and evidenced by certification, if appropriate.

- Collection, tracking and reporting of incident information. Information today is transmitted instantly via the Internet and the 24/7 news channels. While timely information is valuable, it also can be overwhelming. For an effective response, we must leverage expertise and experience to identify what information is needed to support decision-makers and be able to rapidly summarize and prioritize this information. Information must by gathered accurately at the scene and effectively communicated to those who need it. To be successful, clear lines of information flow and a common operating picture are essential.

A revised version of *NIMS* will update existing doctrine based on lessons learned since the first publication of *NIMS* and add additional areas such as:

- Crisis action planning. Deliberative planning during non-incident periods should quickly transition to crisis action planning when an incident occurs. Crisis action planning is the process for rapidly adapting existing deliberative plan and procedures during an incident based on the actual circumstances of an event. Crisis action planning should also include the provision of decision tools for senior leaders to guide their decision-making.

- Exercises. Consistent with the National Exercise Program, all stakeholders should regularly exercise their incident management and response capabilities and procedures to ensure that they are fully capable of executing their incident response responsibilities.

Source: Department of Homeland Security, "Quick Reference Guide for the National Response Plan," May 22, 2006, version 4.0., 14–15, available at http://www.dhs.gov/xlibrary/assets/NRP_Quick_Reference_Guide_5-22-06.pdf.

One highly experienced emergency manager puts it this way:

While NIMS is based on the highly regarded Incident Command System, ICS is primarily a field operating system that is useful for hierarchical paramilitary organizations. In other words, it works for fire, police, and emergency medical services. NIMS fails to take into account, however, the qualitative differences that emerge as one approaches crises of increasing complexity that must be managed by non-hierarchical organizations.

FIGURE 6-4 | Joint Field Office

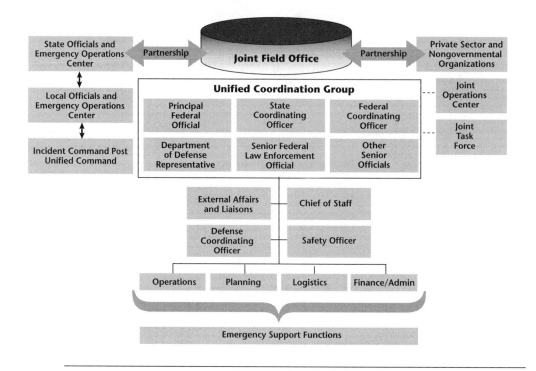

The growing emphasis on terrorism readiness and ICS principles has led to a concomitant emphasis on "first responder" agencies and personnel. In current homeland security parlance, the term "first responder" refers to uniformed personnel (fire, police, and emergency services personnel) that arrive at the scene of a disaster. Missing from this discourse is a recognition that, as numerous studies reveal, ordinary citizens are the true "first responders" in all disasters. For example, in Homeland Security Presidential Directive-8, a mere two sentences are devoted to the topic of citizen participation in preparedness activities. These new policies and programs may leave vast reserves of talent and capability untapped in future extreme events.[50]

Many post-9/11 investigations have highlighted problems associated with "stovepiping" or the tendency for organizations and agencies to closely guard information, carry out their own specialized activities in isolation from one another, and resist efforts to encourage cross-agency collaboration.[51] Indeed, DHS itself was created in order to overcome stovepipes, better integrate disparate agencies and programs, and improve information sharing and cooperation. However, many homeland security initiatives have created new stovepipes, owing to the effects of organizational turf wars and to the imposition of state secrecy requirements in realms that did not have them before.

FIGURE 6-5 | Federal Incident Management Planning Structure

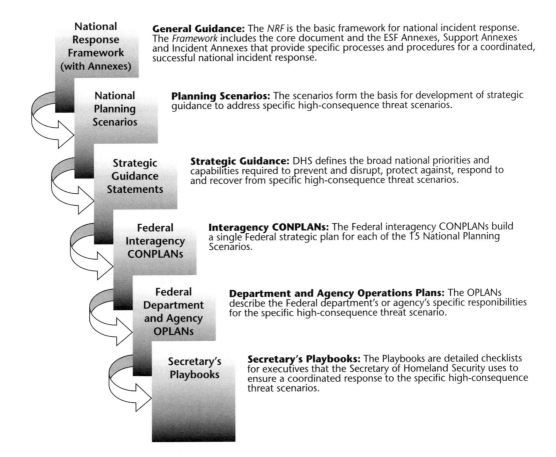

National Response Framework (with Annexes)

General Guidance: The *NRF* is the basic framework for national incident response. The *Framework* includes the core document and the ESF Annexes, Support Annexes and Incident Annexes that provide specific processes and procedures for a coordinated, successful national incident response.

National Planning Scenarios

Planning Scenarios: The scenarios form the basis for development of strategic guidance to address specific high-consequence threat scenarios.

Strategic Guidance Statements

Strategic Guidance: DHS defines the broad national priorities and capabilities required to prevent and disrupt, protect against, respond to and recover from specific high-consequence threat scenarios.

Federal Interagency CONPLANs

Interagency CONPLANs: The Federal interagency CONPLANs build a single Federal strategic plan for each of the 15 National Planning Scenarios.

Federal Department and Agency OPLANs

Department and Agency Operations Plans: The OPLANs describe the Federal department's or agency's specific responsibilities for the specific high-consequence threat scenario.

Secretary's Playbooks

Secretary's Playbooks: The Playbooks are detailed checklists for executives that the Secretary of Homeland Security uses to ensure a coordinated response to the specific high-consequence threat scenarios.

According to a senior disaster sociology scholar,

> although diverse law enforcement agencies at different governmental levels may be making progress in working together on terrorism-related issues, the law enforcement sector itself may have little incentive to take an active role in broader cross-sectoral preparedness efforts. Rather than promoting comprehensive preparedness for all potential threats—including disasters and terrorism—special-purpose initiatives (such as antiterrorism) encourage organizations to interact and plan within their own separate spheres and to focus on particular kinds of threats. Massive infusion of federal funds into specialized . . . intergovernmental programs causes distortions in broad-gauged emergency management conducted by state and local governments.[52]

INTERGOVERNMENTAL DISASTER MANAGEMENT CHALLENGES

In any field of endeavor, the effectiveness of a human system depends upon how well those who are part of that system understand the functions that must be carried out and their own roles and responsibilities in smoothly executing those functions. Certainly, this is true of emergency management. The potential for human suffering and devastation in a disaster makes it critical that emergency managers and related personnel understand fully the character of potential hazards, what can be done about these hazards through the application of emergency management principles and programs, and their role and responsibilities in the system of emergency management.

In the U.S. system of disaster management a broad range of political and managerial transactions take place between and among governments of all levels. Each of the fifty states and each American commonwealth territory has an emergency management agency of some type. These agencies, like their local counterparts, are supposed to be well organized and to have emergency plans, facilities, and equipment. To become and remain eligible for federal emergency management financial assistance, each state must manage a state emergency management program that augments and facilitates local emergency management.

To make an intergovernmental system work, improvisation and flexibility must be part of the ethos of the system. Officials in this system must identify various emergency task domains and they must reach a consensus about who is going to perform each. Nevertheless, many disasters present unanticipated demands, so emergency managers must be able to improvise.

Intergovernmental relations in matters of disaster management are not always affable. For example, federal, state, and local officials are supposed to conduct preliminary damage assessments after a disaster. These assessments help to determine whether the disaster is beyond the response and recovery capabilities of the state and local governments affected. A determination that the disaster has produced damage, or has created ongoing dangers, beyond the response and recovery capabilities of the affected governments serves to justify issuance of a presidential declaration of major disaster or emergency.[53] However, disputes sometimes arise over the matter of how extensive damage actually is and what is "clearly beyond" recovery capability and what is not. Sometimes these disputes must be resolved by the president himself through approval or rejection of a governor's request for a declaration of major disaster or emergency.

Some suspect that after many "disasters" intergovernmental interchanges embody a **crying poor syndrome.**[54] Local governments sustaining disaster losses and costs have every incentive to exaggerate their scales of damage in order to maximize outside state and federal postdisaster aid. If state governments shield their local governments from having to pay little or no money into the state-local matching share required in many federal disaster relief programs, these local governments have even greater incentive to detail every conceivable disaster loss eligible for state and federal assistance. Zero local matching share means that federal and state relief provide a 100 percent local recovery subsidy. Repairs to City Hall do not impose costs on local taxpayers.[55]

States also have an incentive to maximize, if not exaggerate, their magnitudes of disaster loss. Ordinarily, each presidential declaration of major disaster or emergency conveys federal-

HOW THINGS WORK

A SHORT REVISIT TO PRESIDENTIAL DECLARATIONS

For all major disasters, and for emergencies that do not primarily involve federal responsibility and authority, governors of the affected states must request the presidential declaration after certifying that necessary action has been taken under state law; damage estimates have been made; state and local resources have been committed; and, cost-sharing requirements of the statute will be met.[57]

The collection of information on damages involves a collaborative effort involving FEMA staff, state officials, and personnel from affected local governments. Teams of assessors conduct a preliminary damage assessment to estimate the degree of damage and potential costs resulting from the disaster. The assessment is broken down into categories (such as the number of homes damaged or destroyed and the number of public facilities damaged or destroyed) that correspond to the broad categories of disaster relief and assistance that FEMA provides through the individual assistance or public assistance programs authorized by the Stafford Act. Information in the preliminary damage assessments is used to determine whether a declaration will be issued and, if one is issued, whether individual and public assistance programs will be provided to the areas (generally, counties, parishes, and independent cities) included in the declaration.

It is in these interchanges that political and managerial factors often come into play. Mayors press governors for more state and federal aid. A governor, lamenting the high costs of a disaster and the state matching share obligations they produce, sometimes receives permission to borrow from the federal government the money his or her state needs to pay its own match. At least one Government Accountability Office report disclosed that states sometimes fail to repay all or most of the federal money they have borrowed to cover their matching share. In catastrophic disasters, governors sometimes succeed in securing from the president a higher federal match (100 percent for Florida after Hurricane Andrew in 1992); 90 percent for California after the Northridge earthquake in 1994); 90 percent for Louisiana, Mississippi, and Alabama after Hurricane Katrina in 2005. Such generous federal matching shares impel state and local loss estimators to identify every single dollar of eligible disaster cost.

FEMA sets forth criteria its own officials use to judge state and local eligibility for a declaration of major disaster, but as mentioned before, the decision to confer a declaration is the president's alone, and the president can freely use or disregard FEMA's criteria.[58] Each year, FEMA issues a notice that identifies the threshold to be used as one factor to be considered in the determination of whether public assistance or individual assistance or both will be made available after a major disaster declaration has been issued. The regulations establish a minimum threshold of $1 million in public assistance damages for each state.[59] Major disasters declared on or after October 1, 2005, would generally be expected to reach the threshold of $1.18 per capita for public assistance to be authorized. However, the statewide threshold is not the sole factor. Assessments consider concentrations of damages in local jurisdictions even if statewide damages are not severe. Countywide impacts from major disasters declared on or after October 1, 2005, would generally be expected to reach the threshold of $2.94 per capita in order to be authorized for public assistance.[60]

state matching aid of seventy-five to twenty-five. In other words, seventy-five cents of every dollar of state disaster loss is subsidized by federal assistance. When states share their matching burden with localities, the state government derives an even greater subsidy. Since the federal government carries the bulk of financial burden in paying for the public costs of presidentially declared emergencies and major disasters, it is no surprise that FEMA officials are often highly suspicious of state and local estimates of disaster loss.[56] They sometimes suspect state and local government officials of conspiring to maximize federal disaster dollars dispatched to their jurisdictions. Such behavior on the part of these officials exemplifies distributive politics, under which political actors seek resources in excess of their actual need.

Nonprofit Organizations and Volunteers

A great many voluntary nonprofit organizations are involved in disaster mitigation, preparedness, response, and recovery efforts. Disasters trigger an outpouring of individual contributions of money or in-kind donations central to the operation and sustenance of many of these bodies. Government emergency management agencies often interact with these organizations and do so for a variety of reasons. The dynamics of that interchange, the interdependence of public and private disaster management organizations, and the political positives and negatives of relying upon nonprofit voluntary organizational help will be addressed here.

By definition, a voluntary nonprofit organization is one that provides service to a community free of charge or for the minimal cost that is required to defray the cost of the service(s) furnished. Financial support for voluntary agencies is generally through donations, contracts, and grants. Private nonprofit organizations are legally characterized by holding the special nonprofit federal tax exempt status. Many such organizations provide educational, social services, emergency, medical, rehabilitation, and temporary or permanent custodial care facilities (including those for the aged and disabled), or other facilities that produce essential services for the general public.

Voluntary nonprofit organizations, community service groups, and church organizations that provide assistance in the aftermath of a disaster or an emergency are often referred to as VOLAGs, or voluntary agencies. VOLAG involvement in disaster response and recovery has a long history in America. For example, in 1905, the U.S. Congress mandated that the American Red Cross "continue and carry on a system of national and international relief in time of peace and apply the same in mitigating the sufferings caused by pestilence, famine, fire, floods, and other great national calamities, and to devise and carry on measures for preventing the same." [61] Similarly, the Salvation Army, a recognized church, has been providing disaster relief assistance since 1899.

A great many not-for-profit and volunteer organizations in the United States have an interest in, and role to play in, emergency management. Organized volunteer resource groups come in a great variety of forms. Besides the American Red Cross and the Salvation Army there are Volunteers of America, the Mennonite Disaster Service, the Southern Baptist Convention, Catholic Charities, Episcopal Relief and Development, United Jewish Communities, Friends Disaster Service, Church World Services, Save the Children, to name a few (see NVOAD membership, p. 160).

States, localities, and nongovernment organizations respond to many disasters that do not involve federal assistance. These organizations also play a vital role when federal authorities are involved in disaster work under a presidential disaster declaration. However, government emergency managers and those in voluntary assistance organizations do not necessarily share the same definition of disaster or emergency. Even voluntary organizations themselves use different emergency management terminology, follow different methods of budgeting and management, and have different perceptions of government's role in disaster management.

Nonprofit voluntary relief organizations have historically provided considerable disaster assistance to victims, particularly by distributing food, medical supplies, and temporary shelter. Churches, religious orders, and social welfare organizations have established organizations specifically dedicated to providing such assistance. A report issued by the National Academy of Public Administration after Hurricane Andrew noted that volunteer organizations, many nonprofit organizations, and private sector organizations participate in mitigation, preparedness, response, and recovery.[62] They regularly address incidents ranging from minor ones to catastrophes.

In preparedness, VOLAGs assist in developing disaster plans and in training disaster responders; they provide facilities and resources as well as community disaster education; and they join in drills, exercises, and simulations. In the response phase, VOLAGs furnish resources such as trained personnel, masses of untrained but instrumental helpers, and various facilities. In cooperation with local, state, and federal authorities, VOLAGs often provide the bulk of mass care services, sheltering, feeding, and clothing individuals and families; assisting high-risk, "gap group" clients; and, through an extended network of service organizations, helping to coordinate interests not generally involved in disaster response. Gap group clients are those who seem to fall between the cracks of eligible government assistance; they are poor but not poor enough to qualify for government individual and household cash assistance, which is means tested.

In recovery operations, VOLAGs work in partnership with government and affected communities to identify and meet remaining long-term recovery needs of families and individuals. In mitigation, VOLAGs often advocate to elected and appointed officials sound land-use planning and zoning, as well as the adoption and implementation of appropriate building codes and standards aimed at protecting and safeguarding people and property from disaster. Information about what the public can do to safeguard their property is shared through community disaster education activities.

A growing trend is the cooperation and coordination of volunteer organizations that participate in disaster relief. At the national level is the National Volunteer Organizations Active in Disaster (NVOAD), a group of forty-nine national organizations that have made disaster response a priority and coordinate the planning efforts of many voluntary organizations that respond to disaster (see Table 6-3). The group includes the American Red Cross and the Salvation Army. NVOAD grew out of the response to Hurricane Camille in 1969, when organizations that had been involved in providing resources and services to victims and communities affected by the disaster shared their mutual concern about their frequent duplication of services. Representatives of these organizations began to meet together on a regular basis. In those meetings participants learned about their respective activities, concerns, and frustrations, and they labored to prevent duplication and inefficiencies in their responses to future disasters.

TABLE 6-3 — NVOAD Membership List as of May 4, 2007

Adventist Community Services	Medical Teams International
American Baptist Men/USA	Mennonite Disaster Service
American Disaster Reserve	Mercy Medical Airlift (Angel Flight)
American Radio Relay League, Inc. (ARRL)	National Association of Jewish Chaplains
American Red Cross	National Emergency Response Team
America's Second Harvest	National Organization for Victim Assistance
Ananda Marga Universal Relief Team (AMURT)	Nazarene Disaster Response
Catholic Charities USA	Operation Blessing
Christian Disaster Response	Points of Light Foundation and Volunteer Center
Christian Reformed World Relief Committee (CRWRC)	National Network
Church of the Brethren—Emergency Response	Presbyterian Church (USA)
Church World Service	REACT International, Inc.
Churches of Scientology Disaster Response	Salvation Army
Convoy of Hope	Samaritan's Purse
Disaster Psychiatry Outreach	Save the Children
Episcopal Relief and Development	Society of St. Vincent de Paul
Feed The Children	Southern Baptist Convention
Friends Disaster Service, Inc.	The Phoenix Society for Burn Survivors
HOPE Coalition America	Tzu Chi Foundation
Humane Society of the United States	United Church of Christ—Wider Church Ministries
International Aid	United Jewish Communities
International Critical Incident Stress Foundation	United Methodist Committee on Relief
International Relief and Development (IRD)	United Way of America
International Relief Friendship Foundation (IRFF)	Volunteers of America
Lutheran Disaster Response	World Vision

Source: National Voluntary Organizations Active in Disasters, "National Members," May 4, 2007, available at http://www.nvoad.org/membersdb.php ?members=National (accessed November 12, 2007).

Also part of NVOAD are sixty-one distinct state-level umbrella groups, VOADs, working at the state, District of Columbia, or trust territory levels. These state-level VOADS help coordinate the work of many hundreds of smaller organizations. VOAD member organizations provide more effective disaster aid and less duplication in service by getting together before disasters strike. Once disasters occur, NVOAD or an affiliated state VOAD encourages members and other voluntary agencies to convene on site. This cooperative effort helps a wide variety of volunteers and organizations to work together in a crisis.

NVOAD serves member organizations in the following ways:

- Communication: disseminating information electronic mechanisms, newsletters, directories, research and demonstration, case studies, and critique
- Cooperation: creating a climate for cooperation at all levels (including grassroots)
- Coordination: coordinating policy among member organizations and serving as a liaison, advocate, and national voice
- Education: providing training and increasing awareness and preparedness in each organization
- Leadership development: giving volunteer leaders training and support so as to build effective state VOAD organizations

- Convening mechanisms: conducting seminars, special meetings, board meetings, regional conferences, training programs, and local conferences
- Outreach: encouraging the formation of, and furnishing guidance to, state and regional voluntary organizations active in disaster relief

NVOAD policy stipulates: "The role of a VOAD group is not to manage disaster response operations; but it is instead to coordinate planning and preparations in advance of disaster incidents and operations."

Volunteer Organizations in the Field

Most volunteer organizations are involved in immediate emergency response, such as mass care, which includes feeding, sheltering, clothing of victims, and the like. Some are involved in recovery activities, such as rebuilding, clean up, and reconstituting community mental health. Many organizations provide the same or similar services. Problems of overlap or competition usually are avoided if the agencies coordinate and cooperate. VOLAGs must collectively agree to share the work by coordinating their limited resources so that as many agencies as possible are able to take part in the response and recovery effort. By sharing and cooperating, VOLAGs may share credit for the recovery of their communities and for promoting the community healing process. Sometimes VOLAGs fight among themselves at the expense of the people they are trying to serve.

However, VOLAGs by nature compete for the donated dollar. This is not necessarily a problem unless during relief operations various VOLAGs are not provided an opportunity to serve or be publicly recognized for the help they provide. VOLAGs need a chance to demonstrate their abilities to both their supporters and to the community at large. Sometimes government public information officers report on the efforts of just a few VOLAGs without acknowledging the legitimate contributions of all VOLAGs engaged in a response or recovery operation. Such omissions can create rancor and misunderstanding. VOLAGs themselves need to draft cooperative, or joint, press releases to illustrate their collaborative efforts.

VOLAGs are private organizations with their own missions and responsibilities. Local VOLAGs often report to a parent organization whose headquarters are located outside of the disaster area. Sometimes an agency's national headquarters will support their local agency by sending in national leadership or a response team to assist the disaster relief effort. Conflicts sometimes arise when the national teams and the local response element do not coordinate, collaborate, cooperate, or communicate. Occasionally problems and awkwardness result when the national team makes a decision on behalf of its local affiliate without thinking about the long-term ramifications that decision might have on the agency after the national team returns home. Sometimes a national team fails to understand cultural, economic, and political sensitivities of the local community and acts in a way that induces the community to look unfavorably upon the local affiliate. This may undermine years of trust and good faith built up under conditions of normalcy before the disaster. It is important that parent organizations not jeopardize the credibility or funding base of local affiliates during a disaster response or recovery effort.

In addition to those nonprofit voluntary organizations outside of government, some voluntary organizations engaged in disaster response and emergency management are part of

HOW THINGS WORK

THE POLITICS AND PREFERENCES OF VOLUNTEER ORGANIZATIONS

Government emergency management officials can never be sure how much postdisaster help voluntary organizations are able to provide. Often, voluntary organizations augment government assistance and do so admirably. However, sometimes voluntary organizations are overwhelmed by the scale of need they encounter. Clearly, many voluntary organizations were for weeks overwhelmed by the human needs created by Hurricane Andrew in south Florida in 1992 and by Hurricane Katrina in the Gulf Coast in 2005. Sometimes they are only modestly involved in offering assistance and occasionally they choose not to respond to a disaster at all. Some organizations are reluctant to offer assistance if they have problems with those needing help. They may be highly reluctant to aid undocumented aliens, or corrections parolees, or HIV-AIDS victims, or people of religious faiths or cultures drastically different from their own. In 1992, after the Los Angeles riots triggered by police exoneration in the Rodney King case, some organizations were slow or unwilling to help victims, many of whom were racial or ethnic minorities.

The disaster assistance process is based on an interagency referral system. Referrals are made between VOLAGs, between govern-

ments, and between VOLAGs and governments. Government assistance supplements individual and family resources, and VOLAG assistance augments these resources and helps address unmet needs. VOLAG people serve communities after disasters. However, they also know that government programs often provide more assistance, and in recent years, with greater speed than most nonprofit and private organizations do after a disaster. Moreover, VOLAGs must take into account that if they provide certain forms of financial assistance, that assistance may make the client ineligible to receive certain types of government disaster assistance. Ironically, by providing certain forms of aid too quickly, VOLAGs may decrease the total sum of government disaster assistance that might have flowed to the community. VOLAGs must reconcile their desire to respond and assist quickly in recovery efforts with the knowledge that more resources may be conserved if they wait for government to distribute its resources and only then offer help to meet the remaining needs of disaster clients. Perhaps most significant is how such organizations support and nurture disaster victims and their families. Yet, despite this historical and traditional role, it is not possible to measure

government. The Citizen Corps, which is an arm of U.S.A. Freedom Corps, invites people at the community level to volunteer. Citizen Corps councils working at the state and local level regularly receive federal funding used to promote training and education of community volunteers, in some ways helping them to respond to disasters or emergencies in their communities.[63] Moreover, the federal Corporation for National and Community Service administers and, through grants, funds AmeriCorps, Senior Corps, and Learn and Serve America. These three organizations engage in volunteer-based activity, a portion of which is directed to serving emergency management and homeland security purposes.[64] This type of volunteer coproduction activity not only augments the pool of people available to help in times of disaster or accurately the amount of assistance provided through such voluntary efforts.

Another complicating factor is that disasters provide a major impetus for the solicitation of charitable contributions needed to administer these organizations and to fund their assistance programs. Many nonprofit assistance organizations derive income for their budgets from governments both before and after disasters. The federal government may provide reimbursement of some of the costs of relief provided by VOLAGs. However, law and policy dictate that FEMA cannot reimburse a VOLAG that proselytizes its religion in the course of dispensing relief assistance to disaster victims.

Voluntary organizations must generate positive publicity in order to reassure contributors that their donations are getting to where they are intended. However, voluntary organizations compete with each other for donors and donated dollars. Emergency managers must be aware of the possibility that competition among nonprofit organizations may complicate coordination of relief efforts. Certain organizations have strong political backing that they may bring to bear on disaster managers.

Voluntary nonprofit organizations enjoy a special tax status that exempts them from paying many federal, state, and local taxes and that provides their donors with a tax deduction for charitable dollar or in-kind donations. However, this special tax benefit limits these organizations from engaging in political activity, especially lobbying legislatures. Consequently, voluntary organizations appear not to be formally involved in public political issues. However, they are very much involved informally in public and community issues that are part of the world of politics and policy. These organizations and their members are free to express their views and to publish recommendations on matters of public policy. They are less able to make campaign contributions or directly lobby the government for special benefits to their organizations. However, they often champion the causes of the general interests they represent (children, the elderly, the disabled, minorities [racial, ethnic, religious], women, the poor and homeless, victims of crime or abuse, victims of disaster, the seriously ill or those needing hospice care, ex-convicts, people suffering drug addictions or mental illness, health or social welfare clients, and the like). Consequently, by advocating government benefits for the interests they represent, they may gain from government programs indirectly.

emergency, but these programs help foster popular support for the work of local, state, and federal emergency management people and programs.

GOVERNMENT CONTRACTORS AND DISASTER MANAGEMENT

When the federal government hires private businesses to perform specific jobs, the government becomes the customer. Ingrained in the customer-to-supplier relationship is the supplier's obligation to satisfy the customer. If the contracted business is to satisfy the government, the contracted task(s) must be completed in an efficient, effective, and equitable manner.

Ordinarily, contracts are awarded through a competitive bidding process, but in emergency circumstances the federal government may award a firm contract if it is the only applicant, a form of sole source contracting. The federal government can also lump together many tasks into one, large contract and allow the winning contractor to subcontract distinct sections of the prime contract work to other businesses, again in the interest of speed. Because government agencies cannot handle every disaster management task, these agencies award contracts to businesses to handle specific tasks, to engage in certain types of activity, or to produce or supply some type of product or service.

The federal government is quite dependent on contractors, and this is especially so for the Department of Homeland Security and the Federal Emergency Management Agency. One argument in favor of using government contractors is that contractors have more flexibility and freedom to complete work, and often at less cost, than government does. A counterargument is that government contractors, as profit-maximizing businesses, have an incentive to minimally meet the terms of the contract, nothing more. Some government contractors have been accused of being unresponsive to taxpayers or have been prosecuted for fraud and corruption.

Contractors are often rapacious in their effort to win government funding. Some private firms have found a niche in helping other companies win government contracts. One such company is Onvia. Onvia provides a type of brokerage service between businesses looking to win government contracts and government agencies seeking to hire businesses. Winning a government contract is often complicated, and the necessary paperwork is dauntingly exhaustive. Organizations like Onvia provide tutelage to contractors that retain their services.[65]

Few corporations seem to dominate spheres of government contracting more than Halliburton does. Founded in 1919, Halliburton is one of the world's largest providers of products and services to the petroleum and energy industries.[66] Halliburton has many government contracts, and many of those are with the U.S. military. However, Halliburton has expanded its services into disaster relief.[67]

Booz Allen Hamilton, another corporation experienced in winning and completing government contracts, is a consulting firm that has expertise in decision support and technology applications. Booz Allen Hamilton serves the public sector in its information technology work, its national security work, and its services integration work.[68] The firm is noted for its achievements in supporting projects involving water supply, highway construction, airports, housing, telecommunications, and other public improvements.[69]

Booz Allen Hamilton has engaged in a wide variety of government contracts relevant to emergency management. The firm uses a governance committee that works cooperatively with the U.S. Senate, the Department of Defense, and the Department of Homeland Security.[70] The committee was working to improve federal response and resilience well before Hurricane Katrina struck the Gulf Coast in 2005. The vice president of Booz Allen Hamilton said that the committee "builds in the ability to absorb a blow and get operations back up quickly. It integrates different disciplines around mission effectiveness and improves the velocity of recovery." [71]

Booz Allen Hamilton was directly involved in the transportation of Hurricane Katrina victims. The U.S. Department of Transportation at the FEMA-led National Response Coordination Center hired Booz Allen Hamilton to offer consultation on security, emergency management, planning, logistics, operations systems, and technical support services. Booz Allen Hamilton had been working with the National Response Plan's Emergency Support

Function number 1 before Katrina. ESF number 1 is the framework regarding how the federal government aids communities after a disaster. The firm's employees were integrally involved in conducting work for the government before, during, and after Hurricane Katrina.[72]

Another government contractor, Bechtel, is a global engineering, construction, and project management company in existence for more than a century. Bechtel focuses on roads and rail systems, airports and seaports, environmental cleanup projects, telecommunications networks, and pipelines.[73] A company with more than forty thousand employees and forty offices, Bechtel has been a government contractor for such projects as the Hoover Dam, Europe's Channel Tunnel and Rail Link, the Boston Central Artery/Tunnel, Iraq reconstruction, the Three Mile Island cleanup.[74]

As a longtime customer, therefore, FEMA looked to Bechtel to assist in the disaster recovery efforts of Hurricane Katrina. Bechtel immediately supplied temporary housing for almost one hundred thousand Mississippi residents who were displaced.[75] The Department of Homeland Security and FEMA then awarded Bechtel a two-year contract to provide additional temporary housing and other disaster relief support. According to Bechtel, the contract was won through a full and open competitive process. The contract, which has a $250 million upper limit, calls for Bechtel to carry out tasks decided by FEMA officials. Some of these tasks include site assessment and inspection; temporary housing unit hauling, installation, and staging area support; temporary housing group site design; general construction services; and facility management. Bechtel has subcontracted some of the tasks to other federally certified businesses.[76] In a news release in August 2006 the chairman of Bechtel, Thomas Hash, assured the public of its readiness for action: "We stand ready for FEMA's call to partner in relief efforts whenever the need arises. We were pleased to answer FEMA's call during the Hurricane Katrina recovery and I'm proud of our record of success in helping to quickly house nearly 100,000 Mississippians. . . . Bechtel and our team of small business subcontractors are committed to continuing to provide FEMA with first-rate rapid response in support of individuals affected by such disasters." [77]

In July 2006 the Gulf Coast Workforce Development Initiative took effect. The initiative is a public-private partnership involving local businesses; construction trade groups; labor unions; community organizations; academic institutions; and federal, state, and local governments. The group includes an association of 160 chief executive officers from the nation's leading companies. The plan calls for a program in which 20,000 new construction workers will be recruited and trained. The idea is to train and hire individuals from the area and enable them to rebuild the area that they consider home. Bechtel is heavily involved in this project and in Gulf Coast reconstruction. The development program is expected to become an important catalyst and model for disaster recovery in the future.[78]

Last, the Dewberry Company has a half-century of experience providing expert contractor services in architecture, environmental services, geographic information systems, land development, and transportation. Dewberry claims that its government contract work has done much to advance the development of emergency management. Dewberry provides both predisaster and postdisaster assistance to federal, state, and local governments. Dewberry clients include the Department of Homeland Security, FEMA, the Army Corps of Engineers, the U.S. Geological Survey, and more than thirty local government agencies. Dewberry's emergency management specialists have an average of twenty-six years experience in the field.

Dewberry has experience and expertise in all four phases of emergency management: preparedness, response, recovery, and mitigation.[79]

After Hurricane Katrina, FEMA hired Dewberry to help in disaster recovery. The firm dispatched engineers, specialists, and inspectors into the Gulf Coast region to perform a diverse range of tasks. For example, Dewberry was designated to lead the strike team asked to assess damage done to certain justice facilities. Working alongside state and local officials, Dewberry performed on-site assessments of police facilities, fire stations, and courthouses. Dewberry won contracts to provide technical assistance to municipalities seeking repair of their infrastructure. Dewberry holds contracts aimed at helping FEMA advance disaster mitigation and evaluate the performance of various structures in disaster circumstances.[80]

In 2006 FEMA awarded Dewberry a two-year contract to provide temporary housing assistance for future disaster victims. It has a $250 million cost ceiling. [81]

Observations on Government Contractors and Contracting

There has been a significant increase in federal government contracting since 9/11. A great many of these contracts have been awarded by the Department of Homeland Security and FEMA. Is government becoming too dependent on government contractors? Is the process under which contracts are bid and awarded fair, legal, and appropriately monitored? Has the system of bidding and application become so complex and mysterious that small companies cannot expect to be competitive in winning government contracts?

If one examines government contracts, it is often intriguing to discover what specific services government agencies are contracting out to businesses. There obviously are many tasks the government cannot perform themselves, but clearly some tasks could be, and have in the past been, executed by the federal government. For many years FEMA relied on its own force of disaster assistance employees, who are in fact paid volunteers with needed expertise, to handle many disaster recovery duties. However, FEMA has contracted out a considerable portion of these disaster service worker duties to private businesses.

Positive and Negative Aspects of Subcontracting

In federal fiscal year 2005, for example, the year of Hurricane Katrina, the federal government spent over $388 billion on "all" of its federal contracts (for every purpose). Most companies that win contracts rarely do all the work on their own; instead, they subcontract work out to other companies. This has positive and negative consequences. A positive consequence is that smaller firms less capable of competing for prime federal contracts sometimes win business on the rebound via subcontracting. A negative consequence is that government oversight of contracted work becomes extremely difficult when layers of subcontractors are engaged. This practice makes it difficult to ensure accountability to the U.S. Treasury and national taxpayer. The practice also sometimes adds overhead charges such that the ultimate services and products provided are of less volume and of greater per unit cost than what the government expected when it awarded the contract. Waste and misuse become more difficult to ferret out.[82]

FIND THE FAULT?

The Northridge earthquake of January 17, 1994, was a highly destructive U.S. seismic event. The Northridge earthquake occurred along a thrust fault and did most of its damage across the San Fernando Valley and other areas of Los Angeles. Again, just as with the northern California's Loma Prieta earthquake of 1989, Northridge drew protracted national news coverage, often broadcast live with the anchor person in the zone of damage. Political differences between the Democratic president Bill Clinton and the Republican governor Pete Wilson could have interfered with any cooperation between FEMA and California's Office of Emergency Services, but to the credit of all, the federal, state, and local response was generally efficient and lauded.

Federal response to the 1994 Northridge earthquake was also remarkable because it introduced many new applications of information technology. FEMA's inspectors used palm-top computers to receive and send reports. These reports pertained to field visits they made to homes and other structures that sustained damage and whose owners or occupants sought federal assistance. FEMA and California Office of Emergency Services officials generated prodigious numbers of GIS-produced maps that helped in surveying building inspections, damage patterns, and infrastructure problems. Cell phone technology facilitated field operations in a way not seen in previous disaster response and recovery operations.[83]

However, a post-Northridge federal-state disaster rebuilding controversy arose concerning the costs of rebuilding Los Angeles area hospitals. FEMA contributes to disaster recovery costs, including costs of improving health and safety facilities. In March 1996 the agency announced that it would provide nearly $1 billion in federal funds in a new mitigation effort to strengthen the structural integrity of four local hospitals damaged by the Northridge earthquake.[84]

This decision came after a heated dispute between FEMA and California officials. Initially, FEMA officials complained that California had mandated post-quake building code changes that were unfair to the federal government. When thousands of large, medium, and small businesses complained about the high cost of rebuilding under the state's new tougher seismic building codes, California relented and waived the new code requirements for "private-sector" entities. Yet, the state maintained the new building code requirements for "public" structures, those that FEMA would have to rebuild under a federal-state cost-sharing scheme of ninety to ten. President Clinton had waived the seventy-five/twenty-five federal-state match and allowed a more generous ninety/ten federal-state match. Thus, the hospitals and all other government and nonprofit enterprises eligible to receive rebuilding money under the ninety/ten federal-state rule had to comply with the new tougher building codes.

FEMA director James Lee Witt elegantly conceded in the dispute by disclosing that after "comprehensive consultation with the state and the hospitals, FEMA provided the most cost-effective funding package that would ensure that these buildings will be able to operate after another major earthquake."[85] The new hospitals would help preclude the need to evacuate patients in future quakes and would ensure that hospital facilities would be there and intact to help after future seismic disasters. In the end, no California hospitals were put out of operation and, in fact, four completely new hospitals were built with federal postdisaster public assistance funds. This case conveys the complexity of intergovernmental disaster management in the United States and demonstrates how one state shrewdly capitalized on federal disaster relief made available after an earthquake.

CONCLUSION AND SUMMARY

One thing abundantly obvious in U.S. disaster policy and management is the tremendous degree of overlap and interdependence of American governmental jurisdictions. Moreover, U.S. intergovernmental relations are dynamic and ever changing. Sometimes the federal government appears dominant and other times states or localities seem to gain ascendancy. For the United States, homeland security priorities were triggered by acts of terrorism. Counterterrorism efforts demand colossal information collection, processing, and management aimed at preventing or responding to "incidents." These efforts require information sharing, coordination, and considerable centralization of authority. The standardization, security restrictions, and hierarchy of authority needed in homeland security complicates intergovernmental relations, diminishes the role of civilian, and particularly private or voluntary, parties and subsumes all-hazards emergency management under a new form of American civil defense.[86]

Another obvious but unappreciated aspect of disaster policy is how nongovernmental organizations, such as Volunteer Organizations Active in Disasters, play a role in the making of disaster policy and in disaster management. These altruistic organizations do much more than "gap fill" the unmet needs of disaster victims. They are part of the essential bulwark of disaster preparedness, response, and recovery. However, these organizations have their own agendas, work together with varying degrees of success, are not necessarily compelled to respond to a disaster, and depend on the donated dollar and on publicity for the good works they do. However, it is people from these organizations that are likely to help you and your family in the middle of the night when your home has been destroyed by a fire. Local firefighters may have rescued you and extinguished the fire. But in the absence of help from family and friends, it will likely be people from a charitable organization that will provide you and your family clothing, temporary shelter, food, and even short-term financial help.

Finally, as national policy for the last fifteen to twenty years, the federal government has engaged either in outright privatization of many functions previously handled by the government or in outsourcing selective functions and activities to private sector firms. State and local governments have also engaged in privatization and outsourcing as well. On top of this, the federal government has retained private for-profit corporations either to manage various short-term projects and tasks or to produce and distribute certain products. Privatization and outsourcing have corresponded with a simultaneous shrinkage of the full-time federal workforce. The world of "government" programs has become a world heavily occupied by for-profit businesses. Many federal emergency management officials dedicate their workdays to managing and overseeing contracts issued to private firms, firms that today implement gigantic swathes of emergency management duties. Heavy disaster management contracting to private firms has reduced federal need for small armies of voluntary, although government paid, temporary disaster workers. Those who seek to understand the intergovernmental relations of disaster management need to understand the world of government contracting.

KEY TERMS AND CONCEPTS

bottom-up approach   135

bureaucratic "turf wars"   141

command and control strategies   135

compact   146

crying poor syndrome   156

emergency declaration assistance   139

Emergency Management Assistance
    Compact   145

emergent organizations   135

faith-based voluntary organizations   135

federal-state agreements   136

fraudulent claims   138

FEMA's federal regions   137

individual and household assistance   139

major disaster assistance   138

memorandums of understanding   145

mutual aid agreements   145

nonprofit voluntary organizations   135

nonterrorism missions   140

Performance Partnerships   136

private contractors   135

regional directors   137

top-down command and control
    system   134

unemployment assistance   139

CHAPTER **7**

CIVIL-MILITARY RELATIONS AND NATIONAL SECURITY

FOR DECADES, U.S. CIVIL DEFENSE AND HOMELAND SECURITY policy has been enmeshed in the nation's disaster policy. In the 1950s, civil defense against nuclear attack was the platform upon which modern emergency management evolved. In the mid-1990s, the policy of the federal government ensured that national security matters were integrated into FEMA's overall all-hazards approach to emergency management. Today, state and municipal governments carry a considerable portfolio of duties related to national security, many implemented through Department of Homeland Security grant programs. Such grant programs embedded with detailed conditions, requirements, and standards characterize what much of disaster policy and governmental disaster management is today in the United States.

Disaster management in the United States has almost always been referred to as being "bottom-up," that is, local emergency management organizations and governments address disasters and emergencies first, seeking help from their state government or from adjacent local governments. Federal government help is perceived as "last resort" assistance, when a state cannot respond to and recover from a disaster or emergency using its own resources. However, since the terrorist attacks on September 11, 2001, political pressures and national fears surrounding the threat of more spectacular and devastating attacks have created a disaster policy that is very much a "top-down" president-dominated and federal government–dominated system, despite political rhetoric that national emergency management is based on a federal-state-local "partnership." Before the 9/11 attacks, one would have been hard-pressed to identify instances of municipal involvement in national security affairs, but in the months and years following these attacks, many local governments have been expected to shoulder a variety of "homeland" security responsibilities embedded in national security.[1]

This chapter covers the Posse Comitatus Act of 1878, the trend toward the militarization of disaster policy, and the emergence of the Department of Homeland Security. Also discussed

A U.S. Coast Guard rescue helicopter and rescuers winch up a survivor of Hurricane Katrina from a rooftop in New Orleans on August 30, 2005, approximately one day after the hurricane made landfall along the Gulf Coast of Louisiana, Mississippi, and Alabama. The military is a major player in the nation's system of disaster response; however, military capacity to undertake such work and disputes about the nature and duration of the military role in homeland disasters have been matters of controversy. Nonetheless, emergency management in the United States has been, and continues to be, massively affected by military and national security concerns.

is how modern homeland security overlaps domestic emergency and terrorism consequence management at home. The limitations of military response to disaster and the issues of military involvement that have affected disaster policy and politics are included. Finally, this chapter surveys homeland security programs related to national security and their effect on local governments and local emergency managers.

PRESIDENTS, THE U.S. MILITARY, AND *POSSE COMITATUS*

The *Posse Comitatus* Act of 1878 was passed during Reconstruction following the Civil War in order to prohibit the military from enforcing civilian laws. The law sought to codify the long-standing aversion of American citizens to a standing army that would be an instrument of governmental tyranny and control.[2] It established clear boundaries regarding the role the military could play in civil law enforcement.

Under the *Posse Comitatus* Act the armed services are generally prohibited from engaging in law enforcement activities inside the United States, such as investigating, arresting, or incarcerating individuals, except as authorized by federal law. The National Guard, however, enjoys a unique legal status. Guard troops are frequently referred to as citizen soldiers, part of the military's substantial Reserve components. Reserve forces were traditionally called to active service only for limited periods, such as for annual training or for short overseas deployments. Since 2003, however, National Guard units of almost every state have been called up for short- or long-term deployments abroad in Iraq and Afghanistan. When not on active duty, National Guard units remain on call to support the governors of their respective states. If a governor declares marshal law in specific areas of his or her state, the National Guard, not the U.S. military, could take on law enforcement duties and this would not violate *Posse Comitatus* law. *Posse Comitatus* does not apply to National Guard forces when they are mobilized by the president or the national command authority as federal troops; in other words, as "federal" troops they are not legally allowed to engage in criminal law enforcement.[3] As a result, unless federalized, the Guard plays the primary role in augmenting state and local law enforcement under state control, whereas the Department of Defense active-duty military plays a supporting role, providing resources and logistical support.[4]

However, the military's role in civil law enforcement has expanded. In the 1980s specific laws were passed to allow the Defense Department a greater role in drug interdiction and border security. In the 1990s, in response to the terrorist bomb attack in Oklahoma City and growing fears about global terrorism, the military was given an expanded role in responding to terrorist attacks that may use weapons of mass destruction.[5] The 9/11 terrorist attacks gave further impetus to greater military involvement in terrorism prevention and response. There are an immense number of postdisaster tasks that military units are qualified to undertake. Certain types of military services and equipment may be used to augment the services and equipment made available by civilian governments, the private sector, or nonprofit sector organizations. For example, military units may engage in search and rescue; emergency medical care; emergency transport of people; mass feeding; in-kind distribution of food, clothing, and other necessary commodities; epidemiological work and disease control; decontamination (in hazardous materials or radiological circumstances); temporary sheltering; firefighting; help in restoration of electric power and other utility services; debris removal to reopen roads; and bridge repair or temporary bridge replacement, as well as offering security and property pro-tection aid.[6] Under the homeland security regime established in the years after September 11, 2001, the military has been entrusted with invigorated authority to address vast homeland security concerns in matters of bioterrorism and terrorist use of other weapons of mass destruction. There are a small number of military involved in local disaster-related grant pro-grams (for example, in chemical weapons disposal transport and routing agreements with local governments, and military base impact programs aiding local governments), but most of these are for highly specific purposes and some are classified.

When is the military called in? State governors may call up their respective state National Guard in disaster or emergency circumstances. Sometimes, governors choose to deploy select-ed units of the National Guard that have the technical expertise needed to address certain prob-lems that may have overwhelmed or exceeded the capabilities of civilian authorities. The pres-ident may ask the secretary of defense to deploy the military, and military leaders themselves possess authority to independently respond to disasters. For the president and the military, authority to do this resides in Article IV, section 4, of the U.S. Constitution, the Civil Defense Act of 1950, and the National Emergencies Act of 2002. All this can be done independently of the Stafford Act process of governor-requested presidential declarations of major disaster.[7] However, since the early 1900s, presidents have rarely invoked this authority. Military leaders are even more reluctant to exercise their response authority independently except for the most grave circumstances, as when military people and bases directly experience a disaster. The mil-itary, outside the National Guard and other reserve units, ordinarily responds to only presiden-tially declared major disasters and under conditions set forth in the National Response Plan.[8]

In 2005 President Bush publicly advocated amending the *Posse Comitatus* Act to allow the military to become involved immediately and automatically following natural disasters.[9] During his address to the nation on September 15, 2005, following Hurricane Katrina, President Bush stated that he believed the military should play a greater role in future disas-ters: "It is now clear that a challenge on this scale requires greater federal authority and a broader role for the armed forces—the institution of our government most capable of massive logistical operations on a moment's notice." [10] When the military is deployed to a disaster site, its people and resources sometimes dwarf those of civilian authorities.[11]

Thus, the government response to Hurricane Katrina renewed debate over the efficacy of the *Posse Comitatus* Act. Several scholars, among them James Jay Carafano, Gregory M. Huckabee, and James F. Miskel, believe that amending the law to grant federal troops greater authority in restoring order in the wake of a domestic emergency is not a good idea and chang-ing *Posse Comitatus* would be a mistake.[12] One newspaper report disclosed, "Many Pentagon officials have expressed concern about broadening the military's responsibilities to include what would, in effect, be police work, along with its combat role. They argue that it would require very different training, equipment and force levels." [13] An assistant secretary of defense for homeland security said in an interview about the military's response to Hurricane Katrina, "What we ought not do is convert D.O.D. into a department of first responders." [14]

Policymakers may be on firmer political and legal ground, however, if they find ways to use the U.S. military and its resources as supplements to the aid and resources provided by civil-ian public and private organizations. The military must avoid undercutting local and state emergency response. There are relatively few constraints on the military in playing a supportive role in some disaster circumstances. For example, in major disasters the military has been used to transport victims and medical supplies, provide shelter and mass feeding operations, direct traffic, reopen roads and highways clogged by disaster debris, and engage in emergency repair of infrastructure.

If policymakers granted Department of Defense active-duty military people law enforcement authority such that all *Posse Comitatus* Act restrictions were removed, the U.S. military would simultaneously gain and lose. It would gain in the sense that those last vestiges of federal law that inhibit U.S. military law enforcement inside the nation would be removed. The military might be more freely deployed by the president to locations inside the nation when the president determined that the National Guard, along with state and local law enforcement, was incapable of meeting a threat or event of some type. However, the military would lose in the sense that its public image might suffer if its soldiers carried out law enforcement actions improperly and unjustly inside the United States. The military might also suffer if domestic disaster management responsibilities undermined its primary national defense mission.[15]

Owing to the massive deployment of military units to Iraq, Afghanistan, and other places outside the United States, there are those who worry that the military is being asked to do too many things as it is. Assigning the active-duty military law enforcement duties inside the United States for anything less than a condition of constitutionally authorized national emergency is arguably unreasonable.[16]

Regardless, the president always has constitutionally protected authority to declare a national emergency, thus freeing the U.S. military to take part in criminal law enforcement or to support domestic operations. For example, federal forces helped to quell riots by miners in Idaho in 1899; protected James Meredith, the University of Mississippi's first black student, in 1961; and assisted in controlling the 1992 Los Angeles riots.[17] During Hurricane Katrina, tens of thousands of National Guard troops streamed into the damage zone, many of them assisting local law enforcement and operating under state law.[18] In fact, federal forces have been used to enforce laws over 175 times in the past 200 years under the authority of laws such as the Insurrection Act. In short, the federal troops can be there when they are needed.[19]

MILITARIZATION OF DISASTER POLICY

Modern homeland security highlights the overlap of domestic emergency management and terrorism consequence management at home. Owing to the range of weapons and instruments potentially available to modern terrorists and the damage these might cause, antiterror emergency management and conventional disaster management may actually complement each other better today than civil defense and conventional disaster management did during the cold war of 1946–1990.

Many conventional disaster management duties and homeland security obligations are interwoven. Homeland security obligations have contributed to the militarization of more realms of disaster management. Preparation for hazardous materials incidents overlaps much of that for bioterrorism events. Preparedness and response planning for a major urban earthquake parallels some elements of preparedness and response planning in the event of the detonation of a low-yield nuclear weapon in a large metropolitan area. In some ways, hurricane civil evacuation planning dovetails with civil evacuation planning for dirty bomb incidents.

Under current arrangements, the military provides key support and partners with civilian emergency responders, but the overall tasks of assessing needs, interagency coordination, deployment of urban search and rescue teams, and overall management of federal disaster response have been entrusted to DHS and its FEMA. Most of the functions, tasks, and skills that are essential in all phases of emergency management fall outside the scope and mission of the military, whose primary functions are to deter war and provide security for the nation. In the United States most emergency management responsibilities continue to be entrusted to civilian, not military, organizations and institutions.[20]

However, some sixteen state governments require that their state emergency management agencies report daily to the state adjutant general, a military official, under a military-dominated model of state emergency management. In nondisaster circumstances, two additional states have their respective civilian emergency management agencies report to the state adjutant general.[21] States with emergency management organized on a military-dominant model usually assign emergency management work to a state military department or division and employ both military and civilian workers, who work closely with military supervisors. Regardless of whether states organize their emergency management under the state adjutant general military model or not, each state's emergency management is influenced by the military, owing to the prominent place the National Guard holds in disaster response in all states.

Usually after catastrophic disasters proposals for involving the military more intimately in disaster response abound. Proponents for more military involvement point out that the military's command and control structure, plus its logistical systems, would provide the kind of framework and efficiency that was missing in civilian agency responses to Hurricanes Katrina and Andrew, for example. Others underscore the usefulness of military resources such as helicopters and watercraft for rescue and tents and other facilities to provide for human shelter. Just as the U.S. military responds to disasters abroad, it is able to do likewise at home. Still others argue that the military's most important role could be in providing security following the most catastrophic and destabilizing events. The most extreme arguments advocate transferring the responsibility for emergency response from civilian agencies like FEMA to the Department of Defense.[22]

Given the 9/11 terrorist attacks and Hurricane Katrina, the militarization of disaster management has gained considerable traction. For example, the U.S. Coast Guard, a part of the Department of Homeland Security since 2003, has a much higher profile in disaster management today than in the past.[23] President George W. Bush responded to dissatisfaction with civilian agency response to the needs of people in New Orleans and surrounding areas by assigning a Coast Guard admiral, Thad Allen, the lead DHS role in managing disaster response operations in and around New Orleans for a period of weeks.[24]

The U.S. military has engaged in massive studies and preparations gearing up for homeland deployments in catastrophic disasters, most of those envisioned as the result of terrorism. Since 2002 the North American Command (**Northern Command, or NORTHCOM**) has fulfilled many duties under the National Response Plan and the unfolding National Response Framework. The Northern Command, discussed later in this chapter, has the disaster management job of "orchestrating the operational aspects of defense support to civil authorities in all of its forms. . . ."[25]

Military involvement in emergency management work has long been a component of the U.S. Army Corps of Engineers work inside the nation. Since it was formed in 1802, the Corps of Engineers has built, owned, maintained, and managed a colossal amount and variety of public infrastructure inside the United States. A sizable share of this infrastructure promotes structural mitigation of flood threat. Over the years the corps was asked by the federal government to contribute to both military construction and works "of a civil nature," many of these related to water resources, maintenance of navigable waterways, and flood control. Throughout the nineteenth century, the corps supervised the construction of coastal fortifications, lighthouses, jetties, and piers for harbors. It also mapped navigational channels and mapped much of the American West as well. In the twentieth century, the corps became the lead federal flood control agency and significantly expanded its civil works activities, becoming a major provider of hydroelectric energy and water impoundment recreation areas. The corps' role in responding to natural disasters emerged in matters of flood control after the Civil War. Floods on large rivers such as the Mississippi impaired commerce, destroyed property, and cost lives.[26]

The corps' first formal disaster relief mission was during the Mississippi Flood of 1882, when it supported efforts to rescue people and property. Army engineers also played a critical role in responding to the Johnstown, Pennsylvania, flood of 1889 and the San Francisco earthquake of 1906. Under the Disaster Relief Act of 1950 the corps continued to be the lead federal agency during flood disasters.[27] Under the National Response Plan, the corps is the lead agency for one of the working groups of Emergency Support Function 3: Public Works and Engineering. After Hurricane Katrina, the corps "led the effort to repair the levees that flooded New Orleans and its environs."[28]

However, one critic of the corps alleged that "Shoddy Army Corps engineering crippled the Greater New Orleans flood-control system," thus contributing to the hurricane vulnerability of the levees in and around New Orleans.[29] The corps has also been criticized for overreliance on engineered structures to mitigate flood threat. Sometimes these structures provide a false sense of security to people in communities threatened by flood. Yet, to be fair, in the 1990s and beyond, the Army Corps of Engineers has made significant commitments to nonstructural flood mitigation and environmental protection.

Disaster Response and Recovery Efforts

The military is often a magnificent asset in humanitarian disaster response. National Guard and active-duty military people are trained to follow orders, trained to operate in the field, prepared to move into hazard zones with enough equipment to sustain themselves independently for considerable periods, and willing to put themselves in harm's way.

Military people and emergency responders are expected to take these risks if they are so ordered. Certainly, civilian firefighters, police officers, and emergency medical people are willing to take similar risks and often do. Still, civil servants, often dedicated to their work in valiant ways, are not expected to enter danger zones that pose a significant risk to their health and welfare.[30] These civilian officials, including FEMA workers, are in fact prohibited by federal law from taking dangerous personal risks in disaster response.

The U.S. Coast Guard is a military organization highly praised for its Hurricane Katrina disaster response, in which its people carried out a great many rescues. The U.S. Coast Guard rescued more than 33,000 people during and after the storm, often under harrowing conditions. And the Pentagon pitched in as well. By August 31, two days after the hurricane struck Louisiana, the Defense Department had started medical airlifts, and the USS *Bataan,* a multipurpose amphibious assault ship equipped with two search and rescue helicopters dispatched to provide humanitarian assistance, had arrived off New Orleans. Almost 50,000 National Guard forces deployed to support hurricane relief, and more than 17,000 active-duty troops from the Eighty-second Airborne and First Cavalry pitched in as well.[31]

The nation's experience with Hurricane Katrina highlighted the importance of the military in disasters. When local and state assets are overwhelmed during a disaster, it is appropriate for military people and assets to be brought in to bridge the gap until civilian responders can handle the situation. And that did happen in the response to Hurricane Katrina.[32] A second amphibious assault ship and an aircraft carrier arrived on September 6, 2005, in the Gulf Coast damage zone. Twenty ships, 360 helicopters, and 93 fixed-wing aircraft were in the affected area by September 7. It was the largest and fastest deployment of U.S. military forces in support of a natural disaster in the nation's history.[33]

However, military organizations are often ill-equipped to handle many short- and long-term disaster recovery needs: rebuilding homes, managing shelters, feeding the displaced, resettling people, helping businesses resume operation, providing disaster unemployment aid, servicing the long-term medical needs of disaster victims, replacing major public infrastructure, and bringing back public utilities, to name a few.

Owing to changes made after the 9/11 terrorist disaster, the active military now has a greater presence in addressing domestic disaster, but the military is chiefly poised and prepared for various forms of terrorist-caused disasters.

Military and State-level Disaster Management

The National Guard has about 312,000 soldiers nation-wide, who are commanded in each state by the state's governor unless called to federal duty by the president. The troops can perform law enforcement functions under a state's laws but, as explained earlier, cannot enforce criminal law when they are federalized—when they are under the direct control of the president. The National Guard is a principal and major resource for governors who must respond to a disaster event. The National Guard provides well-trained people, "communications systems and equipment, air and road support, heavy construction and earth-moving equipment, and emergency supplies such as beds, blankets, and medical supplies."[34]

In 1992 the Florida National Guard was fully available in the aftermath of Hurricane Andrew. By contrast, in 2005 only about 60 percent of the Mississippi National Guard and 65 percent of the Louisiana National Guard were available to deploy to Hurricane Katrina's (much bigger) zone of devastation because so many were on overseas missions.[35] The issue here is whether or not civilian authorities need to reconsider their disaster management dependence on the National Guard given the Guard's heavy obligations abroad and given concerns about its ability to recruit sufficient numbers of soldiers.

Relatedly, there are disputes over whether National Guard forces should be federalized by the president when the president judges that circumstances warrant doing so. When a president feels compelled to federalize National Guard units, this often signifies that a breakdown in president-governor relations has occurred. However, what matters most is the proper use of the military, including the National Guard, in disasters and the realization that military help is highly temporary. The deployment of the National Guard and active-duty military to a zone of disaster connotes failure on the part of the civil government in that zone. The military would be expected to engage in search and rescue, protect property and life, and maintain civil order. However, **martial law** is a last resort act of desperation in the United States.

After Hurricane Katrina, a reporter quoted a National Guard official as saying that the Guard can handle both international and domestic jobs. "I think the response of the military was more than sufficient, effective and timely for Katrina," and more effective than the response of any other part of the federal government.[36] After Hurricane Andrew, during the administration of George H. W. Bush, proposals were made in Congress that would have broadened the military's role in responding to domestic disasters. They included rolling FEMA into the Defense Department; placing a key portion of FEMA, such as its communications apparatus, in the Defense Department; and increasing the role of the National Guard in emergency response.[37] Few of these proposals won approval, largely because senior military officials told lawmakers that the Pentagon did not want to absorb FEMA and its domestic emergency management responsibilities.

Some counter that local officials, from small-town sheriffs to big-state governors, say Louisiana's problems during Katrina were the exception, not the rule. They say the Department of Homeland Security and the Pentagon overreached in their move to dominate disaster management and that a federal takeover of relief work would make matters worse. In the aftermath of Hurricane Katrina, at a meeting of the Western Governor's Association on November 8, 2005, the U.S. Navy admiral Timothy J. Keating, head of the U.S. Northern Command, advocated giving active-duty military forces complete authority to respond to catastrophic disasters such as Hurricane Katrina.[38] The head of the Washington State National Guard, Maj. Gen. Timothy J. Lowenberg, upon hearing Keating's proposal, responded vociferously. Lowenberg told colleagues that Admiral Keating's suggestion that the military assume a much greater role in domestic disaster management amounted to a "policy of domestic regime change."[39] Some considered Keating's proposal a "power grab" by NORTHCOM because it would have dramatically increased the military role in disaster management inside the nation.

In the end, Admiral Keating's proposal failed. Other similar proposed changes failed because of quiet opposition by the top ranks at the Pentagon and more vocal protests from governors and state emergency management officials, many who feared losing control in a crisis.[40] Assigning the active-duty military a lead role in domestic disaster response raises a host of difficult questions, including whether the active-duty military should have deadly force authority to keep order in a homeland disaster, whether the National Guard or the active-duty military is in charge if both are responding, and what authority governors retain in such situations.[41]

The Rise of the North American Command

The 9/11 terrorist attacks dramatically opened the door to heavier military involvement in disaster policy. One domain of this advance has been air defense. As the *9/11 Commission Report* vividly recounts, civilian and military air controllers and authorities encountered a series of major problems in their efforts to cope with hijacked commercial airliners being used as weapons of terror.

The Northern Command was established to better protect the homeland from attack. NORTHCOM people have worked to find their place in national disaster management. However, military culture is rarely compatible with the culture of civilian emergency management.[42] NORTHCOM's mission is to help prevent another terrorist attack on the homeland by militarily defeating attacks by foreigners if possible, by protecting U.S. borders or air space from encroachment or penetration by attackers, or by aiding in the response to an incident involving a weapon of mass destruction inside the United States.

The Northern Command has occasionally been a target of criticism. One report exclaims:

> Hidden deep inside Cheyenne Mountain, more than 100 intelligence analysts sift through streams of data collected by federal agents and local law enforcers—continually updating a virtual picture of what the command calls the North American "battlespace," which includes the United States, Canada, and Mexico, as well as 500 miles out to sea. If they find something amiss, they have resources to deploy in response that no law enforcement agency could dream of. They've got an army, a navy, an air force, the Marines, and the Coast Guard.[43]

According to *Mother Jones* correspondent Peter Byrne,

> NORTHCOM is designed to take command of every National Guard unit in the country, as well as regular troops, and wield them as a unified force. It has a variety of jobs, including fighting the war on drugs and supporting civilian authorities in cases of natural disaster, civil disorder, or terrorist attack. But it also has the less straightforward task of locating terrorists before they strike, which means, first and foremost, coordinating intelligence work. To this end, the command has been forging a national surveillance system directly linking military intelligence operations to local law enforcement intelligence operations and private security and information companies.[44]

Critics of NORTHCOM acknowledge the need to protect America from terrorist attack, but they also "argue that the delicate task of domestic intelligence gathering should be left to law enforcement." [45]

So it seems apparent that owing to the national security features of homeland security evident in Northern Command operations, and the inclusive requirements of the NRP and the NIMS, disaster policy today is infused with "national securitization" issues. Much of what the Northern Command does is conducted under rules of state secrecy. **Security classification** now shrouds from public view a variety of emergency response plans, including those in place for facilities whose operation may pose a danger to surrounding communities. Homeland security law and policy have infused disaster management with major sums of money, but they have also made disaster policy implementation more closed, more secretive, and more dominated by the military and law enforcement. These are problems likely to become flashpoints of controversy in future disaster circumstances.

HOW THINGS WORK

THE NORTHERN COMMAND AND DISASTER MANAGEMENT

Authorized by President George W. Bush on April 17, 2002, the Department of Defense (DOD) established the U.S. Northern Command to consolidate under a single unified command existing homeland defense and civil support missions that were previously handled by other military organizations. On May 8, 2002, the U.S. Air Force general Ralph E. Eberhart, the commander of the North American Aerospace Defense Command (NORAD) and U.S. Space Command, was nominated by DOD to be the first commander of NORTHCOM. The Northern Command began operations on October 1, 2002. On November 5, 2004, Admiral Timothy J. Keating became the second combatant commander of NORTHCOM and the first navy admiral to command NORTH-COM. He also assumed command of NORAD.

The purpose of the U.S. Northern Command is to provide command and control of Department of Defense homeland defense efforts and to coordinate the defense support the military provides to civil authorities. NORTH-COM considers its primary role as that of defending America's homeland.

NORTHCOM's missions include anticipating and conducting homeland defense and civil support operations within its assigned area of responsibility, that being, to defend, protect, and secure the United States and its interests. Its area of operations includes air, land, and sea approaches to the United States, encompassing the continental United States, Alaska, Canada, Mexico, and the surrounding waters out to approximately 500 nautical miles. This area includes the Gulf of Mexico and the Straits of Florida. The defense of Hawaii and U.S. territories and possessions in the Pacific is the responsibility of the U.S. Pacific Command, not NORTHCOM. The defense of Puerto Rico and the U.S. Virgin Islands is the responsibility of the U.S. Southern Command. The commander of NORTHCOM is responsible for theater security cooperation with the governments of Canada and Mexico.

The Northern Command consolidates under a single unified command several military missions. NORTHCOM officials insist that unity of command is critical to accomplishment of their missions.

NORTHCOM plans, organizes, and executes homeland defense and civil support missions but has few permanently assigned forces. The president and secretary of defense may

HOMELAND SECURITY TERRORISM PROGRAMS

State and local governments have been in the business of managing and budgeting for disasters and emergencies for a great many years, certainly well before federal disaster relief programs were set forth. Virtually every local government municipal charter obligates the jurisdiction to provide for public safety, which encompasses local emergency management and today homeland security. Owing to new homeland security obligations and expanded emergency management duties, state and local governments are now important and active co-participants in the NRP and the National Incident Management System.[46] Let's consider several homeland security programs that have penetrated the world of state and local government since 9/11.

assign additional forces to NORTHCOM whenever they deem it necessary.

Civil service employees and uniformed members representing all service branches work at NORTHCOM headquarters, located at Peterson Air Force Base in Colorado Springs, Colorado.

The commander of NORTHCOM also commands the North American Aerospace Defense Command, a bi-national command responsible for aerospace warning and aerospace control for Canada, Alaska, and the continental United States. NORTHCOM's civil support mission includes domestic disaster relief operations needed to address fires, hurricanes, floods, and earthquakes. Civil support also includes counter-drug operations and managing the consequences of a terrorist event involving a weapon of mass destruction. When asked by the Department of Defense, NORTHCOM provides assistance to a civilian lead agency in cases of natural or human-caused disaster or catastrophe, and for national special security events. In compliance with the *Posse Comitatus* Act, NORTHCOM military forces may provide civil support but cannot become directly involved in law enforcement.

In providing civil support, NORTHCOM generally operates through established joint task forces subordinate to the command. A disaster or emergency must exceed the capabilities of local, state, and federal agencies before NORTHCOM becomes involved. In most cases, support will be limited, localized, and specific. When the scope of the disaster is reduced to the point that the civilian lead agency can reassume full control and management without military assistance, NORTHCOM will exit, leaving experts at the scene of the disaster to finish the job.[47]

NORTHCOM has taken part in many counterterrorism exercises with civilian emergency management agencies. In September 2005, as directed by the secretary of defense and in accord with the National Response Plan, NORTHCOM supported the Department of Homeland Security, FEMA, and other federal agencies in disaster relief efforts in the aftermath of Hurricane Katrina. More than 21,400 active-duty service members and 45,700 Army and Air National Guard members supported the effort in the U.S. Gulf Coast.[48]

The Homeland Security Advisory System

On March 12, 2002, the **Homeland Security Advisory System (HSAS)** was made operational. A threat-based, color-coded system was used to communicate to the American public and safety officials the status of terrorist threat to the nation or to parts of the nation. Government authorities and the public could thereby exercise heightened vigilance that might thwart a terrorist attack, or, should an attack of some sort be imminent, they could take appropriate protective measures.

However, raising or lowering the threat condition to a different color level produced problems. The system was poorly conceived in that it could not simultaneously be a national alert system and an indicator of daily, weekly, or monthly national threat condition status. Many

THE SHIFTING FOCUS
OF EMERGENCY MANAGEMENT

According to former FEMA director James Lee Witt, the civilian nature of the emergency management system is one of the underpinnings of its success in the past. He wrote:

> While I was director of FEMA from 1993–2001, I never had a problem getting the resources needed from the Department of Defense. Under the Federal Response Plan, I had the authority to task the Department of Defense and any other federal agency to marshal the resources that were required. The difference might have been that we put possible items in the pipeline before a hurricane hit, not after it hit. If some of the problems that have surfaced in the emergency management system over the last four years are addressed, a civilian lead emergency management system can prosper again in the future.[49]

The federal government already possesses the ability to tap into the military's resources through memorandums of understanding that were the backbone of the old National Response Plan and that are now part of today's National Response Framework.[50] The issue is to what degree military involvement in disaster management is tolerable and reasonable.

James Lee Witt believes FEMA was dealt a major setback when it was moved into the Department of Homeland Security. This move had the effect of pushing both FEMA and state and local emergency managers further into the realm of national defense and national security. Witt lamented, "The federal government has taken a lead in shifting the focus of our emergency management system over the past . . . years away from all-hazard preparedness and toward a more narrow emphasis on homeland security. This change in focus was not new; the Federal

Emergency Management Agency's priorities had shifted back and forth from natural disaster preparedness to civil defense several times," over its history.[51] Witt agreed that the shift to homeland security and improved domestic preparedness was necessary after the terrorist attacks of 2001. But he also maintained that gains in homeland security have diminished the nation's commitment to all-hazards preparedness. Witt contends that "the wholesale incorporation of FEMA into DHS has seriously hampered FEMA's ability to carry out its all-hazards mission."[52]

A different view is offered by James Jay Carafano. He writes,

> Most disasters, including terrorist attacks, can be handled by emergency responders. Only catastrophic disasters—events that overwhelm the capacity of state and local governments—require a large-scale military response. Assigning this mission to the military makes sense. It would be counterproductive and ruinously expensive for other federal agencies, local governments, or the private sector to maintain the excess capacity and resources needed for immediate catastrophic response. On the other hand, maintaining this capacity would have real utility for the military. The Pentagon could use response forces for tasks directly related to its primary warfighting jobs—such as theater support to civilian governments during a conflict, counterinsurgency missions, and postwar occupation—as well as homeland security. Furthermore, using military forces for catastrophic response would be in accordance with constitutional principles and would not require changing existing laws.[53]

Americans were disturbed, annoyed, and confused by what DHS was doing with the system. HSAS rankled many state and local officials as well, among them law enforcement and emergency management people.

At first, HSAS repeatedly raised and lowered the threat status between elevated (yellow) and high (orange). After two years of the system's operation, DHS reduced its pattern of rapid fluctuation, owing to public opposition and new DHS standards governing the system's use.[54] Nevertheless, few homeland security activities have drawn as much public and political ire and criticism as has the Color-coded Threat Level System. The HSAS program as a whole must observe a careful balance between unduly alarming the public and maintaining an appropriate level of national, state, and local preparedness. State and local officials complain of unreimbursed police and fire overtime costs attributable to high-alert levels. Others complain that the color coding is not specific as to the actual threat Americans need to prepare for. State and local criticism of, and resistance to, the threat-based, color-coded Homeland Security Advisory System will be a problem for DHS until it is either reconceived in a way that satisfies critics or until it is discontinued.

The Urban Area Security Initiative

The **Urban Area Security Initiative** (UASI) is a major DHS program and it involves emergency management. The program is highly complex and a challenge to administer on the federal, state, and, especially, local levels. UASI encapsulates many of the counterterrorism duties and problems that have been imposed on local law enforcement and local emergency management. The aim of UASI, authorized by federal law in 2005, is to facilitate rapid response in the nation's fifty largest cities to attacks from weapons of mass destruction. The urban areas that were selected have high international profiles and large populations.[55] UASI addresses planning, operations, equipment acquisition, training, and exercise needs. The program provides financial assistance to these areas based on a risk-and-needs approach. The amount given to each city is determined by a formula that combines current threat estimates, critical assets within the urban area, and population density. There is no state or local matching fund requirement for this program.

Early in the life of the program DHS officials informed states of their cities' eligibility for the program. The state government must obligate at least 80 percent of all federal funding provided through the program to the designated urban area within sixty days after receipt of funds. The UASI program was part of the consolidated Homeland Security Grant Program and operates on biennial (two-year) cycles, which means UASI recipients do not need to reapply in order to receive second-year funding. UASI-authorized annual funding levels for fiscal years 2005, 2006, and 2007, respectively, were $854 million, $734 million, and $817 million.

Central to UASI's mission is helping state and local governments build and maintain the capability to prevent, protect against, respond to, and recover from threats or acts of terrorism. In the aftermath of Hurricane Katrina in 2005, however, policymakers called for a change in UASI national planning priorities. They required that the program also address issues such as pandemic influenza and catastrophic disaster (as might be caused by a major hurricane or earthquake). Administrators of UASI were asked to accommodate catastrophic events like Hurricane Katrina, something most local emergency managers were happy to see. In effect,

HOW THINGS WORK

THE INFAMOUS FIVE-COLOR THREAT-LEVEL SYSTEM OF THE DEPARTMENT OF HOMELAND SECURITY

Local governments might be expected to do some of the following things under each respective color-coded threat-level condition.

RED—
Severe risk of terrorist attacks

Besides the previously outlined Protective Measures listed below for green, blue, yellow, and orange threat levels, the following may necessary under condition red:

- Assigning emergency response personnel and pre-positioning specially trained teams
- Monitoring, redirecting, or constraining transportation systems
- Closing public and government facilities
- Increasing or redirecting personnel to address critical emergency needs

ORANGE—
High risk of terrorist attacks

Besides the Protective Measures under green, blue, and yellow threat levels, the following may be necessary under threat-level orange:

- Coordinating necessary security efforts with armed forces or law enforcement agencies
- Taking additional precaution at public events
- Preparing to work at an alternate site or with a dispersed workforce
- Restricting access to essential personnel only

YELLOW—
Significant risk of terrorist attacks

Besides the previously outlined Protective Measures under green and blue threat levels, the

following may be necessary under threat-level yellow:

- Increasing surveillance of critical locations
- Coordinating emergency plans with nearby jurisdictions
- Assessing further refinement of Protective Measures within the context of the current threat information
- Implementing, as appropriate, contingency and emergency response plans

BLUE—
General risk of terrorist attack

Beyond the Protective Measures of threat-level green, the following may be needed under threat-level blue:

- Checking communications with designated emergency response or command locations
- Reviewing and updating emergency response procedures
- Providing the public with necessary information

GREEN—
Low risk of terrorist attacks

The following Protective Measures may be applied:

- Refining and exercising preplanned Protective Measures
- Ensuring personnel receive training on HSAS, departmental, or agency-specific Protective Measures
- Regularly assessing facilities for vulnerabilities and taking measures to reduce them[56]

post-Katrina changes in the program reintroduced "dual use" requirements of the type common in the cold war civil defense era. UASI grants could fund nonterror disaster management but only on condition that these activities "also" enhanced the jurisdiction's ability to address terrorism: "dual use."

Although the program dispensed the grants by formula, eligible governments had to apply for UASI funds and win DHS approval. Funds provided were to address the unique needs of large urban municipal government areas and mass transit authority special district governments. As mentioned previously, UASI funds could be used for equipment, training, exercises, and planning but could neither be used to hire new employees nor subsidize salaries of current workers. This program limitation produced considerable managerial and political controversy. Some state and local officials objected to the limited sets of purposes UASI funds could be used to address. The program is heavily biased toward the purchase of DHS-approved equipment. This may appear to be a minor problem, but because almost all of the DHS-approved equipment was geared for counterterrorism purposes and because UASI money came almost exclusively for the purchase of equipment (not for salaries to pay personnel), distortions resulted at the local level.

In some cases, state and local governments were accused of using UASI funds to purchase lavish, unnecessary, and exotic counterterrorism equipment. News investigations of such activity triggered claims of wasteful spending and pork barreling.[57] The counterargument might be that local officials, fearing that seemingly one-time federal UASI or other homeland security grant funds would be lost or would go to other jurisdictions and appreciating that they are rarely the beneficiaries of federal largess, may have felt justified in purchasing vehicles and equipment that were excessive or of questionable necessity. Where that equipment had dual-use application that worked to the benefit of local emergency management, such equipment acquisitions might have been judged acceptable by both the public and journalist investigators.

Regardless, the federal UASI money came with prodigious paperwork demands. Applicant governments had to demonstrate that they had prepared an Urban Area Homeland Security Strategy and that their state government had in place a state program and Capability Enhancement Plan. Even then, applicant governments had to document that their request for UASI funding was consistent with the goals, objectives, and priorities of the national Urban Area Homeland Security Strategy and in conformity with UASI policies and conditions. Applicant local governments also had to prove that their Urban Area Homeland Security Strategy was consistent with their respective state's Homeland Security Strategy. The state government itself was expected to have in place a program and Capability Enhancement Plan, under requirements of the DHS **State Homeland Security Grant Program.**

In fiscal year 2006, DHS identified thirty-five areas eligible to apply for and receive UASI funding. These thirty-five areas encompassed ninety-five cities, and each area had a population that exceeded 100,000. Of late, UASI has sought to build greater regional capabilities across selected geographic areas.

All eligible applicants must submit an "investment justification." This identifies needs and outlines the intended security enhancement plan to be addressed with the funding. That plan is expected to meet the target capabilities outlined in the National Preparedness Goal, itself a product of Presidential Homeland Security Directive-8, issued in December 2005. The purpose of the National Preparedness Goal is to "establish policies to strengthen the preparedness of the United States to prevent and respond to threatened or actual domestic terrorist attacks, major disasters, and other emergencies by requiring a national domestic all-hazards preparedness goal, establishing mechanisms for improved delivery of Federal preparedness assistance to State and local governments, and outlining actions to strengthen preparedness capabilities of Federal, State, and local entities."[58] **Target capability** is homeland security jargon that refers to the ability of a government jurisdiction to prevent, or respond to, a range of different types of terrorist attacks. Investment justifications are reviewed, scored, and prioritized (by DHS officials) along with risk factors to determine which investments should be funded to best address need and minimize risk.

UASI is only one of several homeland security grant programs directed to state and local government. Unfortunately, each of these programs is rife with federal "boilerplate" language that, for many state and local officials (as well as professors, students, and others), makes them unclear and arbitrary. The elaborate complexity of these programs opens the door to considerable misunderstanding. UASI demands that local recipients of government grants collect a massive amount of information and use it to engage in elaborate planning work. More than this, the plans are tested against envisioned scenarios, most of them anticipating some type of terror attack with some type of terror weapon. The burden of UASI paperwork reportage and UASI prohibitions against using federal funds to hire staff in some respects represents a partially unfunded mandate imposed by the federal government on state and local governments.

The Law Enforcement Terrorism Prevention Program

The Law Enforcement Terrorism Prevention Program (LETPP) supports law enforcement communities in their efforts to detect, deter, disrupt, and prevent acts of terrorism. Categories of aid include "information sharing to preempt terrorist attacks; target hardening to reduce vulnerability of selected high-value targets; recognition and mapping of potential or developing threats; interoperable communications; and interdiction of terrorists before they can execute a threat or intervention activities that prevent terrorists from executing a threat.[59] As in other homeland security program grants, federal funding is disbursed first to the state government. Local law enforcement agencies are then advised to work with and seek LETPP funding from the state's lead law enforcement agency.[60]

The LETPP encourages its participating organizations to collaborate with private security organizations, government agencies outside law enforcement, and with the private sector in general. The LETPP has no matching grant provisions.[61] Why mention the LETPP in a study of disaster management? The LETPP pulls local law enforcement into the counterterrorism business. The program's use of so-called fusion centers provides a nexus of local, state, and federal terrorism-focused law enforcement, and local emergency managers are part of this nexus.

The Emergency Management Performance Grant Program

Emergency Management Performance Grants (EMPGs) are allocated to states, which use the money to bolster their intrastate emergency management programs and capabilities. EMPG funds are to "support comprehensive emergency management at the state and local levels and to encourage the improvement of mitigation, preparedness, response, and recovery capabilities for all-hazards." [62] DHS-FEMA wants states to use EMPG money to foster partnerships of government, business, volunteer, and community organizations. DHS-FEMA also suggests that the funds be used to pay for joint operations, mutual aid, local and regional support, and state-to-state cooperation. For many years, EMPGs were based on dual-use cold war funding for local emergency preparedness programs that had evolved from civil defense against nuclear attack.[63]

States are free to decide on their own how much EMPG money they will pass on to their local jurisdictions.[64] EMPGs are designed to help state and local emergency managers develop, maintain, and improve their emergency management capabilities, providing assistance in emergency planning, training, exercising, and interdisciplinary coordination. Although only part of the DHS grants package, EMPG recipients are asked to concentrate on the most likely hazards of their respective local jurisdictions, such as earthquake, hurricane, and flood. Through this program, FEMA provides states the flexibility to allocate funds according to their respective risk and to address the most urgent state and local needs in disaster mitigation, preparedness, response, and recovery. Under the program, DHS-FEMA expects these governments to achieve measurable results in key functional areas of emergency management. All states are eligible.[65] Local governments must apply through their state governments to FEMA. Funding under this program is ultimately used by emergency management organizations.

In 2006, congressional budget makers fashioning the fiscal year 2007 budget of the EMPG program cut funds to this long-standing federal program by approximately $13 million. These cuts came even after the glaring failures of coordination and collaboration during the federal, state, and local response to the catastrophic events of Hurricane Katrina. The president of the Mississippi State Civil Defense/Emergency Management Association pointed out that the program had been seriously underfunded for years and required significant additional funding just to catch up. He added that although it was always supposed to be a 50 percent federally matched program, Mississippi had been fortunate to secure even a 20 percent federal match.[66]

When asked in congressional hearings about the rationale for the EMPG cuts, Secretary Chertoff responded that the department preferred not to fund personnel and indicated that doing so was not "a federal interest." He further stated that "traditionally" the federal government did not fund personnel.[67]

The president-elect of the International Association of Emergency Managers (IAEM), also a director of Emergency Management and Homeland Security in a Kansas county, offered a retort to Secretary Chertoff. He remarked that the secretary had prominently displayed a copy of the National Plans Review requested by Congress and the president. He asserted,

> The information and analysis contained in the N[ational] P[lans] R[eview] was due to the efforts of hundreds of EMPG-funded state and local emergency managers involving thousands of man hours—how is that not a Federal interest? Unfortunately, it appears there's a striking lack of understanding within DHS as to what Emergency managers do. We are in a people-intensive business. We're supposed to be the "honest brokers" who bring all the disciplines together to prepare for and to meet the crisis.[68]

The IAEM Government Affairs chairman, an emergency management director in a Maine county, added, "To imply that the funding of personnel under EMPG is not a traditional function of the Federal Government is astonishing given that the EMPG program has been in existence since the 1950s. If that's not a tradition, I'm puzzled as to what is." [69]

The Assistance to Firefighters Grant Program

The Assistance to Firefighters Grant program, in cooperation with the U.S. Fire Administration, provides financial assistance directly to local fire departments, and this money pays for vehicles, equipment, and training that firefighters and emergency medical service personnel need.[70] The Bush administration budget request for FY 2006 asked Congress to furnish $500 million in competitive grants to fire departments and emergency medical providers.[71]

The Metropolitan Medical Response System

The **Metropolitan Medical Response System** was developed after the 1995 Oklahoma City bombing. Its aim was to ensure that big-city police and fire departments had the training and equipment to care for the victims of a mass casualty event caused by nuclear, biological, or chemical attack.[72]

The Metropolitan Medical Response System (MMRS) helps localities "with funding to write plans, develop training, purchase equipment or pharmaceuticals, and conduct exercises related to catastrophic incidents, whether terrorist or natural disasters. The purpose of the program is to help local governments improve their capacity to respond to mass casualty events during the first hours of a response or until other help arrives. The system also emphasizes enhanced mutual aid with neighboring localities." [73] The MMRS at this writing resides in the Department of Health and Human Services.

HOMELAND SECURITY GRANTS AND THEIR EFFECTS AT THE LOCAL LEVEL

Since the 1980s the all-hazards approach to civil defense and emergency management has developed into a sophisticated system of intergovernmental relations. On September 11, 2001, the United States withstood its most catastrophic terrorist attack. Despite the tragic and heroic losses of a great many firefighters, police officers, and other emergency responders at the site of the World Trade Center, the existing broad-gauged intergovernmental system for disaster and recovery management worked well. The intergovernmental response to the terror attack on the Pentagon has been widely praised. However, the president and other policymakers concluded that prevention should be the focus in addressing future terror threats and attacks. Consequently, prevention was added as a new phase in emergency management.[74]

Homeland Security Presidential Directive-1 (HSPD-1) of October 29, 2001, made terrorism a national security responsibility to be handled in a coordinated way by federal, state, and local officials. Although natural and technological hazards were still viewed as the responsibility of the local and state governments, with federal assistance, HSPD-1 defined terrorism preparedness as "a critical national security function" requiring extensive coordination across all levels of government.[75] Other homeland security presidential directives, several new federal laws, and a battery of new federal grant programs were introduced. Collectively, these measures dictated to local governments the exact steps they were expected to take. These measures placed terrorism preparedness above preparedness for all other types of disaster agents.

After enactment of the Homeland Security Act of 2002, it soon became apparent that the entire federal homeland security mechanism would be dominated by criminal justice officials. Terrorism prevention again took precedence over all other types of mitigation and preparedness.[76] Policymakers used homeland security funding to induce state and local authorities to join a system of reinforcing cross-jurisdictional information sharing regarding "persons of interest." Much of this work came at the expense of preparing for nonterrorism hazards, emergencies, and disasters. The presence of potential terrorists and their supporters, known as "persons of interest," was one of the few bases for rating a locality's vulnerability to terrorism, or "threat level," under the 2004 Urban Area Security Initiative Program.[77]

The State Homeland Security Grant Program, the Urban Area Security Initiative, Emergency Management Performance Grants, Community Emergency Response Teams, and the Metropolitan Medical Response System were at first separate grant-issuing programs with individual purposes. However, in accord with policymaker wishes, DHS consolidated these programs under the State Homeland Security Grant Program to ensure that all would need to operate with state government as an intermediary between federal and local governments. The new homeland security grants did not directly permit funding of conventional disaster mitigation and preparedness. Although the 2002 Homeland Security Act references "major disaster" as defined in the Stafford Act, the mission of the new department focuses on terrorism. Other provisions of the act refer to the phases of the terrorism management cycle (prevention, response, and recovery) for which the department is responsible. Furthermore, the law declares, "the department shall also be responsible for carrying out other functions of the entities transferred to the department as provided by law." Because the law is vague, DHS has been able to funnel its resources almost entirely toward its main priority: terrorism.

Mitigation has changed from public works activities to those related to criminal justice. Preparedness is defined in terms of surveillance capabilities. Owing to these reforms, local emergency planning has been subsumed within a nation-centered, president-dominated authority model.[78] For local emergency managers, compliance with homeland security requirements is both daunting and seemingly never ending.

The National Preparedness Goal aims to create "capability-based planning." This has three components: **national planning scenarios,** a Universal Task List, and a **target capabilities list.** The DHS developed a set of fifteen "planning scenarios" that encompass the range of "plausible" events that could pose the greatest risk to the nation.[79] These scenarios were intended to be used in evaluating the ability of a jurisdiction to manage a major disaster. Local officials were supposed to select those scenarios they thought most likely to occur in their areas and determine if their current capabilities would enable them to save lives, protect property, and revive their local economies.

The fifteen scenarios encompass disasters caused by an improvised nuclear device, aerosol anthrax, pandemic influenza, plague, blister agent, toxic industrial chemicals, nerve agent, a chlorine tank explosion, a major earthquake, a major hurricane, a radiological dispersal device, an improvised explosive device, food contamination, foreign animal disease, and cyber attack.[80] In practice, leaders are asked to count their jurisdiction's response resources and to engage in "tabletop" exercises playing each of these fifteen scenarios.

The 2006 UASI grant guidance changed the exercise from an evaluation of performance to a commitment to using future grant money to correct the deficiencies.[81] The annual exercise cycle topic is dictated by the state, which may select only from the scenario list provided by the federal government. The type of disaster agent selected may not be important for a given location; in other words, the participating UASI local government officials may be asked to conduct an exercise to address what for them is an extremely rare and unlikely event.

The purpose of developing a set of scenarios was to prompt consideration of a wide range of potential disaster events, with a goal of identifying "the critical tasks and capabilities that would be required from all sources in a coordinated national effort to manage major events." [82]

The **Universal Task List** was developed to describe "what tasks need to be performed," "who needs to perform them," and "how to perform them." [83] Individual governments are to use the list to document their existing capabilities to respond to the fifteen planning scenarios. They are expected to create a plan for the use of federal counterterrorism grant funds and locally available funds to address missing capabilities they discover in their planning. The Universal Task List contains an astounding 1,600 different tasks. Moreover, it is impossible for local government officials to maintain a correct list of all the resources needed and available to fulfill each task. Equipment breakdowns, personnel absenteeism, and shift-work schedules all prevent an accurate operational picture of the resources available in a community at any moment. Asking local officials to address 1,600 different tasks as part of the "All Hazards Taxonomy of National Preparedness Tasks," combined with associated planning and preparedness demands, is both daunting and unrealistic.[84]

Mitigation, a core phase of conventional emergency management, is located under "Protect" in the "All Hazards Taxonomy" and is stipulated as "Mitigate Risk to Public," but there is no provision for capital projects. The purpose of physical protection is subjugated under the criminal justice mind-set of "Prevent." The UASI program uses evocative imperatives such as "Detect Threats," "Control Access," and "Eliminate Threats," all of which are focused on human suspects and weapons. Nothing in the taxonomy addresses preventing loss of life and maintaining economic viability in anticipation of natural disasters through mitigation measures like construction of protective structures or the application of building codes.[85]

From 2006 onward, the principal scheme for allocating federal preparedness funds to local governments seems based on a combination of threat analysis and population. The funding distribution scheme also penalizes local emergency response groups when hazards they must prepare for fall outside the accepted threat analysis. For local governments without a significant terrorism threat, there may be little or no funding available for emergency preparedness for disasters previously supported by federal funding assistance. Even those larger and more complex municipalities that have continued to receive homeland security funding under the new system may in fact see erosion in their nonterror emergency management capability.

In 2005, federal agencies undertook an evaluation of critical infrastructure based on the **"CARVER" technique,** developed by the Department of Defense for "the military's target prioritization purposes." [86] Infrastructure was evaluated according to the following criteria:

- **C**riticality. How important is the target? Importance is determined by the impact of its destruction on operations and whether or not substitutes or backups exist for the target.
- **A**ccessibility. How easily can a target be reached, either by infiltration or weapons?
- **R**ecoverability. How long will it take to replace or repair the target once it is damaged or destroyed?

- **V**ulnerability. How susceptible is the target, and its construction, to an attack?
- **E**ffect. What impact will the target's destruction have on the public, including psychological, domestic, and international ramifications? For instance, will it shake the public's confidence in the enterprise's systems, policies, processes?
- **R**ecognizability. How readily can a target be identified and not confused with other structures?[87]

These confidential site lists were developed by a committee within the executive branch of the federal government. The national list of critical sites was kept confidential but was used to estimate threat in the early days of the UASI program. Priority targets tended to be large stadiums and iconic structures (for example, the Golden Gate Bridge); of lower priority were high-technology and utility facilities. Each state was "assigned" a certain number of sites. The state could then contest the priority of the specific sites and substitute other locations the state deemed more critical, provided the number of sites assigned to the state remained the same.

Unfortunately, some infrastructure sites selected by DHS officials were chosen without consulting appropriate local officials. Local jurisdictions were invited to review the list only as a preliminary step in applying for another homeland security grant program. DHS lack of consultation with local governments sometimes resulted in embarrassing gaffs; miniature golf courses and petting zoos were for a time identified as "selected sites" while high-technology companies were overlooked.[88]

CONCLUSION AND SUMMARY

Most disasters, including terrorist attacks, can be handled by civilian emergency responders. However, as mentioned previously, for some truly catastrophic disasters in which civilian authorities and nongovernmental organizations are overwhelmed, a military role is necessary. It may be that catastrophic disasters—events that overwhelm the capacity of state and local governments—require a large-scale military response. Use of the National Guard in domestic disaster response is not as contentious an issue as employing active-duty military personnel in disaster response. The establishment of the Northern Command has opened the door to more frequent introduction of active-duty military people in U.S. disaster management. The active-duty military plays a major role in matters of bioterrorism and weapons of mass destruction attacks, as well as in federal catastrophic disaster planning; this means that active-duty military are now integral participants in the national system of emergency management. The overlap of homeland security and catastrophic disaster management in the United States suggests that it would be both counterproductive and inefficient to bar active-duty military forces from assisting in domestic disaster management.

However, undermining or supplanting the authority of mayors and governors in a moment of national crisis would be a mistake. Rather than tinkering with constitutional relationships, Congress and presidential administrations should focus on creating mechanisms to get these officials the forces they will need to get the job done. "The greatest obstacle to overcome is not the legal barriers, but the tyranny of time and distance and the destroyed infrastructure, such as downed bridges and flooded roads, which might limit access." [89]

"All disasters are local" is an oft-repeated and regularly valid assertion of emergency managers and students of disaster. Nevertheless, the United States is a large nation, operated through a federal system. Emergency management capacity at the local level varies widely across the nation. Large cities and many localities in major metropolitan areas have experienced disasters before and have considerable ability to work all phases of disaster. Still, there is also a vast array of smaller counties, cities, towns, and villages; their emergency response capacity differs, ranging from high quality to merely adequate. A great many localities rely on volunteer firefighters, most of whom are unpaid. The experience, education, and training of these firefighters vary from outstanding to satisfactory. Moreover, the emergency management capability of law enforcement officers also varies dramatically across the nation. It has been maintained in this book that emergency management includes emergency response, but so too mitigation, preparedness, and recovery; local governmental provision for adequate emergency response is only part of the game.

It is ironic that although state and local emergency managers from the 1950s through the 1990s rightfully complained of inadequate federal funding of their work, many states and local governments may well have ignored the need for full service emergency management had they not received federal funding, even federal dual-use, civil-defense-biased funding. The problem has changed today. Many state and local officials appreciate the dramatically scaled-up grant funding they have received in this post-9/11 homeland security era, but many also lament the federal preoccupation with terrorism at the expense of established emergency management, the hierarchical system for dispensing funds, and the immense paper- and computer-work burdens they must now shoulder.

The slowness of government's emergency response in the aftermath of Hurricane Katrina, particularly in areas of New Orleans devastated by levee-failure flooding, and the ensuing blame game, sparked renewed interest in militarizing emergency response, much as happened after Hurricane Andrew.[90] However, top military officials are highly ambivalent about taking over civilian emergency management duties, although the military has been willing to play a more active role in short-term emergency response to homeland disasters, particularly through the new Northern Command. Yet, the military preoccupation remains that of national defense against threats posed to the nation by other nations or by stateless terrorists. The military culture and the civilian emergency management culture are in many ways highly incompatible. Emergency management has paramilitary participants, but most emergency managers, even most of those in paramilitary occupations, appreciate the need to work consultatively, cooperatively, and consensually. The Incident Command System discussed in Chapter 6 implies a military model of decision making, but ICS is fundamentally used as a nexus of cooperative decision making applied to emergency response. The multiagency coordination system employed in emergency management is vital. Clearly, ICS works satisfactorily for concentrated and localized disasters, but command and control regimentation of ICS becomes infeasible in catastrophic disasters covering large areas. It is then that the value of multiagency coordination and cooperation becomes apparent.[91]

The world of state and local homeland security is dramatically influenced by federal laws, rules, funding conditions, and administrative actions. As mentioned previously, federal public policy after the 9/11 terrorist attacks called for the nation to recruit, hire, and oversee state and local government homeland security and emergency management officials so they could better prevent and respond to acts of terrorism. One major result of this policy change was a profusion of federal homeland security programs and a dizzying array of grant programs with far-ranging and sometimes bizarre requirements.

Many of these programs dramatically affected state and local emergency management. Some of these programs represented arms of homeland security and disaster policy implementation. Some of these programs enriched state and local emergency management and law enforcement with major infusions of federal funds. However, some of these programs undercut or distorted state and local emergency management and law enforcement in controversial ways. Some of these programs also imposed massive stress on state and local emergency management and law enforcement officials.

Some studies have demonstrated that substantial federal and state aid to local government in particular policy areas can undermine local control of local government agencies.[92] In local emergency management, heavy federal and state subsidization, combined with conditions these other levels of government attach to the money dispensed, may potentially undercut local control of local emergency management. In other words, the greater the share of federal and state funding in local emergency management budgets, the greater the probability that a condition of dependency will evolve such that local emergency management becomes more an arm of state and federal emergency management and homeland security and less a locally controlled municipal function. Recruiting state and local government to fight the War on Terrorism has had, and will continue to have, major effects on how disaster policy and emergency management is carried out.

KEY TERMS AND CONCEPTS

"CARVER" technique   190

Emergency Management Performance
   Grants   180

Homeland Security Advisory
   System   181

martial law   178

Metropolitan Medical Response
   System   188

national planning scenarios   189

Northern Command   175

security classification   179

State Homeland Security Grant
   Program   185

target capabilities list   189

target capability   185

Universal Task List   190

Urban Area Security Initiative   183

DISASTERS STRIKE ALL NATIONS OF THE WORLD, AND MANY PEOPLE anticipate that future disasters will be larger and more destructive owing to such factors as climate change and environmental degradation. Disaster vulnerability is also growing because the world population is increasing, accelerating the pace of urbanization. A massive share of the world's populace resides along coastlines. The systems and infrastructure to sustain and nurture the world population are of uneven quality and durability. Many disasters befall developing nations that lack financial resources, infrastructure, and adequate preparedness and response capability.[1] Because disaster forces and the effects of disasters often spill over or straddle borders, and because disasters may easily overwhelm individual states, they are sometimes difficult for nation-states to address independently. Owing to the frequency and expansive effects of disasters and catastrophes, disaster management increasingly requires responses that are multinational or even global in scope. International disaster management involves not only the nations themselves but all relevant actors and loci of authority, be they multilateral and multilevel governmental, public, or private. Consequently, international disaster management, most particularly in postdisaster response and relief, constitutes a major domain of emergency management.[2]

The international community, development banks, and nongovernmental organizations (NGOs) must consider ethical and humanitarian criteria before they launch an intervention into disaster-stricken areas of other nations. Rising transnationalism and increased interdependency between developing and developed nations has given new urgency to matters of disaster management. The **globalizing forces** that have characterized the post–cold war era—notably the massive movement of individuals, capital, goods, information, and technologies

The author wishes to thank doctoral student Cédric S. Sage, coauthor of this chapter, for permission to draw from his paper "International Disaster Relief from a Comparative Analysis: The Case of the UN and U.S. Apparatuses," University of Delaware, Newark, 2006.

Fleeing the onslaught of the Indian Ocean earthquake–triggered tsunami on December 26, 2004, these people of Ao Nang, Thailand, confronted a catastrophic disaster that smashed coastlines, killed more than 225,000 across eleven nations, and wreaked havoc all the way from Indonesia to Somalia. The United Nations, the United States, a host of other nations, and innumerable private organizations responded with help.

across borders—further interlace developing nations to new and old industrialized nations. For many developing nations, disasters and this interdependence combine to produce negative, destabilizing effects.[3] Moreover, disaster in developing nations often triggers massive flows of refugees who seek to escape zones of civil strife.[4] Disasters sometimes contribute to security threats. Failed states are not only highly vulnerable to the forces of natural disaster but they may be incapable of preventing the spread of radicalism and terrorism.[5]

More than ever before, security and peace are linked to long-term, sustainable political and economic development. Therefore, the international community as a whole has a stake in preventing developing states from collapsing. By extension, this also entails helping developing nation governments to cope with disaster realities and disaster threats. The international community has a vested interest in assisting many nations whose people and governments have experienced disaster.

In the international realm disasters are commonly categorized as natural disasters, technological disasters, or complex humanitarian emergencies. Among these three, **complex humanitarian emergencies (CHEs)** are often the most difficult to address. CHEs signify that a country or region is at or near complete breakdown of civil authority. CHEs sometimes involve ethnic conflict, displacement of population groups, market collapse, and mass starvation.[6] In a CHE, the success or failure of a disaster relief operation often rests on the degree of coordination, the fairness and equality in relief distribution, and whether the relief effort connects with (or at least does not impede) the country's reconstruction and economic development.[7] CHEs often coincide with natural disasters. For example, the Darfur region of western Sudan, a region of immense human suffering in recent years, is not only riven by ethnic and religious warfare but is also experiencing extended drought, which has added to the misery of hundreds of thousands of people.

Territorial sovereignty—the internationally recognized principle that a government should be the ultimate authority within the boundaries of its jurisdiction and should be free of unwanted external interference—may in some cases constitute a powerful obstacle to extending humanitarian assistance.[8] Leaders of some nation-states, in times of disaster, choose to protect their national sovereignty even if this disadvantages their own citizens. Sometimes leaders of newly independent nations fear that postdisaster intervention by a rival state or a great power may bring about their recolonization or result in subjugation by a neighboring nation. For this reason, humanitarian assistance tends to be more successful when the leaders of recipient nations perceive it as offered by neutral parties and undertaken by the international community rather than by one or a few nations.

The international relief and humanitarian assistance mechanisms and tools of the United Nations are examined in this chapter along with the international disaster management system of the United States. The United States is a world superpower. The United Nations is an international organization of some 192 member states. The UN's enforcement capacity and its resources flow from the permission and goodwill of its members. Both the United States and the UN are constrained in their freedom of action and response capability. Interestingly, the UN, a confederation of nation-states, and the United States, a federal system and representative democracy of fifty states (plus the District of Columbia and trust or commonwealth territories), must deal with a plethora of public and private actors, many having their own standards, procedures, and agendas.

The UN and U.S. agencies involved in international disaster relief are described in this chapter, and the UN and U.S. disaster response and recovery mechanisms are compared, contrasted, and evaluated.

THE U.S. RESPONSE SYSTEM

The United States has a disaster policy and politics within its international relations. First, the United States has committed itself to serving the disaster management needs of its trust and commonwealth territories. Many Americans may be unaware that U.S. trust and commonwealth territories are eligible to request and receive presidential declarations of major disaster and emergency just as are all of the fifty U.S. states. Puerto Rico and the U.S. Virgin Islands, U.S. trust territories in the Caribbean, have emergency management systems. Guam, American Samoa, the Marshall Islands, the Northern Marianas, and the Federated States of Micronesia also maintain an emergency management capability. They too are within the American family of trust or commonwealth territories and so are eligible to receive presidential major disaster and emergency declarations and all of the federal relief assistance these convey. Providing relief and long-term recovery aid to trust or commonwealth governments that experience a disaster and receive a presidential declaration is often a daunting logistical challenge and an exceedingly expensive proposition for the federal government.

Huge hurricanes sometimes sweep through Puerto Rico or the U.S. Virgin Islands and produce massive devastation. Both governments have received a sizable share of presidential declarations of major disaster since 1953. In the Pacific, too, typhoons periodically devastate U.S. trust and commonwealth states. Some of the most expensive per capita federal disaster declaration spending has flowed to U.S. trust and commonwealth states in the Pacific. Sometimes typhoons destroy coastal infrastructure and jeopardize public water supplies. The U.S. military possesses air- and sea-lift capacity to ship food, water, clothing, building materials, and other commodities to these distant locations. Every trust or commonwealth territory of the United States is part of a FEMA region, and FEMA, as well as each additional federal agency called upon to respond, sends both representatives and aid to these governments.

The United States also has treaty obligations to offer disaster help to a great many of its neighboring nations in the Western hemisphere. Long-standing treaties, many of them predicated on defense pacts, obligate the United States to offer help to nations in Europe, Asia, South America, and Africa as well. The United States, then, is part of an international web of disaster response and emergency management. U.S. government organizations active in international disaster management are considered in more detail in the following section.

The U.S. Agency for International Development

The U.S. Agency for International Development (USAID), for many years an independent agency, is now again part of the Department of State. The agency is officially obligated to further U.S. foreign policy interests in expanding democracy and free markets while improving the lives of the citizens in developing countries.[9] Receiving a budget of half of one percent of the total U.S. budget, USAID is the chief U.S. agency in charge of overseas development.

USAID extends assistance to countries recovering from disasters. Rooted in the Marshall Plan, which was designed to reconstruct Europe after World War II, and in President Truman's Point Four Program, USAID was authorized in the Foreign Assistance Act of 1961 and launched under an executive order issued by President Kennedy.[10] USAID symbolized the American recommitment to long-term foreign development and it clearly separated U.S. military and nonmilitary international assistance programs. However, since 1961 the USAID annual budget has been an object of political controversy almost every year.

USAID receives guidance from the U.S. secretary of state. USAID also works closely with more than 3,500 American companies (300 of these companies are domestically based) and the Overseas Private Investment Corporation (a federal corporation).[11] The agency addresses issue areas as broad as economic growth, agriculture, trade, global health, democracy, conflict prevention, and humanitarian assistance. It provides assistance in sub-Saharan Africa, Asia, the Near East, Latin America, the Caribbean, and Europe/Eurasia.[12] Within USAID, the Bureau for Humanitarian Response coordinates the agency's response to emergencies in other nations. Within the bureau, a special office, the Office of U.S. Foreign Disaster Assistance manages all nonfood assistance directed to disaster victims.[13]

The Office of U.S. Foreign Disaster Assistance

Within USAID, the Office of U.S. Foreign Disaster Assistance (OFDA) facilitates and coordinates U.S. emergency response overseas. The OFDA is divided into four units. These are the Operations Support Division, the Program Support Division, the Disaster Response Division, and the Prevention, Mitigation, Preparedness, and Planning Division.

The OFDA is authorized to respond to all natural disasters (earthquakes, volcanic eruptions, cyclones, floods, droughts, fires, pest infestation, disease outbreaks) and man-made disasters (civil conflicts, acts of terrorism, industrial accidents). The OFDA, besides furnishing immediate assistance, funds mitigation activities to lessen the effects of recurring disasters. It also makes available guidance and training intended to help those in other nations develop their own disaster management and response capacity.[14]

U.S. Ambassadors Declare Disasters

When a U.S. ambassador judges that his or her posted nation's capability to address a disaster is overwhelmed, and if the nation's government requests international assistance, the ambassador or the chief of mission can issue a disaster declaration on behalf of the United States. This action initiates a set of U.S. emergency procedures and the ambassador can dispense $25,000 to $50,000 in immediate financial aid.[15] The USAID administrator then dispatches a team to the nation in question. Various response activities then transpire that are scaled to the gravity of the crisis. Such responses evolve from the immediate allocation of discretionary money through the embassy and from the immediate dispatch of regional advisers. Those authorities provide shelter and medical aid supplies. A Disaster Assistance Response Team (DART) assesses the scope of damage, proposes a strategy, and estimates how much assistance is required and what it will cost.[16] The response team often provides logistical support to and coordinates the efforts of all actors and responders involved. These include the UN and other international organizations, NGOs, and governments. DARTs monitor and evaluate U.S. operations as well.[17]

In very great disasters, Response Management Teams are formed in Washington and sent to the field to ensure optimum coordination between the various DARTs involved.[18] A special assistance team, or Technical Assistance Group, composed of experts in fields as varied as agriculture and public health often share their expertise with and assist DARTs and Response Management Teams in their work.[19] The OFDA furnishes direct assistance and may follow this up by also offering a wide variety of project grants to public and private recipients. These are intended to help them develop and share best practices in disaster relief and mitigation.[20]

After the October 8, 2005, earthquake in Pakistan, USAID dispatched a DART team to bolster life-saving efforts. One of the most pressing issues was to assess shelter needs of the population and to prioritize assistance from the OFDA stockpile before the Himalayan winter set in. In less than two days, the OFDA was transporting tents and shelter materials by plane and deploying shelter specialists to provide the resident populations with technical assistance.[21]

Similarly, a magnitude 7.7 earthquake struck the southern coast of Java, Indonesia, on July 17, 2006, producing a tsunami. The tsunami killed more than 300, injured more than 400, and caused extensive destruction of homes and property over a 175-kilometer stretch on the coastline. The U.S. ambassador to Indonesia, B. Lynn Pascoe, declared a disaster, triggering the USAID/OFDA donation of $50,000 for emergency relief assistance to the Indonesian and International Red Cross organizations and the Red Crescent Societies. A team of embassy and USAID personnel was also dispatched to monitor the conditions.[22]

The Role of the Department of Defense and the U.S. Military

The Department of Defense (DOD) has crucial responsibilities in foreign disaster relief and response. A special office within the DOD, the Office of Peacekeeping and Humanitarian Affairs, has the job of leading or coordinating the U.S. military response to disasters beyond U.S. borders. Use of the U.S. military in disaster-stricken nations is sometimes controversial because for many the military's war-oriented mission does not comport well with the humanitarian aspirations of disaster relief. However, the military generally has excellent and necessary equipment, extensive training, and well-entrenched standards of procedure required to handle such operations. A request for military support by USAID/OFDA is usually transferred to the DOD Office for Political/Military Affairs before following the chain of command. International disaster relief by the military is designated as a Humanitarian Assistance Operation or Foreign Humanitarian Assistance, the latter being authorized by the DOD at the request of the OFDA.

Once on foreign soil, U.S. forces involved in a **humanitarian assistance** mission are limited by the principles of force protection and rules of engagement; in other words, they must ensure the security of their own military personnel as well as the security of civilians, facilities, and equipment, and they are restricted in their ability to engage in combat by certain rules ("no fire first," for instance). In conflict-ridden zones of intervention, the priority of the military forces often shifts from providing security and leadership to that of a strict mission of assistance through logistical, physical, and communications support, and the distribution of food and medical relief. During deployments, Humanitarian Assistance Survey Teams are often sent to evaluate the needs on the ground to ensure that the intervention is proceeding effectively.[23] A joint task force is usually set up on site in disaster zones to coordinate the activities of diverse military units and civilian agencies. The commander of this task force is in charge of creating a civil-military operations center. The center's job is to coordinate military-civilian activities, to serve as the connection with the overall response structure, and to provide the effective logistical support to other agencies and responders (for example, the OFDA, the United Nations, and NGOs).

The Department of Defense launched an extraordinary response to the December 26, 2004, tsunami in Southeast Asia, an event triggered by a 9.0 Richter magnitude earthquake. The catastrophic tsunami killed an estimated 225,000 people; fatalities occurred in eleven nations, most of them with coastlines on the Indian Ocean. The DOD supplied the logistic elements of the operation through the use of its airplanes, helicopters, military ships, and other equipment. USAID also coordinated the work of various civilian organizations.[24] In the Indian Ocean tsunami case, more than 15,000 military personnel contributed to the relief effort and were dispatched to the affected nations. More than 2.2 million pounds of supplies were sent by the U.S. military to the region, including 16,000 gallons of water, 113,000 pounds of food, and 140,000 pounds of relief supplies during the first twenty-four hours.[25]

EMERGENCY MANAGEMENT IN OTHER NATIONS

The United States is not the only nation engaged in emergency management. Virtually every developed nation has some system of disaster management. Many have disaster management agencies, and some of those predate FEMA.[26] Some have developed emergency management on a platform of civil defense, but a great many have advanced emergency management as a form of public safety or civil preparedness.

Many nations have had long experience with domestic or international terrorism and so have their own forms of homeland security.[27] It is also true that many developed nations support foreign aid programs and international disaster assistance activities.[28] Many nations belong to treaty organizations or regional alliances that also engage in international emergency management endeavors.

It is developing nations that often have limited capacity to engage in the full range of emergency management activity.[29] Poverty, dangerous patterns of human settlement, unsafe agricultural and infrastructure construction practices, low public awareness of disaster vulnerability, inadequate public warning and sheltering systems, poor transportation infrastructure, deficient power and communications systems, and other problems often confound emergency management in other nations. Many developing nations have little or no history of insurance use and so lack the ability to employ insurance as a disaster mitigation tool. Moreover, some governments of developing nations lack political legitimacy and the public support of their cit-izenry. Some governments do not consider emergency management a priority for their people and so lack the political will to respond to postdisaster needs. In many developing nations the chief governmental arm of disaster response is the military. In some nations the citizenry look upon the national military with suspicion and fear. When national military help is extended to disaster victims in such places, people fear that repression, exploitation, or corruption might ensue. Such problems have given rise to international disaster management activity based on humanitarianism. Much of this activity seeks to at least temporarily fill the gaps in develop-ing nation emergency management capacity.

A wide variety of **development banks** have taken a strong interest in emergency manage-ment, among them the World Bank, the Asian Development Bank, the International Monetary Fund, and the Inter-American Development Bank.[30] Moreover, a host of **emer-gency-management-oriented multinational organizations** have emerged. Among them are the Coordination Center for Natural Disaster Prevention in Central America, the Caribbean Disaster Emergency Response Agency, and the Pan American Health Organization. The North Atlantic Treaty Organization, the European Union, the Organization of American States, and the Southern African Development Community all have programs under way that promote emergency management internationally.[31]

THE UNITED NATIONS AND INTERNATIONAL DISASTER RELIEF

With 192 member states, the United Nations constitutes one of the most experienced inter-national organizational actors in the management of international disaster response and miti-gation. UN agencies are generally involved on the ground in disasters and catastrophes. In the 1990s the UN reformed its capability to respond to disasters in order to better address the increasing complexity of emergencies. In 1987 the UN declared the decade of the 1990s the International Decade for Natural Disaster Reduction. By 1989 the UN had set up an office in Geneva, Switzerland, tasked with coordinating the implementation of the decade's activi-ties across all UN agencies. In 1994 UN member states met at the World Conference on Natural Disaster Reduction in Yokohama, Japan, and developed a strategy and plan of action that embodied a vast array of emergency management principles. In January 2005 the UN convened the World Conference on Disaster Reduction in Hyogo, Japan, a meeting that included representatives from 168 governments and 78 UN specialized agencies and observer organizations. Some 161 NGOs were also represented at the conference. The Hyogo meeting yielded a framework for action and a plan to substantially reduce disaster losses of communi-ties and countries by the year 2015.[32]

The UN Office for the Coordination of Humanitarian Affairs

In 1998 the UN General Assembly established the UN Office for the Coordination of Humanitarian Affairs (OCHA) to be headed by the emergency relief coordinator. The coor-dinator acts as the primary adviser and, as the title implies, coordinates the work of the various relief organizations in humanitarian emergency responses. He or she does so through the Inter-Agency Standing Committee, itself composed of both UN and non-UN humanitarian leaders.[33] OCHA seeks to build consensus and share best practices among all UN partners, and it identifies issues arising from disaster management and response that need to be addressed. OCHA also amasses information from its Disaster Response System, a unit that monitors ongoing disasters, conducts postdisaster assessments and evaluations, and manages a bank of data made available to the international community of responders.

OCHA coordinates the field missions of an assortment of UN agencies. These agencies assess needs, mobilize resources by launching interagency appeals, organize donations, monitor the contributions, and issue follow-up reports to update various actors on postdisaster developments.[34] OCHA advocates conformity to humanitarian norms and principles in its dealings with partners and world governments. Foremost among those norms and principles is respect for human rights. On the matter of financial assistance, OCHA is in charge of the Central Emergency Revolving Fund. The fund operates as a cash reserve available to humanitarian agencies with cash-flow problems. OCHA is able to loan money, but reimbursement is expected within a year.[35]

When a disaster strikes, OCHA works in close cooperation with government groups and NGOs, including USAID/OFDA, to formulate a joint and coordinated course of action in each case. It helps set priorities and prevent overlap in the work of various agencies.[36] OCHA dispatches some of its personnel to provide on-site support to UN agencies. When needed, OCHA can set up a UN Disaster Assessment and Coordination team. The team aids in the coordination of the relief effort, in the assessment of damage, and in gauging the response required. OCHA's responsibility is particularly crucial in the immediate postdisaster phase. It helps restore damaged communications and helps first responders work in harmony.[37]

Other UN agencies also manage and respond to international emergencies. The Office of the United Nations High Commissioner for Refugees (UNHCR), the World Food Program (WFP), the United Nations Children's Fund (UNICEF), and the United Nations Development Program (UNDP) all assist in disaster recovery work. The World Health Organization (WHO), too, plays an important role as a relief agency.

The United Nations High Commissioner for Refugees

Founded in the aftermath of World War II, the UNHCR protects and aids refugees and internally displaced persons.[38] The UNHCR's most basic responsibility is to guarantee refugees' fundamental rights, including their ability to seek asylum. It strives to make sure that no person is involuntarily returned to a country if doing so would subject that person to persecution or otherwise put his or her life in danger.[39] The UNHCR facilitates the necessary movement of masses of people, often refugees, during emergencies. It promotes education, health, and shelter programs and is expected to provide for the well-being of refugees. It manages the repatriation of people who freely wish to return to their home country and resettles those refugees seeking asylum to nations willing to accept them.[40] If refugees do return to their home countries, the UNHCR works closely with other agencies and organizations to prevent disrupting socioeconomic infrastructures of the home country and to facilitate refugee reintegration.

The UNHCR has a long-term commitment to the cause of refugees. Its special mission, the United Nations Relief and Works Agency for Palestine Refugees in the Near East, has provided relief, health care, and education help to Palestine ever since the 1948 Arab-Israeli conflict.[41] The agency originally provided assistance to about 750,000 Palestinian refugees who had lost their homes or livelihoods or both. By the year 2000, it was working to help 3.7 million registered Palestinian refugees dispersed over areas of Lebanon, Jordan, Syria, and the combined West Bank and Gaza Strip.[42]

The United Nations Children's Fund

Formerly known as the United Nations International Children's Emergency Fund, the UN Children's Fund was created after World War II to alleviate the suffering of European children. Since then its mandate has been expanded. UNICEF has an in-country permanent presence in many nations.[43] Thus, the agency may be able to respond rapidly to natural or man-made disasters from its offices in nations where it already has permission to operate.[44] The necessity of a swift response is highlighted by the especial vulnerability of new mothers and families with small children. Children and women caring for small children are often weaker members of their societies and are less capable of rebounding in disasters than others. During natural disasters or complex humanitarian emergencies, UNICEF works with other relief agencies to restore basic services, such as food distribution, water, and sanitation. UNICEF officials also try to make available basic medical services and immunizations. UNICEF is empowered to advocate children's rights worldwide.[45] In conflict-prone areas, the agency has, with help, sometimes managed to negotiate cease-fires so as to provide humanitarian relief and to immunize children.[46]

The United Nations Development Program

The UN Development Program, created in 1965, has jurisdiction over many disaster-related activities, including disaster mitigation, prevention, preparedness, response, recovery, and reconstruction. The UNDP operating norm is that disaster vulnerability remains fundamentally connected to weak or absent infrastructures, the failure or inadequacy of environmental policies, and human settlement in high-hazard zones.[47]

Because disasters hold the potential to quickly reverse a nation's previous progress or set a nation's economic development back decades, UNDP officials consider disaster mitigation and risk reduction to be priorities. The UNDP ties its response and recovery efforts to long-term and sustainable development. In 1995 it reorganized itself and created an **Emergency Response Division,** which accelerated UNDP's capacity to respond to disasters. A response team is now routinely deployed to help coordinate relief and recovery efforts of other UN agencies and NGOs with the efforts of disaster-stricken national governments. The response teams also prepare comprehensive redevelopment projects in disaster recovery operations.

The UNDP has programs adapted to virtually all existing emergency circumstances. In 1997 the Emergency Response Division was granted more extensive duties over disaster and mitigation through the creation of the **Disaster Reduction and Recovery Program.** Through this program, the UNDP makes sure that its long-term development work includes the demobilization of combatants, landmine clearance, the reintegration of refugees and internally displaced persons, and a plan for restoration of governance in the affected country.[48] The close collaboration of the UNDP with national and local officials often yields positive results. The UNDP has stimulated grassroot initiatives, promoted long-term resuscitation, and sought to improve people's living standards. It also facilitates recovery through the use of financial tools, notably microcredit to the poor in Central America. The UNDP often leads interagency workshops that identify potential risks, develop early warning systems, or build states' disaster response capabilities and programs.[49] In addition, the UNDP runs the UN's International Strategy for Disaster Reduction Working Group on Risk, Vulnerability, and Disaster Impact Assessment. The group advocates standardized guidelines aimed at increasing emergency responder sensitivity to the social impact of disasters. It also operates a Disaster Management Training Program.[50]

The World Food Program

The World Food Program is responsible for providing rapid and self-sustaining nutritional relief to the millions of victims of man-made or natural disasters.[51] Most nations that receive WFP aid eventually return to agricultural self-sufficiency. However, those nations that regularly fall victim to civil wars or ethnic conflicts usually also suffer food shortages or famine.[52] In cases of emergency, the WFP attempts quick response, but always with permission of the host government. WFP duties cover transport, delivery, and distribution of food made available by other UN agencies, other national governments, or NGOs. When called upon, the WFP joins in reconstruction and rehabilitation activity.

The WFP works in close collaboration with the UN Food and Agriculture Organization (FAO) of the United Nations, an agency that issues early warnings of potential food crises and assesses food supply problems. Both the WFP and the FAO are critical in meeting the needs of disaster victims living in rural areas and who may be farmers. The FAO facilitates the rehabilitation of food production through the support its Special Relief Operations provides to farmers. Many WFP programs operate under strict conditions and are tied to projects demobilizing combatants or clearing landmines.

The World Health Organization

The World Health Organization is the UN's central agency assigned to manage health and sanitation concerns throughout the world. The WHO uses its people, authority, and expertise to assess and respond to health needs in regions and countries affected by natural and manmade disasters. The WHO operates programs designed to help the governments manage firstaid supplies, improve their medical capabilities, and maintain epidemiological surveillance of disease. All of these purposes are important in the aftermath of disasters. The WHO works to eradicate diseases and reduce the effects of epidemics through campaigns of information and immunization.

U.S. DOMESTIC DISASTER RELIEF VERSUS THE
U.S. INTERNATIONAL RELIEF SYSTEM

Although there are many differences between the way the United States engages domestic disasters and international disasters, there are also striking similarities in the mechanisms and procedures used by FEMA and its foreign disaster aid counterpart USAID/OFDA. Both agencies are involved in activities extending beyond the mission of disaster relief; disaster management encompasses not only relief distribution but also preparedness, mitigation, and recovery work. In both the domestic and international cases, the scope of the disaster must be judged significant enough to overwhelm the authorities theoretically in charge of such activity. In other words, a government must be judged to have been overwhelmed or incapable of meeting the needs created by a catastrophe or disaster, such that help from outside is necessary. In the United States, state governments are generally expected to ask the federal government for help before the president declares a disaster or emergency, although exceptions are permitted. In foreign countries, UN organizations, as well as USAID and its OFDA, expect that their help will be officially requested by the established governments of the disaster-affected nations.

Once approached, both UN agencies and USAID's OFDA first seek to assess the scope of the damages and to evaluate the needs of the victims. Both sets of agencies have an all-inclusive approach as they try to maximize all resources and skills available, as they work in synergy with and try to coordinate the efforts of public and private relief organizations. Finally, both domestic and international relief systems often rely on the U.S. military to provide logistical, physical, and communications support, as was done in 2004 in the tsunami in Southeast Asia and 2005 in the Hurricane Katrina disaster of the U.S. Gulf Coast. Ironically, the use of the U.S. military to respond to disasters inside America is sometimes as controversial as it is when it responds to disasters internationally.

Indeed, whereas the use of the U.S. military can be perceived by foreign governments as the sign of superpower interference, there is in the United States a long-standing tradition of suspicion about the use of the military and the application of martial law. The 1878 *Posse Comitatus* was passed to curtail the powers of the federal government in using federal military personnel for criminal law enforcement. During Reconstruction following the Civil War, federal troops committed many abuses in the South, and the *Posse Comitatus* Act was enacted to prevent future similar abuses by the military at home. However, the Stafford Act of 1988 and other laws have yielded back to the president extensive powers to use the armed forces to restore public order in domestic emergencies and after terrorist attacks.

The United Nations as an organization has no military "combat" forces of its own; it relies on the goodwill of member states and sometimes its **"blue helmeted" peacekeeping soldiers,** comprised of units contributed by various member states. UN peacekeepers are, "soldiers, police officers, and military observers from the United Nations' member countries. UN soldiers are paid volunteers from the armed services of various member states. All member states are invited to send volunteers, however, albeit with a few exceptions soldiers from the developing world do most of the volunteering." [53] Bangladesh, Pakistan, and India at this writing have contributed about 10,000 troops in blue helmets, whereas American soldiers accounted for just 12. The contributing countries continue to pay their soldiers, but they get reimbursed by the UN at a standard rate of $1,028 per month, plus a few hundred dollars extra for specialists. Troops typically are dispatched to peacekeeping missions for at least six months at a time, with the exact details of the deployment schedule left up to the country that sent them.[54] Blue helmet forces and related workers are counted on to provide the logistical and physical contributions necessary to carry out UN disaster relief and recovery missions.

Returning to the U.S. context, there are also some fundamental distinctions regarding the use of FEMA and USAID's OFDA. The U.S. government is ultimately accountable to its own citizens, and therefore is more likely to pay a political price for failing to provide an adequate response to a disaster occurring on American soil (for example, Katrina). As a result, the U.S. government tends to be more responsive to disasters occurring on domestic soil than to international disasters, as would be true in any nation.

FEMA's mission is to protect and assist Americans in times of man-made and natural disaster; this is achieved through FEMA's coordination of the work of federal departments and agencies working under the National Response Plan or Framework. The mission of USAID/OFDA is subordinated to the pragmatic goals of American foreign policy and interests abroad. Although the U.S. federal government needs to consider the needs, powers, and wishes of the state and local governments, federal intervention in disaster response and recovery has been allowed to grow, particularly in response to national concerns about the threat of attacks by terrorists inside the United States. At the international level, relations between nation-states remain profoundly affected by respect for national territorial sovereignty. The capacity and authority of USAID/OFDA abroad remains deeply limited by the U.S. government and by the UN-protected system of international relations. Often USAID/OFDA must work as simply one of many foreign relief agencies. The permission and goodwill of the host government remain conditions of its presence on foreign soil.

Internationally, USAID/OFDA becomes involved in a disaster response after it has received a request from the ambassador or chief of mission. Each request is evaluated according to precise criteria. As mentioned, often after consultation with the White House, an ambassador makes available a sum of up to $50,000 for disaster work to be spent at his or her discretion. In turn, OFDA dispatches its Assessment Team to evaluate the scope of the disaster and the range of unmet needs. In domestic U.S. disasters the president has the authority to approve a state governor's request for a major disaster declaration. For disasters outside the United States and its trust or commonwealth territories, the president may provide help to nations that request it through USAID and through the Department of Defense.

CONCLUSION AND SUMMARY

Both the UN and the United States play a crucial role in international disaster relief. Their competencies both overlap and complement each other. For instance, sometimes the UN and the United States may not be directly involved on the ground in the same operation. The UN might address a nation's disaster through direct field operations while the United States provides aid indirectly by funneling funds and in-kind assistance from U.S.-based NGOs to the affected nation. Sometimes the United States and the UN do work together and are present at the site of devastation, as occurred after the 2004 tsunami in Southeast Asia.

Comparing UN disaster assistance to U.S. foreign disaster assistance may seem inappropriate because the UN is an international organization of some 192 members and is a supranational body, whereas the United States is a territorial-based sovereign state and a superpower. The organizations and disaster response structure of the UN seem better able to deal with disasters in the international realm than are U.S foreign disaster relief organizations. USAID/OFDA might respond faster if it limited the number of agencies involved in its response process, increased its flexibility in postdisaster activities, augmented and diversified its funding and the purposes to which it could be directed, and won government approval of major increases in its overall budget for international humanitarian assistance.

In some respects, U.S. strengths are UN weaknesses and vice versa. The United States is primarily responsible and accountable to its own citizens and their elected representatives. When the American polity judges U.S. international disaster relief programs as a low priority, the U.S. system of relief suffers. U.S. government relief programs, and the missions of its specialized agencies, are supposed to assist people in other nations and at the same time promote U.S. interests abroad. The rationale underlying U.S. humanitarian assistance is that by encouraging democracy and building structures favorable to sustainable political and economic development, the U.S. government gains and keeps allies and promotes other U.S. interests, among them the security of the United States itself. In providing disaster aid to the people of other nations, an American secondary agenda is to prevent recipient nations from political or economic collapse, to forestall their subversion by enemies of the United States, and to prevent the spawning of failed states that may evolve into rogue states.

For these reasons, leaders of some nation-states decline American offers of disaster relief. Some are wary of U.S. motives; many leaders fear the consequences of U.S. intervention and worry that American "help" might destabilize their governing regimes. For these reasons, they often judge UN help as less threatening, because it is coming from an international body founded on humanitarian ideological goals: alleviating human suffering and promoting human rights and peace around the globe. The UN often projects a more neutral and legitimate image than the United States. This legitimacy is reinforced by long-standing relationships that the UN has with most of its member states. To many in the international community, the collective and multilateral character of past UN interventions represents altruistic interests of a confederation of nations rather than the sometimes insincere help of an individual state.

The UN is a capable overall coordinator of disaster relief and recovery programs but an organization poorly suited to separating combatants, forcefully protecting relief workers, their aid stores, and their aid distribution networks. Moreover, the size of the UN budget (and therefore the UN capacity to intervene) depends on the benevolence of its member states and private donors.

In contrast, the United States has its own international disaster relief system, has the manpower to implement its missions, and has the capacity to use its military people and capabilities when it so chooses. In addition, the United States is one of the largest contributors to the UN, although the United States has also resisted paying its full assessment.[55] The U.S. government and the American people also donate funds and in-kind resources to many international organizations capable of dispensing disaster relief. The UN is in many ways dependent on U.S. help and resources. A disagreement between UN and U.S. officials in a matter of international disaster relief has consequences for all parties. The United States remains a vital and fundamental player in the United Nations' disaster response system.

Poor nations can rarely afford to engage in disaster preparedness and mitigation activities without outside help. Moreover, in some cases the leaders of certain poor and developing nations adhere to political ideologies and conduct domestic and foreign policies disliked by other nations. In the twenty-first century, the need to fight terrorism and the dissemination of weapons of mass destruction coexists with the need to advance the moral imperatives of peace and development. Disasters must be addressed by a wide array of state and nonstate actors. Together, the United States and the United Nations do have important stakes in assisting such nations and their peoples. Both the UN and the United States are essential actors in a multilevel/multilateral disaster-relief global regime.

UN and U.S. agencies collaborate with many states, agencies, and NGOs. Each possesses the resources and the capacity to intervene and provide relief in disaster-stricken areas. With so many actors involved in the response process, both the UN and the United States have a stake in maintaining and improving coordination and communication among themselves and with others. Each needs to better allocate the funds of donors, avoiding redundancy and counterproductive outcomes. Effort and aid must be distributed quickly, wisely, and efficiently so as to lessen the effects of disasters.

KEY TERMS AND CONCEPTS

"blue helmeted" peacekeeping
    soldiers   205
complex humanitarian emergencies
    (CHEs)   196
development banks   201
Disaster Reduction and Recovery Program
    (of UNDP)   204

emergency-management-oriented multi-
    national organizations   201
Emergency Response Division
    (of UNDP)   203
globalizing forces   195
humanitarian assistance   199
territorial sovereignty   196

CHAPTER

9

CONCLUSIONS
AND THE
FUTURE

SO WHAT DO I NEED TO KNOW FOR THE TEST? THIS IS A FAIR question that my, and most, students ask after they have completed a set of reading assignments. Regardless of whether or not you are a student, if you consider catastrophes, disasters, and emergencies as "tests," this concluding chapter offers some points worth remembering. As a nation we need to know and appreciate what emergency management is as a profession. Emergency management is an evolving profession that has been advancing on a great many fronts for at least forty years. People do not have to become emergency managers in order to understand the policy and politics of disaster, but they would be wise to have an open-minded grasp of what emergency management involves.

Chapters 1 and 4 demonstrate that the president is an emergency manager. Governors, mayors, city managers, county executives, and others who hold positions of public executive authority are emergency managers as well. Elected chief executives, including the president, cannot be expected to engage in emergency management work all the time, but when disasters and emergencies strike or are imminent those officials must know what to do. Full-time professional emergency managers in government implement disaster policy; they can be found working at all levels of government, and they often work closely with elected executives. Consequently, government emergency managers have some capacity to influence and shape disaster policy and to be part of its politics. Emergency management work is not confined to government. Nonprofit voluntary organizations, as well as for-profit private corporations and businesses, actively engage in emergency management work and so can be considered both actors and stakeholders in the field. Disaster policy encompasses all the actors mentioned in this paragraph and many more: elected lawmakers, the public, a vast array of businesses (foremost, the insurance industry), and a host of nongovernmental organizations.

Odd as it may seem, disaster research is conducted in a great many academic fields. The field of disaster research is diffuse, multidisciplinary, and in some respects interdisciplinary

After the Northridge earthquake hit Southern California in 1994, many buildings were retrofitted to prevent future buckling. The St. John's Health Center in Santa Monica chose to rebuild, rather than retrofit, and this image shows one of the Center's emerging "quake-resistant" buildings. Not only has Southern California seen reconstruction and prevention efforts in the wake of Northridge, the state as a whole will most certainly play a lead role in shaping the future of U.S. disaster policy.

(emerging from and transcending different knowledge disciplines). Disasters, whether from natural sources or from human causes, affect almost every aspect of life for those who experience them. Some scientific research has been dedicated to identifying the causes of hazard threats. Weather forecasting is part of emergency management. Hurricane research and tracking is undoubtedly important in emergency management. Seismologic research plays a central role in calculating the possibility of major earthquakes, as well as the possibility of other geological phenomena likely to affect people and structures on the surface. Floodplain management has become its own specialization. Also, emergency management, particularly in regard to disaster mitigation, owes much to the building sciences. No less important is sociological research concerning human behavior during disasters. Political science and economics have added to useful knowledge in emergency management.

As has been shown, certain disaster agents (for example, tornadoes, severe storms, floods, hurricanes, earthquakes, hazardous materials, terrorism) draw the interest of certain sets of researchers and their organizations. The result is that many specific disaster types have their own circle of special interest groups that engage the policy process. Sometimes, however, those who support work on a specific type of disaster agent have little interest in working cooperatively or in unison with those working on other disaster agents.

Regarding the public perception of disasters, it was explained in Chapter 1 that disaster policy and politics are vulnerable to what Anthony Downs called the "issue attention" cycle, just as the environmental movement was in the past and perhaps still is today. Disaster policy and politics will always suffer from public interest levels that reflect the ups and downs of a fun park rollercoaster. Disasters are episodic, but at the same time, they are increasingly predictable if not in some respects inevitable. Tolerated vulnerabilities to known natural hazards often help natural forces generate effects that are disastrous for humans. When this happens it may be incorrect to refer to them as "natural" disasters.

America has its own politics of hazard vulnerability. Many people build homes as close to the ocean as they can get them. Often the market value of the plots (often only sand lots) closest to the ocean beach, and most vulnerable to storm surges and coastal flooding, exceeds the cost of the houses that will be built on them. In mountainous areas of the nation, more and more people erect homes on steep slopes. In seismically active areas, or in areas vulnerable to erosion or landslides, this practice poses major risks. Rivers or streams are, for many, wonderful amenities. However, they often tempt people to locate new homes and businesses in flood-prone areas. Drawn to the natural beauty and recreational opportunities that these water bodies afford, people often discount or overlook the risks they assume in placing structures in or near floodplains. The same phenomenon applies when people choose to build and reside in homes located inside or adjacent to the fire hazard areas of forest lands or urban/wildland interface zones.

Disaster management is characterized by fragmented government responsibility. Disaster policy itself often overlaps so many other policy domains—many perceived as having a higher priority than disaster management—that developing a coherent and broad-gauged all-hazards disaster policy is politically daunting. Chapter 6, covering the intergovernmental relations realm of disaster policy and emergency management, demonstrated how many different players are involved in disaster policy and disaster management. Many of these players have found ways to organize and to press politically for the interests they judge important. Therefore, the politics of disaster is rich and diverse. It should be examined both in regard to the players and interests interacting within each separate layer of government and in regard to the players and interests interacting across layers of government.

Since Hurricane Katrina in 2005, a catastrophe that came to represent a dark hour for emergency managers everywhere, many people have become interested in how decisions are made under disaster circumstances. Since Katrina, the nation has witnessed a profusion of presidential candidates who promise to be capable leaders and executives in times of disaster. More and more political candidates seeking elected executive offices, or who are hoping to retain them, tout their ability to handle a crisis or emergency. Disaster management is very much an executive-dominated activity. How disasters are managed is increasingly a matter of political importance.

Chapter 1 closed with an overview of the phases of emergency management: mitigation, preparedness, response, and recovery. Some scholars have suggested that other phases could be added in the interest of refining the conceptual framework. Several have asked that people think in terms of short-term disaster recovery and long-term disaster recovery. Some, concerned with homeland security counterterrorism, advocate pairing "prevention" with "mitigation." The phases model, or heuristic, roughly demarcates time-relevant aspects of disasters and emergencies. However, mitigation, called by some the cornerstone of emergency management, is something not bound by time or phase sequencing. In other words, mitigation activities may be a part of preparedness, response, and recovery. Moreover, people and governments should engage in mitigation activities before disasters strike, not simply after they have occurred. The four phases should not be viewed as distinct compartments or categories but as fluid, overlapping, and dynamic. One should not succumb to the spell of news media dramatizations that infer disaster policy and emergency management are only about the "response" phase.

DISASTER MANAGERS AND THEORIES OF POLICY IMPLEMENTATION

Chapter 2 introduced two normative political theories that were applied to the work of emergency managers. The Jeffersonian model posited that emergency management is done at the grassroots local level. Jeffersonian public managers possess skill in consultation, negotiation, and communication, as well as the ability to probe for public understanding that eventually wins public and official consent. Capable Jeffersonian emergency managers rely heavily on community participation. Their work is quite political in the sense that part of their job is to maintain and advance democracy. The skills of Jeffersonian emergency managers are skills one would associate with generalists rather than specialists. Local emergency managers must serve local executives and at the same time respond to the needs of people in their jurisdiction. Education in the liberal arts and law are to the advantage of Jeffersonian emergency managers.

Counterposed to the Jeffersonian model is the Hamiltonian model. Under the Hamiltonian model public managers must put emphasis on getting results. They work under after-the-fact accountability. Hamiltonian model decision makers must be students of organization and must possess executive talents in formulating plans and carrying out duties. They must understand the substance, tools, and processes of their work.

In many respects, Hamiltonian emergency managers are well-educated, professional, technocrats. Much of modern life is dependent on people with technocratic skills: the air traffic controller who guides aircraft and prevents mid-air collisions; the emergency medical technician who offers first aid and life-saving skills to trauma victims; the civil engineer who designs, builds, and maintains massive public infrastructures like highways, water and wastewater systems, and electric power grids. Hamiltonian emergency managers possess special knowledge and expertise that most average citizens do not have, and they often work under the norm of the scientific method and the expectation of political neutrality. They know how to apply geographic information system mapping software to model potential damage from specific types of hazards and disaster agents. They are expected to be familiar with computer programs that help them prepare and test population evacuation plans. They grasp the fundamentals of disaster sociology so as to understand and better predict human behavior in disasters and emergencies. They understand the details of disaster law and policy as these apply to where they work. More than this, Hamiltonian emergency managers are trusted to act independently and decisively when necessary.

Some of the underlying tension within emergency management stems from the cross-cutting and conflicting demands that the Jeffersonian and Hamiltonian models place on the work of emergency managers. This may be why education in disaster study and emergency management is frequently offered through interdisciplinary combinations of education and training.

Some of the bureaucratic politics of disaster policy and emergency management were explored in Chapter 2. FEMA has been both a combatant and a victim of bureaucratic "turf" wars. New problems, calamities, or emergencies, sometimes defined as "disaster" by public opinion, media influence, and political forces, often produce new policies. Which federal executive branch departments, agencies, or offices would win the jurisdiction and resources to implement these new policies often raised the question of who's in charge. FEMA's history is a scatter plot of "who's in charge" negotiations and disputes with officials of other federal departments and agencies. Throughout the 1980s and 1990s FEMA was the only federal agency with large-scale disaster recovery monies and budget authority. FEMA continues to have considerable say in matters of president-declared nonterror disasters.

FEMA's administrative culture has been shaped by its history. The nation's system of disaster management is permeated by military and paramilitary concerns, as demonstrated in Chapter 7. Throughout this book it has been asserted that disaster policy is dominated by the president. Certainly as the "emergency manager" in chief, the president has come to rely on FEMA and related emergency management agencies. Thus, FEMA, although beholden and accountable to Congress in many ways, is a tool of the president. In the American federal system presidents must sometimes work closely with governors, and sometimes mayors, to facilitate the intergovernmental relations necessary in acute disaster management circumstances. Since its inception in April 1979, FEMA administrative culture has been strongly influenced by how presidents have chosen to use the agency in their relations with governors and local elected executives.

A portion of Chapter 2 applied Graham Allison's three models of government decision making. The rational actor model could be applied to explain some presidential decisions on whether to approve or deny a governor's request for a presidential declaration of major disaster or emergency, a subject discussed at length in Chapter 4. Allison's bureaucratic politics model explains presidential decisions on disaster declarations as the outcome of negotiations between senior political appointees (agency heads, cabinet-level secretaries, state emergency management leaders, and so forth) and elected executives (governors, mayors, and the like). The bureaucratic politics model might be used to explain many other aspects of government emergency management, particularly in regard to major disasters. Finally, Allison's organizational process model held that emergency management professionals compile disaster damage information and use it to review gubernatorial requests for declarations (the governor's request itself would be the product of state emergency management agency activity). In the organizational process model the executive has either largely delegated decision authority to lower-level officials or he or she rubber-stamps the official recommendation of emergency management functionaries. Clearly, much of the emergency management decision making that transpires between disasters or that is applied to relatively routine disasters could be explained through organizational process model assumptions and testing.

Chapter 2, anticipating a much broader discussion in Chapter 6, presented a variety of theories about federalism and intergovernmental relations. These theory tools help explain the prospects and problems of intergovernmental relations and program coordination.

First was a discussion of best-practices approaches used to help emergency management grow as a profession. The chapter then covered principal-agent theory, which sounds complex and mysterious but is not. Government emergency managers work in a universe of federal, state, local, and private sector agencies. An immense amount of government emergency management work is contract management (see Chapter 6), which involves private contractors and nonprofit volunteer organizations. In a sense, government officials are principals who retain agents, in this case contractors, who in turn carry out various duties, functions, and tasks. Information flows among agents and principals. It is essential that government officials (principals) use their contract oversight authority to ensure that contractors (agents) do the work they are being paid to do and in the manner and at the pace they are expected. From a different perspective, Congress is a principal seeking to ensure that emergency management officials, as its agents, perform their work appropriately and responsively. Principal-agent theory, emanating from economics, has considerable potential uses in explaining and conducting emergency management, particularly in an era when government relies so heavily on for-profit contractors.

Partisan mutual adjustment, as a theory used to understand and explain various dimensions of disaster policy and emergency management, is the theory most likely to be disputed. Every elected political official still able to draw a breath is likely to decry and deny any claim that disasters involve partisan politics. However, all elected officials who won office through partisan competition are forever conscious of their rivals in opposing political parties. Disaster politics involves the demonstration of political responsiveness and, occasionally, partisanly motivated blame fixing as well. Disaster management sometimes has electoral consequences for public executives. In the partisan mutual adjustment theory, public managers of different agencies clash owing to their respective personal political motivations, their respective obligations to the law and to the agencies they lead, and their respective commitments to their elected executive and legislative overseers. Part of the politics of disasters comes in the form of both competition and mutual accommodation of the partisan political behaviors of elected executives.

Also examined in Chapter 2 were the effects of the "reinventing government" and "new public administration" movements on emergency management. Customer satisfaction is a worthy, although challenging, goal of emergency management.

Not to be overlooked in Chapter 2 is the investigation of the knowledge base of emergency management. Will emergency management knowledge largely advance and proliferate as a product of the training and tacit knowledge of practicing disaster responders, often in occupational specializations, or will it emerge from scientific and academic study of the field and from the scholarly publications of top emergency management practitioners?

HISTORICAL TRENDS IN DISASTER MANAGEMENT

Chapter 3 reminded us that disaster policy in the United States has a long history. This book concentrated on disaster policy and politics since 1950. The Civil Defense Act of 1950 and the Disaster Relief Act of 1950 built the foundation for modern emergency management at the federal level. The system of presidential disaster declarations flowed from the Disaster Relief Act of 1950. That law represented congressional concession of disaster declaration authority to the president. The measure also laid out the process by which governors could ask the president for declarations of major disaster. Moreover, these laws launched an assortment of federal agencies and programs intended to provide a means of securing federal assistance to subnational governments first and disaster victims later. Some of this assistance came as generous federal matching grants to state and local governments. Some of it came as baskets of federal assistance to disaster victims, although for some baskets victims had to make application and prove means-tested need.

Sometimes disasters, particularly catastrophic ones, have transformed presidents and their administrations. Hurricane Camille (1969), and an ensuing weak and highly criticized federal response to that disaster, pressed President Nixon to assign various emergency management duties to an archipelago of federal agencies. The federal-state debacle in managing the response to Hurricane Andrew in August 1992 damaged President George H. W. Bush's image and, although he narrowly carried Florida and so won its electoral votes, may have contributed to his defeat in the November 1992 presidential election. Once in office, President Bill Clinton responded to the Hurricane Andrew controversy by appointing a qualified and experienced state emergency manager to head his FEMA. Clinton, despite other controversial problems of his presidency, left office widely considered a president capable of leading the federal government through natural disasters. His supporters point to his ability to exhibit compassion and his insistence on proactive and capable government response to major disasters. His critics point to his propensity to generously issue major disaster and emergency declarations as well as his ability to occasionally exploit disaster for political advantage. The terrorist attack disaster of September 11, 2001, had a profound effect on President George W. Bush. He quickly redefined his administration's primary mission as one of countering and preventing terrorism attacks inside the nation and prosecuting a "**War on Terrorism.**" Hurricane Katrina and the excoriated federal response to that disaster moved Congress to reconstitute FEMA as a full-service emergency management agency, but one that at this writing remains embedded within the gigantic Department of Homeland Security.

Thomas A. Birkland, in his *Lessons of Disaster: Policy Change after Catastrophic Events* is correct in asserting that disaster policy is very much **event driven.**[1] Donald F. Kettl, in his *System under Stress,* is correct in positing that certain disasters, often catastrophes, not only stress the nation's disaster management system but force massive reforms that produce a "**new normal**" in the national psyche and in the domain of disaster policy and homeland security.[2] James F. Miskel, in his *Disaster Response and Homeland Security,* is correct in his claim that FEMA, whether independent or within DHS, is fairly good at managing "routine" disasters.[3] However, Miskel is also insightful when he declares that no federal agency is invested with sufficient authority to adequately or proficiently cope with a catastrophe. It becomes the job of the president and his staff to orchestrate and oversee the work of many federal disaster agencies in catastrophic circumstances. Such work has to be carried out with the help and cooperation of governors, mayors, and other elected executives. A host of other players are involved as well; these include state and local emergency managers, emergency responders, nonprofit organizations active in disasters, and private corporations, large and small.[4]

Much of Chapter 3 tells the story of FEMA. The agency is, for better or for worse, the institutional embodiment of federal emergency management and a chief implementer of the nation's disaster policy. FEMA's struggle to mature as an agency, to win the confidence and trust of successive presidents, to demonstrate that it can capably manage disaster recovery, and to survive in a hostile sea of power-hungry competing federal agencies, all comprise parts of its history. A recurring theme of FEMA's history is the dialectical "push and pull" about whether the agency is an operational disaster response organization (one lawmaker referred to it as the nation's 911 emergency number) or whether it is more fundamentally a coordinating mechanism used to align and coach portions of other federal agencies called out to work with state, local, and nongovernmental organizations in times of disaster. As in any dialectic, whenever FEMA moves too far toward becoming only a coordinating agency, it is pulled back in the direction of being a disaster response organization. Conversely, when it takes on too much as a response agency, it is pushed in the direction of assuming more exclusively coordinative duties.

The agency's leaders have always understood that FEMA's fortunes rise and fall as a function of how presidents perceive it and choose to use it. FEMA owes much to President Carter because he championed and approved formation of the agency. Presidents have tasked FEMA with different duties and missions at different times. To use a baseball metaphor, FEMA is a utility infielder and coach called out to help the president get out of tough innings. Presidents rely on FEMA in the declaration process, they count on FEMA to coordinate the work of other federal agencies mobilized to respond to a disaster, and they use FEMA to help them deal with anomalous problems and events.

To date and arguably, no president has made better use of FEMA than President Bill Clinton. Presidents Jimmy Carter and Clinton seemed to recognize the importance of disaster policy and politics. President Clinton, inaugurated in January 1993, and his FEMA appointees were blessed by the end of civil defense against nuclear attack concerns as the cold war ended. They would give all-hazards federal emergency management a chance to flourish. Presidents Reagan and George H. W. Bush used FEMA's civil defense role in their foreign policies. President George W. Bush, and Congress, pressed FEMA to assume homeland security duties. In many respects, homeland security mimics civil defense of the past. However, the homeland security mission is addressing terrorism and the threat of terrorism inside the

United States. Federal emergency management today is suffused with a homeland security ethos, and this applies throughout the federal system.

Chapter 3 demonstrated that disaster policy in the United States is very much formulated and implemented through "planning" activities. The word "plan" deserves a capital "P." Planning work is massive. Planning work in disaster policy is never finished. In effect, until a major disaster or emergency strikes, whether caused by natural forces or by an act of terrorism, the broad-gauged planning work done by officials implementing the National Response Plan, or National Response Framework, is the essence of disaster policy implementation. First responders are constantly trained and advised under the National Incident Management System, itself an ever-changing and evolving tactical plan. The NIMS represents the field "application" arm of disaster policy and emergency management.

DISASTER POLICY AND PRESIDENTIAL POWERS

The law and policy of U.S. disaster management accords the president flexibility to decide what does or does not constitute a declarable "major disaster" or "emergency." This declaration authority allows the president to extend both reassurance and meaningful disaster assistance. This flexibility is essential in an era when the nation faces new disaster threats, many unforeseen or nearly impossible to predict. The 9/11 terrorist attacks and the succession of anthrax letter incidents in the months afterward represent extraordinary examples of the uncertainty facing presidents. Yet, it is the exercise of presidential discretion in deciding which calamities deserve declarations that draws some to allege that such decisions are expediently political.

Federal laws enacted since 1950 that have entrusted the president with extensive authority in times of disaster and emergency were examined in Chapter 4. As one would expect, the U.S. Constitution itself entrusts the president with certain emergency authority, particularly within the context of defending the nation. The cold war era of civil defense against nuclear attack, from about 1949 to 1990, encouraged Congress to enhance presidential emergency powers. In 1950 Congress gave the president authority to issue major disaster declarations to states whose governors requested them. Moreover, Congress allowed the president to exercise discretion and judgment in reviewing the worthiness of requests. Presidents could deny them. Congressional intent in 1950 was to limit the president to issuing declarations for a loosely defined set of natural disaster types. However, over time presidents determined that they could use this authority to address various human-caused disasters. They also were free to define the thresholds for differentiating scales and types of natural disasters that deserved declarations.

Federal disaster laws have evolved dramatically since the 1950s and 1960s. Some laws in this early era provided modest federal assistance and most of this went only to state or local governments, not directly to disaster victims. As modern federal disaster laws came to address a wider range of public needs, and as new disaster relief programs were developed and implemented under these laws, presidential disaster declaration authority conveyed a broader and deeper basket of state and local benefits. Added to this basket was a variety of federal assistance that went directly to disaster victims and nongovernmental organizations. Presidential disaster declaration authority therefore assumed greater importance and newsworthiness. Many presidents took notice of this, and for some, disaster declaration authority and discretion became a respected and much-used instrument of presidential power.

When presidents issue approvals for unique primary incidents, they set precedents, and governors take notice. Governors then look for incidents in their state that are comparable to the new disaster type. They then formulate and submit requests for presidential declarations of major disaster or emergency. This helps their state and respective localities address this new type of "disaster." The dynamic has helped introduce presidential distributive politics into disaster policy.[5] Presidents, whether Democratic or Republican, have engaged in the distributive politics of disaster declaration issuance. Governors not only tempt presidents to engage in this behavior but they have sometimes exploited the system in order to maximize federal assistance to their state and affected localities.

Since 1982, the twenty-four-hour news coverage of Cable Network News, satellite broadcasts of live news events from abroad via CNN, and links to broadcasts of other television news organizations from abroad have made White House staffers keenly aware of the president's vulnerability in news coverage. Such wide coverage has also provided presidents greater opportunity to shape the news, particularly when the nation has looked to the president in time of disaster. Presidents have become susceptible to the CNN syndrome of "disaster" news coverage.[6] Presidents Eisenhower, Kennedy, Johnson, Nixon, and Ford may have had less interest in presidential declarations of disaster than later presidents have had because in their times federal emergency management was dispersed over many small, relatively obscure agencies, federal disaster relief provided in law was more limited, and disasters were covered less extensively by the major national television networks.

Presidents often lead in the formulation and legitimation of disaster policy. Presidents are chief executives and many presidents have, either by choice or by the press of emergency circumstances, used their executive authority to move the federal government to address new emergencies, disasters, and exigencies. Today, owing to authority entrusted to President George W. Bush after the 9/11 disaster, presidents are able to mobilize various agencies of federal, state, and local government to address even the "possible" risk of a terror attack in a specific location.

Beyond the matter of presidential emergency powers is the more mundane issue of political appointments to federal emergency management positions. Some presidents have assumed office believing that major disasters and catastrophes are sufficiently infrequent to allow them to appoint disaster-inexperienced FEMA officials who may learn on the job. Some presidents may be confident that civil servant federal emergency managers (ordinarily hugely assisted by state and local emergency management officials and agencies) will be able to manage and cope with the many "routine" and smaller-scale disasters that do occur. This logic has encouraged them to fill some or most senior appointed posts at FEMA through a **"Plum Book" spoils system,** which rewards the people and interests that helped them win office. Every president from Eisenhower through Bill Clinton and George W. Bush engaged in this practice to varying degrees. FEMA has sometimes been called a political dumping ground for spoils system political appointees who are unqualified for the duties of their positions, a claim that was occasionally made in the news before 1993 and was loudly repeated after FEMA's debacle in the Hurricane Katrina response operations of 2005.[7]

THE ROLE OF SCIENCE AND ENGINEERING

Chapter 5 demonstrated that disaster policy encompasses a broad pool of scientific and engineering interests. Using the extensive scientific instrumentation now available—orbiting geoscience satellites, a national system of automated river and stream gauging, a massive array of scientific instruments attached to buoys in the mid–Pacific Ocean, a national and international system of seismographic monitoring, and hurricane hunter aircraft, to name a few—the United States is devoted to researching the environment, the demographics of human settlement and land use, and natural disaster forces themselves.

In many respects, the major infusion of homeland security funding into what were previously established disaster management programs has been a blessing and a curse. It has been a blessing in the sense that the nation's major research laboratories, owing to their incorporation into parts of DHS, now research the broadly reconceived field of disaster. Also, federal, state, and local emergency-management-related agencies now enjoy more federal funding than they have in their previous histories, particularly between-disaster preparedness funding. For local governments in particular, homeland security funding has subsidized the establishment or enhancement of local emergency operation centers, the purchase of new equipment, and the training and education of personnel. This and other factors have made disaster studies a high-demand and growing field of academic study. State and local governments have recruited and hired in substantial numbers graduates of emergency management higher education programs. Massive homeland security and emergency-management-related contracts have been issued to corporations, who in turn need to hire armies of qualified workers.

That disaster policy is a homeland security concern has major ramifications for disaster researchers. The curse is the possibility that disaster-related scientific research is returning to a type of dual-use era in which research on natural disasters is contingent on proving value and relevance in coping with possible terrorist attacks, up to and including those involving the use of weapons of mass destruction. Homeland security is also a curse when it imposes security restrictions on what is researched, what is made public, and who is eligible to receive government research grants. Many areas of disaster research and information sharing, right down to the local level, have been affected by homeland security restrictions.

Scientists and engineers often form effective and knowledgeable **political pressure groups** in disaster policy. Knowledge creation may be one of the best disaster mitigation tools the nation possesses.

Is emergency management too broadly interdisciplinary? Do scientific and engineering professions address disaster in ways that are too parochial? Who researches disaster? How is new knowledge created in the field of disaster policy? Who teaches emergency management and disaster policy? Again, these are all worthy and perhaps provocative questions that deserve to be answered in the future.

INTERGOVERNMENTAL RELATIONS IN DISASTER POLICY

Many have assumed that local governments fundamentally advance disaster policy. "All disasters are local" is an oft-repeated and regularly valid assertion of emergency managers and students of disaster. Nevertheless, the United States is a large nation, operated through a federal system. Emergency management capacity at the local level varies widely across the nation. Most large cities and smaller localities in metropolitan areas have experienced disasters, and most, although not all, have considerable ability to work all phases of disaster. There is also a vast array of more rural or remote counties, cities, towns, and villages that maintain emergency response capacity, again some of it superior and some of it merely adequate. A great many localities rely on volunteer firefighters, the vast majority of whom are unpaid. The experience, education, and training of these firefighters vary from outstanding to satisfactory. Moreover, the emergency management capability of law enforcement officers also varies dramatically across the nation. Emergency medical capacity also varies widely owing to high patient demand, health insurance and liability issues, low pay, expensive and demanding certification requirements, municipal residency requirements in some cities, the closure of too many hospital emergency rooms, limited hospital surge capacity after disasters, and so on. Local governmental provision for adequate emergency response is only part of the game, however; emergency management also includes mitigation, preparedness, and recovery.

In the United States, government management of major disasters is done through intergovernmental relations or it is not done at all. As mentioned before, one thing obvious to anyone who studies U.S. disaster policy and management is the tremendous degree of overlap and interdependence of American governmental jurisdictions. FEMA and the Department of Homeland Security are expected to create an emergency management partnership with other federal agencies, state and local governments, volunteer organizations, and the private sector to better serve customers. DHS and its FEMA are expected to establish, in concert with their state and local partners, a national emergency management system that is comprehensive, risk-based, and all-hazards in approach. Hazard mitigation is supposed to be the foundation of the national emergency management system. The federal government, in conjunction with state and local government, is counted on to provide a rapid and effective response to, and recovery from, declared disasters. The federal government is asked to help strengthen state and local emergency management.

When civil defense against nuclear attack was the federal emergency management priority, disaster policy was imposed from the top down. Today, owing to the political pressures and national fears surrounding the threat of more spectacular and devastating attacks, as occurred on September 11, 2001, and despite political rhetoric that national emergency management is based on a federal-state-local "partnership," disaster policy is again very much a top-down system, dominated by the president and the federal government. Vast homeland security grant programs embedded with detailed conditions, requirements, and standards largely define much of what governmental disaster management is today in the United States. It is ironic that state and local emergency managers from the 1950s through the 1990s rightfully complained of inadequate federal funding of their work. However, many states and local governments may well have ignored the need for full service emergency management had they not received federal funding, even federal funding biased toward dual use and civil defense. The problem has changed today. Many state and local emergency management officials appreciate the dramatically scaled-up grant funding they receive today in this post-9/11 homeland security era, but many also lament the federal preoccupation with terrorism at the expense of established all-hazards emergency management, the hierarchical system for dispensing funds, and the immense paper- and computer-work burdens they must now shoulder.

It is fair to ask, is the federal government moving toward federalizing even more emergency management? Are domestic natural disasters becoming a subset of national counterterrorism policy? Is U.S. federalism a help or a hindrance in disaster management?

Consider as well that, according to Miskel, FEMA is an agency whose "authority" does not match the magnitude of its "responsibility."[8] In catastrophic disasters, it is naive to expect an agency of three thousand to five thousand federal workers to respond operationally and at the same time coordinate the response of a constellation of other federal, state, and local agencies. Expansive and massively destructive catastrophes (of any type) can rarely be addressed to the satisfaction of the public and their elected representatives.[9]

Chapter 5 underscored the immensely important role of nonprofit, nongovernmental organizations active in disasters. These organizations are major participants in the broader governance realm of disaster policy, and they are often significant political actors in the politics of disaster.

No less important is the role of for-profit government contracts retained by federal, state, and local governments to undertake a great variety of tasks and projects. These contractors are often essential in disaster recovery operations, whether short term or long term. Contractors are players who are often astutely capable of securing grants or contracted work assignments paid for by government. For-profit government contractors, just as nonprofit organizations, are capable of doing great good. However, just as nonprofit organizations sometimes do, contractors may capitalize on their association with government for gain.

CIVIL-MILITARY RELATIONS AND NATIONAL SECURITY

Civil defense and homeland security were always tethered to disaster policy. In the 1950s, civil defense against nuclear attack was the platform upon which modern emergency management evolved, although this was done conjointly with thousands of state and local emergency managers. Civil defense of the past and homeland security of the present, both signify that disaster policy has always had a national security and foreign policy component.

The military is often a magnificent asset in humanitarian disaster response (see Chapter 8 for international examples as well). Men and women in the National Guard and the active-duty military are trained to follow orders and operate in the field; they are prepared to move into hazardous zones with enough equipment to sustain themselves independently for considerable periods; and they are willing to put themselves in harm's way. For example, the U.S. Coast Guard, since 2003 a part of the Department of Homeland Security, is a military organization highly praised for its disaster response to Hurricane Katrina, which included many rescues.

Military people and certain types of emergency responders are expected to take risks if they are so ordered. As mentioned, firefighters, police officers, and emergency medical people are willing to take similar risks and often do so regularly, as was dramatically obvious during and after the 9/11 terrorist attacks. However, other, well-meaning, public servants cannot be expected to enter danger zones that pose a significant risk to their health and welfare.[10] This has given rise to a public and media propounded assumption that the military is better suited to conduct emergency management than is civilian government, particularly when people believe that civilian authorities are overwhelmed or incapable of doing the job.

The 9/11 terrorist attack dramatically opened the door to heavier military involvement in disaster policy. The National Guard and active reserve forces have long played an important role in disaster response and short-term recovery. Each governor is able to deploy his or her respective state National Guard in disasters or emergencies they believe warrant such deployment. Unfortunately, the number of available National Guard members in most states has dwindled as the War on Terrorism has called upon the Guard to shoulder military responsibilities in Iraq and Afghanistan.

Breakdowns in president-governor relations are apparent when, during an ongoing domestic disaster, the president considers federalizing (assuming direct control of) National Guard forces that have been deployed by, and are under the command of, a governor. However, as stated previously, what matters most is the proper use of the military in disasters and the realization that military help is highly temporary. The deployment of the National Guard and active-duty military to a zone of disaster means that civil government in that zone has failed. The military can be expected to facilitate rescues, protect property and lives, and maintain civil order. However, martial law quickly becomes intolerable to Americans.

Military organizations are often ill-equipped to handle many short- and long-term disaster recovery needs: rebuilding homes, managing shelters, feeding the displaced, helping businesses resume operation, servicing the long-term medical needs of disaster victims, replacing public infrastructure, bringing back public utilities.

Students of disaster must understand the bounded role of the military in disaster management. Owing to the national security features of homeland security, and the inclusive requirements of the National Response Plan and the National Incident Management System, disaster policy today is suffused with "national securitization" issues. Security classification now shrouds from public view a variety of emergency response plans. The Department of Homeland Security has injected vast sums of money into disaster management and at the same time has made disaster policy implementation more closed, more secretive, and more dominated by law enforcement. These are problems likely to become flashpoints of controversy in future disaster circumstances.

The North American Command has been established to better protect the homeland from attack. NORTHCOM people have worked to find their place in national disaster management. However, the military command and control culture is rarely compatible with the more consensual, grassroots culture of civilian emergency management, which entrusts much authority to field responders and rests on coordination, collaboration, and improvisation.[11] NORTHCOM perceives its mission as preventing another terrorist attack on the homeland, militarily defeating attacks by foreigners if possible, protecting U.S. borders or air space from encroachment or penetration by attackers, or aiding in the response to a weapon of mass destruction incident inside the United States.

Since the formation of DHS there have been cries from the emergency management community that the president went too far in his reorganization. What had been built up as a strong system over recent years was beginning to unravel and become confused in the age of homeland security. Under homeland security, the focus of emergency management shifted from frequent natural disasters to rare but potentially devastating acts of terrorism. With this shift came a new focus on prevention and diminished concern for disaster mitigation. State and local emergency managers were being transformed into intelligence collectors, vigilant surveillance officials, and adjuncts of counterterrorism law enforcement. Federal emergency managers were cast into unfamiliar environments filled with administrative and political "turf" battles inside DHS.

James Lee Witt told a congressional hearing:

> The establishment of DHS has also adversely affected the key partnerships which make the emergency management system function properly. Responsibility for the immediate response to any natural disaster flows up from the local to the state and on to the federal level as it becomes evident that it will overcome the capacity and resources of the previous level of government. Even when the federal government takes over responsibility for a disaster response, however, state and local responders and emergency managers continue to work along side their colleagues at the federal level. During the 1990s, the relationships between FEMA regional offices and their state and local counterparts were fostered through participation in joint exercises and because the relationship was supported by a flow of resources. FEMA had an understanding of the needs of the state and local emergency managers because we administered a number of other programs. These funding programs served as a way of aligning the policies of the local, state, and federal emergency management community and fostering a strong relationship.[12]

Adjusting to the new DHS terrorism-dominated environment was difficult for federal emergency management officials. Similarly, state and local emergency management officials, an imputed interest group and intergovernmental partners of FEMA, were now thrust into the field of homeland security.[13] During the shuffling, a massive new federal department basically swallowed up FEMA. The agency's people represented less than 2 percent of all DHS permanent full-time employees. The FEMA within DHS was dwarfed by other agencies and forced to work through new layers of administration to accomplish the same tasks that a single telephone call might have taken care of in years past. Moreover, according to Witt, under the DHS system, "FEMA's grant making authority was sharply eroded. Taking away this function and instead giving it to other divisions within DHS has also contributed to the nation's slip away from all-hazard preparedness. While homeland security is an important aspect of our nation's readiness, we have seen all too clearly the price that can be paid in not striking an adequate balance between natural and man-made hazard preparedness." [14]

GLOBALIZATION OF DISASTERS

In a sense it was a gradual but increasingly serious wedge of human-caused disasters, some caused by acts of terrorism, that moved the U.S. government toward acknowledging the international as well as domestic implications of federal emergency management. The 1993 World Trade Center bombing perpetrated by international terrorists was not the first attack on the American homeland by foreign nationals. However, that bombing reminded Americans that they were vulnerable to attack by terrorists. The 1995 bombing of the Oklahoma City Murrah federal office building, although committed by Americans, drew FEMA further into **terrorism consequence management.**

The September 11, 2001, terrorist attacks erased the imaginary line between conventional domestic disaster management and defense against foreign attacks inside the United States. President Bush's HSPD-5 states, "The Assistant to the President for Homeland Security and the Assistant to the President for National Security Affairs shall be responsible for interagency policy coordination on domestic and international incident management, respectively, as directed by the President." Both of these officials, "shall work together to ensure that the United States domestic and international incident management efforts are seamlessly united." [15]

The U.S. system of foreign disaster assistance in many respects predates modern federal emergency management of the post–World War II era, although American foreign disaster relief has long emphasized reactive emergency response activity. Through the 1990s to the present, features of U.S. emergency management at home have found their way into international development programs. The World Bank and other international banking institutions, reflecting growing U.S. interest in disaster management, have launched a variety of initiatives aimed at advancing U.S.-style emergency management in developing nations. It can safely be said, however, that U.S. domestic emergency management activity only lightly interweaves its foreign disaster assistance efforts. An exception is the military, which has extensive experience working both domestic and international disasters.

United Nations officials and people in its array of organizations addressing disaster and emergency concerns have learned some lessons from U.S. disaster experience. But UN agencies also have amassed an impressive record of disaster experience on their own. UN agency people have often worked shoulder to shoulder with U.S. foreign disaster responders. Many other nations maintain emergency management agencies and have the capacity to address their respective domestic disasters and offer disaster assistance to people in other nations. More study of international disaster management seems obviously necessary. Disasters have national, international, and sometimes global implications.

Many of the most famous international disaster relief organizations, bodies that routinely respond to humanitarian emergencies stemming from natural disasters, war, or civil strife, have long had domestic U.S. components. Donor communities and altruistic organizations, faith-based or secular, have worked alongside federal, state, and local disaster officials. Nonprofit organizations are today major players in broader disaster policy governance.

SPECIAL ISSUES

Because FEMA has always been a president-serving entity, it should come as no surprise that a change of presidential administration usually triggers wholesale replacement of FEMA's appointed leadership. The transition from Bill Clinton to George W. Bush involved replacing FEMA appointees, just as the transition from George H. W. Bush to Clinton did. This can safely be predicted to occur again when a new president assumes office in January 2009. New politically appointed executives affect the management and performance of the agencies and offices they direct. This is also the case on the state and local level when such turnovers occur. High turnover of politically appointed disaster officials has sometimes hurt agency employee morale, undercut agency performance, and created operational instability. Clinton's FEMA has a generally favorable public image not only because he appointed an experienced and capable emergency manager to head his disaster agency but also because his director was able to serve almost eight full years, the longest tenure of any FEMA director. However, as Miskel contends, the successful operation of the national emergency management system in time of major disaster or catastrophe is often far more important than who holds leadership positions in FEMA.[16]

The congressional reform of FEMA spearheaded in 2006 and 2007 now requires that all future FEMA directors have disaster management experience. Notwithstanding this requirement, the signing statement of President Bush disavows the need to comply with it. Moreover, there is some question as to whether FEMA has an official "director" any longer. As of March 1, 2003, no FEMA director existed in the Department of Homeland Security, but only an undersecretary charged with leading the organizational remnants of FEMA. As of March 31, 2007, the DHS-FEMA leader was referred to as the "administrator." However, it is fair to say that the administrator of FEMA from April 1, 2007, onward has most, although not all, of the authority previously vested in the FEMA directors of April 1979 to March 2003.

Regardless of their experience, expertise, or management brilliance, few FEMA administrators can be expected to retain their posts after a catastrophic disaster. The demands of the job in those circumstances are too great; the expectations of the public and elected representatives are too unrealistic; and a fired FEMA head is a convenient scapegoat for any president seeking political survival after a catastrophe.

Natural and Human-Caused Disasters versus Terror-Caused Disasters

Modern homeland security highlights the overlap of domestic emergency management and terrorism consequence management at home. Owing to the range of weapons and instruments potentially available to modern terrorists and the damage these might cause, modern antiterror emergency management under homeland security and conventional disaster management may actually complement each other today much more than civil defense and domestic emergency management complemented each other during the cold war. In addition, many conventional disaster management duties and many homeland security obligations complement one another under all-hazard emergency management.

Do Americans Expect Too Much?

Early in 2001, President George W. Bush's FEMA director, Joseph Allbaugh, testified before Congress that federal disaster assistance was "an oversized **entitlement program** and a disincentive to effective state and local risk management." [17] An overstatement to be sure, but many Americans expect the federal government to be the insurer of last resort for the disaster misfortunes they experience. This expectation is justifiable in periods of war and economic depression. The expectation is subject to challenge when Americans fail to buy available insurance to help protect them against known risks to their life and property, particularly when they were aware of the risks and had the means to purchase the insurance.

For example, the National Flood Insurance Program, discussed at length earlier in this book, has many worthwhile features that serve to help those whose homes and businesses experience flood damage. Yet, too few Americans have purchased National Flood Insurance policies. And although many local governments across the United States participate in the NFIP, many of those governments have not gone far enough to discourage development in their floodplains and have not done enough to relocate structures from floodplains.

Homeowner's insurance policies in many U.S. coastal areas are becoming prohibitively expensive. Many homeowners have not adequately insured their homes against the hazards they reasonably face. Residential earthquake insurance in documented seismically active zones is often woefully inadequate. Wind, fire, property, casualty, business continuity, accident, and workman's compensation insurance coverage is often insufficient in many locales. Insufficiency is often two pronged. Private insurers choose not to market high-risk policies fearing claims will be too many, too often, and likely to be filed all at once, and those who need to buy the insurance choose not to purchase policies owing to high premiums, high deductibles, difficulty in collecting on claims, or other reasons. Insurance is an important tool of both disaster preparedness and disaster mitigation, but it is often a tool only selectively used.

Winners and Losers in Disaster Policy

Hurricane Katrina reminded Americans that disasters often have profound effects on people who are poor or who are struggling to make ends meet. Disaster relief, especially long-term recovery relief to assist in rebuilding, relocation, and economic recovery, is also a matter of **antipoverty social policy** for the nation. Many sociological studies have analyzed and described the problems of poverty, ethnic and racial discrimination, ageism, and gender bias associated with all phases of disaster. In the United States, disaster policy is "conservative" in the sense that the aim of disaster relief is to return damaged areas, and disaster victims themselves, to the condition they were in before the disaster, albeit with some provision for mitigation against the possible repeat of the same type of disaster in the future. Nonetheless, many millions of Americans, many of whom consider themselves middle class, live only a few lost paychecks away from falling into personal bankruptcy or poverty; disasters often push many disaster victims over an economic ledge they are hard-pressed to climb back to. The winners in a disaster are those people able to find postdisaster help from the government and from other sources such that they and their families recover from the adversities they have suffered. The losers are those people who are unable to fend for themselves, whose postdisaster needs remain unmet, who cannot draw help from a family or community safety net, or who find that the debt they carried before the disaster prohibits them from qualifying for loans and other forms of financial help after a disaster.

Victims of disaster usually expect and often demand full replacement of their damaged private property. What happens when they do not receive all they think they deserve? People often die in disasters. Why should families of those who died on 9/11 get so much government and charitable help when families who lost loved ones in other disasters have never received as much government and charitable assistance? Clearly, the horror and uniqueness of the 9/11 attack and the loss of nearly three thousand people may account for the distinction Congress chose to make between that disaster and all others before or since.

Receiving more or receiving less after a disaster embodies other issues. Individual preparedness and "individual responsibility" are two mantras of emergency management. How is someone to gauge his or her vulnerability? Do individuals consciously engage in disaster risk-taking behavior or is this a myth propounded by critics of government disaster relief? Who is responsible for natural hazard risk assessment, and what is done about its results? Are people who work or live in high-rise buildings engaging in behavior that puts them at high risk of terrorism? Are people who live or work in or near national monuments or other symbols of U.S. power engaging in high-risk behavior?

In times of disaster, it is only natural for the victims of those events to ask for and expect help. That help often comes in many forms. Federal, state, and local law and policy is to provide assistance and relief for some, but not all, types of individual and family losses. Government disaster managers tend to talk in terms of meeting the postdisaster needs of victims. State and local governments, with substantial federal subsidization, will repair, replace, and restore disaster-damaged infrastructure, even that owned and operated by privately owned utilities. However, U.S. disaster law and policy is neither designed nor intended to make disaster victims "whole" after a disaster. Those working for charitable organizations recognize this and so they often seek to fill gaps or unmet needs of government relief through their own aid programs.

Moreover, American social and political cultural norms maintain that people need to make provision for possible disaster losses by purchasing insurance as a hedge. Overly generous government postdisaster relief would undercut the private market as well as the market for National Flood Insurance. In addition, the American political culture manifests an aversion to government-promoted "moral hazard" behavior. Moral hazard applies when overly generous government postdisaster relief provided to victims actually encourages them to engage in disaster hazard risk-taking behavior (for example, building homes on cliff sides vulnerable to failure during earthquakes, heavy rains, or floods; constructing homes and other structures in coastal high-hazard "V-zones" subject to hurricanes and storm surges; erecting shopping malls and other businesses in known floodplains).

Nevertheless, government's effort to avoid encouragement of moral hazard behavior risks producing social inequities and social injustices. Policymakers are forced to revisit this issue after many disasters, as was the case when the 9/11 Victim's Compensation Fund was established. A long-standing issue likely to reemerge in the future is the wisdom of creating a national "all-hazards" insurance program through which Americans could reasonably insure themselves against the full range of disaster hazards they face. Private insurers and reinsurance firms would have to be satisfied that government was not "nationalizing" their casualty and property insurance lines, state government insurance regulation might have to be preempted by the federal government, and the government would have to deny government disaster relief to those who could have purchased all-hazards insurance and did not.[18]

In the United States, just as in most nations, disaster policy is a product of law, program management, and political decision making. In the United States, disaster policy is "distributive" in the sense that costs of disaster recovery are shouldered nationally (with significant payouts by the state governments experiencing the disaster), whereas benefits (aid dispensed) are concentrated at the substate and local levels.

U.S. disaster policy is modestly redistributive in that taxpayers living in areas with few presidentially declared disasters tend to subsidize taxpayers living in areas with relatively many presidentially declared disasters. Some disasters actually transfer resources from low-income taxpayers to high-income taxpayers. Postdisaster federal and state relief to high- and middle-income victims suffering loss of their coastal homes and properties, or loss of their properties in other high-hazard zones (floodplains, mountainsides, wildland areas vulnerable to fire, and the like), often eclipses relief payouts to low-income disaster victims. Wealthy people obviously stand to lose more because they have more to lose. But also, wealthy people often freely choose to take greater risks in where they buy property and build, and they often purchase insurance to share any losses they may sustain from anticipated disaster forces. Certain losses sustained by the wealthy that were not covered by their insurance policies may be eligible for federal postdisaster relief if their property is located in a county included in a presidential declaration of major disaster.

Does government bailout businesses after disasters? The answer is a qualified "yes." Congress passed and President George W. Bush signed into law the Terrorism Risk Insurance Act (TRIA) in November 2002 to stimulate business investment that had slowed to a trickle after the events of September 11, 2001. The initial law created a three-year federal program, which in 2005 was extended by law to December 31, 2007. The Terrorism Risk Insurance Program Reauthorization Act of 2007, signed by the president on December 26, 2007, extends TRIA through December 31, 2014. TRIA backs up insurance companies and guarantees that certain terrorism-related claims will be paid. Under the terms of the act, the federal government has agreed to backstop private insurers who fear they will be swamped and bankrupted by claims filed by those who suffer the consequences of a future large-scale terror attack in the United States.

TRIA asks the secretary of the treasury, in concurrence with the secretary of state and the attorney general of the United States, to determine whether an event should be certified as an act of terrorism. They are to use preestablished criteria in making this judgment. For example, "an individual or individuals acting on behalf of any foreign person or foreign interest" must commit the act. Under TRIA, insurers can now claim government reimbursement for losses in events so certified. The law provides for "a transparent system of shared public and private compensation for insured losses resulting from acts of terrorism." [19]

In the case of 9/11, the federal government through TRIA and other measures helped reinforce the insurance industry, and this bolstered confidence in capital markets, making possible bank loans for major new private construction projects that had been stymied by matters of terrorism risk. Even the 9/11 Victim's Compensation Fund was a partial effort to shield commercial airlines whose planes were lost on 9/11 from lawsuits expected to be filed by families of people killed as a result of the 9/11 attacks. The Gulf Coast Recovery Authority, established to help bring back the infrastructure and economies of Katrina-devastated areas of the south, represents another example of support to public and private endeavors.

However, the federal government is most likely to aid sectors of the national economy, or regional economies, hurt by a disaster rather than only a few specific corporations that sustain disaster loss. Also, federal and state government is sensitive to the needs of people who have lost their jobs owing to a disaster. Government efforts to promote business recovery are also efforts aimed at helping people regain employment.

As stated previously, for many disaster victims the federal government is a kind of insurer of last resort. The federal government often makes available to disaster victims low-interest loans of various types. In cases of presidentially declared major disasters, victims in the counties covered may receive various types of grants and in-kind assistance. Similarly, state and local governments, as well as private businesses and nonprofit organizations, may be eligible to receive various types of federal help.

THE BIG QUESTIONS

What role does private insurance play in disaster mitigation and disaster recovery? What is the relationship between private insurers and the government? Where does National Flood Insurance fit in the scheme of disaster management? Can the government force people to buy insurance against disaster? If not, should the government deny help, especially monetary help, to those who could have bought insurance before a disaster but chose not to?

Has U.S. disaster policy become a modern and growing public works subsidy program for state and local governments? How is infrastructure defined and who pays for its postdisaster repair? Are buyouts and relocations replacing engineered disaster mitigation (flood levies or flood control works)? Should the federal government pay for what is built on the site of ground zero? How much government responsibility attaches to the failure of levees in and around New Orleans during and after Hurricane Katrina?

Volunteers in Disasters

When do volunteers and volunteer organizations make important contributions to disaster relief and recovery and when do they complicate or impede emergency response and recovery? Did volunteers as individuals or groups help or hinder the response to 9/11 or to the Hurricane Katrina disaster? Again, these are questions likely to come up again in the near future. Volunteers, especially through nonprofit organizations active in disasters, are hugely important in disasters. They are often the first on the scene, they frequently aid responders, they are there in varying degrees to help victims during the response and recovery, and their accounts of events are often presented by news organizations. Volunteers, particularly through formal organizations, are a political force to be reckoned with in disaster policy and politics.

Gap Questions

Where are the gaps in American disaster policy? Can federal disaster mitigation succeed in the absence of "federal zoning?" If there are few major federal inducements to press states and localities to engage in land use planning and regulation sensitive to disaster vulnerability, how can national disaster mitigation progress? Is there proof that disaster mitigation consistently works and saves money? How will the structures built on New York's ground zero be less vulnerable to terrorism than the original World Trade Center complex? These are only a few of many "gap" questions in the field.

Answers to these questions will come through both scientific analysis and political interchange. If these "gaps" are to be filled in the future, the political system must do the job. As Peter May has maintained, policymakers, including the president, tend to do a much better job resolving these issues if they act between major disasters, not immediately after them.[20]

FEMA and DHS, In or Out?

A major open question that will likely be revisited in the future is whether or not FEMA should remain in the Department of Homeland Security or be returned to the independent agency status it enjoyed from 1979 to 2003. James Lee Witt is a key spokesperson for FEMA independent agency status. He observed, "During the 1990s, when FEMA was an independent agency I reported directly to the President. Its incorporation into DHS has had a dramatic and negative effect on FEMA's ability to maneuver effectively and agilely. The FEMA Director no longer had direct access to the President, but instead has to go through an extra layer of bureaucracy to get what is needed. Even one extra layer has proved one too many in the critical moments." [21] Under the Post-Hurricane Katrina Act of 2006, the FEMA administrator again has access to the president in times of disaster. However, the secretary of DHS also has direct access to the president when the secretary or the president declares an Incident of National Significance. One can only hope that future FEMA directors and DHS secretaries have better working relationships before disasters than did the DHS secretary Michael Chertoff and the FEMA director Michael Brown shortly before Hurricane Katrina struck in 2005.

Congress debated this issue after Hurricane Katrina and elected to keep FEMA inside DHS. Although FEMA has been part of DHS only since 2003, there are now considerable "sunk costs" that bind FEMA to DHS. Among them, the National Response Plan has interlaced homeland security with emergency management. Taking FEMA out of DHS might fracture administration of the plan. DHS houses a massive set of expensive homeland security grant programs, and FEMA manages in various ways parts of these programs. Most of this program funding is directed to terrorism, but dual-use components of these programs significantly benefit (as well as distort) state and local emergency management. What will happen to these programs if FEMA is moved out of DHS?

An even more speculative question might be what is the future of the Department of Homeland Security? After January 2009, will Congress and the president pull DHS apart? Will DHS shrink? How will a FEMA within DHS be affected by the downsizing of the department? Only time will tell.

It is no surprise that many scholars conclude that the definition of disaster is socially constructed. [22] It is also fair to say that the definition of disaster is "politically constructed" in regard to how the media portrays an event, how the president chooses to define and comprehend the event, and how people in the general public perceive and judge the event. In another sense, the political definition of disaster flows from law, judgments of previous presidents, a sitting president's previous actions modulated by the political circumstances of the time that affect his or her judgments, the strategic behavior of governors seeking federal assistance, and the pressure imposed by elected representatives at the federal, state, and local level. Understanding disaster policy and politics is worthwhile, although it demands work and objectivity. Disaster has become a legitimate domain of policy research, just as health, defense, social welfare, labor, and environmental policies have previously. On this you can bet your life.

KEY TERMS AND CONCEPTS

antipoverty social policy   227
entitlement program   226
event driven   217
new normal   217

"Plum Book" spoils system   219
political pressure groups   220
terrorism consequence management   224
War on Terrorism   216

CHAPTER 1 DISASTER MANAGEMENT IN THE UNITED STATES

1. Ted Steinberg, *Acts of God: The Unnatural History of Natural Disaster* (New York: Oxford University Press, 2000).
2. This book will use the terms "disaster management" and "emergency management" interchangeably. Some scholars of the field may object to this interchangeable use, because "emergency managers" are usually defined as those "who possess the knowledge, skills, and abilities to effectively manage a comprehensive [emergency] management program." Michael K. Lindell, Carla Prater, and Ronald W. Perry, *Introduction to Emergency Management* (Hoboken, N.J.: Wiley, 2007), 445. Canton calls disaster management "the tactical and operational implementation of that [planning] strategy at the time of the crisis." Lucien G. Canton, *Emergency Management: Concepts and Strategies for Effective Programs* (Hoboken, N.J.: Wiley, 2007), 60. Much of this book addresses president-declared emergencies and disasters. It is fair to say that emergency managers in those circumstances are also disaster managers both in strategic and tactical terms. Also, within emergency management are "emergency responders," who respond directly to disaster. Emergency responder occupational specialties include firefighters, police officers, and emergency medical technicians (Lindell, Prater, and Perry, *Introduction to Emergency Management,* 445). Much of this study does not draw distinctions between emergency managers and emergency responders. However, it is important to recognize that emergency managers, broadly construed, and emergency responders, many qualified as emergency managers in accord with the definition above, are in the field of disaster management. Disaster management, as used in this book, includes emergency management and those organizations and individuals outside government—nonprofit organizations active in disasters, disaster insurers, corporate emergency managers, and business continuity managers.
3. James F. Miskel, *Disaster Response and Homeland Security: What Works, What Doesn't* (Westport, Conn.: Praeger Security International, 2006), and Steinberg, *Acts of God.*
4. William L. Waugh Jr., *Living with Disasters: Dealing with Hazards* (Armonk, N.Y.: M. E. Sharpe, 2000).
5. Ibid.
6. Ibid., 4.
7. Ibid., 15.
8. Emergency Management Accreditation Program (EMAP) Web site, http://www.emaponline.org/?105 (accessed April 22, 2007; hereafter cited as EMAP Web site).
9. CNN launched its twenty-four-hour television news organization in 1982 in Atlanta, Georgia.
10. See Louise K. Comfort, ed., *Managing Disaster: Strategies and Policy Perspectives* (Durham, N.C.: Duke University Press, 1988).
11. Richard T. Sylves, "The Politics and Budgeting of Federal Emergency Management" in *Disaster Management in the U.S. and Canada,* ed. Richard T. Sylves and William L. Waugh Jr. (Springfield, Ill.: Charles C. Thomas, 1996).
12. See Rutherford H. Platt, "Shouldering the Burden: Federal Assumption of Disaster Costs," in *Disasters and Democracy: The Politics of Extreme Natural Events,* ed. Rutherford H. Platt, 11–46 (Washington, D.C.: Island Press, 1999). See also Miskel, *Disaster Response and Homeland Security.*
13. Charles R. Wise, "Organizing for Homeland Security," *Public Administration Review* 62 (September 2002): 131–144. William L. Waugh Jr. and Richard T. Sylves, "Organizing the War on Terrorism," special issue, *Public Administration Review* 62 (September 2002): 145–153.
14. The author would like to acknowledge the contributions of William L. Waugh Jr. on these points. See William L. Waugh Jr., "Emergency Management and State and Local Government Capacity," in *Cities and Disaster: North American Studies in Emergency Management,* ed. Richard T. Sylves and William L. Waugh Jr. (Springfield, Ill.: Charles C. Thomas, 1990), 229–233.
15. "policy window": John Kingdon, *Agendas, Alternatives, and Public Policies,* 2nd ed. (New York: Longman, 1995), 166; "blew down a wall . . .": Donald F. Kettl, *System under Stress,* 2nd ed. (Washington, D.C.: CQ Press, 2007), 126.

16. See John W. Kingdon, "Agendas, Alternatives, and Public Policies (1995)," in *Classics of Public Policy,* ed. Jay M. Shafritz, Karen S. Layne, and Christopher P. Borick, 148–159 (New York: Pearson Longman, 2005).

17. Anthony Downs, "Up and Down with Ecology: The 'Issue-Attention Cycle,' " *Public Interest* 28 (Summer 1972): 38–50.

18. Ibid.

19. Although Downs, in "Up and Down with Ecology," is not discussing disaster specifically, his arguments are quite appropriate within the realm of disaster policy and politics.

20. Ibid.

21. Douglas Brinkley, *The Great Deluge* (New York: Morrow, 2006).

22. Downs, "Up and Down with Ecology."

23. Ibid.

24. Ibid.

25. Miskel, *Disaster Response and Homeland Security,* 76.

26. Canton, *Emergency Management,* 28.

27. Charles Perrow, *Normal Accidents* (New York: Basic Books, 1984).

28. See Richard T. Sylves and Thomas J. Pavlak, "The Big Apple and Disaster Planning: How New York City Manages Major Emergencies," in Sylves and Waugh, *Cities and Disaster,* 185–219.

29. Thomas Birkland, *After Disaster: Agenda Setting, Public Policy, and Focusing Events* (Washington, D.C.: Georgetown University Press, 1997), 128.

30. See Peter J. May, *Recovering from Catastrophes: Federal Disaster Relief Policy and Politics* (Westport, Conn.: Greenwood Press, 1985), and Peter J. May and Walter W. Williams, *Disaster Policy Implementation: Managing Programs under Shared Governance* (New York: Plenum Press, 1986).

31. Ibid.

32. Richard T. Sylves, "President Bush and Hurricane Katrina: A Presidential Leadership Study," in *Annals of the American Academy of Political and Social Science* 604 (March 2006): 26–56.

33. Steinberg, *Acts of God,* 103.

34. Gilbert F. White, with others, "Changes in Urban Occupance of Flood Plains in the United States" (Research Paper 57, Dept. of Geography, University of Chicago, 1958).

35. Howard Kunreuther, "Insurability Conditions and the Supply of Coverage," in *Paying the Price: The Status and Role of Insurance against Natural Disasters in the United States,* ed. Howard Kunreuther and Richard J. Roth Sr. (Washington, D.C.: Joseph Henry Press, 1998), 36.

36. Howard Kunreuther, "Has the Time Come for Comprehensive National Disaster Insurance?" in *On Risk and Disaster,* ed. Ronald J. Daniels, Donald E. Kettl, and Howard Kunreuther (Philadelphia: University of Pennsylvania Press, 2006), 188.

37. Howard Kunreuther, "Disaster Mitigation: Lessons from Katrina," *Annals of the American Academy of Political and Social Science* 604 (March 2006): 216.

38. See U.S. Department of Homeland Security, Federal Emergency Management Agency Web site, http://training.fema.gov/emiweb/edu/ for an excellent compendium of information about FEMA's higher education and training programs. Dr. B. Wayne Blanchard of FEMA deserves credit for his years in building and cultivating FEMA's higher education program.

39. EMAP Web site.

40. George D. Haddow and Jane A. Bullock, *Introduction to Emergency Management,* 2nd ed. (Boston: Elsevier, Butterworth-Heinemann, 2006), 58–59.

41. Miskel, *Disaster Response and Homeland Security,* 12.

42. Senate Bipartisan Task Force on Funding Disaster Relief, *Federal Disaster Assistance,* 104th Cong., 1st sess., 1995, S. Doc. 104-4, 4–5.

43. Ibid.

44. Haddow and Bullock, *Introduction to Emergency Management,* 58–63.

45. Ibid.

46. EMAP Web site.

47. Canton, *Emergency Management,* 66.

48. David A. McEntire, *Disaster Response and Recovery* (Hoboken, N.J.: Wiley, 2007), 24.

49. William J. Petak, "Emergency Management: A Challenge to Public Administration," special issue, *Public Administration Review* 45 (January 1985): 3.

50. Haddow and Bullock, *Introduction to Emergency Management,* 131–132.

CHAPTER 2 DISASTER MANAGEMENT AND THEORIES OF PUBLIC MANAGEMENT

This chapter has been adapted from a paper presented by the author at the FEMA Emergency Management Higher Education Conference on June 8, 2004, in Emmitsburg, Maryland. Many of the core ideas and perspectives developed in this chapter are an adaptation of ideas presented in Laurence E. Lynn Jr., *Public Management as Art, Science, and Profession* (Chatham, N.J.: Chatham House, 1996).

1. Thomas A. Birkland, *After Disaster: Agenda Setting, Public Policy, and Focusing Events* (Washington, D.C.: Georgetown University Press, 1997). See also Peter J. May, *Recovering from Catastrophes: Federal Disaster Relief Policy and Politics* (Westport, Conn.: Greenwood Press, 1985), and Peter J. May and Walter W. Williams, *Disaster Policy Implementation: Managing Programs under Shared Governance* (New York: Plenum Press, 1986).
2. The Jeffersonian and Hamiltonian models discussed here stem from work on public management by Lynn, *Public Management as Art, Science and Profession.* See also Richard T. Sylves, "A Precis on Political Theory and Emergency Management," *Journal of Emergency Management* 2 (Summer 2004).
3. David A. McEntire, *Disaster Response and Recovery* (Hoboken, N.J.: Wiley, 2007), 35.
4. Ibid.
5. Ibid.
6. Ibid., 49.
7. Ibid., 55.
8. Ibid., 66.
9. Edwin Jewett, "Coalescing Effective Community Disaster Response: Simulation and Virtual Communities of Practice, December 2005," paper e-mailed to the author, February 23, 2006. Gaming applications are emerging from cross-collaboration between government, industry and academia, or "multiple constituencies coming together to solve problems." See James Paul Gee, Kurt Squire, and Constance Steinkuehler, "How Games Are Re-Shaping Business and Learning," available at http://www.academiccolab.org/initiatives/accelerate.html; this Web site hosts online workshops, advertises grants, and serves as a platform to present papers and ideas about academic distributed learning activities. Gaming technology has been universally adopted by a huge and powerful "gamer generation" of 90 million people in the United States alone, ages fifteen to thirty-five (approximate). We are in an age of media convergence where peoples' fundamental relationships with media are changing. The book *Got Game: How the Gamer Generation Is Reshaping Business Forever* (Boston: Harvard Business School Press, 2004) suggests that "gamers" are leaders in the workplace with a sophisticated set of abilities, and they play to win.
10. Dennis S. Mileti, *Disasters by Design: A Reassessment of Natural Hazards in the United States* (Washington, D.C.: Joseph Henry Press, 1999); Susan L. Cutter, ed., *American Hazardscapes: The Regionalization of Hazards and Disasters* (Washington, D.C.: Joseph Henry Press, 2001).
11. John C. Pine, *Technology in Emergency Management* (Hoboken, N.J.: Wiley, 2007).
12. *Facing Hazards and Disasters: Understanding Human Dimensions* by the National Research Council's Committee on Disaster Research in the Social Sciences (Washington, D.C.: National Academies Press, 2006) is an excellent edited compilation of disaster-related social scientific research.
13. "HAZUS," available at http://www.fema.gov/plan/prevent/hazus/ (accessed November 30, 2007). HAZUS-MH is a powerful risk assessment software program for analyzing potential losses from floods, hurricane winds, and earthquakes. HAZUS-MH (MH refers to Multi-Hazard), current scientific and engineering knowledge, is coupled with the latest GIS technology to produce estimates of hazard-related damage before, or after, a disaster occurs. Potential loss estimates analyzed in HAZUS-MH include:
    * physical damage to residential and commercial buildings, schools, critical facilities, and infrastructure;
    * economic loss, including lost jobs, business interruptions, repair and reconstruction costs; and
    * social impacts, including estimates of shelter requirements, displaced households, and population exposed to scenario floods, earthquakes and hurricanes.

    Federal, state, and local government agencies and the private sector can order HAZUS-MH free of charge from the FEMA Publication Warehouse.
14. Dwight Waldo, *The Administrative State* (New York: Ronald Press, 1948).

15. See also H. George Frederickson and Kevin B. Smith, *The Public Administration Theory Primer* (Boulder, Colo.: Westview Press, 2003), 43.
16. Lynn, *Public Management as Art, Science, and Profession.*
17. Kathleen J. Tierney, Michael K. Lindell, and Ronald W. Perry, *Facing the Unexpected: Disaster Preparedness and Response in the United States* (Washington, D.C.: Joseph Henry Press, 2001), 233–240.
18. Richard T. Sylves, "Political Theory and Emergency Management" (paper presented at the FEMA Emergency Management Higher Education Conference, FEMA Emergency Management Institute, Emmitsburg, Maryland, June 8, 2004), 7.
19. Something addressed in Gary L. Wamsley, "Escalating in a Quagmire: The Changing Dynamics of the Emergency Management Policy Subsystem," *Public Administration Review* 56 (May–June 1996): 235–244, and in Richard T. Sylves, "Ferment at FEMA: Reforming Emergency Management," *Public Administration Review* 54 (May–June 1994): 303–307.
20. Rohit Jigyasu, "Disaster: A Reality or Construct? Perspective from the East," in *What Is Disaster? New Answers to Old Questions,* ed. Ronald W. Perry and E. L. Quarantelli (Philadelphia: Xlibris, 2005), 49, 59.
21. Lynn, *Public Management as Art, Science, and Profession,* 91.
22. Ibid., 91.
23. Laurence E. Lynn Jr. *Public Management as Art, Science, and Profession* (Chatham, N.J.: Chatham House, 1996), 91.
24. Graham T. Allison, *Essence of Decision: Explaining the Cuban Missile Crisis* (Boston: Little, Brown, 1971).
25. Lynn, *Public Management as Art, Science and Profession,* 97, quotes Chester I. Barnard, *Functions of the Executive,* 30th anniversary ed. (Cambridge, Mass.: Harvard University Press, 1968).
26. James L. Witt and J. Morgan, *Stronger in the Broken Places: Ten Lessons for Turning Crisis into Triumph* (New York: Times Books, 2002).
27. Donald F. Kettl, "The Worst Is Yet to Come: Lessons from September 11 and Hurricane Katrina," *Fels Government Research Service,* Report 05-01 (Philadelphia: Fels Institute of Government, University of Pennsylvania, 2005), 7.
28. Naim Kapucu, "Making Matters Worse: Anatomy of Leadership Failures in Catastrophic Events" (paper presented at the annual national conference of the American Society for Public Administration (ASPA), Washington, D.C., March 23–27, 2007).
29. Kettl, "The Worst Is Yet to Come," 14.
30. See Lynn, *Public Management as Art, Science, and Profession.*
31. See Richard T. Sylves and William L. Waugh Jr., *Disaster Management in the U.S. and Canada,* (Springfield, Ill.: Charles C. Thomas, 1996), and William L. Waugh Jr., *Living with Disasters: Dealing with Hazards,* (Armonk, N.Y.: M. E. Sharpe, 2000).
32. Sylves, "Political Theory and Emergency Management," 10.
33. Tierney, Lindell, and Perry, *Facing the Unexpected,* 17.
34. See Robert A. Stallings, *Promoting Risk: Constructing the Earthquake Threat* (New York: Aldine de Gruyter, 1995). See also T. J. Blocker, E. B. Rochford Jr., and D. E. Sherkat, "Political Responses to Natural Hazards: Social Movement Participation Following a Flood," *International Journal of Mass Emergencies and Disasters* 9 (1991): 367–382.
35. Stallings, *Promoting Risk: Constructing the Earthquake Threat,* 13–14.
36. See Tierney, Lindell, and Perry, *Facing the Unexpected,* 194–195.
37. Lynn, *Public Management as Art, Science, and Profession,* 116.
38. For more about principal-agent theory see Kenneth J. Arrow, "The Economics of Agency," in *Principals and Agents: The Structure of Business,* ed. J. W. Pratt and R. J. Zeckhauser (Boston: Harvard Business School, 1988), 37–51.
39. Richard F. Elmore, "Backward Mapping: Implementation Research and Policy Decisions," *Political Science Quarterly* 94, no. 4 (1979–1980): 69–83.
40. See Graham T. Allison, *Essence of Decision: Explaining the Cuban Missile Crisis* (Boston: Little, Brown, 1971).
41. Charles E. Lindblom, *The Intelligence of Democracy: Decision Making through Mutual Adjustment* (New York: Free Press, 1965).
42. Hugh Heclo, *A Government of Strangers: Executive Politics in Washington* (Washington, D.C.: Brookings Institution, 1977).

43. Deil S. Wright, "Models of National/State/Local Relations," *American Intergovernmental Relations*, ed. Laurence J. O'Toole Jr. (Washington, D.C.: Congressional Quarterly, 1985), 59. Many scholars other than Wright have developed theories of federalism, among them Martha Derthick, Daniel Elazar, Richard H. Leach, Vincent Ostrom, and David B. Walker. Wright's IGR theory was used here because it provides a good fit of theory to the reality of U.S. disaster policy.

44. Deil Wright, *Understanding Intergovernmental Relations*, 3rd ed. (Pacific Grove, Calif.: Brooks/Cole, 1988), 58.

45. *Stanford Encyclopedia of Philosophy*, available at http://plato.stanford.edu/entries/federalism/ (accessed November 30, 2007).

46. Eugene Boyd, "Summary" and "Dual Federalism: Part II 1865 to 1901," *American Federalism, 1776 to 1997: Significant Events*, updated January 6, 1997, available at http://usinfo.state.gov/usa/infousa/politics/states/federal.htm (accessed November 30, 2007).

47. Frances Winslow-Edwards, "Federal Intervention in Local Emergency Planning: Nightmare on Main Street," (paper sent to the author, November 9, 2006).

48. Wright, *Understanding Intergovernmental Relations*, 64.

49. Wright, "Models of National/State/Local Relations," 60.

50. See David B. Walker, *The Rebirth of Federalism*, 2nd ed. (New York: Chatham House, 2000), 314.

51. Winslow-Edwards, "Federal Intervention in Local Emergency Planning."

52. Michael Barzelay, *Breaking through Bureaucracy: A New Vision for Management in Government* (Berkeley: University of California Press, 1992).

53. James Lee Witt, "Military Role in Natural Disaster Response," *Disaster Preparedness* 1, no. 1 (Summer 2006), issued by the Center for Defense and Security, Wilburforce University, available at http://www.wilberforce.edu/cdsp/cdsp_art2_01.html.

54. Lynn, *Public Management as Art, Science, and Profession*, 145.

55. See *U. S. Code of Federal Regulations*, Title 44 and Title 6.

56. William R. Cumming, FEMA Office of General Counsel, retired, e-mail exchange with the author, March 15, 2003.

57. Or through transnational organizations such as the United Nations and the World Bank.

CHAPTER 3 HISTORICAL TRENDS IN DISASTER MANAGEMENT

1. James E. Anderson, "Policy Implementation," in *Public Policymaking: An Introduction*, 3rd ed. (Boston: Houghton-Mifflin, 1997).

2. Homeland Security National Preparedness Task Force, *Civil Defense and Homeland Security: A Short History of National Preparedness Efforts* (Washington, D.C.: Department of Homeland Security, 2006), 7.

3. Standard presidential administrations usually begin and end on or about January 21. Republican Dwight David Eisenhower was inaugurated in January 1953 and left office at the end of his second term in January 1961.

4. President Kennedy, a Democrat, was inaugurated in January 1961 and was assassinated in November 1963. His vice president, Lyndon Johnson (LBJ), was then sworn in as president.

5. President Johnson, as mentioned in note 4, was sworn in as president in November 1963 soon after President Kennedy was assassinated. LBJ won the 1964 presidential election and served until January 1969. He opted not to run for reelection in 1968.

6. Homeland Security National Preparedness Task Force, *Civil Defense and Homeland Security*, 13.

7. President Richard M. Nixon, a Republican, was elected in November 1968 and inaugurated in January 1969. He was reelected to office in the presidential election of 1972 but resigned from office owing to the Watergate scandal in August 1974.

8. Keith Bea, "The Formative Years: 1950–1978," 81–109, in *Emergency Management: The American Experience, 1900–2005*, ed. Claire B. Rubin (Fairfax, Va.: Public Entity Risk Institute, 2007), 92.

9. Ibid., 101.

10. Speaker of the House Gerald R. Ford, a Republican, took the presidential oath of office in August 1974, following President Nixon's resignation. Ford ran unsuccessfully for reelection in 1976 and left office in January 1977, with President Carter's inauguration.

11. Homeland Security National Preparedness Task Force, *Civil Defense and Homeland Security*, 16.

12. Ibid.

13. Bea, "The Formative Years: 1950–1978," 106.
14. Homeland Security National Preparedness Task Force, *Civil Defense and Homeland Security*, 14.
15. Ibid.
16. Thomas E. Baldwin, *Revised Historical Chronology of FEMA's Terrorism Consequences Management Role as Assigned by Section 2-103 of E.O. 12148* (Argonne, Ill.: Argonne National Laboratory, 2006), 1. Supplied as e-file to the author March 18, 2007, by William R. Cumming, FEMA General Counsel's Office, retired.
17. Ibid., 14.
18. Homeland Security National Preparedness Task Force, *Civil Defense and Homeland Security*, 16.
19. The American Institutes for Research, The Pacific Institute for Research and Evaluation, and Deloitte & Touche LLP, *A Chronology of Major Events Affecting the National Flood Insurance Program*, prepared for the Federal Emergency Management Agency under contract no. 282-98-0029, October 2005, available at http://www.dhs.gov/xlibrary/assets/privacy/privacy_pia_mip_apnd_h.pdf (accessed December 3, 2007).
20. Ibid.
21. Claire B. Rubin and Irmak R.Tanali, *Disaster Time Line: Selected Milestone Events and U.S. Outcomes, 1965–2001* (Arlington, Va.: Claire B. Rubin and Associates, 2001). Tropical storm Agnes produced widespread damage. Seven states won presidential declarations of major disaster: Florida, Maryland, New York, Ohio, Pennsylvania, Virginia, and West Virginia. New York and Pennsylvania sustained damage.
22. Democrat Jimmy Carter beat the incumbent, though unelected, Republican president Gerald R. Ford in the 1976 general election. Carter was defeated in the 1980 general election and left office in January 1981.
23. Henry B. Hogue and Keith Bea, *Federal Emergency Management and Homeland Security Organization: Historical Developments and Legislative Options*, CRS Report RL33369 (Washington, D.C.: Congressional Research Service, 2006).
24. William C. Nicholson, *Emergency Response and Emergency Management Law: Cases and Materials* (Springfield, Ill.: Charles C. Thomas, 2003), 236.
25. William L. Waugh Jr., *Living with Hazards, Dealing with Disasters* (Armonk, N.Y.: M. E. Sharpe, 2000), 28–29.
26. Baldwin, *Revised Historical Chronology*, 2.
27. Ibid.
28. Ibid.
29. Rutherford H. Platt, "Shouldering the Burden: Federal Assumption of Disaster Costs," in *Disasters and Democracy: The Politics of Extreme Natural Events,* ed. Rutherford H. Platt, (Washington, D.C.: Island Press, 1999), 23–26.
30. Allen K. Settle, "Disaster Assistance: Securing Presidential Declarations," in *Cities and Disaster: North American Studies in Emergency Management,* ed. Richard T. Sylves and William L. Waugh Jr. (Springfield, Ill.: Charles C. Thomas, 1990).
31. Ibid., 51–52.
32. Homeland Security National Preparedness Task Force, *Civil Defense and Homeland Security*, 18.
33. Ibid., 19.
34. Ibid., 6–14.
35. President Ronald Reagan, a Republican, beat incumbent President Jimmy Carter in the 1980 presidential election. Reagan won a second term in 1984 and ultimately left office in January 1989, turning that post over to his former vice president, George Herbert Walker Bush.
36. Keith Bea, *Federal Stafford Act Disaster Assistance: Presidential Declarations, Eligible Activities, and Funding*, CRS Report RL33053 (Washington, D.C.: Congressional Research Service, 2006), 3.
37. President George H. W. Bush, a Republican, was elected in 1988 and inaugurated in January 1989. He served only one term, being defeated in the 1992 presidential election by the Democrat William J. Clinton.
38. *New Georgia Encyclopedia*, CNN, http://www.georgiaencyclopedia.org/nge/Article.jsp?id=h-2643 (accessed December 2, 2007).
39. Bea, *Federal Stafford Act Disaster Assistance*.
40. Mission assignment works in the following way. When other federal agencies besides FEMA are doing emergency management work under a presidential declaration of major disaster or emergency, and the spending authority of those agencies is insufficient for them to carry out their

disaster-related work, officials of those agencies may ask FEMA permission to draw funding from the president's Disaster Relief Fund under a category called mission assignment. A sizable share of spending in many presidentially declared major disasters stems from mission assignment.

41. Hogue and Bea, "Federal Stafford Act Disaster Assistance."

42. It should be noted that when FEMA was reinvigorated by post-Katrina legislation in 2006, it was granted permission to hire additional staff. This has allowed it to exceed its previous usual upper limit of 3,000 full-time federal workers.

43. Aaron Schroeder and Gary Wamsley, "The Evolution of Emergency Management in America: From a Painful Past to a Promising but Uncertain Future," in *Handbook of Crisis and Emergency Management,* ed. Ali Farazmand (New York: Marcel Dekker, 2002).

44. Dianne Rahm, *United States Public Policy: A Budgetary Approach* (Belmont, Calif.: Wadsworth, 2004), 97–113.

45. Kevin Arceneaux and Robert M. Stein, "Who Is Held Responsible When Disaster Strikes? The Attribution of Responsibility for a Natural Disaster in an Urban Election," *Journal of Urban Affairs* 28 (January 2006): 43.

46. Ibid.

47. Homeland Security National Preparedness Task Force, *Civil Defense and Homeland Security.*

48. President William J. Clinton, a Democrat, was elected in 1992, inaugurated in January 1993, reelected in 1996, and left office in January 2001.

49. James F. Miskel, *Disaster Response and Homeland Security* (Westport, Conn.: Praeger Security International, 2006), 89.

50. Homeland Security National Preparedness Task Force, *Civil Defense and Homeland Security,* 23.

51. Ibid.

52. Ibid.

53. Patrick S. Roberts, "FEMA and the Prospects for Reputational Authority," *Studies in American Political Development* 20 (Spring 2006): 16.

54. William R. Cumming and Richard T. Sylves, "FEMA's Place in Policy, Law, and Management: A Hazardous Materials Perspective 1979–2003," in *Homeland Security Law and Policy,* ed. William C. Nicholson (Springfield, Ill.: Charles C. Thomas, 2004), 23–55.

55. Homeland Security National Preparedness Task Force, *Civil Defense and Homeland Security.*

56. Frances L. Edwards, "Homeland Security from the Local Perspective," in *Homeland Security Law and Policy,* ed. William C. Nicholson, (Springfield, Ill.: Charles C. Thomas, 2005), 114.

57. The National Defense Authorization Act of 1995 amended the Robert T. Stafford Disaster Relief and Emergency Assistance Act (Public Law 93-288).

58. Ibid.

59. House Committee on Public Works and Transportation, Subcommittee on Water Resources and the Environment, *Midwest Floods of 1993: Flood Control and Floodplain Policy and Proposals,* hearing, statement of Harold L. Volkmer, 103rd Cong., 1st sess., 1993, serial number 103-57, 241.

60. George D. Haddow and Jane A. Bullock, *Introduction to Emergency Management,* 2nd ed. (Boston: Elsevier, Butterworth-Heinemann, 2006), 12.

61. Ibid., 63.

62. Ibid., 12.

63. Michael K. Lindell, Carla Prater, and Ronald W. Perry, *Introduction to Emergency Management* (Hoboken, N.J.: Wiley, 2007), 361–362.

64. Ibid., 66.

65. Edwards, "Homeland Security from the Local Perspective," 120.

66. President George W. Bush was inaugurated in January 2001, was reelected to a second term in 2004, and will leave office with the inauguration of the next president in January 2009.

67. Kathleen J. Tierney, *Recent Developments in U.S. Homeland Security Policies and Their Implications for the Management of Extreme Events* (Boulder: Natural Hazards Research and Applications Center, Institute of Behavioral Science, University of Colorado, 2005).

68. Ibid.

69. David B. Truman, *The Governmental Process* (New York: Knopf, 1951).

70. Haddow and Bullock, *Introduction to Emergency Management,* 2nd ed., 299.

71. For the full text of Homeland Security Presidential Directive-5 (HSPD-5), see http://www.whitehouse.gov/news/releases/2003/02/20030228-9.html.

72. Tierney, *Recent Developments in U.S. Homeland Security Policies*. See also William C. Nicholson, "The Shape of Emergency Response and Emergency Management in the Aftermath of the Homeland Security Act of 2002: Adopting the National Response Plan (NRP) and the National Incident Management System," in *Homeland Security Law and Policy*, ed. William C. Nicholson, 68–106 (Springfield, Ill.: Charles C. Thomas, 2005).

73. Tierney, *Recent Developments in U.S. Homeland Security Policies*.

74. National Response Plan, FEMA Emergency Management Institute, 7, http://training.fema.gov/EMIWeb/IS/ICSResource/assets/NRPallpages.pdf (accessed December 3, 2007). The National Response Framework eliminated the Incident of National Significance instrument in March 2008.

75. Haddow and Bullock, *Introduction to Emergency Management*, 2nd ed., 98–99.

76. For the full text of Homeland Security Presidential Directive-8 (HSPD-8), see http://www.whitehouse.gov/news/releases/2003/12/20031217-6.html.

77. Tierney, *Recent Developments in U.S. Homeland Security Policies*.

78. Ibid.

79. House Subcommittee on National Security, Emerging Threats, and International Relations and the Subcommittee on Energy Policy, Natural Resources and Regulatory Affairs, statement of James L. Witt, 108th Cong., 2nd sess., March 24, 2004.

CHAPTER 4 UNDERSTANDING DISASTER POLICY THROUGH PRESIDENTIAL DISASTER DECLARATIONS

1. Jack C. Plano and Milton Greenberg, *The American Political Dictionary*, 7th ed. (New York: Holt, Rinehart and Winston, 1985).

2. Thomas E. Cronin, "The Swelling of the Presidency," in *Classic Readings in American Politics*, ed. Pietro S. Nivola and David H. Rosenbloom (New York: St. Martin's, 1986), 413–426.

3. Centralized authority: Donald F. Kettl, *System under Stress: Homeland Security and American Politics* (Washington, D.C.: CQ Press, 2004), 46, 113. Range of authority: Jane A. Bullock, George D. Haddow, Damon Coppola, Erdem Ergin, Lissa Westerman, and Sarp Yeletaysi, *Introduction to Homeland Security* (Boston: Elsevier, Butterworth-Heinemann, 2005).

4. *9/11 Commission Report: Final Report of the National Commission on Terrorist Attacks upon the United States* (New York: Norton, 2004).

5. *Robert T. Stafford Disaster Relief and Emergency Assistance Act, as amended, and Related Authorities*, "Title I—Findings, Declarations and Definitions," sec. 101 (2007), 1, available at http://www.fema.gov/pdf/about/stafford_act.pdf (accessed December 3, 2007).

6. Keith Bea, *Federal Stafford Act Disaster Assistance: Presidential Declarations, Eligible Activities, and Funding*, CRS Report RL33053 (Washington, D.C.: Congressional Research Service, 2006), 10–11.

7. Ibid., 7–10.

8. *9/11 Commission Report: Final Report of the National Commission on Terrorist Attacks upon the United States* (New York: Norton, 2004).

9. Department of Homeland Security, "Final Draft: National Response Plan," 2004, available at http://www.dhs.gov/interweb/assetlibrary/NIMS-90-web.pdf, 8–9, quotation, 9. Under the National Response Framework, which replaced the NRP and went into effect in early 2008, the Incident of National Significance designation and process is discontinued.

10. Ibid., x.

11. Before 2003, presidents had authority to declare NSSEs through mobilizing the U.S. Secret Service. Since 2003, the Secret Service has been part of the Department of Homeland Security. Now NSSEs are interlaced with presidential authority to issue disaster declarations and to declare incidents of national significance. The quotation is from Department of Homeland Security, *Final Draft: National Response Plan*, 4.

12. Department of Homeland Security, *Final Draft: National Response Plan*, 8.

13. See William C. Nicholson, ed., *Homeland Security Law and Policy* (Springfield, Ill.: Charles C. Thomas, 2005), and Bullock et al., *Introduction to Homeland Security*.

14. See William L. Waugh Jr. and Richard T. Sylves, "Organizing the War on Terrorism," *Public Administration Review* 62 (September 2002): 145–153. See also William L. Waugh Jr., "Terrorism, Homeland Security, and the National Emergency Management Network," *Public Organization Review* 3 (December 2003): 373–385.

15. House Select Bipartisan Committee to Investigate Preparation for and Response to Hurricane Katrina, *A Failure of Initiative,* 109th Cong., 2nd sess, February 16, 2006.

16. Waugh and Sylves, "Organizing the War on Terrorism."

17. Senate Committee on Governmental Affairs, *Hearing on Rebuilding FEMA: Preparing for the Next Disaster,* 103rd Cong., 1st sess., May 18, 1993, 151.

18. Rutherford H. Platt, "Shouldering the Burden: Federal Assumption of Disaster Costs," in *Disasters and Democracy: The Politics of Extreme Natural Events,* ed. Rutherford H. Platt, 11–46 (Washington, D.C.: Island Press, 1999).

19. See Peter J. May, (Westport, Conn.: Greenwood Press, 1985). See also Platt, "Shouldering the Burden." *Recovering from Catastrophes: Federal Disaster Relief Policy and Politics* 20. Richard T. Sylves and William L. Waugh Jr., eds., *Disaster Management in the U.S. and Canada* (Springfield, Ill.: Charles C. Thomas, 1996).

21. Saundra K. Schneider, *Flirting with Disaster: Public Management in Crisis Situations* (Armonk, N.Y.: M. E. Sharpe, 1995).

22. James E. Anderson, "Policy Implementation," in *Public Policymaking: An Introduction,* 3rd ed. (Boston: Houghton-Mifflin, 1997): 213–270.

23. Peter J. May and Walter Williams, *Disaster Policy Implementation: Managing Programs under Shared Governance* (New York: Plenum Press, 1986). See also Richard T. Sylves, "President Bush and Hurricane Katrina: A Presidential Leadership Study," *Annals of the American Academy of Political and Social Science* 604 (March 2006): 26–56.

24. Federal Emergency Management Agency (FEMA), "2007 Federal Disaster Declarations," available at http://www.fema.gov/news/disasters.fema?year=2007.

25. Richard T. Sylves, "The Politics and Budgeting of Federal Emergency Management," in Sylves and Waugh, *Disaster Management in the U.S. and Canada.* See also James F. Miskel, *Disaster Response and Homeland Security: What Works, What Doesn't* (Westport, Conn.: Praeger Security International, 2006).

26. Ted Steinberg, *Acts of God: The Unnatural History of Natural Disaster in America* (New York: Oxford University Press, 2000), 181.

27. George D. Haddow and Jane A. Bullock, *Introduction to Emergency Management,* 2nd ed. (Boston: Elsevier, Butterworth-Heinemann, 2006).

28. Thomas A. Birkland, *Lessons of Disaster: Policy Change after Catastrophic Events* (Washington, D.C.: Georgetown University Press, 2007).

29. Donald F. Kettl, *System under Stress,* 2nd ed. (Washington, D.C.: CQ Press, 2007).

30. Miskel, *Disaster Response and Homeland Security.*

31. Ibid.

32. Joseph A. Pika and John Anthony Maltese, *The Politics of the Presidency,* 6th ed. (Washington, D.C.: CQ Press, 2004), 149–153.

33. Executive Office of the President (EOP), President George W. Bush, homepage of the EOP at the White House, available at http://www.whitehouse.gov/government/eop.html.

34. Ibid.

35. *Federal Register* 64, no. 169 (September 1, 1999): 47697–47699. See also Francis X. McCarthy, *FEMA's Disaster Declaration Process: A Primer,* CRS Report RL34146 (Washington, D.C.: Congressional Research Service, 2007).

36. Richard Buck (FEMA, retired), e-mail to author, February 8, 2007.

37. National Academy of Public Administration (NAPA), *Coping with Catastrophe: Building an Emergency Management System to Meet People's Needs in Natural and Manmade Disasters* (Washington, D.C.: NAPA, 1993).

38. Sylves, "President Bush and Hurricane Katrina."

39. Sylves and Waugh, *Disaster Management in the U.S. and Canada,* 27.

40. Kettl, *System under Stress,* 2nd ed., 15.

41. R. Steven Daniels and Carolyn L. Clark-Daniels, "Transforming Government: The Renewal and Revitalization of the Federal Emergency Management Agency," 2000, available at http://www.businessofgovernment.org/pdfs/DanielsReport.pdf.

42. Jason D. Mycoff, "Congress and Katrina: A Failure of Oversight," special issue, *State and Local Government Review* 39, no. 1 (2007): 16–30.

43. For a more thorough description and explanation of the fund, and for a table of Disaster Relief Fund spending from FY1974 to FY2006, see Bea, *Federal Stafford Act Disaster Assistance,* 28–33.

44. Thomas A. Garrett and Russell S. Sobel, "The Political Economy of FEMA Disaster Payments," *Economic Inquiry* 41, no. 3 (2003): 496–509.

45. Ibid., i.

46. Ibid., 2.

47. Ibid., 1.

48. Ibid., 4.

49. Ibid.

50. Sylves, "President Bush and Hurricane Katrina."

51. Government Accountability Office (GAO), *Disaster Assistance: Improvement Needed in Disaster Declaration Criteria and Eligibility Assurance Procedures,* GAO-01-837 (Washington, D.C.: GPO, 2001), 5.

52. Miskel, *Disaster Response and Homeland Security,* 114–115.

53. Ibid.

54. Bea, *Federal Stafford Act Disaster Assistance.*

55. In this book, the word "county" will be used to mean a county or a state's equivalent of a county.

56. Schneider, *Flirting with Disaster,* 32.

57. Allen K. Settle, "Disaster Assistance: Securing Presidential Declarations," in *Cities and Disaster: North American Studies in Emergency Management,* ed. Richard T. Sylves and William L. Waugh Jr. (Springfield, Ill.: Charles C. Thomas, 1990).

58. Ibid. See also Government Accountability Office, *Disaster Assistance.*

59. James L. Witt and J. Morgan, *Stronger in the Broken Places: Nine Lessons for Turning Crisis into Triumph* (New York: Times Books, 2002). See also, Platt, "Shouldering the Burden," and Daniels and Clark-Daniels, "Transforming Government."

60. Sylves, "The Politics and Budgeting of Federal Emergency Management."

61. Ibid. See also Thomas A. Birkland, *After Disaster: Agenda Setting, Public Policy, and Focusing Events* (Washington, D.C.: Georgetown University Press, 1997).

62. William L. Waugh Jr. and Ronald John Hy, *Handbook of Emergency Management* (Westport, Conn.: Greenwood Press, 1990). See also Gary L. Wamsley, Aaron D. Schroeder, and Larry M. Lane, "To Politicize is NOT to Control: The Pathologies of Control in Federal Emergency Management," *American Review of Public Administration* 26, no. 3 (1996): 263–285, and Platt, "Shouldering the Burden."

63. Brian Tarcey, "Flooding the Ballot Box: The Politics of Disaster," *Harvard Magazine,* March–April 2004.

64. Andrew Reeves, "Political Disaster? Presidential Disaster Declarations and Electoral Politics," September 12, 2007, available at http://www.people.fas.harvard.edu/~reeves/papers/fema.pdf (accessed December 5, 2007), 1.

65. Ibid.

66. Ibid.

67. Reeves, "Political Disaster?"

68. Tarcey, "Flooding the Ballot Box."

69. Reeves, "Political Disaster?" 3,

70. Ibid., 11.

71. Ude J. Dymon and Rutherford H. Platt, "U.S. Federal Disaster Declarations: A Geographical Analysis," in *Disasters and Democracy: The Politics of Extreme Natural Events,* ed. Rutherford H. Platt (Washington, D.C.: Island Press, 1999).

72. *American Heritage Dictionary,* 2nd coll. ed., s.v. "overwhelm."

73. Miskel, *Disaster Response and Homeland Security.*

74. Sylves, "The Politics and Budgeting of Federal Emergency Management," 32; Government Accountability Office, *Disaster Assistance,* 9–15.

75. Philip G. Joyce and Amy E. Kneedler, "Emergency Management Competencies and Incentives and Implications for Funding in the Intergovernmental Context" (paper presented at the Sixtieth National Conference of the American Society for Public Administration, 1999), 11.

76. Ibid.

77. Ibid.

78. Ibid., 13–14.

79. Ibid., 14.

80. Government Accountability Office, *Disaster Assistance.*

81. Waugh, *Living with Hazards, Dealing with Disasters.*
82. Platt, "Shouldering the Burden."
83. Wamsley, Schroeder, Lane, "To Politicize is NOT to Control."
84. Sylves, "The Politics and Budgeting of Federal Emergency Management."
85. James David Barber, "Presidential Character," in *American Government: Readings and Cases,* ed. Karen O'Connor (Boston: Allyn and Bacon, 1995), 204.
86. Thomas Anton, *American Federalism and Public Policy* (New York: Random House, 1989); Paul E. Peterson, *The Price of Federalism* (Washington, D.C.: Brookings Institution, 1995); David B. Walker, *The Rebirth of Federalism: Slouching toward Washington* (Chatham, N.J.: Chatham House, 1995); Joyce and Kneedler, "Emergency Management Competencies."

CHAPTER 5 THE ROLE OF SCIENTISTS AND ENGINEERS

1. See Roger A. Pielke Jr., *The Honest Broker: Making Sense of Science in Policy and Politics* (New York: Cambridge University Press, 2007). See also Sylvia Kraemer, *Science and Technology Policy* (Piscataway, N.J.: Rutgers University Press, 2006).
2. Richard T. Sylves, "Federal Emergency Management Comes of Age: 1979–2001," in *Emergency Management: The American Experience, 1900–2005* ed. Claire B. Rubin (Fairfax, Va: Public Entity Risk Institute, 2007), 129. See also John C. Pine, *Technology in Emergency Management* (Hoboken, N.J.: Wiley, 2007).
3. See Louise K. Comfort, ed., *Managing Disaster: Strategies and Policy Perspectives* (Durham, N.C.: Duke University Press, 1988). See also Susan L. Cutter, ed., *American Hazardscapes: The Regionalization of Hazards and Disasters* (Washington, D.C.: Joseph Henry Press, 2001). See David R. Godschalk, David J. Brower, and Timothy Beatley, *Catastrophic Coastal Storms: Hazard Mitigation and Development Management* (Durham, N.C.: Duke University Press, 1989).
4. "For more than thirty years, scholars of many stripes have discussed "big science." The terms of this discussion were framed by the popular writings of the physicist Alvin Weinberg and the physicist-historian Derek de Solla Price in the 1960s. Both authors focused on the rapidly increasing size and expense of scientific projects, both identified this increase in scale as a distinctive feature of science in the post–World War II era, and both worried about the consequences of the "disease" of "big science." Catherine Westfall, "Rethinking Big Science: Modest, Mezzo, Grand Science and the Development of the Bevalac, 1971–1993," *Isis* 94 (March 2003): 32.
5. See also Alexander J. Morin, *Science Policy and Politics* (Englewood Cliffs, N.J.: Prentice-Hall, 1993), 142.
6. National Research Council, *Making the Nation Safer: The Role of Science and Technology in Countering Terrorism* (Washington, D.C.: National Academies Press, 2002).
7. National Research Council, *Risk Analysis and Uncertainty: Flood Damage Reduction Studies* (Washington, D.C.: National Academies Press, 2000).
8. The National Laboratories system includes the Argonne, Brookhaven, Fermi, Idaho, Lawrence-Berkeley, Lawrence-Livermore, Los Alamos, Oak Ridge, Pacific Northwest, and Sandia National Laboratories, as well as the National Renewable Energy Laboratory.
9. National Research Council, *Facing Hazards and Disasters: Understanding Human Dimensions* (Washington, D.C.: National Academies Press, 2006).
10. William L. Waugh Jr., *Living with Hazards, Dealing with Disasters: An Introduction to Disaster Management* (Armonk, N.Y.: M. E. Sharpe, 2000).
11. E. L. Quarantelli, "Disaster Planning, Emergency Management, and Civil Protection: The Historical Development of Organized Efforts to Plan for and to Respond to Disasters" (Newark: University of Delaware, Disaster Research Center, 2000). Available as DRC Preliminary Paper no. 301, 2000, http://www.udel.edu/DRC.
12. See National Research Council, *Facing Hazards and Disasters.*
13. See Dennis S. Mileti, *Disasters by Design: A Reassessment of Natural Hazards in the United States* (Washington, D.C.: Joseph Henry Press, 1999).
14. Dennis S. Mileti, "Opening Plenary Welcoming Speech" (University of Colorado Hazards Center Annual Workshop, Boulder, CO, July 2004).
15. National Research Council, *Facing Hazards and Disasters,* 29.
16. Ibid., 30.

17. Chester Hartman and Gregory D. Squires, eds., *There Is No Such Thing as a Natural Disaster* (New York: Routledge, Taylor and Francis, 2006).

18. National Research Council, *Facing Hazards and Disasters,* 38.

19. George D. Haddow and Jane A. Bullock, *Introduction to Emergency Management,* 2nd ed. (Boston: Elsevier, Butterworth-Heinemann, 2006).

20. National Research Council, *The Impacts of Natural Disasters: A Framework for Loss Estimation* (Washington, D.C.: National Academies Press, 1999).

21. Ibid., 62. See also Howard Kunreuther, "Insurability Conditions and the Supply of Coverage," in *Paying the Price: The Status and Role of Insurance against Natural Disasters in the United States,* ed. Howard Kunreuther and Richard J. Roth Sr. (Washington, D.C.: Joseph Henry Press, 1998).

22. There were limited homeowner buyouts in 1973 under the program—NFIP—to reduce repetitive flood loss claims; on Love Canal: Ted Steinberg, *Acts of God: The Unnatural History of Natural Disaster in America* (New York: Oxford University Press, 2000), 181; on Times Beach: Kathleen J. Tierney, Michael K. Lindell, and Ronald W. Perry, *Facing the Unexpected: Disaster Preparedness and Response in the United States* (Washington, D.C.: Joseph Henry Press, 2001), 146.

23. David A. McEntire, *Disaster Response and Recovery* (Hoboken, N.J.: Wiley, 2007), 414.

24. Lucien G. Canton, *Emergency Management: Concepts and Strategies for Effective Programs* (Hoboken, N.J.: Wiley, 2007), 184.

25. Ibid., 184–185.

26. McEntire, *Disaster Response and Recovery,* 414.

27. Spencer S. Hsu, "U.S. Weighs How Best to Defend against Nuclear Threats: Proven Technology vs. New Advances," *Washington Post,* April 15, 2006, A-03.

28. Ibid.

29. Ibid.

30. See Graham T. Allison, *Nuclear Terrorism: The Ultimate Preventable Catastrophe* (New York: Times Books, 2004).

31. White House, National Security Presidential Directive HSPD-14, April 15, 2005, Washington, D.C., available at http://www.fas.org/irp/offdocs/nspd/nspd-43.html.

32. Ibid., 80.

33. C. V. Anderson, *The Federal Emergency Management Agency (FEMA)* (New York: Nova Science Publishers, 2003), 49.

34. William R. Cumming and Richard T. Sylves, "FEMA's Place in Policy, Law, and Management: A Hazardous Materials Perspective, 1979–2003," in *Homeland Security Law and Policy,* ed. William C. Nicholson, (Springfield, Ill.: Charles C. Thomas, 2005), 34.

35. Haddow and Bullock, *Introduction to Emergency Management,* 2nd ed., 169.

36. Ibid., 170.

37. Cumming and Sylves, "FEMA's Place in Policy, Law, and Management," 34, 36.

38. Anderson, *The Federal Emergency Management Agency,* 52.

39. Haddow and Bullock, *Introduction to Emergency Management,* 2nd ed., 285.

40. Anderson, *The Federal Emergency Management Agency,* 162–163.

41. Haddow and Bullock, *Introduction to Emergency Management,* 2nd ed., 68.

42. Ibid., 285.

43. Jerome M. Hauer, in panel discussion "Clear and Present Danger: Bio-terrorism in America," led by Ted Koppel, *Nightline,* ABC, October 14, 2001, available at http://sunday.ninemsn.com.au/sunday/cover_stories/article_946.asp?s=1.

44. White House, "Project BioShield: Progress in the War on Terrorism," July 21, 2004. Available at http://www.whitehouse.gov/infocus/bioshield (accessed October 1, 2007).

45. Homeland Security National Preparedness Task Force, *Civil Defense and Homeland Security: A Short History of National Preparedness Efforts* (Washington, D.C.: Department of Homeland Security, 2006), 16.

46. The American Institutes for Research, The Pacific Institute for Research and Evaluation, and Deloitte & Touche LLP, *A Chronology of Major Events Affecting the National Flood Insurance Program,* prepared for the Federal Emergency Management Agency under contract no. 282-98-0029, October 2005, available at http://www.dhs.gov/xlibrary/assets/privacy/privacy_pia_mip_apnd_h.pdf.

47. Ibid.

48. Homeland Security National Preparedness Task Force, *Civil Defense and Homeland Security,* 16.

49. Miriam G. Anderson and Rutherford H. Platt, "St. Charles County, Missouri: Federal Dollars and the 1993 Midwest Flood," in *Disaster and Democracy: The Politics of Extreme Natural Events,* ed. Rutherford H. Platt (Washington, D.C.: Island Press, 1999), 215–240.

50. William J. Petak and Arthur A. Atkisson, *Natural Hazard Risk Assessment and Public Policy* (New York: Springer-Verlag, 1982).

51. Ibid., 76–79.

52. Haddow and Bullock, *Introduction to Emergency Management,* 66.

53. Richard T. Sylves, "Earthquakes," in *Handbook of Emergency Management,* ed. William L. Waugh Jr. and Ronald W. Hy (Westport, Conn.: Greenwood Press, 1991).

54. HAZUS, FEMA's Software Program for Estimating Potential Losses from Disasters, http://www.fema.gov/plan/prevent/hazus.

55. MCEER is not the only NSF-supported earthquake engineering research center. There is also the Mid-America Earthquake Center, run by the University of Illinois at Urbana-Champaign, and the Pacific Earthquake Engineering Research Center, administered by the University of California at Berkeley. See National Research Council, *Facing Hazards and Disasters,* 30.

56. Haddow and Bullock, *Introduction to Emergency Management,* 67.

57. See Pielke, *The Honest Broker.*

58. Loran B. Smith and David T. Jervis, "Tornadoes," in Waugh and Hy, *Handbook of Emergency Management,* 106–128.

59. Steve Davis, Senior Vice President of Engineering, Clear Channel, "Company Sets the Record Straight about Aftermath of Minot, North Dakota Train Derailment" (speech, National Alliance of State Broadcasters Associations' 2006 National Summit on EAS and Emergency Communications, Alexandria, Va., February 26, 2006), available at http://www.clearchannel.com/Corporate/PressRelease.aspx?PressReleaseID=1558.

60. Thomas E. Baldwin, *Revised Historical Chronology of FEMA's Terrorism Consequences Management Role as Assigned by Section 2-103 of E.O. 12148* (Argonne, Ill.: Argonne National Laboratory, 2006).

61. Portions of this section were adapted from Sylves, *Emergency Management,* 130–132.

62. U.S. Army Corps of Engineers, Office of History, *The History of the U.S. Army Corps of Engineers* (Stockton, Calif.: University Press of the Pacific, 2004).

63. See Orrin H. Pilkey and Katherine L. Dixon, *The Corps and the Shore* (Washington, D.C.: Island Press, 1996).

64. U.S. Department of Justice, "Protecting America's Critical Infrastructures: PDD-63," available at http://www.cybercrime.gov/factsh.htm.

65. Waugh, *Living with Hazards, Dealing with Disasters,* and Sylves, *Emergency Management.*

66. The Disaster Relief Act of 1974 was one of the first to advance disaster mitigation through augmented federal postdisaster funding to states and localities.

67. Robert Bolin and Lois Stanford, *The Northridge Earthquake: Vulnerability and Disaster* (London: Routledge, 1999).

68. Thomas A. Birkland, *After Disaster: Agenda Setting, Public Policy, and Focusing Events* (Washington, D.C.: Georgetown University Press, 1997).

CHAPTER 6 INTERGOVERNMENTAL RELATIONS IIN DISASTER POLICY

1. David R. Morgan and Robert E. England, *Managing Urban America,* 4th ed. (Chatham, N.J.: Chatham House, 1996), 41.

2. The Department of Homeland Security updated, revised, and renamed the National Response Plan. The NRP is, as of early 2008 to be referred to as the National Response Framework. I discuss the National Response Plan and the National Response Framework in this book..

3. Thomas J. Anton, *American Federalism and Public Policy* (New York: Random House, 1989). See also, David B. Walker, *The Rebirth of Federalism: Slouching toward Washington* (Chatham, N.J.: Chatham House, 1995).

4. Peter J. May, *Recovering from Catastrophes: Federal Disaster Relief Policy and Politics* (Westport, Conn.: Greenwood Press, 1985). See also Peter J. May and Walter W. Williams, *Disaster Policy Implementation: Managing Programs under Shared Governance* (New York: Plenum Press, 1986).

5. Lucien G. Canton, an experienced emergency manager, wrote, "An inviolate premise of federal disaster response is that the local government retains control of the disaster and that federal and state

resources are deployed at the request of local government and used in support of local efforts." Lucien G. Canton, *Emergency Management: Concepts and Strategies for Effective Programs* (Hoboken, N.J.: Wiley, 2007), 45.

6. See Allen K. Settle, "Disaster Assistance: Securing Presidential Declarations," in *Cities and Disaster: North American Studies in Emergency Management,* ed. Richard T. Sylves and William L. Waugh Jr. (Springfield, Ill.: Charles C. Thomas, 1990).

7. David A. McEntire, *Disaster Response and Recovery* (Hoboken, N.J.: Wiley, 2007), 343.

8. There are exceptions. For example, in cases of bioterror attack federal law provides for federal agencies to direct state and local governments in a command and control fashion. In cases of national emergency, as might be expected after a weapon of mass destruction attack on the nation, federal authority is paramount. Some authorities contend that the National Response Plan, or, today, Framework, and the National Incident Management System embody command and control procedures, which they in fact do. However, it should not then be assumed that the federal government or federal agency officials are therefore in command and control relationships with state and local officials under either the NRP/NRF or NIMS.

9. Charles R. Wise and Rania Nader, "Organizing the Federal System for Homeland Security: Problems, Issues, and Dilemmas," *Public Administration Review* 62 (September 2002): 44–57.

10. James Lee Witt and J. Morgan, *Stronger in the Broken Places: Nine Lessons for Turning Crisis into Triumph* (New York: Times Books, 2002).

11. George D. Haddow and Jane A. Bullock, *Introduction to Emergency Management,* 2nd ed. (Boston: Elsevier, Butterworth-Heinemann, 2006), 5.

12. McEntire, *Disaster Response and Recovery,* 252–257.

13. Keith Bea, *Federal Stafford Act Disaster Assistance: Presidential Declarations, Eligible Activities, and Funding,* CRS Report RL33053 (Washington, D.C.: Congressional Research Service, 2006), 7–8.

14. Ibid., 9.

15. George D. Haddow and Jane A. Bullock, *Introduction to Emergency Management,* 2nd ed. (Boston: Elsevier, Butterworth-Heinemann, 2006), 5. Remember, whereas all major disaster declarations require a gubernatorial request and, generally, findings and certifications, emergency declaration requirements are less rigorous. The president may even issue an emergency declaration without a gubernatorial request if there is a significant federal interest in the disaster or if the federal government is in some manner liable for the disaster itself. Also, specific thresholds or calculations of past averages are not considered for emergency declarations, but FEMA officials do assess whether all other resources and authorities available to meet the crisis are inadequate before recommending that the president issue an emergency declaration.

16. FEMA's permanent staff has never exceeded 2 percent of the total DHS permanent staff.

17. "Recruited" may be too strong a word because it may well be that state and local officials were anxious to join the federal effort and do what they could to prevent future 9/11-scale attacks on the nation.

18. For a classical work on federal reorganization politics, see Harold Seidman, *Politics, Position and Power: The Dynamics of Federal Organization,* 5th ed. (New York: Oxford University Press, 1998).

19. BNET Research Center, "Memo of the Month, FEMA," *Washington Monthly,* December 2003, available at http://findarticles.com/p/articles/mi_m1316/is_12_35/ai_111897436, copyright 2003 Washington Monthly Company, and copyright 2004 Gale Group.

20. Frances E. Winslow, "Intergovernmental Challenges and California's Approach to Emergency Management," in *Disaster Management in the U.S. and Canada,* 2nd ed., ed. Richard T. Sylves and William L. Waugh Jr. (Springfield, Ill.: Charles C. Thomas, 1996), 115.

21. Canton, *Emergency Management,* 296.

22. Ibid., 297.

23. Guy E. Daines, "Planning, Training, and Exercising," in *Emergency Management: Principles and Practice,* ed. Thomas E. Drabek and Gerard J. Hoetmer (Washington, D.C.: International City Management Association, 1991), 164–165.

24. CBS News, "The Bridge to Gretna, Why Did Police Block Desperate Refugees from New Orleans?" *60 Minutes,* story filed from Gretna, Louisiana, December 18, 2005, available at http://www.cbsnews.com/stories/2005/12/15/60minutes/main1129440_page3.shtml.

25. Ibid.

26. Douglas Brinkley, *The Great Deluge: Hurricane Katrina, New Orleans, and the Mississippi Gulf Coast* (New York: Morrow, 2006), 469. Brinkley's account of the incident generally corresponds to the *60 minutes* account.

27. CBS News, "The Bridge to Gretna."
28. Ibid.
29. Brinkley, *The Great Deluge,* 469–472.
30. Ibid., 469, and CBS News, "The Bridge to Gretna."
31. CBS News, "The Bridge to Gretna."
32. Ibid.
33. This paragraph is extracted from CBS News, "The Bridge to Gretna."
34. Ibid.
35. Ibid.
36. Ibid.
37. Brinkley, *The Great Deluge,* 472.
38. CBS News, "The Bridge to Gretna."
39. Ibid.
40. This paragraph is extracted from ibid.
41. Brinkley, *The Great Deluge,* 472–473.
42. See William L. Waugh Jr. and Ronald John Hy, "The Utility of All-Hazards Programs," in *Handbook of Emergency Management,* ed. William L. Waugh Jr. and Ronald John Hy (Westport, Conn.: Greenwood Press, 1991).
43. See Thomas J. Anton, *American Federalism and Public Policy* (New York: Random House, 1989), and Walker, *The Rebirth of Federalism.*
44. U.S. Nuclear Regulatory Commission, "About the NRC: Emergency Preparedness, Public Meetings," PowerPoint slide, available at http://www.nrc.gov/about-nrc/emerg-preparedness/public-meetings/ml051300295.pdf (accessed November 12, 2007).
45. The NIMS document is available at http://www.fema.gov/nims.
46. At least one early draft of the NIMS produced by the Homeland Security Department and others was criticized for failing to consult enough state and local emergency management officials.
47. *9/11 Commission Report: Final Report of the National Commission on Terrorist Attacks upon the United States* (New York: Norton, 2004).
48. Holly Harrington, "A Message from Michael D. Brown," *Transitioning Newsletter* (a weekly electronic newsletter with DHS transition information for FEMA employees), March 5, 2003.
49. Kathleen J. Tierney, *Recent Developments in U.S. Homeland Security Policies and Their Implications for the Management of Extreme Events* (Boulder: University of Colorado, Institute of Behavioral Science, Natural Hazards Research and Applications Center, 2005).
50. Canton, *Emergency Management,* 28.
51. *9/11 Commission Report* and the Fifth Annual Report to the President and the Congress of the Advisory Panel to Assess Domestic Response Capabilities for Terrorism Involving Weapons of Mass Destruction (the so-called Gilmore Commission), *Forging America's New Normalcy: Securing Our Homeland, Preserving Our Liberty* (Arlington, Va.: Rand Corporation, 2003).
52. Ibid.
53. Richard T. Sylves, "The Politics and Budgeting of Federal Emergency Management," in Sylves and Waugh, *Disaster Management in the U.S. and Canada.*
54. See Rutherford H. Platt, "Federalizing Disasters: From Compassion to Entitlement," in *Disasters and Democracy: The Politics of Extreme Natural Events,* ed. Rutherford B. Platt (Washington, D.C.: Island Press, 1999).
55. Local governments in most states are obligated to pay some share of the state-local match. Some state governments require their local governments to pay the entire state-local match. However, most states have some type of arrangement for splitting payment of the state-local match between localities and the state government. When the president decides to significantly reduce the state-local match for a specific major disaster, perhaps approving a 90/10 federal/state-local match as was done for Hurricane Katrina, states may have a further incentive to shoulder most of the match in order to maximize federal assistance. However, the incidence of the state matching subsidy needs to be considered. In other words, sometimes states replace revenue dedicated to a generous state-local match by asking counties receiving disaster funds to increase the local sales tax by some percentage with the resulting revenue stream flowing back to the state government.
56. See James F. Miskel, *Disaster Response and Homeland Security* (Westport, Conn.: Praeger Security International, 2006).

57. Bea, *Federal Stafford Act Disaster Assistance*. 3. See the *Robert T. Stafford Disaster Assistance and Emergency Relief Act of 1988, as Amended*, 42 *U.S. Code*, title 42, chap. 68, sec. 5121, para. b, "It is the intent of Congress, by this chapter, to provide an orderly and continuing means of assistance by the federal government to state and local governments in carrying out their responsibilities . . . , " available at http://frwebgate.access.gpo.gov/cgi-bin/getdoc.cgi?dbname=browse_usc&docid= Cite:+42USC5121; also see, sec. 5170, subchap. IV, para. 401, which requires that a gubernatorial request for Stafford Act assistance "be based on a finding that the disaster is of such severity and magnitude that effective response is beyond the capabilities of the state and the affected local governments and that federal assistance is necessary" (available at http://www.disastercenter.com/ stafford/SubChp4.html).

58. Bea, *Federal Stafford Act Disaster Assistance*, 4.

59. See *Code of Federal Regulations*, title 44, chap. 1, part 206.48(a)(1) (2002). The relevant passages can be found at Dennis J. Smith, Florida Division of Emergency Management, "Disaster Recovery Thresholds," available at http://www.floridadisaster.org/brm/PA/thresholds/index.htm (accessed December 12, 2007).

60. Bea, *Federal Stafford Act Disaster Assistance*, 5.

61. American Red Cross, Museum, Explore Our History, "The Federal Charter of the American Red Cross," available at http://www.redcross.org/museum/history/charter.asp (accessed December 12, 2007).

62. National Academy of Public Administration (NAPA), *Coping with Catastrophe: Building an Emergency Management System to Meet People's Needs in Natural and Manmade Disasters* (Washington, D.C.: NAPA, 1993).

63. Jane A. Bullock and others, *Introduction to Homeland Security*, 2nd ed. (Boston: Elsevier, Butterworth-Heinemann, 2006), 117.

64. Ibid., 116–117.

65. Onvia, "Debunking Government Contracting Myths," *Government Contracting 101*, January 17, 2006, Onvia, November 27, 2006, available at http://government.onvia.com/index.php?s= Contracting+Myths (accessed December 12, 2007).

66. Halliburton, "Oilfield Technologies and Services," available at http://www.halliburton.com/ (accessed November 9, 2007).

67. Halliburton Watch Organization, *About Halliburton*, "The Basics of Halliburton's Military Contracts," available at http://www.halliburtonwatch.org/about_hal/costplus.html (accessed December 12, 2007).

68. Booz Allen Hamilton, "Services," available at http://www.boozallen.com/capabilities/services (accessed November 27, 2006).

69. Booz Allen Hamilton, "Government Infrastructure Experience," available at http://www.boozallen .com/capabilities/Industries/industries_article/659010 (accessed December 12, 2007).

70. Booz Allen Hamilton, "Fledgling Organization Is a Strong Voice for Government Security Convergence," available at http://www.boozallen.com/capabilities/services/services_article/ 1077792?lpid=981960 (accessed December 12, 2007).

71. Ibid.

72. Booz Allen Hamilton, "Booz Allen Provides Award Winning Emergency Response Services," January 9, 2006, available at http://www.boozallen.com/capabilities/Industries/industries _article/1078190?lpid=981228 (accessed December 12, 2007).

73. Bechtel Corporation, "Corporate Overview," 2006, available at http://bechtel.com/overview.htm (accessed November 27, 2006).

74. Bechtel Corporation, "Corporate History" 2007, available at http://www.bechtel.com/history.html (accessed December 12,, 2007).

75. Bechtel Corporation, "Bechtel National Wins Contract to Support FEMA," available at http://www.bechtel.com/2006-08-10.html (accessed December 12, 2007).

76. Bechtel Corporation, "Bechtel National Wins Contract to Support FEMA," news releases, August 10, 2006, available at http://www.bechtel.com/2006-08-10.html (accessed December 5, 2007).

77. Ibid.

78. Bechtel Corporation, "Business Roundtable Announces Initiative to Spur Construction Training and Bring Jobs to Thousands of Gulf Region Residents," press releases, July 28, 2006, available at http://www.mywire.com/pubs/PRNewswire/2006/07/28/1720913?&pbl=222 (accessed December 5, 2007).

79. Dewberry, "Dewberry Profile," *Dewberry,* 2006, available at http://www.dewberry.com/profile.asp?id=80 (accessed December 5, 2007).

80. Dewberry, "Dewberry Sending Employees to Assist FEMA in Hurricane Katrina Response," *Emergency Management,* September 22, 2005, available at http://www.dewberry.com/mitigation.asp?id=730 (accessed November 27, 2006).

81. Dewberry. "Dewberry, PaTH Team, Win FEMA Housing Contract," August 16, 2006, available at http://www.dewberry.com/news.asp?id=906 (accessed December 5, 2007).

82. Griff Witte, "Contractors Face More Scrutiny, Pinched Purses; Democrats Vow to Examine Large Deals," *Washington Post,* November 28, 2006, late edition, D01.

83. Robert Klebs and Richard T. Sylves, "The Northridge Earthquake: Memoirs of a FEMA Building Inspector," in Sylves and Waugh, *Disaster Management in the U.S. and Canada.*

84. See U.S. General Accounting Office, *Disaster Assistance: Improvements Needed in Determining Eligibility for Public Assistance,* report to the chairman, Subcommittee on VA, HUD, and Independent Agencies, Committee on Appropriations, U.S. Senate, GAO/RCED-96-113 (Washington, D.C.: GAO, 1996), 41.

85. Federal Emergency Management Agency, Office of Emergency Information and Public Affairs, "FEMA to Provide Nearly $1 Billion for Earthquake-Damaged Hospitals," Internet release, March 12, 1996, http://www.fema.gov, no longer available.

86. William L. Waugh Jr. and Richard T. Sylves, "Organizing the War on Terrorism," special issue, *Public Administration Review* 62 (September 2002): 81–89.

CHAPTER 7 CIVIL-MILITARY RELATIONS AND NATIONAL SECURITY

1. An exception might be the case of municipal emergency plans for protecting foreign embassies and legations within their jurisdictions. Others might be aviation security at a municipal airport, special municipal functions that fall to cities situated on national borders, cooperation in local law enforcement relevant to addressing international narcotic or drug interdiction, and certain port security functions.

2. Kurt A. Heppard and Steve G. Green, "Department of Defense Capabilities in Homeland and Transportation Security," United States Air Force Academy (paper presented at the Annual Conference of the American Society for Public Administration, Denver, Colo., March/April 2006). See also M. C. Hammond, "The *Posse Comitatus* Act: A Principle in Need of Renewal," *Washington University Law Quarterly* 75, no. 20 (1997).

3. There are certain special exceptions, but these relate to primarily military purposes as might apply under the Uniform Code of Military Justice, or which involve the authority of a commander on a military base, or that involve protection of state secrets or protection of military people and Defense Department property. See Gregory M. Huckabee, "Partnering with the Department of Defense for Improved Homeland Security," in *Homeland Security Law and Policy,* ed. William C. Nicholson (Springfield, Ill.: Charles C. Thomas, 2005), 171.

4. James Jay Carafano, "Catastrophic Disaster and the Future of the Military Response," *Disaster Preparedness* 1, no. 1 (Summer 2006), available at http://www.Wilburforce.edu:80/cdsp/cdsp_art2_02.html.

5. Hammond, "The *Posse Comitatus* Act."

6. For an excellent exposition on what the military offers in the way of postdisaster support, see Huckabee, "Partnering with the Department of Defense," 164.

7. Ibid.

8. James F. Miskel documents that the military was often called out by the president to address disasters in the nineteenth century. He explains that institutionalized disaster relief in the United States had its origins in the War Department during World War I. James F. Miskel, *Disaster Response and Homeland Security* (Westport, Conn.: Praeger Security International, 2006), 41.

9. Heppard and Green, "Department of Defense Capabilities."

10. Katherine M. Peters and Jason Vest, "Calling in the Cavalry," *Government Executive,* October 1, 2005, available at http://www.govexec.com/features/1005-01/1005-01s1.htm. See also Heppard and Green, "Department of Defense Capabilities."

11. Miskel, *Disaster Response and Homeland Security,* 55.

12. Carafano, "Catastrophic Disaster." See Huckabee, "Partnering with the Department of Defense," 171–172, and Miskel, *Disaster Response and Homeland Security* (Westport, Conn.: Praeger Security International, 2006), 40–56.

13. David E. Sanger, "Bush Wants to Consider Broadening of Military's Powers during Natural Disasters," *New York Times,* September 27, 2005, available at http://www.nytimes.com/2005/09/27/national/nationalspecial/27military.html.

14. Ibid.

15. L. M. Colarusso, "Air Force Told to Pick Up Noble Eagle Costs," *Air Force Times,* February 7, 2005, 1. See also Heppard and Green, "Department of Defense Capabilities."

16. *Protecting the American Homeland: A Second Look at How We're Meeting the Challenge,* A Brookings Briefing (Washington, D.C.: Brookings Institution, 2003).

17. The president issued the declaration to California on the basis of the fires set by rioters. However, it may well have been that President G. H. W. Bush did not want to set the precedent of issuing a presidential declaration of major disaster for a civil disturbance. The Los Angeles riots were triggered by a jury decision of innocence for Los Angeles police officers who had been videotaped beating Rodney King during his arrest.

18. Tom Bowman and Siobhan Gorman, "Increasing Military's Role Raises Questions," *Baltimore Sun,* September 20, 2005.

19. *Brookings Briefing.*

20. Ibid.

21. National Emergency Management Association, *NEMA Profile of State Emergency Management Directors and Their Agencies: Results of FY 2007* (Lexington, Ky.: National Emergency Management Association, 2007), 4, available at http://www.nemaweb.org/?1814 (accessed January 5, 2008).

22. James Lee Witt, "Military Role in Natural Disaster Response," *Disaster Preparedness* 1, no. 1 (Summer 2006), available at http://www.Wilburforce.edu/cdsp/cdsp_art2_01.html.

23. The U.S. Coast Guard has a long history of involvement in maritime safety and disaster response. For many years the Coast Guard has behaved as a federal emergency management organization but one with an on-the-water focus. The Coast Guard has been highly active in matters of port and maritime disaster mitigation, planning, response, and recovery as well as drug interdiction, boater safety, facilitation of marine navigation, port security, border patrol, fisheries regulation, and environmental protection along coasts and waterways.

24. For a time after Hurricane Katrina, Coast Guard commandant Adm. Thad Allen was FEMA's deputy director for Gulf Recovery.

25. Miskel, *Disaster Response and Homeland Security,* 53.

26. U.S. Army Corps of Engineers, "Introduction" and "Responding to Natural Disasters," in *U.S. Army Corps of Engineers: A Brief History,* available at http://www.hq.usace.army.mil/history/Brief/09-disasters/disaster.html (accessed January 5, 2008).

27. U.S. Army Corps of Engineers, *U.S. Army Corps of Engineers: A Brief History,* available at http://www.hq.usace.army.mil/history/Brief/09-disasters/disaster.html.

28. Miskel, *Disaster Response and Homeland Security,* 54.

29. Douglas Brinkley, *The Great Deluge* (New York: Morrow, 2006), 196.

30. Civil servants are not trained or compensated to enter danger zones that pose a significant risk to their health and welfare. According to William Cumming, "It is an Occupational Safety and Health criminal law violation to send untrained, unprotected workers into harm's way." Cumming (FEMA, Office of General Counsel, retired) to author, June 2, 2007.

31. Ibid.

32. Carafano, "Catastrophic Disaster."

33. Ibid.

34. George D. Haddow and Jane A. Bullock, *Introduction to Emergency Management,* 2nd ed. (Boston: Elsevier, Butterworth-Heinemann, 2006), 85.

35. Bowman and Gorman, "Increasing Military's Role Raises Questions."

36. Ibid.

37. Ibid.

38. Christopher Cooper and Robert Block, *Disaster: Hurricane Katrina and the Failure of Homeland Security* (New York: Times Books, 2006), 282.

39. Robert Block and Amy Schatz, "Storm Front: Local and Federal Authorities Battle to Control Disaster Relief," *Wall Street Journal,* December 8, 2005.

40. Bowman and Gorman, "Increasing Military's Role Raises Questions."

41. Ibid.

42. National Research Council, *Facing Hazards and Disasters: Understanding Human Dimensions* (Washington, D.C.: National Academies Press, 2006).

43. Peter Byrne, "Battlespace America," *Mother Jones,* May–June 2005, available at http://www.motherjones.com/news/outfront/2005/05/battlespace_america.html.

44. Ibid.

45. Ibid.

46. Federal Emergency Management Agency, *National Emergency Management System: The NIMS Homepage,* http://www.fema.gov/nims (accessed July 8, 2005). See also Department of Homeland Security, "National Response Plan," 2004, http://www.dhs.gov/interweb/assetlibrary/NRP_FullText.pdf (accessed July 8, 2005), 1–426.

47. U.S. Northern Command, "About USNORTHCOM," available at http://www.northcom.mil/About/history_education/history.html (accessed January 7, 2008).

48. Ibid.

49. Witt, "Military Role in Natural Disaster Response," 3.

50. Ibid., 4.

51. Ibid.

52. Ibid.

53. Carafano, "Catastrophic Disaster," 8–9.

54. Haddow and Bullock, *Introduction to Emergency Management,* 14.

55. Frances L. Edwards, "Federal Intervention in Local Emergency Planning: Nightmare on Main Street," *State and Local Government Review* 39, no. 1 (2007): 34.

56. Cumberland County, Penn., "Understanding the Homeland Security Advisory System," at http://www.ccpa.net/cumberland/cwp/view.asp?A=1148&Q=481113 (accessed January 8, 2008).

57. Veronica de Rugy and Nick Gillespie, "The War on Hype: America's Fleecing in the Name of Security," *San Francisco Chronicle,* February 19, 2006, available at http://www.sfgate.com/cgi-bin/article.cgi?f=/c/a/2006/02/19/INGDDH8E311.DTL.

58. Department of Homeland Security, Federal Emergency Management Agency, "HSPD-8 Overview," available at http://www.ojp.usdoj.gov/odp/assessments/hspd8.htm (accessed January 7, 2008).

59. Jane A. Bullock and others *Introduction to Homeland Security,* 2nd ed. (Boston: Elsevier, Butterworth-Heinemann, 2006), 324.

60. Department of Homeland Security, Office of Domestic Preparedness, *2005 Homeland Security Grant Guidance* (Washington, D.C.: Government Printing Office, 2004), 75–78.

61. Department of Homeland Security, "State Contracts and Grant Award Information," 2006, available at http://www.dhs.gov/interweb/assetlibrary/states.htm (accessed June 11, 2006).

62. Bullock and others, *Introduction to Homeland Security,* 324.

63. Edwards, "Federal Intervention in Local Emergency Planning," 34.

64. Department of Homeland Security, *Fiscal Year 2005 Homeland Security Grant Program,* 85.

65. This includes the District of Columbia and territories and possessions of the United States.

66. Refers to Kent Buckley. See Dawn Shiley-Danziesen (communications director of the International Association of Emergency Managers), "Local Emergency Managers Take Issue with DHS on Emergency Management Performance Grants (EMPG)," 2006, http://www.iaem.com/documents/LocalEmergMgrsTakeIssuewithDHSonEMPG02-21-2006.pdf (no longer available).

67. Ibid.

68. Michael Selves, currently the president of IAEM, in ibid.

69. Robert Bohlmann, quoted in Shiley-Danziesen, "Local Emergency Managers Take Issue with DHS."

70. Bullock and others, *Introduction to Homeland Security,* 103.

71. Lennard G. Kruger, *Assistance to Firefighters Program,* CRS Report RS21302 (Washington, D.C.: Congressional Research Service, 2005), 1, available at http://www.ncseonline.org/NLE/CRSreports/05may/RS21302.pdf.

72. Edwards, "Federal Intervention in Local Emergency Planning," 34

73. Department of Homeland Security, *Fiscal Year 2005 Homeland Security Grant Program,* 91.

74. Edwards, "Federal Intervention in Local Emergency Planning," 32–33.

75. President George W. Bush, Homeland Security Presidential Directive-1, October 29. 2001.

76. Edwards, "Federal Intervention in Local Emergency Planning," 34.

77. Department of Homeland Security, Office of Domestic Preparedness, *2005 Homeland Security Grant Guidance* (Washington, D.C.: Government Printing Office, 2004), cited in Edwards, "Federal Intervention in Local Emergency Planning," 34.

78. Edwards, "Federal Intervention in Local Emergency Planning," 42.

79. Department of Homeland Security, "Strengthening National Preparedness: Capabilities-Based Planning" fact sheet dated April 13, 2005, distributed at Regional Planning Conference, San Francisco, August 2005. See also Edwards, "Federal Intervention in Local Emergency Planning."

80. Department of Homeland Security, "Strengthening National Preparedness."

81. Department of Homeland Security, *FY 2006 Homeland Security Grant Program: Program Guidance and Application Kit* (Washington, D.C.: Department of Homeland Security, 2005), available at http://www.ojp.usdoj.gov/odp/docs/fy2006hsgp.pdf (accessed January 7, 2008).

82. Department of Homeland Security, *Strengthening National Preparedness,* 205. See also Edwards, "Federal Intervention in Local Emergency Planning."

83. Department of Homeland Security, *Strengthening National Preparedness,* 205.

84. Ibid.

85. See Edwards, "Federal Intervention in Local Emergency Planning."

86. Cornell University, "Look to the CARVER Method," available at http://counties.cce.cornell.edu/monroe/ag/isyourfarmcrimeproof.htm (accessed November 16, 2007). See also Edwards, "Federal Intervention in Local Emergency Planning."

87. Ibid.

88. Joel Stein, "The Terrorists Hate Our Baby Animals—Why Are the Evildoers Targeting America's Petting Zoos?" *Los Angeles Times,* July 18, 2006, http://www.latimes.com/news/opinion/editorials/la-oe-stein18jul18,0,5653711.column (article no longer available).

89. Bowman and Gorman, "Increasing Military's Role Raises Questions."

90. Senate Committee on Governmental Affairs, *Hearing on Rebuilding FEMA: Preparing for the Next Disaster,* 103rd Cong., 1st sess., 1993.

91. Lucien G. Canton, *Emergency Management: Concepts and Strategies for Effective Programs* (Hoboken, N.J.: Wiley, 2007), 275.

92. Allen K. Settle, "Disaster Assistance: Securing Presidential Declarations," in *Cities and Disaster: North American Studies in Emergency Management,* ed. Richard T. Sylves and William L. Waugh Jr. (Springfield, Ill.: Charles C. Thomas, 1990), 33–57.

CHAPTER 8 GLOBALIZATION OF DISASTERS

1. George D. Haddow and Jane A. Bullock, *Introduction to Emergency Management,* 2nd ed. (Boston: Elsevier, Butterworth-Heinemann, 2006). Haddow and Bullock mention UNICEF figures. They report that 90 percent of related injuries and deaths are sustained in countries that have per-capita income levels under $760 per year. Ibid., 219.

2. See Adrian Wood, Raymond Apthorpe, and John Borton, eds., *Evaluating International Humanitarian Action* (London: Zed Books, 2001).

3. For a thorough analysis of the security threat posed by developing nations to the industrialized world, see Robert Cooper, *The Breaking of Nations: Order and Chaos in the Twenty-First Century* (New York: Atlantic Monthly Press, 2003), 180.

4. For an excellent examination of how natural disasters relate to complex humanitarian emergencies in developing nations, see Ed Tsui, "Initial Response to Complex Emergencies and Natural Disasters," in *Emergency Relief Operation,* ed. Kevin M. Cahill, 32–54 (New York: Fordham University Press, 2003).

5. See Department of State and U.S. Agency for International Development, *Security, Democracy, Prosperity—USAID-State Strategic Plan, Fiscal Year 2004–2009* (Washington, D.C.: U.S. Department of State, 2003).

6. See Haddow and Bullock, *Introduction to Emergency Management,* 220–221.

7. Ibid., 221–222.

8. Ibid.

9. See U.S. Agency for International Development, *Policy Framework for Bilateral Aid, Implementing Transformational Diplomacy through Development* (Washington, D.C.: USAID, 2006). See also

Department of State and U.S. Agency for International Development, *Security, Democracy, Prosperity.*

10. U.S. Agency for International Development, *At Freedom's Frontiers: A Democracy and Governance Strategic Framework* (Washington, D.C.: USAID, 2005).

11. Ibid.

12. U.S. Agency for International Development, *Fragile States Strategy* (Washington, D.C.: USAID, 2005).

13. Other offices under the Bureau for Humanitarian Response provide humanitarian assistance: among others, the Office of Food for Peace and the Office of Transition Initiatives. See Haddow and Bullock, *Introduction to Emergency Management,* 237–238.

14. See Haddow and Bullock, *Introduction to Emergency Management,* 235.

15. See Damon P. Coppola, *Introduction to International Disaster Management* (Boston: Elsevier, Butterworth-Heinemann, 2007), 309.

16. Haddow and Bullock, *Introduction to Emergency Management,* 237.

17. Ibid.

18. Ibid.

19. Ibid.

20. Ibid.

21. See U.S. Agency for International Development, *USAID Administrator Natsios Tours Pakistan Earthquake Areas, Promises Continued U.S. Support for Survivors,* press release, Islamabad, Pakistan, November 18, 2005, available at http://www.state.gov/p/sca/rls/pr/2005/57178.htm (accessed October 31, 2007).

22. Ibid.

23. Haddow and Bullock, *Introduction to Emergency Management,* 239, argue that Humanitarian Assistance Survey Teams remain focused on technical military matters rather than on the purely humanitarian-based issues of the nonmilitary organizations and agencies.

24. See Department of State, "Going the Distance: The U.S. Tsunami Relief Effort 2005: Americans Respond to Tragedy," 2005. available at http://usinfo.state.gov/products/pubs/tsunami/ (accessed January 15, 2008). The operation involved twenty-five ships and ninety-four cargo planes.

25. Ibid.

26. See Brian Toft and Simon Reynolds, *Learning from Disasters* (Oxford: Butterworth-Heinemann, 1994).

27. See Edward P. Borodzicz, *Risk, Crisis, and Security Management* (West Sussex, England: Wiley, 2005).

28. See Uriel Rosenthal, R. A. Boin, and Louise Comfort, *From Crises to Contingencies: A Global Perspective* (Springfield, Ill.: Charles C. Thomas, 2002).

29. See E. L. Quarantelli, *Future Disaster Trends and Policy Implications for Developing Countries* (Newark: Disaster Research Center, University of Delaware, 1994).

30. Coppola, *Introduction to International Disaster Management,* 507–516.

31. Ibid., 500–507.

32. Ibid., 5–10.

33. See Haddow and Bullock, *Introduction to Emergency Management,* 228.

34. OCHA launches an average of twenty-seven appeals each year and has raised $12 billion since 1992. In 2000 alone, the Office for the Coordination of Humanitarian Assistance launched sixteen inter-agency appeals, which eventually raised $1.4 billion to assist 35 million individuals in sixteen countries. United Nations, Office for the Coordination of Humanitarian Affairs, Reliefweb, http://www.reliefweb.int/rw/hlp.nsf/db900ByKey/AboutReliefWeb (accessed October 29, 2007).

35. The fund has lent $127 million in more than fifty transactions since 1992. United Nations, Office for the Coordination of Humanitarian Affairs, Reliefweb, http://www.reliefweb.int/rw/hlp.nsf/db900ByKey/AboutReliefWeb (accessed October 29, 2007).

36. See Haddow and Bullock, *Introduction to Emergency Management,* 228.

37. Ibid.

38. The UNHCR spends an average of $22 million per deployment. Haddow and Bullock, *Introduction to Emergency Management,* 228.

39. Refugees are those who have fled their home countries due to their fears of persecution or for their lives, which fears are connected to issues of race, religion, nationality, or political or social group membership, and do not wish to return home. Their legal status, rights, and obligations are defined

by the 1951 Convention Relating to the Status of Refugees, and by its 1967 protocol. Kate Jastram and Marilyn Achiron, Office of the United Nations High Commissioner for Refugees, *Refugee Protection: A Guide to International Refugee Law* (Geneva, Switzerland: Inter-Parliamentary Union 2001), available at http://www.unhcr.org/publ/PUBL/3d4aba564.pdf (accessed January 15, 2008). By November 1, 2007, 147 states had signed either the treaty or protocol or both. For information regarding treaty or protocol signatories, see UNHCR, United Nations High Commissioner for Refugees, States Parties to the 1951 Convention Relating to the Status of Refugees and the 1967 Protocol, available at http://www.unhcr.org/protect/PROTECTION/3b73b0d63.pdf (accessed January 15, 2008). See also http://www.reliefweb.int/rw/lib.nsf/doc205?OpenForm.

40. Ibid.
41. Ibid.
42. Ibid.
43. See UNICEF, "UNICEF in Emergencies," available at http://www.unicef.org/emerg/index.html.
44. See Haddow and Bullock, *Introduction to Emergency Management,* 228.
45. These rights include minimum requirements for survival as well as an increase of children's opportunities for a successful future. Women are included under the mandate of UNICEF as they are considered to be vital to the care of children. See Haddow and Bullock, *Introduction to Emergency Management,* 228–229.
46. UNICEF has sometimes successfully managed to impose "days of tranquility" and "corridors of peace" in war zones. Also, UNICEF has special programs that assist traumatized children and help reunite children with their families. In 1999, UNICEF provided humanitarian aid in thirty-nine countries. See UNICEF, "UNICEF in Emergencies," available at http://www.unicef.org/emerg/index.html.
47. See Haddow and Bullock, *Introduction to Emergency Management,* 225.
48. Among the types of emergency programs, Haddow and Bullock emphasize: emergency interventions; programming for peace and recovery; area rehabilitation to resettle uprooted populations; the reintegration of demobilized soldiers; de-mining programs; rebuilding institutions and government improvement; the organization of national elections; and the management of aid delivery. See ibid., 226–227.
49. See ibid., 227.
50. Coppola, *Introduction to International Disaster Management,* 9.
51. In 1999 the WFP provided food to 29 million refugees, internally displaced people, and returnees, as well as to 41 million natural disaster victims. See UN sources http://www.un.org/issues/m-humani.html and http://www.reliefweb.int/rw/lib.nsf/doc205?OpenForm.
52. Ibid.
53. Daniel Engber, "Where's My Blue Helmet? How to Become a U.N. Peacekeeper," *Slate,* July 25, 2006, available at http://www.slate.com/id/2146479/ (accessed October 29, 2007).
54. Ibid.
55. Since about 1997, the U.S. has tried to negotiate reforms it seeks at the UN by withholding payment of a portion of its full national UN assessment. See table of U.S. debt to UN from 1996 to 2007 in "Global Policy Forum, U.S. vs. Total Debt to the UN: 1996–2007," available at http://globalpolicy.igc.org/finance/tables/core/usvtotalgraph.htm (accessed January 15, 2008). See also UN General Assembly GA/AB/3800, "Under-Secretary-General for Management Briefs Fifth Committee on Financial Situation; Says Regular Budget Position Weaker Now Compared to Last Year," May 18, 2007, available at http://www.un.org/News/Press/docs/2007/gaab3800.doc.htm (accessed January 15, 2008).

CHAPTER 9 CONCLUSIONS AND THE FUTURE

1. Thomas A. Birkland, *Lessons of Disaster: Policy Change after Catastrophic Events* (Washington, D.C.: Georgetown University Press, 2007).
2. Donald F. Kettl, *System under Stress,* 2nd ed. (Washington, D.C.: CQ Press, 2007).
3. James F. Miskel, *Disaster Response and Homeland Security: What Works, What Doesn't* (Westport, Conn.: Praeger Security International, 2006).
4. Ibid.

5. For an excellent study of distributive politics in the defense sector, see Barry S. Rundquist and Thomas M. Carsey, *Defense Spending: The Distributive Politics of Military Procurement* (Norman: University of Oklahoma Press, 2002).

6. National Academy of Public Administration, *Coping with Catastrophe: Building an Emergency Management System to Meet People's Needs in Natural and Manmade Disasters* (Washington, D.C.: NAPA, 1993).

7. Saundra K. Schneider, *Flirting with Disaster: Public Management in Crisis Situations* (Armonk, N.Y.: M. E. Sharpe, 1995), 163.

8. Miskel, *Disaster Response and Homeland Security*, 37.

9. Ibid. This is a central part of the thesis presented throughout Miskel's book.

10. Civil servants are not trained or compensated to enter danger zones that pose a significant risk to their health and welfare. According to William Cumming, "It is an Occupational Safety and Health criminal law violation to send untrained, unprotected workers into harm's way." William Cumming (FEMA, retired) to the author, June 2, 2007.

11. National Research Council, *Facing Hazards and Disasters: Understanding Human Dimensions* (Washington, D.C.: National Academies Press, 2006).

12. James L. Witt, "Military Role in Natural Disaster Response," *Disaster Preparedness* 1, no. 1 (Summer 2006), available at http://www.wilberforce.edu/cdsp/cdsp_art2_01.html.

13. For more information about imputed interest groups, see Robert H. Salisbury, "An Exchange Theory of Interest Groups," *Midwest Journal of Political Science* 13, no. 1 (February 1969): 1–32.

14. Witt, "Military Role in Natural Disaster Response."

15. See White House, *Homeland Security Presidential Directive/HSPD-5*, "Management of Domestic Incidents," press release, February 28, 2003, available at http://www.whitehouse.gov/news/releases/2003/02/20030228-9.html.

16. Miskel, *Disaster Response and Homeland Security*.

17. David Drum, "Political Animal," *Washington Monthly*, September 12, 2005, available at http://www.washingtonmonthly.com/archives/individual/2005_09/007104.php.

18. Denial of government relief is something always threatened in communities with recurring flood disasters. FEMA has proposed denying postdisaster relief to homeowners flooded in the past and warned that they must buy National Flood Insurance but did not. Every time FEMA attempts to deny relief in such cases, a political intercession by the area's senators and representatives to the president results in a withdrawal of the threat.

19. U.S. Department of the Treasury, *Terrorism Risk Insurance Program, Overview*, January 7, 2008, available at http://www.treas.gov/offices/domestic-finance/financial-institution/terrorism-insurance/claims_process/registration_process.shtml (accessed January 18, 2008).

20. Peter J. May, *Recovering from Catastrophes: Federal Disaster Relief Policy and Politics* (Westport, Conn.: Greenwood Press, 1985).

21. Witt, "Military Role in Natural Disaster Response."

22. Dennis S. Mileti, *Disasters by Design: A Reassessment of Natural Hazards in the United States* (Washington, D.C.: Joseph Henry Press, 1999); Enrico L. Quarantelli, *Disaster Planning, Emergency Management, and Civil Protection: The Historical Development of Organized Efforts to Plan for and to Respond to Disasters* (Newark: University of Delaware, Disaster Research Center, 2000), available at http://www.udel.edu/DRC/preliminary/227.pdf; Kathleen J. Tierney, Michael K. Lindell, and Ronald W. Perry, *Facing the Unexpected: Disaster Preparedness and Response in the United States* (Washington, D.C.: Joseph Henry Press, 2001).

Allison, Graham T. *Essence of Decision: Explaining the Cuban Missile Crisis.* Boston: Little, Brown, 1971.
———. *Nuclear Terrorism: The Ultimate Preventable Catastrophe.* New York: Times Books/Henry Holt, 2004.
Anderson, James E. "Policy Implementation." In *Public Policymaking: An Introduction.* 3rd ed. Boston: Houghton Mifflin, 1997.
Anderson, Miriam G., and Rutherford H. Platt. "St. Charles County, Missouri: Federal Dollars and the 1993 Midwest Flood." In *Disaster and Democracy: The Politics of Extreme Natural Events,* edited by Rutherford H. Platt, 215–240. Washington, D.C.: Island Press, 1999.
Anton, Thomas. *American Federalism and Public Policy.* New York: Random House, 1989.
Arceneaux, Kevin, and Robert M. Stein. "Who Is Held Responsible When Disaster Strikes? The Attribution of Responsibility for a Natural Disaster in an Urban Election." *Journal of Urban Affairs* 28 (January 2006): 43–54.
Arrow, Kenneth J. "The Economics of Agency." In *Principals and Agents: The Structure of Business,* edited by J. W. Pratt and R. J. Zeckhauser, 37–51. Boston: Harvard Business School, 1988.
Baldwin, Thomas E. *Revised Historical Chronology of FEMA's Terrorism Consequences Management Role as Assigned by Section 2-103 of E.O. 12148.* Argonne, Ill.: Argonne National Laboratory, 2006.
Barber, James David. "Presidential Character." In *American Government: Readings and Cases,* edited by Karen O'Connor. Boston: Allyn and Bacon, 1995.
Barnard, Chester I. *Functions of the Executive.* 30th anniversary ed. Cambridge, Mass: Harvard University Press, 1968.
Barzelay, Michael. *Breaking through Bureaucracy: A New Vision for Management in Government.* Berkeley: University of California Press, 1992.
Bea, Keith. *Federal Stafford Act Disaster Assistance: Presidential Declarations, Eligible Activities and Funding.* CRS Report RL33053. Washington, D.C.: Congressional Research Service, 2006.
———. "The Formative Years: 1950–1978." In *Emergency Management: The American Experience, 1900–2005,* edited by Claire B. Rubin. Fairfax, Va.: Public Entity Risk Institute, 2007.
Beauchesne, Ann M. *A Governor's Guide to Emergency Management.* Washington, D.C.: National Governor's Association, 1998.
Bechtel Corporation. "About Bechtel." http://bechtel.com/about_bechtel.html.
———. "Bechtel Wins Contract to Support FEMA," August 10, 2006. http://www.bechtel.com/2006-08-10.html.
———. "Corporate Overview." http://bechtel.com/overview.htm.
Birkland, Thomas A. *After Disaster: Agenda Setting, Public Policy, and Focusing Events.* Washington, D.C.: Georgetown University Press, 1997.
Blocker, T. J., E. B. Rochford Jr., and D. E. Sherkat. "Political Responses to Natural Hazards: Social Movement Participation Following a Flood." *International Journal of Mass Emergencies and Disasters* 9 (1991): 367–382.
BNET Research Center, "Memo of the Month, FEMA." *Washington Monthly,* December 2003. http://findarticles.com/p/articles/mi_m1316/is_12_35/ai_111897436.
Borodzicz, Edward P. *Risk, Crisis, and Security Management.* Hoboken, N.J.: Wiley, 2005.
Booz Allen Hamilton. "Booz Allen Provides Award Winning Emergency Response Services." January 9, 2006. http://www.boozallen.com/.
———. "Fledgling Organization Is a Strong Voice for Government Security Convergence." http://www.boozallen.com/.
———. "Government Infrastructure." http://www.boozallen.com/.
———. "Services." http://www.boozallen.com/.
Brinkley, Douglas. *The Great Deluge.* New York: Morrow, 2006.
Brookings Institution. *Protecting the American Homeland: A Second Look at How We're Meeting the Challenge.* Brookings Briefing. Washington, D.C.: Brookings Institution, 2003.
Bullock, Jane A., George D. Haddow, Damon Coppola, Erdem Ergin, Lissa Westerman, and Sarp Yeletaysi. *Introduction to Homeland Security.* Boston: Elsevier, Butterworth-Heinemann, 2005.
———. *Introduction to Homeland Security.* 2nd ed. Boston: Elsevier, Butterworth-Heinemann, 2006.

Burby, Raymond J., ed. *Cooperating with Nature: Confronting Natural Hazards with Land-Use Planning for Sustainable Communities.* Washington, D.C.: Joseph Henry Press, 1998.

Canton, Lucien G. *Emergency Management: Concepts and Strategies for Effective Programs.* Hoboken, N.J.: Wiley, 2007.

Carafano, James Jay. "Catastrophic Disaster and the Future of the Military Response." *Disaster Preparedness* 1, no. 1 (Summer 2006). http://www.Wilburforce.edu:80/cdsp/cdsp_art2_02.html.

A Chronology of Major Events Affecting the National Flood Insurance Program. Prepared for the Federal Emergency Management Agency by the American Institutes for Research, the Pacific Institute for Research and Evaluation, and Deloitte & Touche LLP. 2005. http://www.dhs.gov/xlibrary/assets/privacy/privacy_pia_mip_apnd_h.pdf.

Colarusso, L. M. "Air Force Told to Pick Up Noble Eagle Costs." *Air Force Times,* February 7, 2005.

Comfort, Louise K., ed. *Managing Disaster: Strategies and Policy Perspectives.* Durham, N.C.: Duke University Press, 1988.

Cooper, Robert. *The Breaking of Nations—Order and Chaos in the Twenty-First Century.* New York: Atlantic Monthly Press, 2003.

Coppola, Damon P. *Introduction to International Disaster Management.* Boston: Elsevier, Butterworth-Heinemann, 2007.

Cornell University. "Look to the CARVER Method." http://counties.cce.cornell.edu/monroe/ag/isyourfarmcrimeproof.htm.

Cronin, Thomas E. "The Swelling of the Presidency." In *Classic Readings in American Politics,* edited by Pietro S. Nivola and David H. Rosenbloom. New York: St. Martin's, 1986.

Cumming, William R., and Richard T. Sylves. "FEMA's Place in Policy, Law, and Management: A Hazardous Materials Perspective 1979–2003." In *Homeland Security Law and Policy,* edited by William C. Nicholson. Springfield, Ill.: Charles C. Thomas, 2004.

Cutter, Susan L., ed. *American Hazardscapes: The Regionalization of Hazards and Disasters.* Washington, D.C.: Joseph Henry Press, 2001.

Daines, Guy E. "Planning, Training, and Exercising." In *Emergency Management: Principles and Practice,* edited by Thomas E. Drabek and Gerard J. Hoetmer. Washington, D.C.: International City Management Association, 1991.

Daniels, R. Steven, and Carolyn L. Clark-Daniels. *Transforming Government: The Renewal and Revitalization of the Federal Emergency Management Agency.* 2000 Presidential Transition Series. Arlington, Va.: Pricewaterhouse Coopers Endowment for the Business of Government, 2000.

de Rugy, Veronica, and Nick Gillespie. "The War on Hype: America's Fleecing in the Name of Security." *San Francisco Chronicle,* February 19, 2006. http://www.sfgate.com/cgi-bin/article.cgi?f=/c/a/2006/02/19/INGDDH8E311.DTL.

Dewberry. "Dewberry Profile." http://www.dewberry.com/profile.asp?id=80.

Downs, Anthony. "Up and Down with Ecology: The 'Issue-Attention Cycle.' " *Public Interest* 28 (Summer 1972): 38–50.

Downton, Mary W., and Roger A. Pielke. "Discretion without Accountability: Politics, Flood, Damage, and Climate." *Natural Hazards Review* 2, no. 4 (2001): 157–166.

Drabek, Thomas E. "The Evolution of Emergency Management." In *Emergency Management: Principles and Practice for Local Government,* edited by Thomas E. Drabek and Gerrard J. Hoetmer. Washington, D.C.: ICMA, 1991.

———. *Also see* U.S. Federal Emergency Management Agency.

Drum, David. "Political Animal." *Washington Monthly,* September 12, 2005. http://www.washington-monthly.com/archives/individual/2005_09/007104.php.

Dymon, Ude J., and Rutherford H. Platt. "U.S. Federal Disaster Declarations: A Geographical Analysis." In *Disasters and Democracy: The Politics of Extreme Natural Events,* edited by Rutherford H. Platt. Washington, D.C.: Island Press, 1999.

Edwards, Frances L. "Federal Intervention in Local Emergency Planning: Nightmare on Main Street." *State and Local Government Review* 39, no. 1 (2007): 31–43.

———. "Homeland Security from the Local Perspective." In *Homeland Security Law and Policy,* edited by William C. Nicholson. Springfield, Ill.: Charles C. Thomas, 2005.

Elmore, Richard F. "Backward Mapping: Implementation Research and Policy Decisions." *Political Science Quarterly* 94, no. 4 (1979–1980): 69–83.

Engber, Daniel. "Where's My Blue Helmet? How to Become a U.N. Peacekeeper." *Slate,* July 25, 2006. http://www.slate.com/id/2146479/.

Frederickson, H. George, and Kevin B. Smith. *The Public Administration Theory Primer.* Boulder, Colo.: Westview Press, 2003.

Garrett, Thomas A., and Russell S. Sobel. "The Political Economy of FEMA Disaster Payments." *Economic Inquiry* 41, no. 3 (2003): 496–509.

Gee, James Paul, Kurt Squire, and Constance Steinkuehler. "How Games Are Reshaping Business and Learning." http://www.academiccolab.org/inititatives/accelerate.html.

Gilmore Commission. "The Fifth Annual Report to the President and the Congress of the Advisory Panel to Assess Domestic Response Capabilities for Terrorism Involving Weapons of Mass Destruction." In *Forging America's New Normalcy: Securing Our Homeland, Preserving Our Liberty.* http://www.rand.org/nsrd/terrpanel/volume_v/volume_v.pdf.

Giuliani, Rudolph. *Leadership.* New York: Miramax Books, 2002.

Godschalk, David R., David J. Brower, and Timothy Beatley. *Catastrophic Coastal Storms: Hazard Mitigation and Development Management.* Durham, N.C.: Duke University Press, 1989.

Haddow, George D., and Jane A. Bullock. *Introduction to Emergency Management.* Boston: Butterworth-Heinemann, 2003.

———. *Introduction to Emergency Management.* 2nd ed. Boston: Elsevier, Butterworth-Heinemann, 2006.

Halliburton. "Oilfield Technologies and Services." http://www.halliburton.com/.

Halliburton Watch Organization. *About Halliburton.* "The Basics of Halliburton's Military Contracts." 2006. http://www.halliburtonwatch.org/about_hal/costplus.html.

Hammond, M. C. "The *Posse Comitatus* Act: A Principle in Need of Renewal." *Washington University Law Quarterly* 75, no. 20 (1997).

Harrington, Holly. "A Message from Michael D. Brown." *Transitioning Newsletter,* March 5, 2003. [A weekly electronic newsletter with DHS transition information for FEMA employees.]

Hartman, Chester, and Gregory D. Squires, eds. *There Is No Such Thing as a Natural Disaster.* New York: Routledge, Taylor and Francis, 2006.

Heclo, Hugh. *A Government of Strangers: Executive Politics in Washington.* Washington, D.C.: Brookings Institution, 1977.

Heppard, Kurt A., and Steve G. Green. "Department of Defense Capabilities in Homeland and Transportation Security." Paper presented at the Annual Conference of the American Society for Public Administration, Denver, Colo., March/April 2006.

Hogue, Henry B., and Keith Bea. *Federal Emergency Management and Homeland Security Organization: Historical Developments and Legislative Options.* CRS Report 33369. Washington, D.C.: Congressional Research Service, 2006.

Homeland Security National Preparedness Task Force. *Civil Defense and Homeland Security: A Short History of National Preparedness Efforts.* Washington, D.C.: Department of Homeland Security, 2006.

Jigyasu, Rohit. "Disaster: A Reality or Construct? Perspective from the East." In *What Is Disaster? New Answers to Old Questions,* edited by Ronald W. Perry and E. L. Quarantelli. Philadelphia: Xlibris, 2005.

Joyce, Philip G., and Amy E. Kneedler. "Emergency Management Competencies and Incentives and Implications for Funding in the Intergovernmental Context." Paper presented at the Sixtieth National Conference of the American Society for Public Administration, 1999.

Kapucu, Naim. "Making Matters Worse: Anatomy of Leadership Failures in Catastrophic Events." Paper presented at the Sixty-eighth Annual American Society for Public Administration National Conference, Washington, D.C., March 23–27, 2007.

Kettl, Donald F. *System under Stress.* 2nd ed. Washington, D.C.: CQ Press, 2007.

———. "The Worst Is Yet to Come: Lessons from September 11 and Hurricane Katrina." *Fels Government Research Service.* Report 05-01. Philadelphia: Fels Institute of Government, University of Pennsylvania, 2005.

Kingdon, John W. "Agendas, Alternatives, and Public Policies (1995)." In *Classics of Public Policy,* edited by Jay M. Shafritz, Karen S. Layne, and Christopher P. Borick, 148–159. New York: Pearson Longman, 2005.

Klebs, Robert, and Richard T. Sylves. "The Northridge Earthquake: Memoirs of a FEMA Building Inspector." In *Disaster Management in the U.S. and Canada,* edited by Richard T. Sylves and William L. Waugh Jr. Springfield, Ill.: Charles C. Thomas, 1996.

Kraemer, Sylvia. *Science and Technology Policy.* Piscataway, N.J.: Rutgers University Press, 2006.

Kunreuther, Howard. "Disaster Mitigation: Lessons from Katrina." *The Annals of the American Academy of Political and Social Science* 604 (March 2006): 208–227.

———. "Insurability Conditions and the Supply of Coverage." In *Paying the Price: The Status and Role of Insurance against Natural Disasters in the United States,* edited by Howard Kunreuther and Richard J. Roth Sr. Washington, D.C.: Joseph Henry Press, 1998.

Lindblom, Charles E. *The Intelligence of Democracy: Decision Making through Mutual Adjustment.* New York: Free Press, 1965.

Lindell, Michael K., Carla Prater, and Ronald W. Perry. *Introduction to Emergency Management.* Hoboken, N.J.: Wiley, 2007.

Lynn, Laurence E., Jr. *Public Management as Art, Science, and Profession.* Chatham, N.J.: Chatham House, 1996.

May, Peter J. *Recovering from Catastrophes: Federal Disaster Relief Policy and Politics.* Westport, Conn.: Greenwood Press, 1985.

May, Peter J., and Walter W. Williams. *Disaster Policy Implementation: Managing Programs under Shared Governance.* New York: Plenum Press, 1986.

McCarthy, Francis X. *FEMA's Disaster Declaration Process: A Primer.* CRS Report RL34146. Washington, D.C.: Congressional Research Service, 2007.

McEntire, David A. "Issues in Disaster Relief: Progress, Perpetual Problems, and Perspective Solutions." *Disaster Prevention and Management* 8, no. 5 (1999): 351–361.

———. *Disaster Response and Recovery.* Hoboken, N.J.: Wiley, 2007.

Mileti, Dennis S. *Disasters by Design: A Reassessment of Natural Hazards in the United States.* Washington, D.C.: Joseph Henry Press, 1999.

———. "Opening Plenary Welcoming Speech." University of Colorado, Hazards Center Annual Workshop, Boulder, July 2004.

Miskel, James F. *Disaster Response and Homeland Security: What Works, What Doesn't.* Westport, Conn.: Praeger Security International, 2006.

Morgan, David R., and Robert E. England. *Managing Urban America.* 4th ed. Chatham, N.J.: Chatham House, 1996.

Morin, Alexander J. *Science Policy and Politics.* Englewood Cliffs, N.J.: Prentice-Hall, 1993.

National Academy of Public Administration (NAPA). *Coping with Catastrophe: Building an Emergency Management System to Meet People's Needs in Natural and Manmade Disasters.* Washington, D.C.: NAPA, 1993.

National Research Council (NRC). Commission on Geosciences, Environment, and Resources. Committee on Assessing the Costs of Natural Disasters. Board on Natural Disasters. *The Impacts of Natural Disasters: A Framework for Loss Estimation.* Washington, D.C.: National Academies Press, 1999.

———. Committee on Disaster Research in the Social Sciences. *Facing Hazards and Disasters: Understanding Human Dimensions.* Washington, D.C.: National Academies Press, 2006.

———. *Making the Nation Safer: The Role of Science and Technology in Countering Terrorism.* Washington, D.C.: National Academies Press, 2002.

———. *Risk Analysis and Uncertainty: Flood Damage Reduction Studies.* Washington, D.C.: National Academies Press, 2000.

Nicholson, William C. *Emergency Response and Emergency Management Law: Cases and Materials.* Springfield, Ill.: Charles C. Thomas, 2003.

———, ed. *Homeland Security Law and Policy.* Springfield, Ill.: Charles C. Thomas, 2005.

9/11 Commission Report: Final Report of the National Commission on Terrorist Attacks upon the United States. New York: Norton, 2004.

Onvia. "Small Business Government Contracts: Myths and Facts." *Government Contracting Best Practices.* May 2007. http://government.onvia.com/index.php?s=contract+myths.

Perrow, Charles. *Normal Accidents.* New York: Basic Books, 1984.

Petak, William J. "Emergency Management: A Challenge to Public Administration." Special issue. *Public Administration Review* 45 (January 1985).

Petak, William J., and Arthur A. Atkisson. *Natural Hazard Risk Assessment and Public Policy.* New York: Springer-Verlag, 1982.

Peters, Katherine M., and Jason Vest. "Calling in the Cavalry." *Government Executive,* October 1, 2005. http://www.govexec.com/features/1005-01/1005-01s1.htm.

Peterson, Paul E. *The Price of Federalism.* Washington, D.C.: Brookings Institution, 1995.

Pielke, Roger A., Jr. *The Honest Broker: Making Sense of Science in Policy and Politics.* New York: Cambridge University Press, 2007.

Pika, Joseph A., and John Anthony Maltese. *The Politics of the Presidency.* 6th ed. Washington, D.C.: CQ Press, 2004.

Pilkey, Orrin H., and Katherine L. Dixon. *The Corps and the Shore.* Washington, D.C.: Island Press, 1996.

Pine, John C. *Technology in Emergency Management.* Hoboken, N.J.: Wiley, 2007.

Plano, Jack C., and Milton Greenberg. *The American Political Dictionary.* 7th ed. New York: Holt, Rinehart and Winston, 1985.

Platt, Rutherford H. "Federalizing Disasters: From Compassion to Entitlement." In *Disasters and Democracy: The Politics of Extreme Natural Events,* edited by Rutherford B. Platt. Washington, D.C.: Island Press, 1999.

———. "Shouldering the Burden: Federal Assumption of Disaster Costs." In *Disasters and Democracy: The Politics of Extreme Natural Events,* edited by Rutherford H. Platt. Washington, D.C.: Island Press, 1999.

Platt, Rutherford H., and Claire B. Rubin. "Stemming the Losses: The Quest for Hazard Mitigation." In *Disasters and Democracy: The Politics of Extreme Natural Events,* edited by Rutherford H. Platt. Washington, D.C.: Island Press, 1999.

Public Entity Risk Institute (PERI). "All About Presidential Disaster Declarations." http://www.peripresdecusa.org.

Quarantelli, E. L. "Disaster Planning, Emergency Management, and Civil Protection: The Historical Development of Organized Efforts to Plan for and to Respond to Disasters." DRC Preliminary Paper 301. Disaster Research Center, University of Delaware, 2000. http://www.udel.edu/DRC.

———. *Future Disaster Trends and Policy Implications for Developing Countries.* Newark: Disaster Research Center, University of Delaware, 1994.

Rahm, Dianne. *United States Public Policy: A Budgetary Approach.* Belmont, Calif.: Wadsworth, 2004.

Reeves, Andrew. "Political Disaster? Presidential Disaster Declarations and Electoral Politics." 2005. http://www.people.fas.harvard.edu/~reeves/papers/fema.pdf.

Relyea, Harold C. "Organizing for Homeland Security." *Presidential Studies Quarterly* 33, no. 3 (2003): 602–624.

Roberts, Patrick S. "FEMA and the Prospects for Reputational Authority." *Studies in American Political Development* 20 (Spring 2006): 1–31.

Rosenthal, Uriel, R. A. Boin, and Louise Comfort. *From Crises to Contingencies: A Global Perspective.* Springfield, Ill.: Charles C. Thomas, 2002.

Rubin, Claire B., and Irmak R. Tanali. *Disaster Time Line: Selected Milestone Events and U.S. Outcomes (1965–2001).* Arlington, Va.: Claire B. Rubin, 2001.

Salisbury, Robert H. "An Exchange Theory of Interest Groups." *Midwest Journal of Political Science* 13, no. 1 (February, 1969): 1–32.

Sanger, David E. "Bush Wants to Consider Broadening of Military's Powers during Natural Disasters." *New York Times,* September 27, 2005. http://www.nytimes.com/2005/09/27/national/nationalspecial/27military.html.

Schneider, Saundra K. *Flirting with Disaster: Public Management in Crisis Situations.* Armonk, N.Y.: M. E. Sharpe, 1995.

Schroeder, Aaron, and Gary Wamsley. "The Evolution of Emergency Management in America: From a Painful Past to a Promising but Uncertain Future." In *Handbook of Crisis and Emergency Management,* edited by A. Farazmand. New York: Marcel Dekker, 2002.

Settle, Allen K. "Disaster Assistance: Securing Presidential Declarations." In *Cities and Disaster: North American Studies in Emergency Management,* edited by Richard T. Sylves and William L. Waugh Jr. Springfield, Ill.: Charles C. Thomas, 1990.

Shiley-Danziesen, Dawn. "International Association of Emergency Managers, Communications Director, Local Emergency Managers Take Issue with DHS on Emergency Management Performance Grants (EMPG)," February 21, 2006. http://www.iaem.com/documents/LocalEmergMgrsTakeIssuewithDHSonEMPG02-21-2006.pdf.

Simendinger, Alexis. "Disaster Response Threatens to Swamp Bush Administration." *National Journal,* September 5, 2005.

Simon, Herbert A., Donald W. Smithburg, and Victor A. Thompson. *Public Administration.* New York: Knopf, 1950.

Smith, Loran B., and David T. Jervis. "Tornadoes." In *Handbook of Emergency Management,* edited by William L. Waugh Jr. and Ronald John Hy. Westport, Conn.: Greenwood Press, 1991.

Stallings, Robert A. *Promoting Risk: Constructing the Earthquake Threat.* New York: Aldine de Gruyter, 1995.

Steinberg, Ted. *Acts of God: The Unnatural History of Natural Disaster in America.* New York: Oxford University Press, 2000.

Sylves, Richard. "Earthquakes." In *Handbook of Emergency Management,* edited by William L. Waugh Jr. and Ronald W. Hy. Westport, Conn.: Greenwood Press, 1991.

———. "Federal Emergency Management Comes of Age: 1979–2001." In *Emergency Management: The American Experience, 1900–2005,* edited by Claire B. Rubin. Fairfax, Va.: Public Entity Risk Institute, 2007.

———. "Ferment at FEMA: Reforming Emergency Management." *Public Administration Review* 56 (1994): 303–307.

———. "The Politics and Budgeting of Federal Emergency Management." In *Disaster Management in the U.S. and Canada,* edited by Richard T. Sylves and William L. Waugh Jr. Springfield, Ill.: Charles C. Thomas, 1996.

———. "A Precis on Political Theory and Emergency Management." *Journal of Emergency Management* 2, no. 3 (Summer 2004): 1–6.

———. "President Bush and Hurricane Katrina: A Presidential Leadership Study." In *Annals of the American Academy of Political and Social Science* 604 (March 2006): 26–56.

Sylves, Richard T., and Thomas J. Pavlak. "The Big Apple and Disaster Planning: How New York City Manages Major Emergencies." In *Cities and Disaster: North American Studies in Emergency Management,* edited by Richard T. Sylves and William L. Waugh Jr. Springfield, Ill.: Charles C. Thomas, 1990.

Sylves, Richard T., and William L. Waugh Jr., eds. *Disaster Management in the U.S. and Canada.* Springfield, Ill: Charles C. Thomas, 1996.

Tarcey, Brian. "Flooding the Ballot Box: The Politics of Disaster." *Harvard Magazine,* March–April 2004.

Tierney, Kathleen J. *Recent Developments in U.S. Homeland Security Policies and Their Implications for the Management of Extreme Events.* Boulder: Natural Hazards Research and Applications Center, Institute of Behavioral Science, University of Colorado, 2005.

Tierney, Kathleen J., Michael K. Lindell, and Ronald W. Perry. *Facing the Unexpected: Disaster Preparedness and Response in the United States.* Washington, D.C.: Joseph Henry Press, 2001.

Toft, Brian, and Simon Reynolds. *Learning from Disasters.* Oxford: Butterworth-Heinemann, 1994.

"Tornado-Associated Fatalities—Arkansas, 1997." *Morbidity and Mortality Weekly Report* 46, no. 19 (May 16, 1997): 412–416. http://www.cdc.gov/epo/mmwr/preview/mm4619.html#article2.

"Tornado Disaster—Alabama, March 27, 1994." *Morbidity and Mortality Weekly Report* 43, no. 19 (May 20, 1994): 356–359. http://www.cdc.gov/epo/mmwr/preview/mm4319.htm#TOC.

Truman, David B. *The Governmental Process.* New York: Knopf, 1951.

Tsui, E. "Initial Response to Complex Emergencies and Natural Disasters." In *Emergency Relief Operation,* edited by Kevin M. Cahill. New York: Fordham University Press, 2003.

United Nations. "UN System Humanitarian and Disaster Relief Assistance." http://www.un.org/issues/m-humani.html.

United Nations. Office for the Coordination of Humanitarian Affairs. *Reliefweb.* http://www.reliefweb.int/rw/hlp.nsf/db900ByKey/AboutReliefWeb.

United Nations Childrens Fund (UNICEF). "UNICEF in Emergencies." http://www.unicef.org/emerg/index.html.

U.S. Agency for International Development (USAID). *At Freedom's Frontiers: A Democracy and Governance Strategic Framework.* Washington, D.C.: USAID, 2005.

———. Bureau for Policy and Program Coordination. *U.S. Foreign Aid: Meeting the Challenges of the Twenty-First Century.* Washington, D.C.: USAID, 2004.

———. *Foreign Aid in the National Interest: Promoting Freedom, Security, and Opportunity.* Washington, D.C.: USAID, 2002.

———. *Fragile States Strategy.* Washington, D.C.: USAID, 2005.

———. *Policy Framework for Bilateral Aid: Implementing Transformational Diplomacy through Development.* Washington, D.C.: USAID, 2006.

———. "USAID Administrator Natsios Tours Pakistan Earthquake Areas, Promises Continued U.S. Support for Survivors." Press release, Islamabad, Pakistan, November 18, 2005. http://www.state.gov/p/sca/rls/pr/2005/57178.htm.

U.S. Army Corps of Engineers. Office of History. *The History of the U.S. Army Corps of Engineers.* Stockton, Calif.: University Press of the Pacific, 2004.

U.S. Congress. House. Committee on Public Works and Transportation. Subcommittee on Water Resources and the Environment. *Midwest Floods of 1993: Flood Control and Floodplain Policy and Proposals.* Serial no. 103-57. Hearing before the Subcommittee on Water Resources and the Environment. 103rd Cong., 1st sess., 1993.

———. Select Bipartisan Committee to Investigate Preparation for and Response to Hurricane Katrina. *A Failure of Initiative.* 109th Cong., 2nd sess., 2006.

U.S. Congress. Senate. "Bipartisan Task Force on Funding Disaster Relief." In *Federal Disaster Assistance.* Report of the Senate Task Force on Funding Disaster Relief, 104th Cong., 1st sess., 1995.

———. Committee on Governmental Affairs. *Hearing on Rebuilding FEMA: Preparing for the Next Disaster.* 103rd Cong., 1st sess., 1993.

U.S. Department of Homeland Security. "Final Draft: National Response Plan." 2004. http://www.dhs.gov/interweb/assetlibrary/NIMS-90-web.pdf.

———. *Homeland Security Grant Guidance.* Washington, D.C.: Department of Homeland Security, 2006.

———. National Preparedness Task Force. *Civil Defense and Homeland Security: A Short History of National Preparedness Efforts.* Washington, D.C.: Department of Homeland Security, 2006.

———. Office of Domestic Preparedness. *2005 Homeland Security Grant Guidance.* Washington, D.C.: Government Printing Office, 2004.

———. Office of State and Local Government Coordination and Preparedness. *Target Capabilities List: Version 1.1.* Washington, D.C.: U.S. Department of Homeland Security, Office of State and Local Government Coordination and Preparedness, 2005.

———. *Quick Reference Guide for the National Response Plan.* Version 4.0, May 22, 2006. http://www.dhs.gov/xlibrary/assets/NRP_Quick_Reference_Guide_5-22-06.pdf.

U.S. Department of Justice. "Protecting America's Critical Infrastructures." PDD-63. http://www.cyber-crime.gov/factsh.htm.

U.S. Department of State. "Going the Distance: The U.S. Tsunami Relief Effort 2005: Americans Respond to Tragedy." http://usinfo.state.gov/products/pubs/tsunami/.

U.S. Department of State and U.S. Agency for International Development. *Security, Democracy, Prosperity—USAID-State Strategic Plan, Fiscal Year 2004–2009.* Washington, D.C.: U.S. Department of State, 2003.

U.S. Federal Emergency Management Agency (FEMA). "National Response Framework." http://www.fema.gov/pdf/emergency/nrf/nrf-core.pdf.

———. *Social Dimensions of Disaster, Instructor Guide,* by Thomas Drabek. Washington, D.C: U.S. Federal Emergency Management Agency, 1996.

———. "2005 Federal Disaster Declarations." http://www.fema.gov/news/disasters.fema?year=2005.

———. "2007 Federal Disaster Declarations." http://www.fema.gov/news/disasters.fema?year=2007.

U.S. General Accounting Office. *Disaster Assistance: Improvements Needed in Determining Eligibility for Public Assistance.* Report to the Chairman, Subcommittee on VA, HUD, and Independent Agencies, Committee on Appropriations, U.S. Senate. GAO/RCED-96-113. Washington, D.C.: U.S. General Accounting Office, 1996.

U.S. Government Accountability Office. *Disaster Assistance: Improvement Needed in Disaster Declaration Criteria and Eligibility Assurance Procedures.* GAO-01-837. Washington, D.C.: Government Printing Office, 2001.

U.S. Nuclear Regulatory Commission. "About the NRC: Emergency Preparedness, Public Meetings." PowerPoint Slide. http://www.nrc.gov/about-nrc/emerg-preparedness/publicmeetings/ml051300 295.pdf.

Waldo, Dwight. *The Administrative State.* New York: Ronald Press, 1948.

Walker, David B. *The Rebirth of Federalism: Slouching toward Washington.* Chatham, N.J.: Chatham House, 1995.

Wamsley, Gary L. "Escalating in a Quagmire: The Changing Dynamics of the Emergency Management Policy Subsystem." *Public Administration Review* 56 (1996): 235–244.

Wamsley, Gary L., Aaron D. Schroeder, and Larry M. Lane. "To Politicize Is NOT to Control: The Pathologies of Control in Federal Emergency Management." *American Review of Public Administration* 26, no. 3 (1996): 263–285.

Waugh, William L., Jr. *Living with Hazards, Dealing with Disasters: An Introduction to Disaster Management.* Armonk, N.Y.: M. E. Sharpe, 2000.

———. "Terrorism, Homeland Security, and the National Emergency Management Network." *Public Organization Review* 3 (2003): 373–385.

Waugh, William L., Jr., and Richard T. Sylves. "Organizing the War on Terrorism." *Public Administration Review* 62 (2002): 145–153.

Waugh, William L., Jr., and Ronald John Hy. *Handbook of Emergency Management.* Westport, Conn.: Greenwood Press, 1990.

White, Gilbert F., and others. "Changes in Urban Occupance of Flood Plains in the United States." Research paper 57. University of Chicago, Department of Geography, 1958.

White House. "Management of Domestic Incidents." *Homeland Security Presidential Directive-5.* Washington, D.C.: White House, 2003. http://www.whitehouse.gov/news/releases/2003/02/20030228-9.html.

———. *The National Security Strategy of the United States of America.* Washington, D.C.: White House, 2006. http://www.whitehouse.gov/nsc/nss/2006/.

———. *Project BioShield: Progress in the War on Terror.* http://www.whitehouse.gov/infocus/bioshield/.

Winslow, Frances E. "Intergovernmental Challenges and California's Approach to Emergency Management." In *Disaster Management in the U.S. and Canada.* 2nd ed., edited by Richard T. Sylves and William L. Waugh Jr. Springfield, Ill.: Charles C. Thomas, 1996.

Wise, Charles R. "Organizing for Homeland Security." *Public Administration Review* 62, no. 2 (2002): 131–144.

Wise, Charles R., and Rania Nader. "Organizing the Federal System for Homeland Security: Problems, Issues, and Dilemmas." *Public Administration Review* 62 (2002): 44–57.

Witt, James Lee. "Military Role in Natural Disaster Response." *Disaster Preparedness* 1, no. 1 (Summer 2006). http://www.wilburforce.edu/cdsp/cdsp_art2_01.html.

Witt, James L., and J. Morgan. *Stronger in the Broken Places: Ten Lessons for Turning Crisis into Triumph.* New York: Times Books, 2002.

Wood, A., R. Apthorpe, and J. Borton, eds. *Evaluating International Humanitarian Action.* London: Zed Books, 2001.

Wright, Deil S. "Models of National/State/Local Relations." *American Intergovernmental Relations,* edited by Laurence J. O'Toole Jr. Washington, D.C.: Congressional Quarterly, 1985.

———. *Understanding Intergovernmental Relations.* 3rd ed. Pacific Grove, Calif.: Brooks/Cole, 1988.

abstract reasoning   Helps produce testable propositions and knowledge that is generalizable and applicable in many contexts. Helpful in mathematical computation, in logic, and in making comparisons and identifying various associations among different types or sets of data and information.

all-hazards emergency management   Assumes common sets of emergency preparedness and response procedures and practices are applicable in any locality and that an economy of scale is achieved by planning and preparing for disaster in generic terms rather than for each unique type.

analytical approaches   Approaches and models that allow for experimentation, trial, and error. They were the early basis of public policy analysis.

applied heuristics approach   Based on heuristics, verbal explanatory sketches, or conceptual frameworks that help public managers produce adequate explanations for puzzling things. Heuristics embody propositions subject to confirmation or disconfirmation; that is, their usefulness can be tested.

best-practices approach   Stems from wisdom gained from practice. If followed in accord with the social scientific approach, this approach may help produce scholarship that is a basis for practice.

big science   A term used to refer to fields of disaster study that require substantial outside funding and expensive technical equipment in order for scientists to pursue their research and experimentation, putting many disaster researchers in the world of government lobbying. One assumption of big science is that the growing dependence of researchers on government funding and participation means that more and more research has to be conducted under terms acceptable to the government.

"blue helmeted" UN peacekeeping soldiers   Contributed by various member states, UN peacekeepers are "soldiers, police officers, and military observers" from the UN member countries. UN blue helmeted soldiers are paid volunteers, counted on to provide the logistical and physical contributions necessary to carry out UN disaster relief and recovery missions.

bottom-up approach   In U.S. intergovernmental relations, the assumption that primary responsibility for emergency management lies with local political subdivisions (towns, cities, and counties) and the local officials and emergency managers or responders within those respective jurisdictions.

bureaucratic politics   A set of theories that strives to explain the motives of public executives and managers as they make decisions. They suggest that the desire of these public officials to protect or promote their own and their agency's special interests, as they compete with other agencies, forms a major motivating factor in shaping the timing and the content of their decisions.

bureaucratic "turf wars"   An expression that denotes heavy competition for jurisdiction and budget funding among government bureaus and agencies, even those within the same department of the executive branch.

buyout programs   Programs, usually noncompulsory, involving the direct government purchase of houses or other structures from owners on account of extremely high disaster risk or repeated damage to the structures by the same disaster agent. Federal emergency managers sometimes use buyouts to help stanch the problem of recurring national flood insurance loss claims and to reduce government postdisaster relief spending.

camcorder politics   Politicization of major and minor disasters before, during, and after the time they occur fueled by the ability, since the early 1980s, of television news programs to cover breaking stories worldwide through the use of portable camcorders and other technology. News commentators and reporters as well as political officials and pundits help create a "politics of a disaster" and so are customarily parts of the phenomenon.

"CARVER" technique   A technique designed to evaluate the nation's critical infrastructure, used by federal agencies since 2005. Developed by the Department of Defense for military target prioritization purposes, the CARVER acronym stands for Criticality, Accessibility, Recoverability, Vulnerability, Effect, and Recognizability.

catastrophic incidents   Any natural or manmade incident, including terrorism, that results in extraordinary levels of mass casualties, damage, or disruption severely affecting the population, infrastructure, environment, economy, and national morale or government functions.

chemical, biological, radiological, or nuclear (CBRN)   Types of weapons of mass destruction that terrorists may seek to acquire and use. A core mission of U.S. homeland security policy is to prevent terrorists from obtaining, transporting, and detonating such weapons; denying them the opportunity to develop CBRN weapons on their own; and developing countermeasures and recovery strategies in the event a CBRN weapon is detonated or released.

civil defense   A U.S. national policy since World War I aimed at preparing the nation for possible attack by enemy nations. After 1949, civil defense policy transitioned to preparation for nuclear attack but became defunct after the end of the cold war.

civil defense preparedness   During the cold war, from about 1949 to 1990, various civil defense measures taken against the possibility of nuclear attack. Tools of civil defense preparedness have included mass evacuation planning, public shelter programs, and home fallout shelters.

codified knowledge   Impersonal knowledge that is learned through thinking and reasoning, not through social relationships. Such knowledge is often conveyed through scholarly publications.

command and control strategies   The hierarchical relations in which those in subordinate positions working in a bureaucratic organization are expected to strictly comply with the orders or instructions of their immediate supervisor, thus creating a chain of command.

complex humanitarian emergencies (CHEs)   The designation of a CHE signifies that a country or region is at or near complete breakdown of civil authority, something occasionally resulting from a major natural disaster. CHEs sometimes involve ethnic conflict, displacement of population groups, market collapse, and mass starvation. In a CHE, the success or failure of a disaster relief operation often rests on the degree of coordination, the fairness and equality in relief distribution, and whether the relief effort connects with (or at least does not impede) the country's reconstruction and economic development.

congressional dominance model   Postulates that the political geography of presidential disaster declaration issuance over time demonstrates FEMA's effort to reward congressional lawmakers on its authorizations and appropriations oversight committees.

coordinate-authority model   A theory of intergovernmental relations that assumes a sharp and distinct boundary between separate national and state governments. National and state governments appear to operate independently and autonomously, and they are linked only tangentially. In the model, local governments are abjectly dependent on their respective state governments.

counterterrorism   Offensive measures taken to prevent, deter, and respond to terrorism and terrorist attacks. Along with antiterrorism, it is the core mission of U.S. homeland security policy and involves threat detection, prevention, mitigation, target hardening, policing, and other preparedness and response activities.

Crisis Relocation Plan (CRP)   Part of civil defense planning against nuclear attack. Done at the state level with federal funds, common CRP activity included provision for population relocation, food distribution, and medical care.

crying poor syndrome   An expression sometimes voiced by federal officials to characterize the behavior of governors, mayors, or other government leaders seeking presidential declarations of major disaster. They allege that these leaders "cry poor" after relatively small-scale disasters by insisting that their respective jurisdictions are unable to respond to or recover from the "disaster" without the federal help a disaster declaration would provide. Sometimes, governors and other state officials accuse local government officials of engaging in the same behavior in order to secure undeserved state disaster relief.

decentralization   Refers to the decentralized nature of the U.S. government and its functions; it is necessary due to the great size and population of the nation, the thousands of subnational governments, and the U.S. system of federalism. It is also part of a national policy of devolution of certain federal powers back to the state and local levels.

development banks   Institutions, called multilateral development banks and multilateral financial institutions, that provide financial support and professional advice for economic and social development activities in developing countries. Many have taken considerable interest in disaster management.

disaster management   The tactical and operational implementation of an emergency planning strategy at the time of a crisis. In presidentially declared emergencies and disasters, emergency managers are also disaster managers both in strategic and tactical terms. The terms "disaster management" and "emergency management" are often used interchangeably in this book.

Disaster Reduction and Recovery Program   A UN program focused on the demobilization of combatants, landmine clearance, the reintegration of refugees and internally displaced persons, and a plan for restoration of governance in a disaster-affected country.

disaster research   Conducted by a broad array of experts in the physical sciences and engineering, the geosciences, the atmospheric sciences, biomedicine, physical geography, and the information sciences. Researchers also include disaster sociologists, political scientists, economists, social geographers, demographers, and urban planners.

disciplinary parochiality Lack of interdisciplinary collaboration that often works to the detriment of broad-based hazard research and disaster studies important in educating emergency managers. People working within specific and specialized academic disciplines, and whose reputations are built as the result of their achievements in their respective discipline, have a tendency and incentive to ignore the work of those in other disciplines.

domestic incidents Acts of terrorism and disasters in the homeland stemming from natural or other human causes. Their management was addressed by the secretary of homeland security in the National Response Plan and the National Incident Management System. In official terms, domestic incidents came to represent a marriage of conventional disaster management and terrorism consequence management.

Doppler radar A type of detection technology used by the National Weather Service at facilities across the country. The early detection of tornadoes that Doppler radar may provide could allow authorities to issue life-saving watches or warnings before a tornado forms or in advance of its impact.

dual federalism A government system in which sovereignty is constitutionally split between at least two territorial levels so that units at each level have final authority and can act independently of the other in some areas. Citizens thus have political obligations to two authorities. In U.S. history, the period from 1789 to 1901 has been termed the era of "dual" federalism, because there was little collaboration between the national and state governments.

dual-use approach Approved in law in 1973, an approach in which civil defense activities could also be used conjointly to prepare for natural disasters. The merging of civil defense and natural disaster management.

earthquake retrofitting Structural improvements made to existing buildings or infrastructure that enable these structures to retain their integrity and protect their occupants against seismic forces greater than those they were originally designed to withstand.

EMAP Standard The Emergency Management Accreditation Program, a joint project of FEMA, the International Association of Emergency Managers, and the National Emergency Management Association, sets forth an appropriate level of emergency management. State and local governments, through a series of steps, are peer reviewed and ultimately judged worthy or unworthy of EMAP Standard accreditation.

emergency declaration A category of presidential declaration authorized in law in the Disaster Relief Act of 1974 and issued as a matter of life and safety before an event or when a disaster is still transpiring. Unlike major disaster declarations, emergency declarations can be issued by the president with or without a governor's request, and governors are not required to document need or estimate losses as a condition of their request.

emergency declaration assistance Type of assistance provided by the federal government under a presidential declaration of emergency, which confers a more modest range of assistance than does a declaration of major disaster. State and local governments receive support and technical help and various forms of federally dispensed emergency aid and furnish debris removal grants. Disaster victims are entitled to receive grants for temporary housing and for uninsured personal needs, as well as medicines, food, and consumables.

emergency management The discipline and profession of applying science, technology, planning, and management to deal with extreme events that can injure or kill great numbers of people, do extensive property damage, and disrupt community life. Efforts are made to limit losses and costs through the implementation of strategies and tactics reflecting the full life cycle of disaster: preparedness, response, recovery, and mitigation.

Emergency Management Assistance Compact Originally an agreement between fourteen states and territories made during 1995–1996 that committed them, through their respective governors, to cooperate in planning for state-to-state extension of emergency management help. Today all the states belong to EMAC.

emergency-management-oriented multinational organizations Organizations working independently or through multistate arrangements that promote emergency management work and capabilities in developing nations.

Emergency Management Performance Grants (EMPGs) Allocated by FEMA to state and local governments to improve their intrastate emergency management programs and their mitigation, preparedness, response, and recovery capabilities for disasters of any type.

emergency manager   A person who manages a comprehensive program for hazards and disasters, and who is responsible in whole or in part for disaster mitigation, preparedness, response, and recovery within his or her government jurisdiction or organization.

Emergency Response Division   A division of the UN Development Programme created in 1995. It deploys response teams to disaster sites to help coordinate relief and recovery efforts of other UN agencies and nongovernmental organizations with the efforts of disaster-stricken national governments. The teams also prepare comprehensive redevelopment projects in disaster recovery operations.

emergency supplementals   Congressional appropriations often used to pay for megadisasters or catastrophes that swallow up all available spending authority in the President's Disaster Fund. Legislators sometimes use this almost veto-proof legislation to add nongermane spending riders (special amendments) that would not win majority votes or enactment any other way.

emergent organizations   Organizations that form spontaneously after a disaster.

entitlement program   A type of government program that provides individuals, and sometimes corporations or state or local governments, with financial benefits or special government-provided goods or services under terms in which potential beneficiaries have a legal right (enforceable in court, if necessary) to the benefits whenever they meet eligibility conditions that are specified by the law that authorizes the program.

ethical code   Expresses principles and practices of behavior. Often adopted by a profession and promulgated by a government agency responsible for licensing a profession. Violations of these codes may be subject to remedies that are administrative (for example, loss of license), civil, or criminal.

event driven   Decisions on policy and politics influenced by the latest memorable disaster or catastrophe. The flaws of event-driven policymaking include a preoccupation or fixation with the type of major disaster that most recently occurred; a failure to maintain a coherent, balanced, all-hazards emergency management capability; and a tendency to be underprepared for disasters that do not mimic or parallel the last major disaster or catastrophe.

faith-based voluntary organizations   Organizations established by recognized and organized religions. Those that accept federal disaster relief funding are prohibited from engaging in unlawful forms of discrimination and from proselytizing their religion or distributing religious materials in the course of dispensing disaster relief.

federalism   The theory or advocacy of federal political orders, where final authority is divided between subunits and a center. Unlike a unitary state system, in a federal system sovereignty is constitutionally split between at least two territorial levels so that units at each level have final authority and can act independently of the others in some area or domain of policy.

federal-state agreements   Usually, negotiated agreements between specific federal agencies and their state government agency counterparts. From about 1979 through 2003, FEMA's relationship with states and localities was primarily through agreements with state offices of emergency management and then, by extension, with local emergency management offices.

federal zoning   Zoning by the authority of the federal government. It is fiercely contested by protectors of local land-use authority, who perceive it as federal encroachment into matters of local land use, zoning, and building regulation. This perception has sometimes impeded federal efforts to promote disaster mitigation at the local level, such as National Flood Insurance Program risk mapping of local governments.

FEMA federal regions   Ten regions geographically distributed in accord with the ten standard federal region format used by most federal departments and agencies. Each is directed by a politically appointed regional director, whose regional offices are located in a major city of the respective region.

fraudulent claims   False documentation or other forms of deceit in people's applications for government assistance.

functional federalism   A theory that identifies distinctive areas of competence for each level of government and that assumes that local governments are best suited to design and implement development programs, particularly those involving physical and social infrastructure. Assumes local governments are best suited to determine their own needs and make provision for their fulfillment in accord with local taxpayer preferences and willingness to pay.

generalists   Broadly educated people, who in public management are likely to be highly politically responsive and able to fulfill government executive obligations of public responsiveness. It is assumed that generalists are better able than specialists to address humanitarian aspects of disaster assistance and are better able to work compatibly with others in the intergovernmental world of domestic disaster management.

generalized knowledge   Furnishes reasoning tools or conceptual lenses that hold explanatory power applicable within or across a wide variety of cases and circumstances.

globalizing forces   The massive movement of individuals, capital, goods, information, and technologies across borders, which bonds developing nations to new and old industrialized nations. Disasters and this interdependence combine to produce negative, destabilizing effects in many developing nations.

governmental politics model   Also the "bureaucratic politics model," developed by political scientist Graham Allison, which posits that presidential decision making may be explained as the result of recommendations of senior political appointees and other elites, these often thrashed out after considerable argument, competition, bargaining, and negotiation.

Hamiltonian public managers   A normative theory of public management in which public managers must learn and apply a growing body of knowledge, some of it practical knowledge and some of it academic knowledge. Hamiltonian public managers embody an authority of expertise, have mastered a specialized field of theoretical and applied knowledge, and are considered technocratic officials.

HAZUS and HAZUS-MH   HAZUS, an earthquake computer simulation applicable and adaptable to most of the nation developed by FEMA in the 1990s, is a powerful risk assessment software program for analyzing potential losses from earthquakes. HAZUS-MH, a newer generation of HAZUS, models potential losses from hurricanes, winds, and floods as well as earthquakes for specific locations across the nation.

Homeland Security Advisory System (HSAS)   A threat-based, color-coded five-tiered system used to communicate to the American public and safety officials the status of terrorist threat to the nation or to parts of the nation.

horizontal fragmentation   What sometimes happens when a disaster or emergency must be addressed by many competing government agencies, all working at the same level of government but with different duties and functions and sometimes overlapping jurisdictions. It occurs when officials of these agencies fail to coordinate their responsibilities with one another, act too independently of one another, duplicate their efforts, or work at cross-purposes.

humanitarian assistance   Involves concern for human welfare and social reforms. Within the realm of disaster humanitarian assistance, acute postdisaster concerns involve providing emergency food, water, shelter, medical services and supplies, clothing, and other items to disaster victims in order to ensure their immediate survival.

incidents of national significance   High-impact events that, under the National Response Plan, require an extensive and well-coordinated multiagency response to save lives, minimize damage, and provide the basis for long-term community and economic recovery. The president or the secretary of homeland security may declare incidents of national significance, which may be acts of terrorism or major disasters or emergencies. The concept of incidents of national significance was discontinued in 2008 under the National Response Framework.

inclusive authority model   A model of intergovernmental relations in which each level of government has a diminishing proportion of responsibilities, from the national to the state to the local government level. The federal government coordinates and shares power and responsibility; however, the authority is essentially hierarchical (top-down control).

Individual and Family Grant (IFG) program   Funds state-administered programs that, under a presidential declaration of major disaster, provide disaster victims cash help for essential needs. Established by the Disaster Relief Act of 1974, IFG operates under a 75/25 federal/state matching requirement and is one of eight human services programs managed by FEMA.

individual and household assistance   A set of federal postdisaster assistance programs available to individuals, families, or household groups under terms of a presidential declaration of major disaster or emergency. Among types of aid are financial grants to rent alternative housing, direct assistance through temporary housing units (mobile homes), limited financial assistance for housing repairs and replacement, and financial assistance for uninsured medical, dental, funeral, personal property, and transportation expenses.

intergovernmental relations   The interaction and exchanges of public and private organizations across all layers of government. Intergovernmental relations reflect the growth of societal interdependence, in economic and technological terms, and have created a webbed and networked system of governance.

issue-attention cycle   A pattern of public perception of certain domestic problems. The cycle has five stages and concerns the way major communications media interact with the public.

issue salience   The importance of an issue to the public and to elected leaders.

Jeffersonian public managers A normative theory of public management in which public managers possess skill in consultation, negotiation, and communication and deftness in probing for public understanding and consent. Jeffersonian public managers are broadly educated generalists who are strictly accountable to the public and to elected overseers.

limited federal response The tendency of Congress to pass a new law in the aftermath of each major disaster that provides additional routine relief funding, often largely symbolically, but which does little to address either the fundamental underlying causes of the disaster or problems in the system of disaster management as a whole.

major disaster assistance Postdisaster federal assistance made available to disaster victims, as well as to state and local governments, under the terms of a presidential declaration of major disaster.

major disaster declaration A category of presidential declaration established initially by the Federal Disaster Act of 1950 and revised and augmented by the Stafford Act of 1988. It opens the door to federal disaster assistance, mobilizes federal agencies to respond in accord with a national response plan or framework, specifies one or more political jurisdictions (a state and eligible counties), delineates who is eligible for relief, and contains an initial statement about the kinds of assistance people or subnational governments may request. Acting on a governor's request for such a declaration, the president has authority to approve it or turn it down.

martial law Temporary rule by military authority imposed upon a civilian population in time of war or when civil authority is unable to maintain public safety. In the United States both the president and state governors hold authority to declare martial law. Presidents are likely to apply it only under extreme conditions of war, national emergency, or crisis. Governors sometimes declare martial law in state emergencies and disasters, using the state National Guard to carry it out.

memorandums of understanding (MOU) Administrative agreements, usually voluntary and usually negotiated by officials of various government agencies, which in emergency management establish commitments regarding how each agency will cooperate with the others and what specific duties will be performed in future disasters or emergencies.

Metropolitan Medical Response System (MMRS) Developed after the 1995 Oklahoma City bombing to ensure that big-city police and fire departments had the training and equipment to care for multiple victims of a nuclear, biological, or chemical attack. MMRS provides funding to write plans, develop training, purchase equipment or pharmaceuticals, and conduct exercises related to catastrophic incidents, whether caused by terrorists or natural forces.

mitigation Activities, laws, or policies that attempt to prevent disasters or reduce potential losses from disasters. Mitigation is often between-disaster activity. Mitigation may be structural (engineered) or nonstructural (behavior changes, zoning laws, land-use restrictions, and the like).

moral hazard An increase in the probability of loss caused by the behavior of a holder of insurance. In the realm of the insurance market, those whose homes are insured behave carelessly or dishonestly by failing to take reasonable measures to protect their homes from a known disaster threat because they expect that insurance will cover their losses if a disaster transpires. In the realm of government, this applies when lower-level governments forgo reasonable disaster mitigation measures because their leaders expect postdisaster assistance from upper-level government to cover their losses and so they believe they have realized a savings by not spending money on predisaster mitigation.

multihazard approach An approach in which the government would manage all kinds of hazards, rather than maintaining unique and separated capacities to deal with different types of disaster agents. To the extent possible, methods and tools used to address one type of disaster would be applied to a variety of types.

mutual aid agreements Written agreements, often formal and matters of law, between agencies or government jurisdictions to assist one another on request by making available personnel, equipment, and expertise in a specified manner.

National Incident Management System (NIMS) The elaborate tactical arm of the National Response Plan, designed to help federal, state, and local governments address domestic incidents, whether acts of terrorism or disasters stemming from natural or other human causes. All federal agencies were required to adopt NIMS and to make its adoption a requirement for other governmental entities receiving federal assistance.

national planning scenarios Fifteen "planning scenarios" developed by the Department of Homeland Security, intended to be used in evaluating the ability of a jurisdiction to manage a major disaster. They encompass the range of "plausible" events, most of them stemming from terror attacks involving weapons of mass destruction, that are assumed to pose the greatest risk to the nation.

national preparedness A set of goals established by the secretary of homeland security under Homeland Security Presidential Directive-8 (HSPD-8), primarily focused on preparedness for terrorism-related events, especially the training and equipping of emergency response agencies.

National Response Plan (NRP) A comprehensive all-hazards approach and master plan intended to strengthen and improve the ability of the United States to manage domestic incidents. Under the NRP, the secretary of homeland security has the primary responsibility for managing domestic crises and requires federal, state, and local authorities to work in unison, or at least in more coordinated ways, to manage domestic incidents. In 2008 the federal government officially reissued the NRP, with some changes, as the National Response Framework.

National Special Security Events (NSSEs) An "incident of national significance" category. NSSEs are designated by the president and usually encompass any high-profile, large-scale event the president believes may be vulnerable to terror attack.

new normal A new view of normalcy in the national psyche and in the domain of disaster policy and homeland security brought about by certain disasters, often catastrophes, that stress the nation's disaster management system and force massive policy reforms. First postulated by Donald F. Kettl, in *System under Stress.*

nonprofit voluntary organizations Organizations composed largely, but not exclusively, of volunteers. Faith-based or not, they are often part of both the official and unofficial response to a disaster or emergency, and all enjoy a nontaxable federal income tax status, as well as exemption from various state and local income and property taxes. Those who make cash and in-kind donations to these organizations often enjoy a federal income tax deduction that effectively subsidizes their contributions. Some of these organizations operate internationally as well as inside the United States.

nonstructural hazard mitigation The use of "soft" engineering and other approaches, such as zoning laws, building codes, land-use regulations, and education of the public, to buffer wetlands against flooding, protect coast lines and barrier islands from erosion and development, encourage the use of landscaping that protects structures from flooding or wildfires, and otherwise protect hazard-prone, high-risk areas.

nonterrorism missions The original missions of FEMA and other agencies that became part of the Department of Homeland Security in 2003. These agencies, including FEMA, are still struggling to fulfill both their terrorism-related duties and their original nonterrorism missions.

Northern Command (NORTHCOM) Refers to the North American Command, which provides command and control of Department of Defense homeland defense efforts and coordinates the defense support the military provides to civil authorities. NORTHCOM's mission is to help prevent terrorist attacks on the homeland by militarily defeating attacks by foreigners if possible, protecting U.S. borders or air space from encroachment or penetration by attackers, and aiding in the response to an incident involving a weapon of mass destruction inside the United States.

occupations Categories of jobs, livelihoods, or vocations. People in certain occupations may be represented by labor unions or trade unions, but the occupations themselves may not necessarily conform to the definition of a "profession."

organizational process model Model developed by political scientist Graham Allison, which posits that presidential decisions are essentially a routine administrative determination handled by a stovepipe-connected assortment of lower-level government officials. In this model the president or executive has either largely delegated decision authority to someone else or rubber-stamps the official recommendation of his or her functionaries.

overlapping-authority model A model of intergovernmental relations in which substantial areas of governmental operations involve national, state, and local governments simultaneously. Areas of autonomy or single-jurisdiction independence and full discretion are relatively small. Power and influence for any one jurisdiction is substantially limited, and authority patterns involve heavy bargaining.

partisan mutual adjustment A political theory that posits that public managers clash owing to their respective personal political motivations, their respective obligations to the law (laws differ from agency to agency) and to the agencies they lead, and their respective commitments to their elected executive and legislative overseers. Political appointees and top civil servant administrators work in a system of organic interdependence.

performance partnerships A type of negotiated agreement, which for many years FEMA used in its administrative transactions with state emergency management organizations, and through these state organizations, local emergency management organizations. Performance partnerships were based on collaborative schemes through which various federal funds were disbursed by FEMA to state and local emergency management agencies under pre-arranged levels and terms of agency performance.

"Plum Book" spoils system   A listing of presidentially appointed positions within the federal government, published every four years by a House or Senate committee. Plum Book positions are a reward for, or acknowledgment of, personal or political support (often owing to campaign work or campaign contributions). Most Plum Book positions do not require Senate confirmation.

political pressure groups   Organized interest groups that apply pressure, through lobbying or other avenues, to government officials, including agency administrators and legislators, in order to advance their own interests or other interests they consider important.

preparedness   Activities, laws, or policies designed to increase readiness or improve capabilities for disaster response and recovery operations. A predisaster activity aimed at helping the public survive and cope with the effects of possible future disasters.

President's Disaster Relief Fund   The main repository of federal disaster spending authority available to the president. Funded from an annual congressional appropriation and from residual, accumulated spending authority on previous disasters, it is often replenished and expanded to pay for extremely costly disasters by congressionally approved disaster supplemental appropriations.

principal-agent theory   Assumes that managers (the principals) function in an environment in which they cannot observe whether their agents (subordinate workers and contractors) in fact carried out the instructions they issued. The theory, from economics and used extensively in performance-based government contracting studies, also assumes that agents hide information from principals and may use the information to act in ways contrary to what principals intended.

private contractors   For-profit government contractors, often corporations and other business entities. They are used by the federal government, as well as by subnational governments, as part of the official response to a disaster and to carry out certain tasks or to produce certain products for the short or long term. Although government contractors usually have to go through a public bidding process, sometimes the slowness of that process has prompted the issuance of "no-bid" contracts, which have often become subjects of political controversy.

profession   A vocation that is esoteric, complex, and discretionary and embodies self-directing work. It requires theoretical knowledge, skill, and judgment that others may not possess or cannot easily comprehend. Theory-grounded knowledge, acquired through higher education, is the basis of most professions.

professional body   Sets examinations of competence for a profession, acts as licensing authority for practitioners of the profession, and enforces adherence to an ethical code of conduct adopted by the professional association it serves. Most professions are regulated by respective professional bodies or organizations of some type.

Project BioShield   Seeks to develop and make available modern, effective drugs and vaccines to protect against attack by chemical, biological, radiological, or nuclear weapons. The project was launched by President George W. Bush in 2004.

public works   A constructed internal improvement that augments a government's economic infrastructure. The term is often used interchangeably with "municipal infrastructure" or "urban infrastructure."

rational actor model   Model set forth by political scientist Graham Allison and widely applied in international relations and in organizational theory that posits that the president (or national leader of some type) makes decisions largely on his or her own, as a unitary actor, on behalf of the entire national government. It also assumes that individual rationality inheres in that decision making.

recovery   Begins as a disaster is ending or at the close of the disaster response phase. Involving activities, laws, or policies that return disaster-affected governments, communities, and people to their predisaster conditions, it may take months or years to complete and is usually the most expensive phase in the disaster cycle.

response   Begins when a disaster event occurs or is imminent. It is also activities, laws, or policies applied in the immediate aftermath of a disaster to protect life and property, prevent secondary disaster effects, and reconstitute government operation.

reinventing government movement   An extension of the New Public Management movement of the 1990s, a movement that offered low-level administrators more power and, informed by modern management consultants, concluded that organizations need to rediscover the importance of customer satisfaction. It also advocated broader governance, under which public and private sector organizations might work together under more cooperative or blended arrangements.

securitization   Involves extension of national security concerns into other domains of public policy, including emergency management. Securitization also involves development of new types of security-related research and technologies.

security classification   A means of government protection of sensitive information from unauthorized disclosure. The federal government maintains a tiered system of security classification, and individuals may be granted security clearances following background checks, their taking of legal oaths that they will not divulge secret information, and other requirements.

seismic building codes   Intended to protect people inside or near buildings by preventing collapse and allowing for safe evacuation. Structures built according to code are earthquake resistant, not earthquake proof. They should be able to resist minor earthquakes undamaged, moderate earthquakes without significant structural damage, and severe earthquakes without collapse.

seismic mapping   Serves as the basis for seismic provisions used in building codes and influences how and where new construction or seismic retrofitting takes place every year.

self-help   A government policy of encouraging individual responsibility for disaster preparedness, and conversely, less public dependence on government for the same purpose.

social catastrophe   Catastrophic disaster in which forces of structural racism and social inequality cause the poor and people of color to suffer disproportionately.

social constructivism   Explains problems and policy issues by focusing on people's behavior and beliefs rather than on the putative "conditions" that are the object of those actions. Social constructivists maintain that it is the actions and persuasiveness of people, perhaps amplified through mass communications, which define what a phenomenon is or is not.

stakeholders   Persons, singly or in a group, who have, or think they have, something to gain or lose. In emergency management, they are people and organized interests affected by the decisions of policymakers and emergency managers. Some stakeholders unselfishly seek benefits or protections for the people or groups whose interests they champion.

State Homeland Security Grant Program   A Department of Homeland Security program that provides funds to state and local governments for help in planning, equipping, and training, a well as exercise activities intended to improve their ability to prepare for, prevent, and respond to terrorist attacks and other disasters. The program also supports the implementation of state homeland security strategies and key elements of the national preparedness architecture, including the National Preparedness Goal, the National Incident Management System, and the National Response Plan.

structural hazard mitigation   Efforts to contain a hazard, such as building dams and other flood abatement works and coastal infrastructure, or strengthening buildings and other structures to withstand disaster stresses. Often entails use of "hard" engineered structures.

tacit knowledge   Vague and ambiguous knowledge that depends on sharing expectations and values through social relationships. Neither easily conveyed nor learned from the outside, this form of knowledge is often acquired through internships, apprenticeships, mentoring, or on-the-job socialization experiences.

target capability   A term that refers to the ability of a government jurisdiction to prevent, or respond to, a range of different types of terrorist attacks on specific likely targets within a jurisdiction.

technocrat   Official of a public bureaucracy who possesses special knowledge and expertise most average citizens do not have and who works under norms of objectivity and political neutrality.

territorial sovereignty   The internationally recognized principle that a government should be the ultimate authority within the boundaries of its jurisdiction and should be free of unwanted external interference.

terrorism consequence management   All government activities undertaken to address the effects or aftermath of a terrorist-caused disaster or emergency. These include not only emergency responder functions but also law enforcement, intelligence work, and the like.

tolerated disaster vulnerabilities   Unintentionally overlooked, discounted, or deliberately dismissed disaster risk vulnerabilities, which are thus tolerated. Human settlement patterns, commercial and government building decisions and infrastructure construction, and known geophysical and meteorological phenomena often combine to create a realm of tolerated disaster vulnerabilities.

top-down command and control system   A form of command and control under which federal officials get to assume top-down leadership positions, and state and local authorities are expected to submit to their direction.

unemployment assistance   A program of disaster assistance administered by states as agents of the federal government. It provides financial help to individuals whose employment or self-employment has been lost or interrupted as a direct result of a major disaster declared by the president.

Universal Task List Developed by the Department of Homeland Security to describe what tasks need to be performed, who needs to perform them, and how to perform them in the event of terrorist attack disaster or natural or human-caused (nonterror) disaster. The Universal Task List contains some 1,600 different tasks, and local government officials are expected to maintain a correct list of all the resources needed and available to fulfill each task.

Urban Area Security Initiative (UASI) Authorized by federal law in 2005 to facilitate rapid response in the nation's fifty largest cities to attacks from weapons of mass destruction. UASI addresses planning, operations, equipment acquisition, training, and exercise needs and provides financial assistance based on a risk-and-needs approach. Funding allotments are determined by a formula that combines threat estimates, critical assets within the urban area, and population density.

vertical fragmentation Occurs in disaster management when officials of these the levels of government—federal, state, and local—fail to coordinate their responsibilities, act too independently of one another, duplicate their efforts, or work at cross-purposes, or when one level of government fails to carry out its obligations in an intergovernmentally organized system.

volition Refers to a conscious choice or decision made by an individual or group. In the realm of disaster risk, individuals use volition when they are aware of the degree of risk or the extent of vulnerability and intentionally decide to assume that risk or accept that vulnerability in some action they take.

voluntary risk A risk accepted on one's own initiative or from one's own free will. The reverse, involuntary risk, implies that a risk is imposed upon someone without that person's agreement, permission, or perhaps even knowledge.

War on Terrorism Also known as the War on Terror, a policy authorized by Congress under the Authorization for Use of Military Force against Terrorists resolution enacted into law following the September 11, 2001, attacks on the United States. Both the phrase "War on Terrorism" and the policies it denotes have been a source of ongoing controversy, as critics argue they have been used to justify unilateral preemptive war, perpetual war, human rights abuses, and other violations of international law.

Abstract reasoning, 32
Accreditation, 7, 20–21, 33
Active-duty military, 172. *See also* Military response
The Administrative State (Waldo), 31
Afghanistan, 172, 174, 223
Africa, 8, 197, 198
Agency for International Development (AID),
   197–200, 202, 205–207
Agnes (tropical storm), 19, 55
Agriculture Department, 57
Airline hijackings, 60, 70
Airport security, 111
Alabama, 157
"Alarmed discovery" stage, 10–11
Alaska, 8, 50, 124, 181
Allbaugh, Joseph, 226
Allen, Thad, 175
All-hazards management, 112
      concept explained, 17
      intergovernmental relations, 221
      policy evolution, 50, 55, 56, 58, 65–70, 75, 79,
         171, 217
      terrorism focus, 4, 43, 67, 70, 73, 134, 150,
         185, 188
Allison, Graham T., 35, 39, 116, 214–215
Ambassadors, 198–199, 206
American Hospital Association, 63
American Medical Association, 63
American Planning Association, 6
American Public Works Association, 6
American Red Cross, 134, 146, 158, 159
American Samoa, 197
American Society for Public Administration
      Section on Emergency and Crisis Management, 6
AmeriCorps, 162
Analytical approaches, 37–38
Anthrax-laced letter attacks, 111, 119
Antiballistic missile program, 60, 64
Antipandemic preparedness, 85
Antipoverty social policy, 227
Applied heuristics approach, 36–37
Arceneaux, Kevin, 63
Architecture, 7
Arkansas, 65
Armed Services Committee, 66
Army Corps of Engineers, 8, 19, 90, 110, 129, 131,
   165, 176
Army Department, 44
Asia, 197, 198, 200
Asian Development Bank, 201
"Assignment of Emergency Preparedness
   Responsibilities" (Reagan executive order), 64–65
Assistance to Firefighters Grant Program, 118, 188
Assistance to individuals and households, 139
Atmospheric research, 3, 109

Atomic bomb, 5, 48
Attorney General, 116
Aum Shinrikyo cult, 118
Australia, 96
Automobile insurance, 97
Aviation security, 111

Bangladesh, 205
Bayh, Birch, 50
Bechtel Corp., 165
Best-practices approaches, 34–37, 215
"Big science," 110
bin Laden, Osama, 66
Biological warfare, 118–120
Biomedical research, 109
Bioterrorism preparedness, 85, 109, 111
Birkland, Thomas A., 217
Blanco, Kathleen, 144
Bloomberg, Michael R., 15, 36
"Blue-helmeted" peacekeeping soldiers, 205–206
Bomb disposal, 111
Booz Allen Hamilton Corp., 164
Border security, 172
Bottom-up approach, 73, 135, 171
Botulin antitoxin, 119
Bradley, Ed, 142
Bradshaw, Larry, 142, 144
Brinkley, Douglas, 142
Brown, Harold, 59
Brown, Michael, 83, 141, 144, 231
Building sciences, 17, 30, 110, 212
Building supply stores, 111
Building trades, 63
Bureaucratic politics, 56
      model, features and use of, 34, 35, 39, 45,
         214–215
      New York City example, 14–15
      organization culture of, 34
      turf wars, 42–43, 141, 144, 214
Bureau for Humanitarian Response, 198
Bush, George H. W., 60–62, 64, 65, 85, 86, 92,
   101, 216, 217, 225
Bush, George W., 226
      appointment politics, 219, 225
      disaster declarations, 24, 79, 84, 95, 99, 101
      homeland security policy, 70, 72, 73, 217
      management style, 87
      militarization of disaster policy, 173, 175,
         180
      nuclear detection policy, 115–117
      Project BioShield, 119
      public relations, 92
      terrorism focus, 85, 111, 216, 219, 229
Buyout programs, 123, 128
Byrne, Peter, 179

Cabinet Committee to Combat Terrorism, 51
Cable News Network (CNN), 61, 219
California, 61, 65, 69, 113, 124, 130, 145, 157, 167
Camcorder politics, 61, 92
Canada, 96, 180, 181
Capability-based planning, 189
Capability Enhancement Plan, 185
Carafano, James Jay, 173, 182
Caribbean Disaster Emergency Response Agency, 201
Caribbean region, 197, 198
Carter, Jimmy, 64, 74, 75
    disaster declarations, 61, 92, 103
    FEMA politics, 56–59, 217
    management style, 86
    Mariel boatlift, 24, 65, 85
"CARVER" technique, 190–191
Castro, Fidel, 24, 65, 85
Catastrophic incidents, 82, 83, 106, 112, 157
Categories of assistance, 138
Categories of disasters, 196
Catholic Charities, 158
CBS News, 142
Centers for Disease Control and Prevention, 131
Central America, 204
Central Emergency Revolving Fund, 202
Certification, 7, 33
Certified Emergency Manager program, 7
Challenger space shuttle, 61
"Changes in Urban Occupance of Flood Plains in the
    United States" (White), 19
Charitable organizations. *See* Nonprofit organizations
Chemical warfare, 118–120
Chernobyl nuclear power plant, 61
Chertoff, Michael, 115, 187, 231
Cheyenne Mountain, 179
Chiefs of mission, 198, 206
Church World Services, 158
Citizen Corps, 162
Citizens, as first responders, 154
City managers, 4, 5, 211
Civil defense
    emergency management component, 5, 14, 49–51,
        58, 60, 65–66
    FEMA jurisdiction, 56–59
    intergovernmental relations, 221
    roots of policy, 5, 48, 171, 218, 222
    shift to homeland security, 64–65, 217
Civil Defense Act of 1950, 48, 50, 56, 66, 173, 216
Civil-military relations. *See* Military response
Civil Preparedness Agency, 50, 53, 56
Civil servants, 176, 219, 222
Civil War, 78
Clans, 44
Clear Channel, 126
Climate research, 3, 30, 37, 109, 110, 130
Clinton, Bill, 85, 167
    all-hazards management, 65–67, 69
    cyber security, 129
    disaster declarations, 101, 120, 122
    FEMA politics, 74, 92, 120, 216, 217, 219, 225

management style, 86
    terrorism focus, 111
    Y2K preparedness, 127
Coast Guard, 175, 177, 222
Code of Federal Regulations, 44
Codified knowledge, 43–44
Cold War, 5, 48–51, 59, 64, 65, 218
Color-coded Threat Level System, 181, 183, 184, 189
Columbia space shuttle, 24
Command and control strategies, 134–136
Commerce Department, 54, 57
Communications infrastructure, 129
Communications Office, 87
Communities of stakeholders, 13–14
Community Emergency Response Teams, 189
Community rating system, 23
Compacts, 145–146
Complex humanitarian emergencies, 196
Computer technology, 30, 37, 109, 111
Congressional dominance model, 94
Congressional role, 4, 83, 91, 93–95, 111
Constitutional powers, 4, 77–78, 173, 174, 218
    state powers, 12, 17, 134
Construction industry, 17, 63
Contractors, 131, 134, 135, 163–168, 215, 222
Coordinate-authority model, 39–40
Coordination Center for Natural Disaster Prevention
    in Central America, 201
Corporation for National and Community Service,
    162
Cost-awareness stage, 11
Council on Emergency Management, 6
Counterterrorism, 9, 110, 111, 134, 168
County executives, 5, 63, 211
Crisis evacuation and relocation, 49, 51, 59, 60, 64
Crisis Relocation Plan, 51
"Crying poor" syndrome, 96, 156
Cuban immigrants, 24, 65, 85
Cuban missile crisis, 34, 35
Cult of personality, 44
Cumming, William, 44
Customer satisfaction, 41–43, 45, 216
Cyber security, 129

Dam safety, 57
Darfur region, 196
Data mining, 111
Davis, Steve, 126
Decentralization, 15–18
Decision-making assumptions, 21
Deerfield Beach, Florida, 69
Defense Civil Preparedness Agency, 50, 53, 56
Defense Department (DOD/Pentagon)
    CARVER technique, 190–191
    creation, 70
    domestic disaster policy, 50, 56, 57, 79, 116, 138,
        177, 182
    foreign disaster response, 199–200, 206
    government contractors, 164
    Northern Command, 178–181

terrorist attack, 70, 92, 99, 188
    See also Military response
Demobilization, 128
Demography, 30, 111–112
Department of. *See* specific department names
Department of Defense Authorization Act of 1996,
    Title XIV, 4
Deservedness criteria, 102
Development banks, 195, 201
Devolution, 64
Dewberry Corp., 165–166
Diffused knowledge, 43–44
Dioxin contamination, 114
Diplomatic Corps, 44
Disaster Assistance Response Team, 198–199
Disaster declarations
    by ambassadors, 198–199
    by presidents. *See* Presidential disaster declarations
Disaster insurance. *See* Insurance; specific types of
    insurance
Disaster management
    "emergency management," term compared, 233*n*.2
    See also Emergency management; International
        disaster management
Disaster Management Training Program, 204
Disaster mitigation. *See* Mitigation
Disaster Mitigation Act of 2000, 69
Disaster policy history, 46–75
    all-hazards management, 65–70
    civil defense preparedness, 5, 48–51, 59–60
    dual-use preparedness, 5, 49–51, 57–58
    evolution of disaster policy, 3–5
    FEMA as instrument of presidential power, 62–63
    FEMA established as single coordinating agency,
        56–57
    from civil defense to homeland security, 64–65
    from state and local to federal emergency
        management, 64
    nationwide emergency management focus, 51–56
    overview, 74–75, 216–218
    stakeholders in disaster policy, 63
    television news coverage effects, 61
    terrorism effects, 67, 70, 72–73
    theory and practice, 47–48
Disaster preparedness. *See* Preparedness
Disaster Reduction and Recovery Program, 204
Disaster relief, 3–4, 57
Disaster Relief Act of 1950, 49, 54, 78, 79, 91,
    176, 216
Disaster Relief Act of 1966, 50
Disaster Relief Act of 1974, 54–57, 60, 78
Disaster research, 108–131
    case studies, 121–128
    disciplines involved, 7–9, 30, 32–33, 109–113,
        130–131, 211–212
    funding, 110, 113, 130
    homeland security nexus, 220
    mitigation, 114–115
    preparedness, 115–117
    public infrastructure repair, 128–130

    recovery, 120–121
    response, 117–120
Disaster Research Center, 112
Disaster response. *See* Response
Disaster Response and Homeland Security (Miskel),
    217
Disaster Response System, 202
Disaster Roundtable, 110
Disaster services industry, 9
Disaster vulnerability, 195
Disasters, categories of, 196
Disease research, 109
Distributive politics, 69, 100–106, 158, 219, 228–229
Domestic incidents, 72, 79, 82
Domestic Nuclear Detection Office, 116
Domestic Policy Council, 87
Donations, 135, 158, 163
Dopplar radar, 8, 126
Downs, Anthony, 212
Drought, 3, 8, 109
Drug interdiction, 172
Dual federalism, 40
Dual-use preparedness programs, 5, 49–51, 58, 60,
    65, 184, 220, 221

Earth Observation Satellites, 8
Earthquake insurance, 3, 227
Earthquake monitoring, 8, 30
Earthquake research, 3, 57, 117, 121–125, 212
Earthquakes, 97
    incidents mentioned, 50, 61, 65, 92, 129, 131,
        157, 167, 176, 199, 200
Eberhart, Ralph E., 180
Economic development interests, 63
Economics, 8, 30, 37, 111–112, 212, 215
Eisenhower, Dwight D., 5, 49, 55, 58, 84, 219
Electoral politics, 63, 92, 100–106, 215
Electric power blackouts, 13
Elites, 35
EMAP Standard, 7, 25
Emergency
    major disaster compared, 78, 99
    term defined, 60, 78
Emergency Alert System, 126, 128
Emergency declaration assistance, 139
Emergency declarations. *See* Presidential disaster
    declarations
Emergency management, 2–25, 211–213
    definition and professional requirements, 5–6,
        31–33, 211
    development of, 3–5
    "disaster management," term compared, 233*n*.2
    fragmented responsibility, 12–18, 22, 212–213
    fundamental challenges and special issues, 9–21,
        225–232
    international assistance. *See* International disaster
        management
    issue attention cycle, 10–12, 212
    phases of, 21–24, 213
    professional organizations and standards, 6–7

research disciplines, 7–9, 211–212. *See also* Disaster research
technical expertise needed, 20–21
theories of. *See* Public management theories
Emergency Management Accreditation Program (EMAP), 7, 20–21
Emergency Management Assistance Committee, 146
Emergency Management Assistance Compact, 145–146
Emergency Management Institute, 20, 150
Emergency Management Performance Grant Program, 150, 186–187, 189
Emergency managers
    credentials needed, 21, 27
    definition and responsibilities, 5–6, 211, 217, 233n.2
    Jeffersonian and Hamiltonian models, 28–31
    presidents as, 211, 214
    as stakeholders, 63
Emergency medicine, 6, 37
Emergency powers, 77–78
Emergency Preparedness and Response Directorate, 144
Emergency responders, 6, 217, 233n.2
Emergency Response Division, 203–204
Emergency supplemental appropriations, 93–94
Emergency support functions, 146, 147, 164–165, 176
Emergency support services, 6
Emergent organizations, 135
Empiricism, 37–38
Energy Department, 44, 110, 116
Engineering research, 7, 37. *See also* Disaster research
Entitlement program, 226
Environmental issues, 18
Environmental movement, 51
Environmental Protection Agency, 8, 51, 110, 131
Environmental science, 30, 110
Epidemiology, 37
Episcopal Relief and Development, 158
Ethical code, 31
"Euphoric enthusiasm" stage, 10–11
Europe, 97, 197, 198
European Union, 201
Evacuation and relocation plans, 49, 51, 59, 60, 64
Event-driven policy, 86, 217
Executive orders, 47, 64–65
Explosives monitoring, 111
Exxon Valdez oil tanker, 10

Faith-based voluntary organizations, 135
Farmers Home Administration, 57
Federal Bureau of Investigation (FBI), 44, 67, 90, 152
Federal Civil Defense Act, 67
Federal Civil Defense Administration, 48
Federal coordinating officer, 100
Federal Disaster Assistance Administration, 53, 56
Federal Disaster Relief Act of 1950, 49, 54, 78, 79, 91, 176, 216
Federal Disaster Relief Act of 1974, 54–57, 60, 78

Federal Emergency Management Agency (FEMA), 178
    all-hazards management, 65–67, 216
    bureaucratic politics, 214
    congressional oversight, 93
    congressional politics, 94
    creation and purpose, 56–57, 75, 87
    cyber security, 129
    director's role, 86, 87, 92, 225–226
    disaster mitigation focus, 21–22, 68–69
    disaster response role, 16, 58–61, 64–65, 175, 176, 217
    earthquake research and response, 30, 124–125, 129–130, 167
    firefighting programs, 117, 118
    flood mitigation, 114
    flood response, 120–123
    government contractors, 164–166
    government reorganization effects, 52–53, 74, 139–141, 144, 182, 224, 226, 231
    grant programs, 186–187
    as instrument of presidential power, 62–63, 214, 217, 219
    intergovernmental relations, 134–141, 144–146, 158, 167, 217, 221, 222
    mismanagement noted, 42, 61, 65
    national response plan, response framework, and incident management system, 146–155
    presidential disaster declarations, 9, 82–91, 96–99, 101–105, 134, 138, 157
    public management theories, 35, 37, 42–43
    regions, 137, 197
    research and research support, 8, 110, 130–131
    stakeholder support, 63
    terrorism consequence management, 67, 224
    training programs, 20, 44
    USAID/OFDA compared, 205, 206
    voluntary nonprofit organizations, 163
Federal Energy Regulatory Commission, 13
Federal Housing Administration, 23
Federal Insurance Administration, 54, 56, 114
Federalism, 40, 64, 215
Federal Preparedness Agency, 51, 56
Federal Response Plan, 64, 73, 125, 146, 148, 182
Federal-state agreements, 136
Federal-state relations. *See* Intergovernmental relations
Federal zoning, 52, 114, 230
Federated States of Micronesia, 197
FEMA. *See* Federal Emergency Management Agency
Fiefdoms, 44
Fire Administration, 117–118, 186
Fire Department of New York (FDNY), 15
Firefighters, 13, 14, 63, 192, 221, 222
Fire Investment and Response Enhancement (FIRE) grants, 117, 118
Fire Prevention and Control Administration, 117
Fire services, 6, 8, 57, 114, 117–118
First Responder Initiative, 117
First responders, 154
Flexible response, 50

Flood Control Act, 19
Flood insurance, 3, 11, 18–20, 54, 57, 114, 227, 228, 230
Flood Plain Management Service, 19
Flood protection, 51, 110, 128–129, 176, 212
Floods, 3, 18, 109, 117, 212
    incidents mentioned, 49, 65, 68, 92, 103, 120, 122–123
Florida, 65, 69, 85, 103, 145, 157, 162, 177, 216
Food and Drug Administration, 119
Ford, Gerald R., 50, 54, 219
Foreign disaster relief. *See* International disaster management
Foreign Assistance Act of 1961, 198
Foreign Humanitarian Assistance, 199
Forest Service, 8, 114
Fragmented government responsibility, 12–13, 24, 212–213
Fraud, 138
Friends Disaster Service, 158
Functional federalism, 104–105
Funding issues
    civil defense and disaster relief, 48, 51, 54, 216
    FEMA programs, 57, 136
    homeland security grants, and their effects, 180–193, 220, 221
    spending percentages (box), 22

Galloway Report, 123
Gaming technology, 30
"Gap group" clients, 159
Gaza Strip, 203
Generalists, 27, 28, 42, 213
Generalized knowledge, 32
General-purpose governments, 133
General Services Administration, 53, 56, 57
Geographic information system (GIS) technology, 30, 37, 109
Geography, 30, 37, 109, 110, 111
Geological Survey, 8, 22, 110, 124, 125, 130, 165
Giuliani, Rudolph, 14–15, 35, 36
Globalization of disasters. *See* International disaster management
Globalizing forces, 195–196
Golden, Cathey, 142
Gorbachev, Mikhail, 60
Gore, Al, 136
Government Accountability Office, 157
Governmental politics model, 34, 35
Government contractors, 131, 134, 135, 163–168, 215, 222
Governors
    as emergency managers, 4, 211
    intergovernmental relations, 136–137, 157
    requests for emergency declarations. *See* Presidential disaster declarations
    requests for National Guard assistance, 173
    as stakeholders, 63
Grant programs. *See* Funding issues
The Great Deluge (Brinkley), 142

Great Midwest Flood (1993), 65, 68, 120, 122–123
Gretna, Louisiana, 142–144
Guam, 197
Gulf Coast, 9, 11, 162, 166, 177, 181
Gulf Coast Recovery Authority, 12, 229
Gulf Coast Workforce Development Initiative, 165

Halliburton Corp., 164
Hamiltonian approach, 29, 41
Hamiltonian public managers, 29–31, 45, 213–214
Hardware stores, 111
Harris, Ronnie, 142–143
Hash, Thomas, 165
Hawaii, 8, 124, 180
Hazard mitigation. *See* Mitigation
Hazard Mitigation and Relocation Assistance Act of 1993, 68
Hazards Research Center, 112
HAZUS, 30, 37, 125
HAZUS-MH, 30, 125
Health and Human Services Department (HHS), 63, 186
Health maintenance organizations, 63
Health policy, 63
Heuristics, 36–37, 213
Holloman, Shauron, 142
Home Depot, 111
Homeland security
    emergence of concept, 15, 64–65
    grants, and their effects at local level, 188–191, 220
    national response plan, response framework, and incident management system, 146–155
    state departments, 140
    terrorism preparedness as focus, 9, 13, 43, 70, 72–73, 134, 140, 182, 189, 216, 223–224
    terrorism programs, 180–188
Homeland Security Act of 2002, 41, 52, 70, 72, 79, 82, 87, 95, 111, 116, 148, 189
Homeland Security Advisory System, 181, 183
Homeland Security Council, 87, 148
Homeland Security Department (DHS), 22, 222
    congressional oversight, 93
    counterterrorism as primary mission, 9, 13, 43, 182, 189, 223–224
    creation and purpose, 41, 70, 87
    disaster response role, 175, 178
    FEMA positioned within, 16, 52–53, 85, 216, 217, 226, 231
    government contractors, 164–166
    grants, and their effects at local level, 188–191, 220
    intergovernmental relations, 134–135, 139–141, 144, 221
    national response plan, response framework, and incident management system, 146–155
    nuclear detection system, 115–117
    organization chart, 71
    presidential disaster declarations, 9, 83, 94, 99
    Project BioShield, 119
    research and research support, 111, 113, 130–131, 220

secretary's role, 72, 73, 87, 95
terrorism programs, 180–188
Homeland Security Grant Program, 183, 185, 189
Homeland Security Operations Center, 150
Homeland Security Presidential Directive-1, 188
Homeland Security Presidential Directive-5, 72–73, 79, 148, 150, 151, 225
Homeland Security Presidential Directive-7, 129
Homeland Security Presidential Directive-8, 73, 154, 185
Hoover, J. Edgar, 44
Horizontal fragmentation, 12, 17
House Committee on Homeland Security, 93
House Select Bipartisan Committee to Investigate Preparation for and Response to Hurricane Katrina, 83
Housing and Urban Development Act of 1968, 54
Housing and Urban Development Department (HUD), 23, 53, 54, 56, 57
Huckabee, Gregory M., 173
Humanitarian assistance. *See* International disaster management
Humanitarian Assistance Operation, 199
Humanitarian Assistance Survey Teams, 200
Hurricane Andrew, 61, 65, 85, 157, 159, 162, 177, 178, 192, 216
Hurricane Betsy, 50
Hurricane Camille, 51, 85, 159, 216
Hurricane Hilda, 50
Hurricane Hugo, 61
Hurricane Katrina
    "bridge to Gretna" incident, 142–144
    government contractors, 164–166
    military response, 173–178, 181, 192, 222
    policy failures and lessons learned, 9–12, 19, 20, 22, 36, 39, 42, 83, 85, 92, 112, 120, 141, 157, 162, 187, 213, 216, 219, 227, 229–231
Hurricane Rita, 12
Hurricanes, 65, 97, 197
    protection needed, 11, 111
    research, 3, 109, 117, 212
    tracking and forecasting, 8
Hussein, Saddam, 118

I-35 bridge collapse, 24, 90, 130
Idaho, 174
Incident Command System (ICS), 148, 150–154, 192
Incidents of national significance, 16, 73, 82, 95, 106, 148, 231
Inclusive-authority model, 39–41
India, 61, 205
Indiana, 50
Indian Ocean, 200
Individual and Family Grant program, 54, 55, 57
Individual and Household Grants, 57
Indonesia, 199
Infrastructure repair, 128–130
Institute of Medicine, 110
Insurance, 57, 211, 230
    business and economic considerations, 3–4, 8–9, 63, 97, 227

federal assistance as disincentive to purchase, 11, 226–227
    flood insurance policy history, 54
    as mitigation tool, 23, 30, 114
    "moral hazard" behavior risks, 228
    policy limitations, 18–20
    redistributive nature, 229
Insurrection Act, 174
Interagency Incident Management Group, 150
Inter-American Development Bank, 201
Intergovernmental relations, 75, 132–169
    bureaucratic politics, 14–15, 34
    disaster management challenges, 156–158
    federal-state relations, 136–145
    first response and management by locals, 134–135
    fragmented responsibility, 12–18, 22, 212–213
    goals, 137
    government contractors, 163–168, 222
    memorandums of understanding, 145
    mutual aid agreements, 145
    national response plan, response framework, and incident management system, 146–155
    nonprofit organizations and volunteers, 158–163, 168, 222
    state-to-state relations, 145–146
    statutory precedent, 49
    term defined, 13, 133
    theory and practice, 39–41, 45, 131, 134–136, 146, 220–222
International Association of Emergency Managers, 7, 187
International City/County Management Association, 6
International Decade for Natural Disaster Reduction, 8, 201
International disaster management, 194–209
    development banks and multinational organizations, 201
    military role, 199–200, 205–206
    other nations' systems, 200–201
    UN and U.S. roles compared, 206–208
    United Nations, 201–204, 225
    U.S. response system, 197–200, 205–206, 224–225
The International Emergency Management Society, 7
The International Journal of Mass Emergencies and Disasters, 8
International Monetary Fund, 201
International Red Cross, 199
International Sociological Association, 7
Internet security, 129
Interstate compacts, 145–146
Interstate Emergency Preparedness Compacts, 67
Iowa, 120
Iraq, 118, 172, 174, 223
Iraq War, 92
Issue attention cycle, 10–12, 212
Issue salience, 10–12, 24

Japan, 201
Java, 199

Jeffersonian approach, 28, 41, 42
Jeffersonian public managers, 28–31, 33, 45, 213, 214
Johnson, Lyndon B., 50, 54, 55, 58, 219
Johnstown flood, 176
Joint Field Office, 150, 151, 154
Jordan, 203
The Journal of Contingency and Crisis Management, 8
The Journal of Emergency Management, 8
The Journal of Homeland Security and Emergency Management, 8
Jurisdictional fragmentation, 12–18, 22, 42–43, 212–213
Justice Department, 65, 67, 116, 152

Keating, Timothy J., 178, 180
Kennedy, John F., 49, 55, 58, 198, 219
Kettl, Donald F., 217
King, Rodney, 162
Knowledge codification and diffusion issues, 43–44, 216, 220
Knowledge-skills-abilities (KSAs), 20

Land-use control, 114
Latin America, 198
Law enforcement
    emergency management authority and capability, 6, 14–15, 192, 221, 222
    military prohibited from civilian law enforcement, 172–174
    as stakeholder group, 13–14
Law Enforcement Terrorism Prevention Program, 186
Lawson, Arthur, 143, 144
Leadership (Giuliani), 36
Learn and Serve America, 162
Lebanon, 60, 203
Legacy agencies, 52–53
Lessons of Disaster: Policy Change after Catastrophic Events (Birkland), 217
Levee repair, 11
Limited federal response, 49
Lincoln, Abraham, 78
Loan programs, 57
Local emergency management committees (LEMCs), 29
Local government responsibilities, 4, 6, 103, 104
    effects of homeland security grants, 188–193
    terrorism programs, 180–181, 183–188
    See also Intergovernmental relations
Loma Prieta earthquake, 61, 92, 167
Los Angeles, 129–130, 162, 167, 174
Louisiana, 11, 19, 92, 157, 177, 178
    "bridge to Gretna" incident, 142–144
Love Canal, 85, 114
Lowenberg, Timothy J., 178
Lowe's Co., 111

Macy, John W., 57
Major disaster, 189, 218
    emergency compared, 78, 99
Major disaster assistance, 138–139

Major disaster declarations. *See* Presidential disaster declarations
Manhattan Project, 111
Marginal disasters, 103, 105, 106
Mariel boatlift, 24, 65, 85
Marshall Islands, 197
Marshall Plan, 198
Martial law, 172, 178, 205, 223
Maryland, 69
May, Peter, 231
Mayors
    as emergency managers, 4, 15, 86, 211, 217
    requests for state and federal aid, 157
    as stakeholders, 63
McVeigh, Timothy, 67
Media coverage, 9, 42, 61, 92, 101, 106, 219
Medical community, 14, 221, 222
Memorandums of understanding, 145
Mennonite Disaster Service, 158
Meredith, James, 174
Meteorology, 3, 7, 30, 37, 109, 110
Metropolitan Edison, 58
Metropolitan Medical Response System, 188, 189
Mexico, 180
Micronesia, 197
Midwest floods, 49, 65, 68, 120, 122–123
Mileti, Dennis, 112
Military response
    foreign disaster relief, 199–200, 205
    militarization of disaster policy, 174–181, 191, 192, 222–223
    statutory limitations, 172–174
    UN peacekeeping forces, 205–206
Minneapolis, 24, 90, 130
Miskel, James F., 173, 217, 222, 226
"Mission assignment" authority, 62, 238*n*.40
Mississippi, 19, 69, 157, 177, 187
Mississippi River, 11, 24, 92, 176
Missouri, 114, 122
Mitigation, 16, 30, 230
    funding, 22
    as phase of emergency management, 21–23, 114–115, 189, 190, 213, 221
    policy formulation, 51, 55, 56, 66, 68–70
    role of voluntary organizations, 159
Mobile homes, 128, 139
Moral hazard, 19, 123, 228
Mount Saint Helens, 92
Multidisciplinary Center for Earthquake Engineering Research, 125
Multihazard approach, 55. *See also* All-hazards management
Multinational organizations, 201
Murrah Office Building, 65, 67, 99, 224
Mutual aid agreements, 17, 145

The National Academies, 110
National Academy of Engineering, 110
National Academy of Public Administration, 159
National Academy of Science, 110

National Aeronautics and Space Administration (NASA), 44, 130–131
National Center for Atmospheric Research, 131
National Center for Earthquake Engineering, 131
National Climate Data Center, 131
National Commission on Terrorist Attacks Upon the United States, 72, 151
National Counterterrorism Center, 152
National Defense Authorization Act, 66, 67
National Earthquake Hazard Reduction Program, 113
National Earthquake Hazards Reduction Act of 1977, 124–125
National Earthquake Mitigation Program Office, 125
National Emergencies Act of 2002, 173
National emergency declaration, 174
National Emergency Management Association, 7, 146
National Emergency Management System, 72
National Emergency Training Center, 44
National Exercise Program, 153
National Fire Academy, 117, 118
National Fire Protection and Control Administration, 56
National Fire Protection Association 1600 standards, 7, 23
National Flood Insurance Act, 54
National Flood Insurance Program (NFIP), 11, 19–20, 22, 23, 54, 56, 114, 122–123, 227, 228, 230
National Governors Association, 56, 58
National Guard, 14, 95, 140, 172–179, 181, 191, 222, 223
National Hurricane Center, 8, 131
National Incident Management System (NIMS), 13, 41, 72, 82, 133, 146, 150–155, 180, 218, 223
National Institute of Standards and Technology (NIST), 8, 110, 124, 125, 130
National Institutes of Health, 119
National Laboratories (DOE), 110–111
National Oceanic and Atmospheric Administration (NOAA), 8, 110, 130
National Operations Center, 152
National Performance Review, 136
National planning scenarios, 189
National Plans Review, 187
National preparedness, 73. *See also* Preparedness
National Preparedness Directorate, 131
National Preparedness Goal, 185, 189
National Response Coordination Center, 152, 164
National Response Framework (NRF), 133, 134, 146, 148–150, 182, 218
National Response Network, 149
National Response Plan (NRP), 79, 82, 164, 180, 218, 231
    creation, purpose, and elements of, 13, 16, 41, 72–73, 146, 148–150
    military disaster response, 173, 176, 182, 223
    revision, 133, 134
National Research Council, 110, 113
National Science Foundation (NSF), 8, 110, 112, 113, 124, 125, 131
"National securitization," 111, 179, 223

National Security Council, 65, 87
National Security Decision Memorandum 184, 50
National security policy. *See* Disaster policy history; Homeland security
National Security Steering Group, 66
National Severe Storm Center, 8
National Severe Storm Laboratory, 128, 131
National Special Security Events, 73, 82
National Volunteer Organizations Active in Disaster (NVOAD), 159–161, 168
National Weather Service, 8, 126, 128
"Natural disasters," 112, 196, 212
Natural Hazards Observer, 8
Near East, 198
New Madrid fault, 124
"New normal" condition, 217
New Orleans, 10, 11, 50, 92, 120, 131, 176, 177, 192, 230
    "bridge to Gretna" incident, 142–144
News media, 9, 42, 61, 92, 101, 106, 219
New York (city), 14–15, 36, 67, 70, 97
New York (state), 13, 70, 85, 97, 114
New York Police Department (NYPD), 14–15, 36
Niagara Falls, 114
9/11 Commission Report, 79, 151, 178–179
9/11 terrorist attacks. *See* September 11, 2001, terrorist attacks
9/11 Victim's Compensation Fund, 228, 229
911 emergency call system, 15
Nixon, Richard M., 50, 51, 53–54, 85, 216, 219
NOAA weather radios, 127, 128
Nongovernmental organizations (NGOs), 195, 199–204, 206, 208, 211, 222
Nonprofit organizations, 138
    definition, 158
    as recipients of disaster aid, 84
    role and activities, 3, 4, 12, 17, 45, 86, 133, 158–163, 168, 211, 217, 222, 225, 230
    as stakeholder groups, 60, 63
    types of (box), 135
Nonstructural mitigation, 51
Nonterrorism missions, 140
Normative political theories, 26–31, 45, 213–214
North American Aerospace Defense Command (NORAD), 180, 181
North Atlantic Treaty Organization, 201
North Carolina, 69
Northern Command (NORTHCOM), 175, 178–181, 191, 192, 223
Northern Marianas, 197
Northridge earthquake, 65, 92, 129, 131, 157, 167
Nuclear attack, defense against. *See* Civil defense
Nuclear detection policy, 115–117
Nuclear power plant accidents, 58–59, 61
Nuclear Regulatory Commission (NRC), 44, 58–59
Nunn-Lugar-Domenici Act, 4
Nursing homes, 145

Occupation, 31
Office for Political/Military Affairs, 199

Office of Cabinet Liaison, 87
Office of Civil Defense (OCD), 50, 53
Office of Domestic Preparedness, 150
Office of Emergency Management, 15, 36
Office of Emergency Planning, 53
Office of Emergency Preparedness, 53
Office of Emergency Services, 167
Office of Management and Budget, 130
Office of Peacekeeping and Humanitarian Affairs, 199
Office of the United Nations High Commissioner for
    Refugees (UNHCR), 202–203
Office of the Vice President, 87
Office of U.S. Foreign Disaster Assistance (OFDA),
    198–200, 202, 205–207
Ohio, 13
Oil industry, 9
Oil spills, 10
Oklahoma, 103
Oklahoma City, 65, 67, 99, 172, 224
Onvia Co., 164
Oregon, 124
Organizational process model, 34, 35, 215
Organization for American States, 8, 201
Organization studies, 31–43
Overlapping-authority model, 39–41
Overseas Private Investment Corp., 198

Pacific Command, 180
Pacific states, 197
Pakistan, 199, 205
Palestinian refugees, 203
Pan American Health Organization, 201
Pandemics, 109
Partisan mutual adjustment, 39, 45, 215
Partnership for a Safer Future for America, 68
Pascagoula, Mississippi, 69
Pascoe, B. Lynn, 199
Pataki, George, 70, 85
Pennsylvania, 13, 58, 70, 176
Pentagon. See Defense Department
Performance Partnerships, 136
"Persons of interest," 189
Petak, William, 6
Peterson Air Force Base, 181
Physical geography, 30, 37, 109, 110
Physical sciences, 32–33
Planning activities, 218
Planning scenarios, 189
Plum Book, 219
Point Four Program, 198
Police. See Law enforcement
Policy formation. See Disaster policy history
Policy implementation theories. See Public manage-
    ment theories
Policy studies, 37
Policy windows, 10
Political Affairs Office, 87
Political appointments, 219
Political aspects of disaster, 18
Political pressure groups, 220

Political science, 8, 30, 111–112, 212
Pork-barrel politics, 104–105
Port security, 111
Posse Comitatus Act of 1878, 172–174, 181, 205
Post-Katrina Emergency Management Reform Act of
    2006, 87, 231
"Post-problem" stage, 12
Predisaster preparedness and response agreements, 146
Preliminary damage assessment (PDA), 89
Preparedness, 16
    FEMA jurisdiction, 56, 57
    funding, 22
    as phase of emergency management, 23, 115–117,
        189, 213
    policy formulation, 5, 41. See also Disaster policy
        history
    predisaster agreements, 146
    role of voluntary organizations, 159
"Pre-problem" stage, 10
Presidential Commission on Critical Infrastructure and
    Protection, 129
Presidential directives, 72–73, 79, 129
Presidential disaster declarations, 76–107
    approvals and turndowns, 61, 99, 100
    congressional role, 91, 93–95
    constitutional authority, 77–78
    cooperating officials and agencies, 86, 217
    DHS secretary role, 87
    discretionary nature, 83–85
    distributive politics, 100–106
    as emergency management tool, 9, 41, 47, 57–59,
        62, 64
    FEMA role, 87–91, 98–100
    governors' role, 40–41, 79, 86, 95–98, 134
    major disaster and emergency declarations com-
        pared, 55
    overview of process, 88–89, 156–158, 218–219
    public relations, 92
    selected examples of, 13, 24, 67, 70
    statutory basis, 49, 55, 60–61, 78–83
    subjective criteria (boxes), 96–97, 102
    types of federal assistance available, 138–139
    White House staff assistance, 86–87
Presidents
    as emergency managers, 4, 211, 214
    policy formation. See Disaster policy history
President's Disaster Relief Fund, 54–55, 62, 93, 103
Prevention, 115, 188–189, 213
Principal-agent theory, 38–39, 45, 215
Profession, 31–32
Professional body, 31
Project BioShield, 119, 120, 131
Project Impact, 69
Public Assistance Program, 84, 91
Public Health Service, 120
Public infrastructure repair, 128–130
Public interest, 10–12, 212
Public management theories, 26–45, 213–216
    analytical approaches versus social constructivist
        theories, 37–38

best-practices approaches, 34–37
bureaucratic politics, 34, 214–215
customer satisfaction, 41–43
emergency management applications, 27–28, 45
emergency management as profession, 31–33
intergovernmental relations theory, 39–41
Jeffersonian and Hamiltonian theories, 28–31,
    213–214
knowledge codification and diffusion, 43–44
partisan mutual adjustment, 39, 215
principal-agent theory, 38–39, 215
Public-private partnerships, 69
Public relations, 61, 92
Public safety directors, 63
Public works, 128, 131, 189, 230
Puerto Rico, 180, 197

Radio warnings, 126–128
Rational actor model, 34, 35, 214
Reagan, Ronald R., 59–62, 64, 86, 92, 217
Recovery, 22, 24, 66, 120–121, 159, 213
Red Crescent Societies, 199
Reeves, Andrew, 101
Refugees, 202–203
Regional directors, 137–138
Regional offices, 137
Reinsurance, 3, 97, 228
Reinventing government, 41–42, 216
Relocation and evacuation plans, 49, 51, 59, 60, 64
Reorganization Plan No. 1 (Nixon), 53
Reorganization Plan No. 2 (Nixon), 53
Reorganization Plan No. 3 (Carter), 56–57
Research. See Disaster research
Research Committee on Sociology of Disasters, 7
Reserve forces, 172
Response
    funding, 22
    as phase of emergency management, 23, 117–120,
        213
    policy formulation, 56, 66
    predisaster preparedness and response agreements,
        146
    role of voluntary organizations, 159
Response Management Teams, 199
Riders, 93
Ridge, Tom, 141
Risk analysis, 110
Robert T. Stafford Disaster Relief and Emergency
    Assistance Act of 1988. See Stafford Act
Rogers Commission, 61
Roosevelt, Franklin D., 78

Salvation Army, 158, 159
San Francisco, 92, 176
Santa Clara County, 145
Sarin nerve gas, 118
Satellite telemetry, 8, 30, 109
Save the Children, 158
Scientific research. See Disaster research
Secret Service, 87

Section on Emergency and Crisis Management, 6
Securitization, 111, 179, 223
Security classification, 179, 223
Seismic activity. See Earthquake entries
Seismic building codes, 121
Seismic mapping, 124
Seismology, 7, 30, 37, 110, 212
Self-help, 48
Senate, 164
Senate Bipartisan Task Force on Funding Disaster
    Relief, 22
Senate Committee on Homeland Security and
    Governmental Affairs, 93
Senate Governmental Affairs Committee, 93
Senior Corps, 162
September 11, 2001, terrorist attacks, 10, 92, 99
    effect on military response role, 172–173, 175
    funding and policy shifts, 15, 18, 22, 24, 52, 70,
        72–73, 79, 82–83, 85, 95, 216, 225
    Giuliani leadership, 36
    impact on federal-state relations, 41, 139–141,
        144, 188
    9/11 Commission, 72, 151
    research responses to, 110–111
    terrorism insurance, 3–4, 229
Shelter-building programs, 48, 49, 60
60 Minutes, 142
Slonsky, Lorry Beth, 142
Small Business Administration, 57, 90, 138
Smallpox vaccine, 119
Social catastrophes, 112
Social constructivist theories, 37–38
Social geography, 30, 111–112
Social sciences, 8, 30, 32–33, 111–113
Sociology, 8, 30, 37, 111–112, 212, 227
South America, 197
Southern African Development Community, 201
Southern Baptist Convention, 158
Southern Command, 180
Southern Governors Association, 145
Soviet Union, 5, 48–50, 59, 60, 64
Special district governments, 45, 133
Special Relief Operations, 204
Spoils system, 219
St. Charles County flood, 121, 122
Stafford Act, 73, 157, 173, 189
    policy changes, 60–61, 66–69, 79, 82, 83, 88–89,
        95, 96, 100, 101, 138, 205
    text excerpt, 80–81
Stakeholders, 13–14, 54, 60, 63, 75
Standard federal regions, 137
Statecraft, 34
State Department, 44, 116, 197, 198
State government responsibilities, 4, 95, 103
    civil defense, 48
    homeland security terrorism programs, 180–188,
        192–193
    See also Intergovernmental relations
State homeland security departments, 140
State Homeland Security Grant Program, 183, 185, 189

State-to-state relations, 145–146
State University of New York, 125
Stein, Robert M., 63
Storms, 3, 109, 111, 212. *See also* Hurricane entries; Tornado entries
"Stovepiping," 154
Strategic Arms Limitation Talks, 59
Strategic Information and Operations Center, 152
Structural hazard mitigation, 51
Subcontracting, 166
Sub-Saharan Africa, 198
Sudan, 196
Surveillance technologies, 111
Syria, 203
System under Stress (Kettl), 217

Tacit knowledge, 43–44
Target capabilities list, 189
Target capability, 185
Technical Assistance Groups, 199
Technical expertise, 20–21
Technocratic groups, 31
Technocrats, 29, 214
Technological disasters, 196
"Technology forcing," 115, 117
Telecommunications, 111
Television news coverage, 61, 219
Tenth Amendment, 12, 134
Territorial sovereignty, 196
Terrorism consequence management, 4, 67, 134, 224
Terrorism insurance, 3–4, 229
Terrorism programs, 180–191
Terrorism Risk Insurance Act of 2002, 229
Terrorism Risk Insurance Program Reauthorization Act of 2007, 229
Terrorist attacks
    disaster policy shaped by, 9, 13, 18, 60, 65–67, 134, 140, 146, 216
    See also September 11, 2001, terrorist attacks
Theories of public management. *See* Public management theories
Threat-based, color-coded alert system, 181, 183, 184, 189
Three Mile Island, 58, 59
Tierney, Kathleen J., 74
Times Beach, 114
Tokyo, 118
Tolerated disaster vulnerabilities, 113, 212
Top-down command and control system, 41, 134, 171, 221
Tornadoes, 8, 50, 109, 212
Tornado research, 3, 121, 125–128
Training and Exercises, 66
Transportation Department, 90, 130, 164
Treasury Department, 54
Treaty obligations, 197
Tree pruning, 13
Truman, Harry S., 5, 48, 49, 58, 70, 74, 75, 99, 198

Trust and commonwealth territories, 197
Tsunami incidents, 199, 200
Tsunami research, 8
Tsunami Warning Center, 131
Turf wars. *See* Bureaucratic politics
Turndowns, 61, 99, 102, 105
    approvals and turndowns, 1953–2005 (table), 100
Turner, Ted, 61
Typhoons, 197

Ukraine, 61
Undiffused knowledge, 43–44
UN Disaster Assessment and Coordination team, 202
Unemployment assistance, 139
UNESCO, 7
UN Food and Agriculture Organization, 204
Unified Program for Floodplain Management, 114
Unitary actor, 35
United Airlines Flight 93, 70
United Jewish Communities, 158
United Nations (UN), 8, 196–197, 201–208, 225
United Nations Children's Fund (UNICEF), 202, 203
United Nations Development Program, 202, 203
United Nations High Commissioner for Refugees, Office of (UNHCR), 202–203
United Nations Relief and Works Agency for Palestine Refugees in the Near East, 203
United States response system, 196–200, 205–208, 224–225
Universal Task List, 189, 190
University of Colorado, 112
University of Delaware, 112
University of Mississippi, 174
UN Office for the Coordination of Humanitarian Affairs, 201–202
UN's International Strategy for Disaster Reduction Working Group on Risk, Vulnerability, and Disaster Impact Assessment, 204
Urban Area Homeland Security Strategy, 185
Urban Area Security Initiative (UASI), 118, 183–186, 189–190
Urban planning, 30, 111–112
U.S.A. Freedom Corps, 162
USS *Bataan*, 177

Vaccines, 109, 111, 119
Vertical fragmentation, 12, 13, 16, 17
Veterans Affairs Department, 23
Vice President, 87
Vietnam War, 50
Virgin Islands, U.S., 180, 197
Volcanoes, 3, 92
Volcanology, 7, 37
Volition, 112–113
Volkmer Amendment, 68
Voluntary nonprofit organizations. *See* Nonprofit organizations
Voluntary risk, 112–113
Volunteers, 230
Volunteers of America, 158

War Department, 247 n.8
War of 1812, 5
War on Terrorism, 140, 146, 216
Washington (state), 69, 92, 124
Washington, D.C., 70
Weapons of mass destruction (WMD)
    defense against nuclear attack. *See* Civil defense
    nuclear detection policy, 115–117
Weather Channel, 8, 128
Weather research, 109, 212
West Africa, 8
West Bank, 203
Western Governors Association, 178
West Nile virus, 85
West Virginia, 69
Wetlands, 11, 51
White, Gilbert F., 19
White House package, 98
White House staff, 86–87
Wildfires, 117

Wilmington, North Carolina, 69
Wilson, Pete, 167
Wind damage, 20
Witt, James Lee, 40
    as FEMA director, 35, 36, 42, 65, 66, 68–69, 92,
        96, 120–121, 136, 167
    FEMA politics, 43, 74, 182, 224, 231
World Bank, 201, 225
World Conference on Disaster Reduction, 201
World Conference on Natural Disaster Reduction, 201
World Food Program, 202, 204
World Health Organization, 8, 202, 204
World Meteorological Organization, 8
World Trade Center
    1993 terrorist attack, 65–67, 97, 224
    See also September 11, 2001, terrorist attacks
World War I, 5, 247 n.8
World War II, 5, 78, 111

Year 2000 (Y2K) preparedness, 115, 121, 127